CONSERVATIVE AT THE CORE

This book was selected as the 2024–25 Giles Family Fund Recipient. The University of Notre Dame Press and the author thank the Giles family for their generous support.

GILES FAMILY FUND RECIPIENTS

2019   *The Glory and the Burden*, Robert Schmuhl (expanded edition, 2022)

2020   *Ars Vitae: The Fate of Inwardness and the Return of the Ancient Arts of Living*, Elisabeth Lasch-Quinn

2021   *William Still: The Underground Railroad and the Angel at Philadelphia*, William C. Kashatus

2022   *An Inconvenient Apocalypse: Environmental Collapse, Climate Crisis, and the Fate of Humanity*, Wes Jackson and Robert Jensen

2023   *Generals and Admirals, Criminals and Crooks: Dishonorable Leadership in the U.S. Military*, Jeffrey J. Matthews

2024–25   *Conservative at the Core: A New History of American Conservatism*, Allan J. Lichtman

The Giles Family Fund supports the work and mission of the University of Notre Dame Press to publish books that engage the most enduring questions of our time. Each year the endowment helps underwrite the publication and promotion of a book that sparks intellectual exploration and expands the reach and impact of the university.

CONSERVATIVE

AT THE

CORE

A New History of American Conservatism

ALLAN J. LICHTMAN

University of Notre Dame Press

Notre Dame, Indiana

Library of Congress Control Number: 2025934548

ISBN: 978-0-268-21030-4 (Hardback)
ISBN: 978-0-268-21028-1 (WebPDF)
ISBN: 978-0-268-21027-4 (Epub3)

GPSR Compliance Inquiries:
Mare Nostrum Group B.V., Mauritskade 21D, 1091 GC Amsterdam, The Netherlands
gpsr@mare-nostrum.co.uk | Phone: +44 (0)1423 562232

To Karyn, always my inspiration

CONTENTS

ACKNOWLEDGMENTS

I want to thank my research assistant, Zac Heidenry, for his outstanding work on this project. Special thanks go to Steve Wrinn, my former student and now the extraordinary director of the University of Notre Dame Press. I also thank Steve's excellent staff, including Megan Levine and Matthew Dowd, and copyeditor Scott Barker. All errors, of course, I claim for myself.

1

DISPENSABLE VERSUS CORE CONSERVATIVE VALUES

Representative Jim Jordan (R-OH), a former wrestling champion known for his combative style, comes to work each day, typically without a jacket, ready to challenge liberals. Despite failing to advance a single bill through Congress during his nine terms, Jordan leveraged his seniority and persistent criticism of Democrats to become the chair of the House Judiciary Committee after Republicans regained control of the chamber in 2023. Beyond his confrontations with Democrats, Jordan has championed what conservatives view as fundamental principles, particularly advocating for states' rights to manage their affairs without federal interference. When Democrats proposed national voting rights legislation in 2021, Jordan condemned it as "another brazen attempt to seize power from state control and transfer it to partisan bureaucrats in Washington."[1]

Other prominent Republicans who became committee chairs in the U.S. House of Representatives in 2023 also voiced their commitment to states' rights. Bryan Steil of Wisconsin, chair of the Administration Committee, joined Jordan in opposing the Democrats' voting rights bill, instead sponsoring an alternative he claimed would "protect our federalist principles." Steil argued that his proposal would equip states with the tools to enhance election integrity without dictating specific actions. He emphasized that the U.S. Congress "must restrain itself from acting improperly and unconstitutionally."[2] Similarly, in a 2021 U.S. Supreme Court amicus brief concerning COVID-19 mandates, Representative James Comer (R-KY), chair of the House Oversight Committee, joined 183 Republican U.S. representatives and senators to assert that state residents should have the autonomy to "craft local solutions to problems facing their States and districts. Federalism concerns should be addressed before requiring federally-imposed solutions."[3]

However, the chairs' commitment to states' rights wavered when Alvin Bragg, district attorney for New York County (elected locally) covering Manhattan, announced his intention to indict former president Donald Trump for falsifying business records to conceal election and tax fraud. The chairs demanded that Bragg justify his prosecutorial decision under state law to the U.S. House: "You are reportedly about to engage in an unprecedented abuse of prosecutorial authority: the indictment of a former President of the United States and a current declared candidate for that office." Given "the serious consequences of your actions, we expect you to testify about what seems to be a politically motivated prosecutorial decision."[4]

In response, Bragg defended states' rights. He argued that House actions "threaten the sovereign powers of the states, the confidentiality of grand jury proceedings, and the integrity of an ongoing criminal prosecution." Bragg cited a U.S. Supreme Court ruling that stated, "Federal intrusions into state criminal trials frustrate both the states' sovereign power to prosecute offenders and their efforts to uphold constitutional rights."[5]

Similarly, when Fani Willis, district attorney of Fulton County, Georgia (Atlanta), indicted Trump and eighteen others under the state's racketeering law, Jordan demanded that Willis provide documents and communications to justify her prosecutorial decisions. In her nine-page response, Willis rejected this demand: "There is no justification in the Constitution for Congress to interfere with a state criminal matter, as you attempt to do." She emphasized that "your efforts at intruding upon the State of Georgia's criminal authority violate constitutional principles of federalism."[6]

The House committee chairs' sudden shift on states' rights highlights the need to examine conservative rhetoric and critically uncover conservatism's realities. My objective is not to compare conservatism with liberalism, which also has contradictions. I will not generally fact-check conservative claims or assess whether conservative policies are better or worse than liberal ones. My sole objective is to understand conservatism on its own terms by deconstructing conventional myths and revealing the true essence of what the U.S. conservative movement truly represents. To present conservatism authentically, I have allowed conservatives to speak for themselves.

In addition to politicians, I have drawn on conservative activists, operatives, intellectuals, and opinion-makers. Attention to the often inflammatory rhetoric of the past century debunks the myth of a lost golden age of civility in U.S. politics. During the 1930s, for example, conservatives branded President Franklin D. Roosevelt a "socialist," a "fascist," a "dictator," the "first Communist President of the United States," and the puppet of "fanatical and communistic Jew professors." Such accusations were not one-sided. Although the study of liberalism is beyond the scope of this book, liberals responded by slamming conservatives as "fascists," "union-busters," and sellouts to predatory businesses. George D. Aiken, the moderate Republican governor of Vermont, lamented in 1938, "Sometimes it seems that there never before has been a time in the history of America when there have been so many diverse elements arrayed against each other in bitterness and distrust."[7]

The late Imre Lakatos, a distinguished epistemologist, offers an analogy from research programs in hard science to understand conservatism as a political program. Every scientific program rests on a hard core of immutable principles, Lakatos says, surrounded by an "outer belt" of auxiliary ideas that can be revised, altered, or even discarded to protect the immutable inner core. A crack in the core could bring down the system with it. In political analysis, the challenge is cutting through the "outer belt" of dispensable ideas to uncover the fixed core of conservative principles. The unpacking of conservatism reveals that two hard core principles guide practice and policy: protecting private enterprise (not free enterprise) and advancing the conservative, though not the only, version of traditional Christian values.[8]

From the publication of Russell Kirk's *The Conservative Mind* (1954), through John Keke's *A Case for Conservatism* (1998) and Yoram Hazony's *Conservativism: A Rediscovery* (2022), with many in between, eminent thinkers have plumbed the philosophical foundations of conservatism.[9] These sages present intriguing, if contradictory, abstractions that cannot explain the meaning of conservativism in the United States as a practical political program. Conservatives cling to the status quo but recognize the need for change. They exalt the rugged individual but decry human imperfections and uphold the value of community. Conservatives are religious but also secular. They reject ideologies but formulate ideologies of their own. Conservatives support ordered authority and enforced morality but cherish individual liberty. They respect tradition but not the inherited traditions of the liberal state. Conservatism is a personal disposition but also a political program. Its ardent followers uphold a strict meritocracy but race, religion, and heritage matter. Conservatives exalt the will of the people but support countermajoritarian restraints.

Even Sherlock Holmes could not deduce the practical political program of conservatives from the abstractions. The elementary truth about conservativism is found by climbing down from the heights of philosophy to probe conservatives' down-to-earth claims about what their movement represents. Novelist Umberto Eco wrote in *The Name of the Rose*, "Those things about which we cannot theorize, we must narrate." Conservative representative Mike Johnson (R-LA), elected Speaker of the House in 2023, narrated a familiar litany of core conservative principles, including "limited government," "fiscal responsibility," "free market," (free enterprise), "the rule of law," and "human dignity" based on "religion and morality," which he grounds in his version of traditional Christian values.[10]

The Heritage Foundation, the conservative flagship think tank, in its "True North" of "fixed" conservative principles, affirmed Johnson's formulations, and added:

- Thomas Jefferson said, "The government closest to the people serves the people best." Powers not delegated to the federal government, nor prohibited by the Constitution, are reserved to the states or to the people.
- Judges should interpret and apply our laws and the Constitution based on their original meaning, not upon judges' own personal and political predispositions.

- International agreements and international organizations should not infringe on Americans' constitutional rights, nor should they diminish American sovereignty.[11]

Ronald Reagan, the iconic conservative president, predicated his presidency on the precepts of "free enterprise and personal responsibility," which Jim DeMint (R-SC), former U.S. senator and Heritage Foundation president, reaffirmed in 2014: "Limited government and individual responsibility" are "fundamental American ideals."[12]

These self-described conservative principles are summarized unsurprisingly as traditional Christian values, free enterprise, limited government, fiscal responsibility, states' rights, personal morality and responsibility, law and order, strict construction, and U.S. sovereignty.

Lakatos reminds us that political systems, no less than scientific ones, are valid only through reliable real-world predictions. The rejection of states' rights by conservatives in Trump's state criminal cases challenges the consistency between conservative rhetoric and practice. The flexibility of states' rights ideals among conservatives is not an anomaly. When scrutinized, conservatism reveals truths that differ significantly from what its adherents claim. Principles such as states' rights are not sacred tenets for conservatives but are instead expendable "outer belt" ideas meant for public consumption. Throughout a century of conservative politics in the United States, this disconnect between rhetoric and reality extends to every principle conservatives publicly espouse. The truth of conservatism lies elsewhere, in the indispensable principles that the "outer belt" of professed ideals protects. "All truths are easy to understand once they are discovered; the point is to discover them," said Galileo.

Not only in our time with Trump but throughout the past century, conservatives have violated their "outer belt" claims to protect the core of their political program:

— **Traditional Christian Values:** Conservatives frequently invoke Christianity to justify their positions on moral issues, such as abortion, gay rights, and school prayer, while also condemning liberal positions on taxes, welfare, and regulation. They claim that liberal economic programs betray Christian teachings by fostering sloth, dissolution, and dependency. Yet, conservatives often cherry-pick parts of the Christian tradition, ignoring its teachings on the dangers of wealth, greed, and deceit and its concern for the poor, oppressed, and marginalized.

— **Free Enterprise:** Conservatives have championed free enterprise, free from government interference, to counter liberal proposals for regulating business. However, they have consistently supported government intervention in the marketplace when it benefits businesses. Conservative presidents, including Warren Harding, Reagan, and Trump, have long supported protectionist tariffs to shield American enterprises from foreign competition. They have carved out exceptions to free markets through favorable regulations, antiunion measures, and "corporate welfare" via business loans, subsidies, and tax breaks.

— **Limited Government:** Conservatives criticize Democratic presidents' big government programs while building their own versions of big government. They have leveraged government power to regulate matters such as alcohol, drugs, gambling, prostitution, LGBTQ rights, pornography, and abortion. They have backed robust military and police establishments, coercive countersubversion measures, mass deportations of undocumented immigrants, censorship in education, and book bans. *The dispute between liberals and conservatives is not about the size of government but the purposes of government.*

— **Fiscal Responsibility:** Conservatives have railed against reckless spending and budget deficits when out of power but, when in control, have accumulated record deficits through tax cuts and spending. Reagan, who promised limited spending and balanced budgets, set new records for federal deficits. Subsequent Republican presidents, including George H. W. Bush, George W. Bush, and Trump, continued this pattern of fiscal irresponsibility.

— **States' Rights:** Despite invoking states' rights to oppose national voting rights and antigerrymandering measures, conservatives have abandoned states' rights to support federal bans on alcohol, constitutional amendments to restrict marriage to heterosexual unions, and nationwide abortion bans. They have also pushed for federal mandates requiring states to implement voter ID laws and abolish diversity, equity, and inclusion programs. Additionally, conservatives have sought to undermine state welfare programs and stringent environmental regulations, such as California's auto emission standards.

— **Personal Morality and Responsibility:** Conservatives condemned President Bill Clinton's personal moral failings, arguing that they disqualified him from holding public office. However, they have overlooked the more egregious transgressions of conservatives such as President Harding, Newt Gingrich, Dennis Hastert, Trump, Herschel Walker, and leaders of the Southern Baptist Convention, none of whom have taken responsibility or shown remorse. Conservatives often blame their misdeeds on a "left-wing" or "deep-state" conspiracy against them.

— **Law and Order:** Conservatives have invoked "law and order" to suppress civil rights demonstrations and justify harsh policing tactics, labeling liberals as "soft on crime" and tolerant of civil disorder. Yet, conservatives have undermined the rule of law in some of the worst scandals of the last century, including Teapot Dome under President Harding, Watergate under Richard Nixon, Iran–Contra under Reagan, and multiple scandals under Trump. Supporters of Trump's "big lie" about a stolen election in 2020 violently stormed the U.S. Capitol, injuring more than 140 Capitol police officers.

— **Strict Construction:** Conservatives have criticized liberal Supreme Court decisions of the 1950s and 60s for abandoning strict constitutional construction in favor of contemporary political leanings. Yet, neither conservatives nor liberals have consistently adhered to strict construction. Liberals criticized the conservative Court of the 1930s for abandoning strict construction to overturn key elements of President Roosevelt's New Deal. Recently, liberals have criticized the conservative-dominated Court under Chief Justice John Roberts for infusing political values into decisions on campaign finance, gun control, abortion, presidential immunity, and the disqualification clause in section 3 of the Fourteenth Amendment.

— **U.S. Sovereignty:** Conservatives have emphasized the importance of maintaining U.S. sovereignty free from foreign interference. They have opposed on this ground international treaties on genocide, racial discrimination, the arms trade, and rights for women and children.

Yet, they have sacrificed U.S. sovereignty in favor of multinational corporations, and leaders of the America First movement hesitated to defend U.S. sovereignty against the Nazi threat. As a candidate and president, Trump and his associates engaged with foreign nations in ways that compromised democracy.

However, Lakatos notes, simply discrediting a theory is insufficient: "There is no refutation without a better theory." The search for a better theory to explain conservatism begins with the origins of modern conservatism after World War I, as thoroughly explored in my earlier book, *White Protestant Nation: The Rise of the American Conservative Movement* (2008). Conservatism is more than a reaction to the rise of the liberal state. The Right's political philosophy, organizing strategy, and grassroots appeal go beyond mere opposition to liberalism. Modern conservatism has its own life, history, and logic. It emerged not just in opposition to the liberal state but alongside it as a potent response to profound social and economic changes in the early twentieth century. U.S. conservatism is as robust and forward-looking as liberalism, but with a different vision for the country's future.

Many historians and commentators incorrectly trace the movement's origins to William F. Buckley Jr.'s founding of *National Review* in 1955 or Barry Goldwater's 1964 presidential campaign. Like liberalism, modern conservatism arose during a national crisis. For liberalism, that moment was the Great Depression. For conservatism, it was a decade earlier, with the events surrounding U.S. involvement in World War I.

By the 1920s, a deep divide had formed between Americans who remained devoted to a national identity rooted in late nineteenth-century Victorian values and those who embraced the increasingly pluralistic religious, racial, and cultural forces of the twentieth century. Conservatives worried about the influx of Jewish and Catholic immigrants from Eastern and Southern Europe, the migration of African Americans to northern cities, and the permissive culture of the Jazz Age. The conservatives who dominated U.S. politics in the 1920s established the core principles that continue to ground the modern political Right. Anti-pluralists joined forces with business leaders to forge a new conservative consensus in the 1920s, uniting support for private enterprise with a version of white Protestant values, or, as conservatives preferred to call them, broadly Christian values. The conservative consensus of the 1920s was more than a brief period of prosperity and reaction wedged between two eras of reform. It was more than just another cycle of political activism and retrenchment. Despite the rise of the liberal state since the 1930s, conservatives have shaped U.S. history as profoundly as liberals have.

At the heart of right-wing politics in the 1920s and beyond was the antipluralistic ideal of the United States as a white Christian nation united under a specific version of Christianity. This version emphasized the salvation of souls, preservation of the traditional family, control over immoral behavior, and spiritual, not secular, solutions to the nation's problems. This interpretation of traditional Christian values remains central to modern conservatism as one of the two core values protected by an "outer belt" of ideas meant for public consumption.

Race, religion, gender, nationality, and class have shaped the country's antipluralist tradition. However, the strength of this tradition lies in an evolving cultural nationalism that has combined these factors in various ways over time. Conservatives have consistently upheld the values of America's Anglo-Saxon pioneers, warning that pluralism would destroy the civilization they built. Virtually every dispute over radicalism, loyalty, reproduction, race, immigration, sexuality, crime, permissiveness, creationism, and school prayer had its precursor in the 1920s.

The moral aspirations of the modern Right center on upholding the so-called traditional family. Since World War I, conservative politics have consistently focused on controlling women's perceived dangerous sexuality and autonomy. From this perspective, a morally ordered society requires a morally ordered family, with clear lines of divinely ordained masculine authority and the containment of women's erotic allure. Conservatives view displays of female bodies that are salacious or nonmotherly, sex education in schools, abortion rights, and easy divorces as threats to the reproduction and orderly progress of civilization.

Since the 1920s, feminist demands to challenge traditional gender roles and undermine patriarchy have been viewed by conservatives as defeminizing women and feminizing men, thereby opening the family and the nation to conquest (rape) and subversion (seduction). Conservative physician Arabella Kenealy wrote in 1922, "The history of failed civilizations shows one striking feature common to most of these great decadences. In nearly every case, the dominance and [sexual] license of their women were conspicuous."[13] A century later, conservative author Stephen Wolfe echoed this sentiment: "We live under a de facto gynocracy where masculinity is pathologized in the name of 'fairness' and 'equity.' To achieve acceptance or relevance today, men must become female-adjacent; that is, to adjust to toxic feminine conditions of empowerment. . . . Men can succeed only if they are effeminate or female-adjacent (viz. they participate under feminine terms)."[14]

This system of gender control and authority also appeals to conservative maternalist women, who embrace the inherent differences between the sexes and women's unique role in raising children as healthy, moral, and productive citizens. These maternalists urge women to embrace their motherly responsibilities and raise courageous sons and domesticated daughters rather than challenge traditional gender roles. They oppose reforms that blur gender roles, undermine traditional male-led families, or replace parental responsibility with state paternalism. Patriotic mothers must uphold family morals and avoid competing with men in business, politics, and war. As conservative maternalism weakened in the mid-to-late twentieth century, a gender gap in political support emerged. In the 2020 presidential election, exit polls showed that 57 percent of women voted for Joe Biden, compared to 42 percent for Trump—a gender gap of 15 percent, which dropped to 8 percent for Kamala Harris's losing 2024 campaign (see my epilogue).

Conservatives have portrayed their religious values as broadly Christian rather than explicitly Protestant, and by the late twentieth century, white Protestants reached a rapprochement with conservative white Catholics. This evolution on the Right reflects a crucial shift in U.S. history: the decline of anti-Catholicism among white Protestants and the rise of a politically and theologically conservative Catholicism that prioritizes sexual morality, traditional gender roles, biblical truth, and the protection of Christianity over Catholic Church teachings on labor, the death penalty, and social welfare. In an ironic twist, white evangelical Protestants provided Catholic conservative candidate Patrick J. Buchanan with his most enthusiastic support in the 1996 Republican primaries, while the most devout Catholics preferred evangelical Protestant George W. Bush over Catholic John Kerry in the 2004 presidential election. Catholics such as Senator Joseph McCarthy, Governor Ron DeSantis, Buckley, Bill O'Reilly, Phyllis Schlafly, Christopher Rufo, Justice Antonin Scalia, and Justice Samuel Alito have influentially shaped modern conservatism.

After World War I, conservatives united to protect private enterprise from Progressive Era regulations, President Woodrow Wilson's free trade policies, and wartime tax hikes. Antipluralists joined forces with business leaders in the 1920s to forge a new conservative consensus. Despite rhetoric championing free enterprise, conservatives have consistently supported private enterprise, even at the expense of free markets. The conservative Republicans who gained government control in the 1920s reinstated high protective tariffs, contradicting the principles of a market economy. They enacted regulations that benefited businesses, suspended antitrust laws for exporting associations, and facilitated access to raw materials while claiming to support free enterprise. Protecting private enterprise, not free enterprise, is the second core value of modern conservatism.

Within the conservative core, the commitment to the Right's version of Christianity and private enterprise typically reinforce one another: God and Mammon. Social conservatives have praised private enterprise as both efficient and virtuous. Despite the shift in society from savers and craftsmen to producers and consumers, conservatives have maintained the connection between virtue and enterprise. From their perspective, private enterprise enforces discipline and morality in its workforce, especially as unions have weakened.

The business community has provided the Right with essential expertise, influence, and resources for political campaigns. Social issues have given the Right a mass base and a passion that economic conservatism lacks. Religiously motivated conservatives have largely exempted capitalism from accusations of cultural corruption, creating space for big capital to unite politically with ordinary shopkeepers, farmers, and workers—an alliance that liberal critics see as uniting victims with their victimizers.

Conservatives developed a revolving litany of supposed principles to serve as publicly appealing ideas. These principles have typically polled well since the advent of scientific surveys in the 1930s. Thus, conventionally accepted conservative principles serve the political goal of rallying voters and vilifying liberals while shielding the two core values at the heart of conservatism. In response to the liberal reforms of the New Deal era, the conservative movement refined its public appeals, sharpening its rhetoric against government intervention. "Anti-New Dealers developed an enduring language of opposition to government and governing. . . . Their rhetoric about the dangers of government has been the background music for opposition to liberal reform ever since," noted historian Lawrence Glickman. "While the critics lost in the short term, in the long run, they helped develop an enduring vocabulary that has fundamentally shaped our political culture, becoming a core component of conservative discourse."[15]

In the 1930s, as today, Republicans recognized that they couldn't outdo the Democrats in providing government benefits, the so-called Santa Claus approach to winning votes. Instead, they focused on appealing to those who harbored deep mistrust of the government, feared the rise of socialism, clung to the values of pioneer America, believed in a Christian nation, and were anxious about the perceived replacement of "real Americans" by Jews, foreigners, and racial minorities. For a century, conservatives have galvanized their base and marginalized their opponents by exploiting a divisive "us versus them" mentality: Christians versus Jews, whites versus Blacks, immigrants versus natives, men versus women, straight versus gay, and binary versus nonbinary gender identities.

Shifting cultural norms posed an existential threat to the conservative vision of right and wrong and to the country. From the Ku Klux Klan in the 1920s to the rise of white Christian nationalism today, conservatism has tapped into a visceral ethnocentrism that gives it a powerful emotional appeal. David M. Elcott, Taub Professor of Practice in Public Service and Leadership at New York University, and his coauthors explain, "This union of nationalism and populism cultivates a belief in divisions between 'us' and 'them.'" Their followers see themselves as "deeply patriotic, yet they are the forgotten, virtuous, struggling, and hard-working majority against a corrupt, self-serving elite consumed with political correctness." They seek to "defend national purity and protect it from institutions and foreign intruders who would rob them of their way of life."[16] Trump didn't emerge from nowhere to win the 2016 Republican presidential nomination by challenging conservative beliefs; he succeeded because he vocalized what Republican primary voters already believed but other candidates dared not say.

Conservatives reject the notion that they mislead ordinary Americans into voting against their economic interests. Instead, they assert that people benefit more from free markets, limited government, and fiscal restraint than from government handouts. Everyone succeeds, they claim, with government off their backs and out of their pockets, to paraphrase Reagan, who won presidential election landslides in 1980 and 1984.

Conservatives further argue that people are motivated by more than just material needs; they respond to an uplifting moral vision. The cultural politics of conservatism has had enduring appeal to Americans who seek the comfort and clarity of absolute moral codes, clear standards of right and wrong, swift and sure penalties for wrongdoers, a patriotic call to American greatness, and established lines of authority in public and family life. "When working-class people vote conservative, as most do in the US, they are not voting against their self-interest; they are voting for their moral interest," says Jonathan Haidt, a professor of psychology at New York University.[17]

Anthropologist Scott Atran states that "empirical studies" from around the world indicate that a sincere attachment to sacred values involves a commitment to doing what is morally right, regardless of risks or rewards. This commitment does not follow from a utilitarian calculus of costs and benefits. Instead, it is often "immune to material trade-offs" and can produce a "backfire effect" when posed against incentives to abandon sacred values, which only heightens the refusal to compromise.[18]

This book focuses on conservatism rather than on the Republican Party itself. Today, conservatives mostly align with the Republican Party and liberalism with the Democratic Party, with little overlap. However, until the late twentieth century, conservatives were divided between most Republicans and white southern Democrats, with a smattering of conservative Democrats in the North. For nearly a century, the conservative southern faction of the Democratic Party imposed Jim Crow discrimination in their region and collaborated with Republicans to block liberal initiatives.[19] Southern Democrats drafted and supported the "Conservative Manifesto" of 1937, which condemned Roosevelt and his New Deal reforms. They also joined with Republicans to form the "conservative coalition" in Congress, which thwarted liberal initiatives, such as President Harry Truman's Fair Deal and President John F. Kennedy's New Frontier proposals. Conservative southern Democrats also joined with Republicans to override Truman's veto of the pro-business Taft–Hartley Act of 1947, and they provided the necessary votes for President Reagan to enact his conservative economic program in 1981.[20]

Until recently, the Republican Party included a moderate wing, exemplified by President Dwight Eisenhower and New York governor Nelson Rockefeller. Eisenhower received nearly unanimous bipartisan support for his legislation to create the federal highway system. Republicans joined with northern Democrats to break the southern Democratic filibuster against the Civil Rights Act of 1964. However, the 1964 Republican presidential candidate, Senator Barry Goldwater of Arizona, who defeated Rockefeller for the nomination, voted against the act, courted the votes of white southern conservatives, and became the first Republican since Reconstruction to sweep the Deep South states.

The ideological mix across parties shifted dramatically in the later twentieth century, culminating in the realigning election of 1994 that largely achieved the conservative dream of uniting its northern and southern wings. For the first time in U.S. history, a majority of southern white Protestants joined their northern counterparts in voting for Republican candidates. The consequence was shifting the once solidly Democratic South into a Republican-dominated region. Realignment in the South advanced the ongoing polarization of U.S. politics by pushing Democrats to the left and Republicans to the right. Moderate southern Democrats were replaced in the Senate by conservative Republicans and in the House by either conservative Republicans or liberal Black and Hispanic Democrats.

According to Gallup polling, conservative affiliation has flatlined for decades at about 36 percent, but conservatives have converged on a single party.[21] However, "Democrats on average have become somewhat more liberal, while Republicans on average have become much more conservative." Further, "The geographic and demographic makeup of both congressional parties has changed dramatically. Nearly half of House Republicans now come from Southern states and are almost all white. House Democrats predominantly represent Northern states, and about half of party members are Black, Hispanic, Asian, or others," compared to relatively few Republicans.[22]

Although no party is monolithic in its ideology, today's Republican and Democratic Parties come close. Per a Gallup survey in 2022, 72 percent of Republicans identified as conservative, compared to just 10 percent of Democrats.[23] The American Conservative Union (ACU) rates lawmakers according to their votes in Congress. In 2021, on conservative scores, Republicans in the House averaged 82 percent, compared to 6 percent for Democrats. Senate Republicans averaged 77 percent, compared to 6 percent for Democrats. The most conservative Democratic representative, Jared Golden of Maine (22%), was more liberal than the most liberal Republican representative, Brian Fitzpatrick of Pennsylvania (33%). The most conservative Democratic senator, Joe Manchin of West Virginia (33%), was still more liberal than the most liberal Republican senator, Susan Collins of Maine (42%).[24] Per Pew Research, in 1971–72, "144 House Republicans were less conservative than the most conservative Democrat, and 52 House Democrats were less liberal than the most liberal Republican."[25]

Conservatives have followed the north star of advancing their social and business agenda for a century. Their discarding of other professed but "outer belt" auxiliary ideas is not random but predicted by these unshakable core principles. Not everyone who identifies as conservative shares these core values, but as a general proposition, they have typified the modern conservative movement. Adherence to these principles explains virtually every deviation from conventionally accepted conservative beliefs, complemented by rallying an electoral base and discrediting opponents, as in the intervention against Democratic prosecutors Bragg and Willis. "He does not believe that does not live according to his belief," said Sigmund Freud.

CHAPTER

2

TRADITIONAL CHRISTIAN VALUES

"I am a Bible-believing Christian," declared Mike Johnson (R-LA) upon his election as Speaker of the House in 2023: "What does Mike Johnson think about any issue under the sun? I said, well, go pick up a Bible off your shelf and read it—that's my worldview. That's what I believe, and I make no apologies for it." Johnson's statement reflects his deeply ingrained Christian values, which he views as inseparable from his political beliefs. In 2016, he explained, "You know, we don't live in a democracy," likening it to "two wolves and a sheep deciding what's for dinner." Instead, he argued the United States is a "constitutional republic" established by the founders who, according to him, adhered to biblical principles. For Johnson, Christian teachings drawn from the Bible sanctify his conservative principles, which he has codified in his "7 Core Principles of Conservatism." Notably, Johnson presumes that the Bible self-evidently ratifies his politics; he does not acknowledge alternative interpretations of the Bible that might contradict his assumptions about scriptural guidance.[1]

Johnson's embrace of Christian nationalism—the belief that the United States is defined and guided by Christianity—resonates with conservatives. According to a 2023 poll, 55 percent of Republicans identified as Christian nationalists.[2] Another poll from late 2022 revealed that 60 percent of Americans believe the founders intended the United States to be a Christian nation, with 45 percent agreeing that the country should be a Christian nation today.[3] Although Christian nationalism is rooted primarily in white, native-born culture, it also appeals to some minorities. For instance, 55 percent of Hispanic Protestants—the fastest-growing group among Hispanics—and 29 percent of all Hispanics either adhere to or sympathize with Christian nationalism. These affiliations help explain why Republicans have made some inroads into the Hispanic vote despite their anti-immigrant rhetoric and policies. A third of Blacks also exhibit an affinity for Christian nationalism; however, for distinct historical reasons, this has not translated into comparable support for Republicans. According to the 2024 exit polls for president, 57 percent of non-Hispanic whites, 46 percent of Hispanics, and 13 percent of Blacks voted for Trump. White and Black support for Trump remained essentially unchanged from 2020, but the Hispanic vote soared from 32 percent to 46 percent.[4]

For a century before Johnson's speakership, modern conservatives have mobilized in support of a religiously based vision of traditional culture. Conservative cultural politics has long resonated with people who seek the comfort of absolute moral codes, clear distinctions between right and wrong, swift penalties for transgressors, and established authority in both public and family life. Christian conservatives have mobilized a massive effort to sway public opinion, built an extraordinary network of support organizations, and deployed the coercive power of government in support of this vision.

Conservatives such as Johnson claim that they faithfully represent traditional Christian values. However, Peter Wehner, a senior fellow at the Trinity Forum—a Christian-based think tank—and former speechwriter in three Republican administrations, says, "Faith, including the Christian faith, manifests itself in many different ways, with a wide range of presuppositions and perspectives. There is no single worldview among Christians—nor in the Bible itself, which is multivocal, written over thousands of years by dozens of different writers. Christians today disagree profoundly on countless doctrinal issues."[5]

The rise of religious activism among conservatives in the early twentieth century coincided with three critical developments. First, millions of Catholic and Jewish immigrants from Eastern and Southern Europe arrived in the United States, challenging the hegemony of native white Protestants. Second, religious modernism, grounded in evolutionary theory, began to take hold within many mainstream Protestant denominations. For religious conservatives, evolution contradicted the book of Genesis, conflated humans with beasts, and cast doubt on humanity's immortal soul. Third, Protestant fundamentalism gained momentum after World War I. Despite deep historical roots, fundamentalism emerged as a self-conscious movement when British and American theologians, funded by California oil magnates Lyman and Milton Stewart, published and widely circulated *The Fundamentals: A Testimony to the Truth*, twelve volumes of conservative theological writings, between 1910 and 1915. Fundamentalists upheld the literal truths of the Bible: that Jesus, the Son of God, was born of a virgin mother, lived a sinless life, and performed mighty miracles. They believed that Jesus died to atone for human sins, was bodily resurrected, ascended to heaven, and would return to pass final judgment on the saved and the damned. Salvation, they argued, required attending church, affirming proper doctrine, and accepting Jesus as a personal Lord and Savior.

The line between fundamentalists and the broader evangelical movement is often blurred. They share similar theology and denominational affiliations, but whereas fundamentalists tend to be more inward-focused, evangelicals actively engage with the world. Commentators used the terms interchangeably in the early twentieth century, and today, few distinguish between them, as the term "fundamentalist" has largely fallen out of use. Conservative evangelical Protestants, including those identifying as fundamentalists, reacted strongly against modernist Protestants who sought to achieve social perfection through science rather than scripture and prioritized social progress over saving souls. They viewed Christian-based social reform as a trap that led believers to embrace secular remedies for humanity's ills, thereby diverting attention from the salvation of souls. They supported compassion and charity but delivered by individuals and communities of faith, not by a distant secular bureaucracy.[6] Historian George Marsden observed that "by the 1920s, the one really unifying factor in fundamentalist political and social thought was the overwhelming predominance of political conservatism."[7]

White conservative evangelicals had sufficient influence to challenge modernists for control over mainstream denominations, such as northern Presbyterians and Baptists. Although evangelicals failed to gain control of mainstream churches, their movement surpassed modernist Protestants in dynamism and growth by proclaiming a singular divine truth with no shades of gray as everyman's guide to life on earth and the journey to heaven. The evangelical ethos maintained a strong presence within mainstream churches, and explicitly evangelical churches grew far more rapidly than their rivals, none more so than the Southern Baptist Convention, which expanded from 3.2 million members in 1920 to 13.7 million in 1980, becoming the country's largest Protestant denomination.

Modernist pastors struggled to fill empty pews, but evangelicals thrived within their distinctive culture of Bible schools, conferences, summer camps, missionary ventures, Christian colleges, and independent parachurch organizations. With new radio networks allotting free public service airtime to the mainstream Federal Council of Churches (FCC), evangelicals pioneered the commercial use of radio in the 1920s, creating what became known as the "electronic church."

Not all evangelicals are conservative, and not all conservatives are evangelicals. Still, evangelicals have formed an indispensable conservative voter base since the early twentieth century and have significantly influenced the Right's policy agenda. The prominent conservative theologian Harold John Ockenga, board chair of the conservative journal *Christianity Today*, remarked at a 1959 board meeting that they were "always keeping in mind the close inter-relation between socio-economic issues and theological beliefs. . . . Liberalism in theology almost inevitably leads to liberal socio-economic philosophies."[8] J. Howard Pew, a devout evangelical Protestant, head of Sun Oil, and financier of *Christianity Today* and other conservative ventures, added, "You cannot take life and divide it into separate compartments—one for your Christianity, another for your economics, another for your social relations, etc." "I have never known a minister who was conservative in his theology, who was not at the same time sound in his social and economic philosophy."[9]

In the 2020 presidential election, 76 percent of self-identified white evangelical or born-again Christians voted for Donald Trump, compared to just 36 percent of all other voters. In 2024, this group voted 82 percent for Trump.[10] This evangelical base is so integral to the conservative movement that if it were to fracture, it would significantly weaken conservatism itself. However, political scientist Michele F. Margolis demonstrates that religious and partisan affiliations reinforce one another, with political commitments often deepening religious identity.[11] Another study found that the ties between religion and politics are more robust in the United States than in most other democracies.[12]

Since the rise of the evangelical movement in the 1920s, conservatives have consistently committed to a vision that merges traditional Christian values with conservative politics. The Reverend Samuel Robinson Allison, who identified as a "broadly conservative Christian," stated in 1948 that the greatest commandment for Christians is to pursue "Father's business" in the world, urging Christians to stand united against anti-Christian forces.[13] In 1951, the editors of *Fortune* magazine, along with contributor Russell Davenport, argued that the "American Proposition" was grounded in Christianity, asserting that "man was created by God in the 'image' of God,'" which gave every individual a special status and the right to live by God's laws rather than merely by human directives.[14]

Russell Kirk, a leading conservative scholar of the twentieth century, further anchored conservatism in Christian orthodoxy. In *The Conservative Mind* (1954), Kirk cited Edmund Burke as the originator of modern conservatism, emphasizing that "Christian orthodoxy is the kernel of Burke's philosophy." "And what is our purpose in this world?" Kirk asked. "Not to indulge our appetites, but to render obedience to divine ordinance." Kirk was not the conservative movement's creative architect, but its chronicler, like Dr. Johnson's Boswell; he channeled conservative ideas through the lens of Burke.[15]

On the 2016 campaign trail, Trump called for a return to the country's Christian heritage to uplift the nation's soul: "Now, in these hard times for our country, let us turn again to our Christian heritage to lift up the soul of our nation."[16] In 2021, Ryan Williams, president of the Claremont Institute, an influential conservative think tank, said, "The mission of the Claremont Institute is to save Western civilization," which he identified with his vision of Christianity. He warned of the disintegration of Christianity's core in the United States: "The Founders were pretty unanimous, with Washington leading the way, that the Constitution is really only fit for a Christian people."[17]

Christian conservative politics in the United States follows four main approaches to religion and society.

First, Christian conservatives advocate for a construct of freedom that differs from the liberal notion of individual autonomy. Instead, they believe freedom means living according to what they see as binding Christian values. Jim Daly, the president of Focus on the Family, said that "true freedom" does not mean "personal independence—the ability to make our own decisions and choose our own path in life, to do whatever we want, whenever we want." "This is not the freedom in Christ that we have been given." Rather, Jesus "was freeing us to do what we ought to do."[18]

Conservative Catholics, who politically allied with conservative Protestants in the late twentieth century, share this vision of freedom as submission to divine authority. The U.S. Conference of Catholic Bishops states, "If our obligations and duties to God are impeded, or even worse, contradicted by the government, then we can no longer claim to be a land of the free, and a beacon of hope for the world."[19] Reflecting this shift, the white Catholic vote, which leaned Democratic through the mid-twentieth century, was 56 percent for Trump in 2020 and 61 percent in 2024.[20]

In 2019, Catholic William Barr, Trump's attorney general, asserted that the founding generation believed in the Judeo-Christian moral system, which they saw as essential for a free government. He warned that "the campaign to destroy the traditional moral order has brought with it immense suffering, wreckage and misery. And yet, the forces of secularism, ignoring these tragic results, press on with even greater militancy."[21]

Freedom thus means living a moral Christian life, as conservatives understand it. Christian conservative activist Onalee McGraw explains, "In humanism, self-fulfillment, happiness, life and justice are found by each man individually, without reference to any divine source. In the Judeo-Christian ethic, there is and can be no real self-fulfillment, happiness, love or justice on earth that can be found which does not ultimately issue from Almighty God, the Creator and the Sustainer."[22] This vision of submission to traditional Christian values prioritizes men as leaders in society and the family, assigning a subordinate role to women and "others," broadly defined.

Second, Christian conservatives guard against government actions they believe subvert Christian virtues or fundamental institutions, such as the church, the school, and the family. They oppose such policies as affirmative action, abortion, contraception, sex education, no-fault divorce, and protections for LGBTQ and transgender rights, which they see as weakening the moral fabric of the nation.

Third, conservatives pair this government restraint with regulation to protect Christian virtues. The conservative push for government-compelled virtue, evident since the 1920s, gained renewed urgency after the cultural shifts of the 1960s and 70s. This agenda has continued with vigor into the present day, with conservatives using government power to enforce their vision of traditional Christian values.

Fourth, conservatives promote a particular notion of "religious liberty," which they define as the right for Christians to deny equal treatment to those with whom they disagree on religious grounds, whether gays and lesbians, women seeking reproductive care, or children seeking gender-affirming care. "This concept goes beyond traditional religious freedom to claim that (certain) religious groups and perspectives should have the right to trump those civil laws of which they disapprove on religious grounds," explains Katherine Stewart.[23]

In support of their demand for religious liberty, conservatives have long claimed that Christianity is under assault. "We are at war today," said Pew in 1964. It is "the most serious and devastating war that has ever been waged, a war against Scripture, against the faith of our fathers."[24] In the twenty-first century, Christian conservative Ken Ham argued that "there is a war in society," with "Christianity under attack." "These are challenging days. On the whole, society is becoming more anti-Christian . . . Christians are fighting for their freedom even in so-called 'Christian' nations."[25] Christian conservative influencer Tomi Lahren warned that "the evil far Leftists in this country have been targeting, attacking, demonizing and demeaning Christians and Christianity as a whole."[26] Mike Huckabee, the former Republican governor of Arkansas, warned that with the advance of LGBTQ rights, "Christian convictions are under attack as never before. Not just in our lifetime, but ever before in the history of this great nation. We are moving rapidly towards the criminalization of Christianity."[27] Speaker Johnson echoed these concerns, asserting that Christian viewpoints are uniquely censored and silenced.[28]

In a 2016 campaign speech, Trump claimed that "Christianity is under tremendous siege." If elected, he said, "Christianity will have power. If I'm there, you're going to have plenty of power, you don't need anybody else."[29] In early 2024, he said, the loss of "religion and Christianity" is why "our country is going haywire. We've lost religion in our country."[30] During the 2024 campaign, Trump called upon "my beautiful Christians" to vote for him: "In four years, you don't have to vote again. We'll have it fixed so good, you're not gonna have to vote."[31]

For more than a century, conservatives have pursued this religiously guided agenda. For 1920s conservatives, Prohibition was seen not as a restriction but as a liberation, revitalizing the traditional family and saving the souls of those afflicted with alcohol abuse. The Prohibition movement targeted working-class immigrants, particularly Catholics, who frequented saloons and vice dens. In the South, prohibitionists argued that alcohol symbolized a dangerous freedom for Blacks, leading to social disharmony and crime.

Conservatives also led the first war on drugs in the 1920s, seeing narcotics as a national calamity that undermined family discipline and moral self-mastery. The decade's most energetic anti-narcotics crusader, Richmond P. Hobson, an evangelical Christian who headed the International Narcotic Education Association, claimed that "nine-tenths of all crime is due to the influence of narcotics." Drugs had become "a national calamity more devastating than the Black Death of the Middle Ages." For moral reformers, drugs and alcohol undermined the family and threatened the purity of women. Even more than drink, however, enslavement to narcotics undercut discipline, self-mastery, and the free will needed to follow a Godly life. The nation closed its public drug treatment clinics and adopted an enduring moral and law enforcement approach to narcotics.[32]

In the early twentieth century, conservatives targeted pornography, contraception, and abortion as violations of Christian morality. The modern crusade against these vices began when Congress enacted the Comstock laws under the Comstock Act of 1873, which criminalized the distribution of obscene material, including contraceptives and abortion-related items. These laws formed the basis for censoring obscenity and restricting access to birth control and abortion. By the mid-1920s, a state-sponsored morality campaign had gained international attention, with British historian A. F. Pollard describing the United States as the "rising hope of stern and unbending Tories." Pollard noted that U.S. laws "were not so much a means of change as a method of putting on record moral aspirations.[33]

During the 1920s, most states enacted similar broad-based laws covering material deemed obscene, indecent, lewd, vulgar, lascivious, or disgusting, with no clear definitions specified.[34] The Comstock Act further prohibited the importation of any drugs or medicines "or any article whatever for the prevention of conception or for causing unlawful abortion." Nationally, the Smoot–Hawley Tariff (1930) banned the importation of "any obscene book, pamphlet, paper, writing, advertisement, circular, print, picture, drawing or other representation."[35]

Conservatives also campaigned against efforts to ban prayer and Bible reading in public schools, viewing such bans as a secular governmental intrusion on their rights. By the turn of the twentieth century, many states permitted prayer and Bible reading in schools, and about half of the nation's school districts practiced it. Similarly, conservatives blocked the reauthorization of the Sheppard–Towner Act (1921), which provided aid for maternal and infant health care, arguing that federal intervention weakened traditional family life and upheld secular values. Conservative opposition led to the act's expiration in 1929.

The Ku Klux Klan and the American Legion played significant roles in shaping the conservative social consensus that emerged after World War I. The Klan, which restricted its membership to Protestants, aggressively promoted its vision of Protestant morality. Its influence was intensely local, as it sought to enforce Prohibition, combat crime, limit immigration, ban obscene materials, and close down dance parlors, pool halls, and brothels. Additionally, the Klan boycotted businesses owned by Jews and Catholics, reinforcing its exclusionary agenda. The American Legion, the largest veterans' organization in the United States, pursued a mission encapsulated in the motto "For God and Country." Though seemingly nondenominational, the American Legion turned to four white Christian chaplains to shape its mission, consistently privileging Christianity in its subsequent activities.

The advent of President Franklin Roosevelt's New Deal prompted conservatives to link what they perceived as moral decline with liberal policies. They criticized the New Deal for undermining traditional values, which they said were essential for redeeming a failed economy and a morally compromised society. Reverend Louis S. Bauman of the Church of the Brethren captured this sentiment in 1933: "Bad bankers, rather than bad banking; bad investors, rather than bad investments; bad politicians, rather than bad politics; bad citizenry, rather than bad legislation" had caused the Great Depression. Bauman and other evangelical leaders typically refrained from endorsing candidates, joining campaigns, or donating to partisan causes in the 1930s. Still, they actively debated policy and political philosophy, primarily through evangelical newspapers and magazines. Although some evangelicals supported some liberal initiatives, such as the Civilian Conservation Corps, and criticized greedy businessmen during the early New Deal years, those with a public profile usually faulted the New Deal's secular activism, relativistic ethics, and collectivist measures.[36]

A liberal state could not redeem a nation that "leaves out God and leaves out sin" from economic calamity, warned the *Sunday School Times*. Perilous times demanded the revival of the Holy Spirit, which redeemed people's souls and inspired them to live moral, productive lives. "The Gospel of Christ is an individual message to the individual heart," declared *The Teacher*. "There is no gospel to men in the mass." In the *Moody Monthly*, published by the prestigious Moody Bible Institute of Chicago, Reverend James Edward Congdon disparaged the idea "that the elevation of the race will be the product of reformatory and regulatory legislation," which "overlooks or rejects the fact of a fallen humanity."[37]

Evangelicals argued that the New Deal discouraged the Christian virtues of self-help, thrift, and charity, and encouraged sloth, dissolution, and dependence. Liberal programs ignored the corruption of liquor, prostitution, and gambling while hobbling the private enterprise system that rewarded disciplined virtue through freedom of choice. *The Teacher* assailed "wrong track" government policies that offered secular solutions to spiritual problems and were "penalizing industry, thrift, economy, self-denial, for the benefit of the shiftless and wasters." Presbyterian minister Daniel Russell denounced "the delusion that the church is outmoded, and that the trend is toward some sort of humanism or scientific philosophy." Instead, "a steady emphasis must be put on the fact that there is no morality without the aid of the church."[38] Dan Gilbert, the general secretary of the World Fundamentalist Association, called the

New Deal "anti-Bible and anti-Christian in its economics, its morality, and its politics." "It has held up to ridicule the so-called Puritan virtue derived from the Holy Scriptures. Thrift, industry, self-denial, sobriety are being flouted by the masterminds of the Brain Trust regime. The Ten Commandments have been torn to shreds." He added, "The Bible warns us against anti-Christ dictatorships.[39]

J. Howard Pew condemned the Social Security Act (1935) for creating dependence on the government and crushing the moral fiber of Americans. "Inherent in this scheme," he said, is "the destruction of the character of individuals . . . which leads to disaster." The system "is unjust, regressive, anti-moral, and anti-social." Once "an individual ceases to depend on his own resources, he develops the psychology of the serf."[40] "New Dealism, Socialism, and Communism are substantially the same thing and all of them are the very antithesis of Christianity."[41]

Conservative Republicans joined in this religiously infused critique of secular, liberal reform. In a 1938 address, former president Herbert Hoover called for restoring "morals as the first objective of government." He accused FDR and fellow liberals of inflicting the same immoral forces that destroyed freedom in foreign dictatorships. "If being conservative on dragging America into the morass of political immorality or the dead sea of reaction is conservatism, then I gladly join that party," Hoover said. Hoover denounced the "moral corruption" of the Roosevelt administration and asked, "Do you wonder that our own people lose faith in honesty? Do they not lose faith in democracy? Does it not disintegrate the moral standards of our people?"[42] Senator John Bricker (R-OH) said, "The very foundations of public morality, of public decency, simple honesty, and fundamental human decency are being eaten away by the unblushing political immorality of the New Deal in its relation to human needs and relief."[43]

To combat the anti-Christian New Deal, Pew joined Protestant minister James Fifield to form Spiritual Mobilization, the country's first Christian Right organization. Spiritual Mobilization avoided a specific theology and claimed to be nondenominational. However, its staff and advisors were all white Protestants with business connections, including Donald J. Cowling, the president of Carleton College, and celebrity preacher Norman Vincent Peale. Spiritual Mobilization exemplified the fusion of business and social conservatives. Business leaders who believed that the right politics followed from the right religion bankrolled Spiritual Mobilization, fusing Christianity and corporate capitalism as "political soul mates, first and foremost," according to historian Kevin M. Kruse. They hoped to inspire ordinary Americans, like peasants after the French Revolution, to demand religion and the old regime. According to Pew's compilation, businesses "contributing $5,000 a year to Spiritual Mobilization" included fifteen of the nation's largest companies, among them, Carnation, Chrysler, Colgate, Firestone, General Motors, Gulf Oil, Sun Oil, Standard Oil, and U.S. Steel. "Corporate America Invented Christian America," Kruse noted.[44]

Spiritual Mobilization aimed to rally "Protestant pastors" to defend the pre-Crash blend of Christian principles and business practices, particularly during a time when "government was placing controls and restrictions on many areas of life" and when "secular religions were offered to replace the genuine faiths." Although the organization did not openly endorse specific candidates or political parties, it established a broader public platform than more narrowly focused religious lobbies, such as the Anti-Saloon League. Spiritual Mobilization argued that religion should inform all policy matters, not just those explicitly tied to moral issues, and it strongly advocated for pro-business policies with a purported spiritual foundation.

The organization disseminated its message widely through a monthly journal, numerous brochures, and a bimonthly magazine mailed free to ministers. It produced a radio program on 600 stations nationwide, organized regional conferences, and recruited clergy to spread its political message. Spiritual Mobilization made "the religious case for individual liberty" and opposed liberal New Deal programs that, in its view, infringed upon man's "inalienable rights and responsibilities." The group urged "the Church and clergy to champion those rights and the spiritual, Capital 'F' Freedom upon which they depend." It denounced the "pagan collectivism [that] lies at the heart of communism, socialism, the Welfare State, and all varieties of the planned economy," arguing that these systems violated scripture by pitting class against class. According to the organization, the country could not rely on "mere recommendations for new political machinery [or] mere economic palliatives," which they saw as replacing God with the false idol of a secular government. Instead, the nation's solutions had to be rooted "at the level of religion and theology."[45]

Following Spiritual Mobilization's example, other Christian Right organizations emerged to further conservative causes. In 1937, conservatives in Chicago established the Church League of America to promote a blend of conservative theology and politics. The League recruited clerical and lay members to spread its message that Christian teaching "elevates and dignifies human personality in contrast to the so-called 'Collectivist' or Marxian doctrines." That same year, conservatives founded the National Christian Businessmen's Association to unite Christianity and private enterprise.

The most significant and enduring organization formed by evangelical leaders was the National Association of Evangelicals (NAE), established in 1943. The NAE sought to reach a broad audience with conservative views on religion, culture, and politics. The NAE created the National Religious Broadcasters to amplify their message, ensuring airtime for evangelical perspectives. The association's membership grew from about 300,000 to 1.3 million by 1950. Although it claimed to accept members "regardless of race or nationality," in practice, the NAE primarily recruited white evangelicals and initially limited full membership to men, relegating women to an auxiliary role. The NAE strongly endorsed "competitive free enterprise and private ownership," arguing that social progress required a confrontation with "man's condition as a sinner. . . . Good things come out of a man's heart only when cleansed (regenerated) by the saving faith in Christ and not out of a good council, a good planning board, nor a good tax."[46]

In 1945, evangelicals brought the gospel to young people when Pastor Torrey Johnson, radio host Percy Crawford, and former jazz band leader Jack Wyrtzen founded Youth for Christ International. This unlikely trio hoped to win young people to Christ by spicing up evangelism with Christian music and movies, personal testimonies, Bible games, vaudeville acts, and discussion groups. Rallies featured sports stars, repentant hoodlums, and even a pious horse that kneeled at the cross and stomped his foot three times to worship the Trinity.[47]

The group's first professional organizer, the charismatic young evangelist Billy Graham, helped attract an estimated 1 million young people to rallies in 1946. Youth for Christ leaders denied any interest in politics but fostered a conservative political culture wary of radical subversion, secularism, and delinquency. The group rejected secular social reforms. Graham said "only a spiritual awakening" could save the country. "If we don't have it, we are done for." He warned that "materialism, secularism, humanism, socialism, and Marxism have all infiltrated most of our Protestant denominations."[48] Evangelicals extended their outreach to students in colleges and universities through the Campus Crusade for Christ.[49]

In 1944, Christian minister Abraham Vereide founded the International Council for Christian Leadership to spread conservative Christianity and politics in the United States and worldwide. In 1950, Christian evangelist Billy James Hargis founded the Christian Crusade. Hargis targeted not only communists but also others he considered anti-Christian, including alleged labor racketeers and proponents of sex education, ecumenism, world government, pacifism, and civil rights. In 1953, an Australian physician and lay preacher named Fred Schwarz organized the Christian Anti-Communism Crusade. Schwarz taught of the "historical link between liberal theology, Modernism and Communism," saying that "the best way to enlist anti-Communist fighters is to enlist them in the army of Jesus."[50]

In 1956, Pew joined Graham to form the theologically and politically conservative journal *Christianity Today*. "God has given to me the ear of millions," Graham wrote to Pew. "He has given to you large sums of money. It seems to me that if we can put these two gifts of God together, we could reach the world with the message of Christ."[51] *Christianity Today* "could change the entire course of the American Protestant Church," Graham said. "Instead of being liberal, like so many are, it will be conservative, evangelical, and anti-Communist. I sincerely believe it is the greatest possible investment an American businessman can make in the Kingdom of God at this moment."[52]

In the 1950s, conservatives rallied once again to combat what they saw as a new threat to Christian values and American life: homosexuality. During the early Cold War, conservatives perceived homosexuals as a multiheaded menace. They believed that homosexuals not only engaged in immoral and illegal activity—anti-sodomy laws remained in force across most states—but also groomed children into a degraded "homosexual lifestyle," undermined traditional family structures, and posed a significant national security risk. In the minds of conservatives, homosexuals represented a unique danger to national security as the country's "closeted" other. They gathered in hidden places, communicated in coded (Aesopian) language, engaged in subversive role reversals, and lived in constant fear of being "outed." This "Lavender Scare" suggested that homosexuals were highly susceptible to blackmail and, as perceived weak and perverted individuals, were prime targets for recruitment by communist agents.[53]

Senator Joseph McCarthy (R-WI), known for his ruthless anti-communist crusade, targeted homosexuals with the help of his aide Roy Cohn, a closeted homosexual himself. The autocratic McCarthy had little regard for constitutional protections for the accused, which his conservative Republican supporters acknowledged and tolerated. Senator John Bricker put it bluntly, "Joe, you're a dirty son of a bitch, but there are times when you've got to have a son of a bitch around, and this is one of them." McCarthy basked in his bullying reputation: "If you want to be against McCarthy, boys, you've got to be either a Communist or a cocksucker."[54]

The push for integration in the 1950s also provoked a conservative Christian backlash that invoked scripture to justify segregation. The South's first pro-segregation White Citizens Council called upon every white Southerner to defend "the God-given right to keep his blood white and pure." Many evangelical ministers from segregated southern churches equated integration with religious liberalism that defied biblical injunctions for segregation. In 1957, *Christianity Today* published an article titled "Segregation on the Kingdom of God" by E. Earle Ellis of the Southwestern Baptist Theological Seminary, which criticized Christians who ignored "the evil implicit in a consistent integrationist philosophy." Ellis defended the South's right "to preserve its European racial and cultural heritage," condemned the civil rights movement for "worsening race relations in the South," and declared integration a failure in the North. He argued that the same flawed theology seduced Christians into supporting integration, "Christian socialism," and "world government and world citizenship."[55]

Bob Jones Sr., one of the nation's most prominent evangelical preachers, argued in 1960 that scripture mandated the separation of the races. "If you are against segregation and against racial separation, then you are against God Almighty" because "God is the author of segregation." Jones warned that if the "satanic" forces who rejected Christian teachings succeeded in erasing the line separating the races, "the Antichrist will take over and sit down on the throne."[56]

In the 1950s, evangelical Christians made significant efforts to weave Christianity into the fabric of national culture. For decades, Abraham Vereide had organized prayer groups for political and business leaders to spread the gospel of Jesus and counter secular, liberal reforms. Vereide's Council for Christian Leadership became influential when it began sponsoring the annual Presidential Prayer Breakfast (later renamed the National Prayer Breakfast), which President Eisenhower inaugurated in 1953. "Members of the Congress of the United States of America" sent invitations to the breakfast, creating the impression of an official government function. The group's chair, Senator Frank Carlson (R-KS), said in 1955 that their mission was a "worldwide spiritual offensive" to defeat communism and establish the rule of Christ globally.

During Eisenhower's presidency, Vereide's council became one of the nation's most influential yet least known. By 1961, it claimed to have organized eighteen small prayer groups in Washington, DC, two hundred more nationwide, and additional groups in more than thirty countries, all funded by secretive, wealthy Christians. Vereide's inner circle during the 1950s was exclusively male, white, and Christian. It included figures such as Billy Graham, hotel magnate Conrad Hilton, industrialist R. G. LeTourneau, Senator Carlson, and more than twenty other Republican and Southern Democratic senators and members of Congress—nearly all of them politically conservative.[57]

In the 1970s, several alarming events galvanized conservative Christians. Beginning in 1970, through executive orders and court decisions, the federal government revoked tax exemptions for white private Christian academies that segregationists had established to evade the integration of public schools. In 1972, two-thirds of both chambers of Congress voted to send the Equal Rights Amendment (ERA) to the states for ratification. In 1973, the U.S. Supreme Court's *Roe v. Wade* decision established abortion as a constitutional right under certain conditions.

Conservatives framed their support for tax exemptions as a defense of religious freedom, not segregation. They argued that Christians should be free to follow their religious convictions without government interference. When the IRS inquired into the racial practices of his Lynchburg Christian schools, televangelist Jerry Falwell lamented, "In some states, it is easier to open a massage parlor than a Christian school." When the IRS revoked the tax exemption for Bob Jones University, one of its administrators, Elmer L. Rumminger, remarked that the decision "alerted the Christian school community about what could happen with government interference" in the affairs of evangelical Christian institutions. "That was really the major issue that got us all involved," he said.[58]

Although this policy shift began under President Richard Nixon (R-CA), conservatives were especially outraged by stricter regulation under President Jimmy Carter (D-GA) in 1978. This regulation targeted private schools that lacked "significant" minority enrollment or thwarted the desegregation efforts in public schools. Senator Jesse Helms (R-NC) warned that the regulations could lead to the government mandating co-ed sports programs, co-ed dormitories, the hiring of homosexual teachers, the availability of abortion counselors, and the abolition of gender-specific choirs, all under the guise of public policy. Religious lobbyist Reverend Robert Grant remarked, "Jimmy Carter has disappointed Biblical Christians," while political strategist Richard Viguerie noted that the Carter regulations "kicked the sleeping dog . . . it was the real spark that ignited the religious right's involvement in politics." Conservatives accused Democrats of meddling in their religious freedom, a theme that resonated in the elections of 1978, 1980, and beyond.[59]

Phyllis Schlafly, the most prominent female conservative activist, led the opposition to the ERA, which stated, "Equality of rights under the law shall not be denied or abridged by the United States or by any state on account of sex." Schlafly organized the STOP ERA movement, which, in collaboration with other groups, prevented the ERA from being ratified by the necessary three-quarters of the states. She argued that the ERA was another attempt by secularists to impose their antireligious views on women and the family. According to Schlafly, the ERA contradicted God's will and represented "a step down for most women," who had long benefited from male protection since the "Christian age of chivalry." She invoked the image of the pure Southern white woman needing protection, arguing that the ERA would dissolve men's obligation to support their wives and children, push women into the workforce, and consign their children to daycare centers. She also warned that the ERA would force women to share bathrooms and foxholes with men, strip them of protections provided by age-of-consent and antirape laws, and create unworkable unisex marriages that would jeopardize women's alimony, child support, and custody over children. Moreover, she claimed it would legalize homosexual marriage and require the government to fund abortions.

Conservative Catholics led the campaign against the *Roe* decision, later joined in the mid-1970s by evangelical Protestants and Republicans. Opposition to so-called aborted babies fostered a broader reconciliation between conservative Catholics and Protestants. *Roe*'s opponents took to the streets and pushed for a constitutional amendment to protect the unborn, a cause that became a lasting pillar of the Republican Party platform in 1976.

Adherents of the movement they named "right-to-life" filed lawsuits challenging *Roe*, ultimately succeeding in *Dobbs v. Jackson Women's Health Organization* (2022) when a conservative majority of 6 to 3 in the Supreme Court overturned *Roe*. Reflecting on the period after the *Dobbs* decision leaked, Chief Justice John Roberts remarked, "The hardest decision I had to make was whether to erect fences and barricades around the Supreme Court," suggesting that this decision weighed more heavily on him than overturning *Roe* itself. By the fall of 2024, twenty-two Republican-led states had either banned abortion outright or imposed restrictions far beyond the limits set by *Roe*.[60]

Conservative state supreme courts adopted additional post-*Dobbs* restrictions. In February 2024, the Alabama State Supreme Court declared that frozen embryos used in in-vitro fertilization (IVF) were legally recognized as persons, stating that personhood rights apply "to all unborn children without limitation. And that includes unborn children who are not located in utero at the time they are killed." Similarly, in April 2024, the Arizona State Supreme Court reinstated a law from 1864—predating both Arizona's statehood and women's suffrage—that criminally banned all abortions, with the sole exception of saving the mother's life.[61] At least publicly, conservative leaders backed away from these unpopular positions.

In 2023, conservatives launched another legal challenge to abortion rights, urging the courts to revoke or limit access to the abortion pill, mifepristone. Plaintiffs revived the Comstock Act of 1873, arguing that it prohibited the mailing of abortion drugs.[62] Although the Supreme Court did not take the mifepristone case on standing grounds, the ruling left the door open for future challenges.[63]

Despite the actions of Red State legislators, voters in states that backed Trump in 2024, including Ohio, Missouri, Montana, and Arizona, have approved referenda to establish reproductive rights. A similar amendment gained 57 percent support in Florida but fell just short of the 60 percent needed to enact a constitutional amendment.[64] Although Republicans, who won control of Congress and the presidency in the 2024 elections, made the politically savvy decision to omit a nationwide abortion ban from their 2024 platform, the party had advocated such a ban for several decades. Trump indicated that he would not sign the ban but could change his mind once released from the pressure of the campaign.

In the late 1970s, Christian conservatives established new organizations reminiscent of the Spiritual Mobilization of the 1930s, but with critical differences. In 1979, several conservative operatives convinced Reverend Jerry Falwell to launch the Moral Majority, a group aimed at uniting "the vast majority of Americans against 'humanism.'" Falwell, who led the Thomas Road Baptist Church in Lynchburg, Virginia, and founded Lynchburg Baptist College (later Liberty University), became a national figure through his television ministry, *Old Time Gospel Hour*.

Falwell and other televangelists, including Jimmy Swaggart, James Robison, Rex Humbard, Oral Roberts, Jim Bakker, and Pat Robertson, built nationwide followings through television ministries that combined simple gospel messages with fundraising appeals. Many of these televangelists, particularly Falwell, Robertson, and Robison, intertwined revivalism with conservative stances on communism, abortion, homosexuality, apartheid, feminism, economic policy, and national defense.

Like Pew, Falwell understood the synergy between religious conservatism and political conservatism. Similar to Schlafly, Falwell emphasized the connection between Christian teachings and traditional gender roles. In *Listen America!* (1980), Falwell asserted, "We would not be having the present moral crisis regarding the homosexual movement if men and women accepted their proper roles as designated by God." He admonished that women "are to be feminine and . . . in the Christian home the woman is to be submissive."[65]

Although the Moral Majority drew from precedents set by Spiritual Mobilization and other early Christian Right groups, it diverged by entering politics on behalf of the Republican Party and endorsing candidates. Commentators labeled Falwell's group as part of a "new Right," because it was the first to actively encourage ministers to register voters, mobilize them at the polls, and direct them toward conservative candidates. The Moral Majority was not a political action committee (PAC) authorized to endorse candidates, but Falwell explained how his network of conservative pastors could engage in partisan politics. "What can you do from the pulpit?" He asked. "You can register people to vote. You can explain the issues to them. And you can endorse candidates, right there in the church on Sunday morning." He clarified that individual pastors, but not tax-exempt churches, could make such endorsements. Falwell reiterated these points in his monthly *Moral Majority Report*, which guided people of faith in influencing politics.[66]

Other Christian Right organizations emerged alongside the Moral Majority. The Christian Voice founded a year earlier, established a PAC that rated members of Congress based on a sixteen-point "moral report card" that included issues such as balancing the federal budget, supporting the white-dominated government of Rhodesia, and opposing strategic arms control, teachers unions, and funding for the National Science Foundation. The Christian Voice also set up Christians for Reagan, which criticized President Carter for "turning his back on God."[67] In 1979, the National Christian Action Coalition created a similar "Family Issues Voting Index," and conservative activist Edward McAteer founded the Religious Roundtable, modeled after the lobbying group for big business, the Business Roundtable, with preacher James Robison as its public face.

Several other organizations, created with less fanfare, had a more enduring influence than the widely recognized Christian Right groups of the time. These organizations similarly linked conservative Christianity with conservative positions on political issues such as abortion, LGBTQ rights, marriage, the family, the role of women, creationism, education, school prayer, anti-communism, welfare, taxes, and regulations.

After Vereide died in 1969, his deputy, Douglas Coe, took control of the Council for Christian Leadership, which sponsored the National Prayer Breakfast and prayer groups worldwide. Coe restructured the organization as the secretive Fellowship Foundation, informally known as

"The Family." Under Coe's leadership, the group expanded its influence, tapping wealthy business leaders, the Lilly Foundation, and the Pew Charitable Trusts to raise its annual budget from about $400,000 in 1971 to $1.3 million in 1977. The Family sponsored prayer groups in business trade associations, civic organizations, and colleges and universities, but its most significant presence was within the government. The Family organized prayer groups in the judiciary, the military, Congress, state legislatures, and various government agencies. It cosponsored prayer breakfasts with the president, U.S. House and Senate members, governors, mayors, and state legislators. The organization conducted informal diplomacy through its contacts with foreign officials and arranged trips abroad for members of Congress affiliated with The Family.[68]

Coe continued leading the growing Fellowship Foundation movement into the twenty-first century's first decade, when its annual budget reached $10 million. For eight decades, the Fellowship cultivated a male-dominated insider's world of power and influence, open exclusively to those who professed belief in Christ. With little public scrutiny or controversy, the Fellowship came closer to establishing Christianity as the official American religion than any other movement in modern U.S. history. The vision of the United States as a Christian nation persisted among Republicans. A 2022 poll revealed that 61 percent of Republicans supported declaring the United States a Christian nation, with support rising to 78 percent among those who identified as evangelical or born-again Christians.[69]

In 1974, D. James Kennedy, the pastor of the massive Coral Ridge Presbyterian Church in Fort Lauderdale, Florida, founded the nationwide Coral Ridge Ministries. This venture included a weekly television show, *The Coral Ridge Hour*, which eventually attracted an audience of 3.5 million viewers, as well as a daily radio program, *Truths That Transform*, broadcast on 400 stations. Kennedy explicitly combined his spiritual message with conservative views on various issues, advocating for the integration of Christianity into government. He continued preaching until his retirement in 2006, after which other pastors took over the ministry and its mission.

Ralph Drollinger founded Capitol Ministries in 1997 to spread his Christian conservative views to political leaders. Drollinger claims that a "nonbiblical system"—socialism—controls Democrats. He regards undocumented immigrants as "invaders" and opposes efforts to combat climate change, abortion, and rights for women, LGBTQ, and transgender individuals. Drollinger has established strictly male-led ministries in forty-three state capitals and Washington, DC. He stated that scripture forbids female leadership in marriage or the church. Drollinger organized U.S. House and Senate Bible study groups and provided biblical guidance to President Trump. He also formed Bible study groups for high-ranking officials in the Trump administration, including Secretary of Agriculture Sonny Perdue, Housing Secretary Ben Carson, Secretary of State Mike Pompeo, Education Secretary Betsy DeVos, Energy Secretary Rick Perry, and Attorney General Jeff Sessions. "No matter what the institution is—the family, commerce, education—it needs the bulwark precepts of the word of God in order to function correctly," said Drollinger.[70]

Kenneth Copeland built his Kenneth Copeland Ministries, founded in 1967, into a massive operation promoting conservative theology and politics. Copeland's ministries held televised conventions nationwide and launched two national television programs, *The Believer's Voice of Victory* and *The Prayer Hour*. His ministry in Texas expanded to employ 500 people on a 1,500-acre campus. He also established the Copeland Bible College on this campus and built a tax-exempt mansion as his residence. Like other televangelists, Copeland declared that the United States was a Christian nation under Jesus's rule. "I'm telling you right now," he said. "Jesus of Nazareth is Lord over the United States."[71]

Beyond preaching conservative views, Copeland immersed himself in Republican politics. In 2007, he hosted Christian Right presidential candidate Mike Huckabee six times on his *The Believer's Voice of Victory* television program, drawing the attention of U.S. Senate investigators. In 2016, he joined Trump's evangelical advisory board and urged voters to support Trump: "You're going to be guilty of an abomination of God. You're going to be guilty for every baby that's aborted from this election forward."[72]

James Dobson, a PhD psychologist trained in child-rearing rather than ministry, quietly founded the influential Focus on the Family in 1977. Dobson's tax-exempt organization aimed to "cooperate with the Holy Spirit in disseminating the Gospel of Jesus Christ to as many people as possible, and, specifically, to accomplish that objective by helping to preserve traditional values and the institution of the family." Dobson pledged loyalty to "the Creator Himself, who ordained the family and gave it His blessing." The group became a prominent lobbyist for conservative causes. Susan B. Ridgley, director of religious studies at the University of Wisconsin-Madison, found in her research on Focus on the Family that from 1977 to 2009, it served as "a model for and a creator of alternative news" that linked "proper Christianity" with conservative politics. This precedent "led seamlessly to the creation of Fox News, and, later, to the formation of internet communities around outlets such as Breitbart."[73]

With women's activism among conservatives largely confined to single-sex groups, the Christian Right organization Concerned Women for America (CWA) emerged as the leading membership group for conservative women, surpassing Schlafly's Eagle Forum. Beverly LaHaye, the wife of conservative Reverend Tim LaHaye, the author of the best-selling *Left Behind* series, founded CWA in 1979 to counter the influence of the "radical" National Organization for Women (NOW). LaHaye organized CWA to recruit evangelical Protestant women with the mission "to protect and promote Biblical values among all citizens—first through prayer, then education, and finally by influencing our society—thereby reversing the decline in moral values in our nation."[74]

After the Moral Majority lost momentum in the 1980s, the Christian Right regained its footing in 1989 when Pentecostal preacher Pat Robertson transformed the "invisible army" of his former presidential campaign into the Christian Coalition. Robertson served as the Coalition's public face, but practical politicians, led by Executive Director Ralph Reed, strategically managed its operations. The Moral Majority had expanded the reach of Christian Right politics beyond Spiritual Mobilization, but the Christian Coalition exceeded the Moral Majority's legacy.

The Coalition mobilized thousands of evangelical churches in support of the Republican Party, filling a crucial gap on the Right, an organized and dedicated force to advocate for candidates and issues. In 1994, Tony Blankley, spokesperson for Representative Newt Gingrich (R-GA), soon to be Speaker of the House, remarked, "The organized Christian vote is roughly to the Republican Party today what organized labor was to the Democrats. It brings similar resources: people, money, and ideological conviction."[75] The Christian Coalition didn't just support the

Republican Party; in collaboration with other conservative Christian groups, it became the Republican Party. The Coalition recruited and trained Christian conservatives to run for state and local party positions. From these county-level roles, activists advanced to state Republican committees and national convention delegations, influencing national party platforms, rules, and nominees.[76]

In a similar vein to their defense of racially segregated Christian academies, conservatives upheld the right to discriminate against LGBTQ persons, not as oppression, but as an affirmation of Christians' religious liberty—their freedom to act according to their doctrinal beliefs. In *303 Creative LLC v. Elenis* (2023), conservative justices on the Supreme Court ruled that religious convictions could override laws protecting LGBTQ individuals from discrimination. By a 6 to 3 majority, the Court upheld the right of a Christian conservative web designer in Colorado to refuse services for same-sex marriages, citing it as a violation of her religious beliefs. The justices invoked the free speech clause of the First Amendment to strike down a Colorado law prohibiting discrimination based on sexual orientation.[77] Defending the ruling, Brent Leatherwood, president of the Southern Baptist Convention's Ethics and Religious Liberty Commission, said, "If the government can compel an individual to speak a certain way or create certain things, that's not freedom—it's subjugation."[78]

Conservatives' commitment to their slant on traditional Christian values has sometimes conflicted with their support for private enterprise. Such tensions became evident during President Obama's second term, particularly over immigration. A bipartisan "Gang of Eight" U.S. senators proposed comprehensive immigration reform, which included a pathway to citizenship for undocumented immigrants, tighter border security, and a requirement for employers to verify workers' legal status. The proposal, which the U.S. Chamber of Commerce backed, passed the Senate 62 to 38. However, conservative Republicans in the House, who opposed the citizenship provision, blocked the bill.

Christian conservatives see their political views enshrined in scripture, but alternative interpretations can lead to different lessons. Before the rise of evangelical Christianity in the twentieth century, the Social Gospel was a prominent nineteenth- and early twentieth-century movement that drew different conclusions from Christian teachings than modern conservatives do. Social Gospel theologians and activists emphasized applying Jesus's teachings on charity, truthfulness, and justice to social and economic reforms, stressing his warnings against greed and wealth. They sought to improve life on earth rather than waiting for the Kingdom of Heaven. The Social Gospel inspired the antislavery movement and early twentieth-century progressive reforms, such as slum clearance, minimum wage and hours laws, workers compensation, unemployment insurance, enhanced health and education, the eight-hour workday, and the abolition of child labor.[79]

Walter Rauschenbusch, a pathbreaking Social Gospel theologian and reformer, wrote, "The crisis of society is also the crisis of the Church," noting that "the unjust absorption of wealth on one side and the poverty of the people on the other" threatens both society and the church. He believed that "the reconstruction of the whole of human life in accordance with the will of God and under the motive power of religion was the moving purpose," as reflected in the prophetic vision of the Old Testament and the aims of Jesus Christ.[80]

David Elcott and his coauthors argue that "it is not Christianity per se that provides the core of this union between Christian identity and illiberal politics, but a self-serving construction of biblical text and "nostalgia for a past in which Christianity was the norm, as was segregation (black churches and white churches), and a very clear heteronormative and male-dominant society." In this view, politics shapes conservatives' interpretation of biblical truth rather than biblical truth shaping their politics.[81]

For instance, conservatives often claim, with little basis, that the teachings of Jesus justify discrimination against LGBTQ individuals. William O. Walker, the Jennie Farris Railey King Professor Emeritus of Religion at Trinity University in San Antonio, Texas, observes, "Most people apparently assume that the New Testament expresses strong opposition to homosexuality, but this simply is not the case." "There is not a single Greek word or phrase in the entire New Testament that should be translated into English as 'homosexual' or 'homosexuality.' In fact, the very notion of 'homosexuality'—like that of 'heterosexuality,' 'bisexuality,' and even 'sexual orientation'—is essentially a modern concept that would have been unintelligible to the New Testament writers." He adds that "the word 'homosexuality' only came into use in the latter part of the nineteenth century."[82]

Conservatives often cite the binary definition of gender, relying on Genesis 1:27: "male and female, he created them." However, Tony Keddie, a professor of ancient Mediterranean religions at the University of Texas at Austin, argues that Jesus recognized more than just binary genders. Keddie points to Jesus's words in Matthew 19:12: "For there are eunuchs who were born that way from their mother's womb, and there are eunuchs who have been made eunuchs by others, and there are eunuchs who have made themselves eunuchs for the sake of the kingdom of heaven. Let the one who is able to receive this receive it." Keddie further observes that in the celestial realm of heaven, Jesus suggests the absence of gender distinctions: "For in the resurrection they neither marry [male] nor are given in marriage [female], but are like angels in heaven" (Matthew 22:30).[83] (All biblical quotations are from the English Standard Version.)

Regarding abortion, both the Old and New Testaments are notably silent. The most relevant passage from the Old Testament suggests that life does not begin at conception and that a fetus is not equivalent to a living human being. This passage prescribes only a fine if a fight causes a woman to miscarry. In contrast, the death of the woman results in the death penalty: "When men strive together and hurt a woman with child, so that her fruit depart from her, and no harm: he shall be surely punished according as the woman's husband will lay upon him; and he shall pay as the judges determine. But if there is harm, then you shall pay life for life, eye for eye, tooth for tooth, hand for hand, foot for foot, burn for burn, wound for wound, stripe for stripe" (Exodus 21:22–25).

Nancy Hardesty, a professor in the Department of Philosophy and Religion at Clemson University, explains, "It can be inferred the fetus was not considered a human life, or 'life for life' would have been demanded as it was for the mother's life, or at least a 'fetus for a fetus.'" Patricia Wilson-Kastner, the Trinity Church Professor of Preaching at General Theological Seminary in New York City, agrees: "The distinction made between the woman and the fetus is important. The woman is valued as a person under the covenant; the fetus is valued as property. Its status is certainly inferior to that of the woman. This passage gives no support to the parity argument that gives equal religious and moral worth to woman and fetus."[84]

Anti-abortion Christians often turn to another Old Testament passage to argue that life begins at conception: "Before I formed you in the womb I knew you, and before you were born I consecrated you; I appointed you a prophet to the nations" (Jeremiah 1:5). However, Presbyterian pastor Katherine Pater notes that there are other plausible interpretations. For centuries, Jewish authorities have understood this passage as referring to "Jeremiah's prophetic mission and just how young Jeremiah is to be offering reprisals of Israel's behavior; for Rashi [a renowned eleventh-century Jewish sage], the phrase 'before you were born I consecrated you' emphasizes Jeremiah's inevitable call and destiny to be a prophet, not when fetal life or personhood begins." David Galston, the ecumenical chaplain at Brock University, says, "When one refers to being called, the point is destiny. Both Jeremiah and Paul [in a similar passage in Galatians 1:15] mean that it was not human beings who appointed them; it was divine irresistible destiny that accounted for the offices they held. These passages are not about their mothers being pregnant."[85]

Conservatives often pay homage to Judeo-Christian values, but they tend to avoid any serious engagement with the Judeo component. The Golden Rule of Christianity is, "Do unto others as you would have them do unto you." However, the Golden Rule of Judaism, which conservatives frequently overlook, is distinct. As the iconic Hebrew teacher Hillel explained in the first century BCE, "That which is hateful to you, do not do to your fellow," which carries different implications for conduct and policy.

Rabbi and biblical scholar Yehuda Shurpin asks, "Is Hillel's Teaching the Same as the [Christian] Golden Rule?" His answer is no: "It can perhaps be argued that the common phraseology seems to emphasize that the reason to treat others well is in order that you be treated well. In Hillel's phraseology, it is almost the opposite. It isn't about you figuring out how to get others to treat you well. It's about you not mistreating others. But how do you know what mistreatment is? By what is hurtful to yourself. While the classic formulation is essentially all about you, in Hillel's phraseology, it's all about the other person."[86]

Moreover, the Judaic tradition does not teach that life begins at conception. Given their history of persecution, Jews generally oppose state-enforced versions of Christian religious beliefs. It's not surprising, then, that a Pew Research Survey found 83 percent of American Jews support keeping abortion legal in all or most cases. Rabbi Danya Ruttenberg highlights that the "long-standing [Jewish] tradition of embracing *machloket,* or divergent opinions, allows a Jew who is personally opposed to abortion more able to see the possibility that someone else might legitimately understand the world in a different way, and to value that perspective." This tradition supports "allowing each individual or community to make the decisions that make the most sense for them."[87]

Keddie critiques how conservatives distort biblical teachings for political gain and to justify discrimination against those who do not fit the mold of white, heterosexual men:

> Republican influencers, who disseminate their discriminatory biblical interpretations to Christian voters through television, the internet, and the pulpit, use three strategies in particular: they *garble* the text by mistranslating or limiting the meaning of its words (whether in the ancient languages or English translation); they *omit* relevant parts of the text by extracting a verse from its literary context and sometimes cutting out sections of verses; and they *patch* this cut-up text together with other cut-up texts into the framework of a carefully designed quilt that's backed by ignorance, stuffed with hatred, and sewn with self-interest. When Republican influencers interpret the Bible in this way, they manipulate the ancient texts to promote modern Republican political positions.[88]

The Right's interpretation and use of so-called traditional Christian values is an example of what historian Emilio Gentile calls "political religion," which is "a form of sacralization of politics that has an exclusive and fundamentalist nature. It does not accept the coexistence of other political ideologies and movements; it denies the autonomy of the individual in relation to the collectivity; it demands compliance with its commandments and participation in its political cult." In its extreme form, "it sanctifies violence as a legitimate weapon in its fight against its enemies and as an instrument of regeneration."[89]

Other religious scholars emphasize that the teachings of Jesus are not harsh and punitive, but they exalt love, compassion, and inclusivity. Jesus does not explicitly address abortion or same-sex love, but he speaks extensively about the dangers of greed and the moral imperative to care for the poor, the oppressed, and the stranger. He warns, "Woe unto you that are rich! For ye have received your consolation" (Luke 6:24). "Take care, and be on your guard against all covetousness, for one's life does not consist in the abundance of his possessions" (Luke 12:15). "You cannot serve God and money" (Matthew 6:24). "It is easier for a camel to go through the eye of a needle than for a rich person to enter the Kingdom of God!" (Matthew 19:24).

According to the Christian Bible Reference Site,[90] Jesus teaches that "the love of money is a root of all kinds of evil." Theologian Tim Chester further reminds us that Jesus teaches "God's rule is a liberating rule, a rule of justice and blessing." "But far from being a reason for inaction, the continuing presence of the poor is the basis for the continuing command to be openhanded."[91] Elcott and his coauthors argue that Christian conservatism "can be unmoored from democratic traditions," often focusing solely on "its notions of exclusion and apocalyptic war and conquest." They point out that this approach frequently seems disconnected from critical Christian traditions, such as caring for strangers, attending church, and emulating Jesus's outreach to those most vulnerable and despised.[92]

Conservatives, they argue, also overlook one of the New Testament's most explicit teachings: fidelity to truth. In John, Jesus urges his followers, "My little children, let us not love in word or talk but in deed and in truth" (1 John 3:18). The Apostle Paul reinforces this: "Let each one of you speak the truth with his neighbor, for we are members one of another" (Ephesians 4:25). Paul also emphasizes, "Rather, speaking the truth in love, we are to grow up in every way into him who is the head, into Christ" (Ephesians 4:15). The book of Proverbs further underscores this wisdom: "Lying lips are an abomination to the LORD, but those who act faithfully are his delight" (Proverbs 12:22), and "Better is a poor man who walks in his integrity than a rich man who is crooked in his ways" (Proverbs 28:6).

The alternative vision inspired by Jesus's teachings has fueled movements such as the Social Gospel and contemporary liberal evangelism. Adherents stress the importance of societal cooperation to aid and uplift the poor, ensure the wealthy contribute their fair share in taxes, regulate enterprises in the public interest, curb business abuses, and protect human and civil rights. The Social Gospel ethos has significantly influenced modern-day Protestant evangelism, seen in Martin Luther King Jr., Barbara Jordan, Jimmy Carter, and Senator Raphael Warnock (D-GA), and the Catholicism of John, Robert, and Ted Kennedy, Alexandria Ocasio-Cortez, and Joe Biden.

Shawn Fain, the head of the United Auto Workers, evoked the Social Gospel tradition during the successful 2023 strike against the major automakers. "It sounds like there's very much an emphasis on Jesus is for the worker. Jesus stands in solidarity with the laborers," noted Christopher Evans, a professor of the history of Christianity at Boston University. "That's his consistent message, and it runs through a lot of the tradition of the Social Gospel going back to the late 19th century." Yet today, the thunderous passion of the Christian Right often mutes the voice of the Social Gospel. "The real novelty of our own time is not the prominence of the religious Right but the silence of the religious Left," historian Alec Ryrie said.[93]

Liberal evangelism is not the sole interpretation of Christian teachings, but it does highlight the dubious and often self-serving nature of conservative constructions. It is challenging to find examples of conservative Christian leaders and their political allies making tough moral decisions that go against their self-interest. Christian Right pastors have notably reaped significant financial rewards from their ministries, amassing substantial fortunes despite Jesus's admonition to accumulate "only what you need" and the guidance in 1 Timothy 3:1–7 that a church leader must not be "a lover of money." Prominent conservative ministers have acquired considerable wealth, ranging from an estimated $5 million for James Robison to $110 million for Pat Robertson and at least $700 million for Kenneth Copeland.[94] Moreover, their tax-exempt religious organizations often subsidize their opulent lifestyles. For instance, Robison resides on a 2,000-acre ranch in Texas in a church-financed, tax-free mansion with luxurious amenities, including an indoor swimming pool, basketball court, and tennis courts. Susan B. Anthony famously remarked in response to religious arguments against women's suffrage, "I distrust those people who know so well what God wants them to do, because I notice it always coincides with their own desires."[95]

The restrictions on abortion, LGBTQ rights, and nonbinary gender identities do not stem solely from conservative interpretations of scripture. Authoritarian regimes hostile to Christianity also suppress these practices and identities, as seen in countries such as North Korea, Malaysia, Pakistan, Saudi Arabia, Somalia, and Syria. In 2018, composer Frank Wilhoit offered a widely quoted critique: "Conservatism consists of exactly one proposition, to wit: There must be in-groups whom the law protects but does not bind, alongside out-groups whom the law binds but does not protect."[96]

CHAPTER

3

FREE ENTERPRISE

As professed by conservatives, free enterprise is a lofty ideal that extols the magic of a free market economy. Since the 1920s, conservative Christian teaching has fit seamlessly into support for free enterprise, which requires the discipline and virtues of Christianity; otherwise, the economy would collapse under the weight of employer greed and worker apathy, leaving the government to restore order by draconian means. Evangelical reverend A. B. Kendall of the United Society of Christian Endeavor, like many religious leaders of the 1920s, agreed that the United States did not have to choose between God and Mammon. "Material prosperity and godliness go hand in hand," he said in 1927. "The nation that sows morality and spirituality will reap peace and prosperity." Conservative journalist Edward Bok, who wrote in 1926, agreed: "In fact the successful outcome of industry depends upon certain moral standards. Thrift, for instance, a higher standard of honor, the keeping of a man's word, steadiness, sobriety, a recognition of honorable dealings—all these Christian virtues have been brought directly into the life of civilized nations by Industrialism. The whole fabric of Business rests upon these moral forces."[1] In 1930, Bible teacher and statistician William Ridgeway told the World Christian Fundamentals Association, "Every one of the 400 largest establishments of the United States is administered by Christian men. No great business success ever was attained by a corporation the founders and operators of which lacked faith in God."[2]

J. Howard Pew reflected on his five decades of business in 1952: "The free market cannot stand alone. It must be erected on a Christian foundation. A free market can exist only in a community where the people generally accept honesty, truthfulness, and fairness as a rule of conduct." You find these attributes "only in a Christian community."[3]

With the advent of the New Deal, conservatives, now entering a political wilderness, refined and amplified their support for free enterprise. Conservatives went beyond advocating for free enterprise. In *Selling Free Enterprise*, the historian Elizabeth Fones-Wolf explained that they effectively sold it to the American people through public relations campaigns. This initiative permeated schools, churches, factories, political organizations, civic groups, trade associations, and the print and broadcast media. Conservative business leaders founded free enterprise think tanks like the Foundation for Economic Education. They bankrolled the Free Market Project at the University of Chicago and the runaway bestseller *Capitalism and Freedom* (1962) by its star, Milton Friedman.[4]

An economy free from government interference has a compelling appeal for empowering individuals to make personal economic decisions guided by impersonal market forces. Free enterprise conservatives argue that it creates a meritocracy where individuals rise or fall based on their merits. It produces goods and services more abundantly and efficiently than any other economic system, benefiting all, not just the rich. Eventually, meddling in the market, even with the best intentions, will compromise individual freedom and lead to tyranny. In a typical homage to free enterprise, editors of the business journal *Barron's* wrote in 1954 that "the foundation of the American system is the individual whose political freedoms can only survive as economic arrangements release, rather than inhibit, his initiative and choice. To this end the government must maintain open markets, in which competition acts as the regulator and energizer of the whole complex process of production and distribution."[5]

Conservatives have not wavered over many decades in applauding the virtues of free enterprise. President Calvin Coolidge said in a 1925 speech before the New York State Chamber of Commerce, "We are a politically free people and an economically free people." Business, he affirmed, "should be unhampered and free."[6] Critics offered little challenge to this celebration of free enterprise during the prosperous 1920s despite wide gaps in income and wealth between the rich and the poor. No new generation of muckrakers replaced crusading journalists of the Progressive Era.

During Franklin D. Roosevelt's (FDR) first term (1933–37), the conservative National Association of Manufacturers (NAM) launched an energetic public relations campaign "to sell free enterprise," a term that NAM sought to make a "part of the American vocabulary, routinely." NAM expanded its public relations budget to promote free enterprise from $36,500 in 1933 to $467,759 in 1936. It established its National Industrial Information Committee to coordinate public relations and a Church–Industry Committee to educate ministers on economics. In tandem with such companies as Ford, General Motors, DuPont, and Texaco, it entered show business by threading pro-business themes into programs it sponsored on the radio.[7]

During World War II, NAM sponsored *This Nation at War*, a weekly program aired on ninety stations to highlight the contributions of free enterprise to the war effort. After the war, NAM, other business groups, and their conservative allies in politics again rallied to sell free enterprise to the nation. Marion Martin, the vice-chair of the Republican National Committee, hailed the Republican victories in the 1946 midterm elections as a "triumph of free enterprise."[8]

During his 1964 presidential campaign, Barry Goldwater, the most conservative Republican presidential candidate since the 1920s, said, "Wherever men are today reasonably free and relatively prosperous, they have gained their freedom and earned their prosperity through a system based on private property, free enterprise, and free markets. There is not a single exception."[9] Conservative activist Phyllis Schlafly gained fame on the Right with her self-published *A Choice Not an Echo* (1964), which foreshadowed a Republican campaign slogan and sold 3 million copies. She, too, extolled free market virtues: "Free competition has been the secret of American greatness. Honest competition between our producers, our transporters, our merchants, has made the American economic system the envy of the world. . . . The Republican Party is especially dedicated to preserving and fostering competition."[10]

For President Ronald Reagan, "Free enterprise is not just the province of the rich, but a system of free choice in which everyone has rights, and that business, large or small, is something in which everyone can own a piece of the action."[11] Senator Ted Cruz (R-TX) agreed. "What folks here understand is that jobs and economic growth, they come from the private sector, they come from entrepreneurs putting capital at risk and they come from small businesses," Cruz said in 2017.[12] In his 2018 recounting of core conservative principles, Representative Mike Johnson (R-LA) listed "free markets": "Government often stands as the greatest obstacle to the progress and prosperity of free people. . . . The free enterprise system rewards hard work and self-sacrifice and is the basis and the genius of the American economy."

The conservative sales pitch for free enterprise worked. A 1955 Opinion Research Corporation poll found that 71 percent of respondents chose "the workings of the free enterprise system" as giving them the best chance for a better life, 17 percent chose "help from government," and 12 percent had no opinion. Later, a Greenberg Quinlan Rosner Research poll for February 2012 found that 59 percent of respondents were more likely to support a Republican candidate who said, "We must rebuild the foundations of the American economy on the principles of free enterprise, hard work, and individualism"; 19 percent declared themselves unlikely, and the rest were indifferent. A Gallup poll from 2021 found that 84 percent of those surveyed had a positive image of free enterprise.

Since the 1930s, conservatives have charged liberals with promoting socialist or communist ideas that sabotaged free markets, regimented the people, and created cadres of hapless dependents. Conservatives criticized FDR's reforms for imposing excessive regulations and placing the government in competition with private enterprises. They charged Democrats with contradicting their 1932 platform pledge for "the removal of government from all fields of private enterprise except where necessary to develop public works and natural resources in the common interest."[13] Representative Bertrand H. Snell (R-NY), the House minority leader, charged in 1935 that New Deal programs have "the government assume the functions heretofore carried out by private enterprise and exercised by the individual." The New Deal "attempts to place a whole people in lockstep" and "reduce every citizen to the status of an automaton, taking orders from a government bureaucrat."[14]

Frank Knox, the 1936 Republican nominee for vice president, declared, "The issue before the country is the preservation of free enterprise. On this issue the Republican Party appeals to the whole people." The Roosevelt administration "has set up a system of regimentation in industry that reduced production and prevented re-employment," Knox said. "By coercion of Congress it forced the passage of reform measures so recklessly drawn that they have hamstrung the revival of enterprise and the renewal of investment."[15]

Eugene Talmadge, the conservative Democratic governor of Georgia, blasted the New Deal as "pure Communism":[16] "The crowd in Washington aren't Democrats." Instead, "a Communist stole the Democratic nomination."[17] Senator Simeon Fess (R-OH) claimed that Roosevelt had adopted fascist tactics to remake the United States in the image of Soviet Russia. Roosevelt was seizing "complete power of Fascism," Fess said, "in order that he may inaugurate the Soviet recommendations that are emanating from his inner cabinet of professors who are steeped in socialism."[18] Senator Thomas David Schall (R-MN) attributed Roosevelt's election in 1932 to an international communist conspiracy: "The Russian newspapers during the last election [1932] published the photograph of Franklin D. Roosevelt over the caption, 'The first communistic President of the United States.'" "Evidently the Russian newspapers had knowledge concerning the ultimate intent of the President, which had been carefully withheld from the voters in this country."[19]

Conservatives became so alarmed over the New Deal's threat to enterprise and the entrenchment of liberals in government that they contemplated seizing power through a violent insurrection, prefiguring the assault on the U.S. Capitol on January 6, 2021. In 1935, Representative Samuel Dickstein (D-NY) convened the special committee he co-chaired on Nazi Activities in the United States to hear retired General Smedley Darlington Butler testify that agents for titans of enterprise had pressured him to recruit veterans led by the American Legion for a citizen's army to overthrow the Roosevelt administration and put the nation under martial law. The committee found Butler's testimony credible. It concluded that "attempts to establish a fascist organization in the United States . . . were discussed, were planned, and might have been placed in execution when and if the financial backers deemed it expedient."[20]

With recovery from the Great Depression faltering during the 1937–38 recession, conservative academic Glenn Frank, the chair of the Republican Program Committee, declared that Americans must have faith in free enterprise: "America was built on two basic institutions, a democratic government and a system of free enterprise," which "is the world's most dependable hope for the much heralded hope for a more abundant life."[21] Wendell Willkie, the Republican presidential nominee in 1940, a moderate on foreign affairs but a conservative on domestic matters, warned that "the free enterprise system, once lost cannot be easily regained . . . we shall go down into the totalitarian pit and the next generation will struggle in darkness to rise out of it." "It is getting late. In fact, it is just about five minutes to midnight."[22]

FDR's death and Harry Truman's succession to the presidency did not dissuade conservatives from charging Democrats with throttling free enterprise. In a 1946 speech, Senator Robert A. Taft (R-OH), known as "Mr. Republican" for his party leadership, said, "Only a Republican Congress can assure real and liberal progress through the restoration of freedom and individual opportunity." "More progress can come from freedom than from all the planned economy in the Communist or New Deal handbook."[23]

Business leader and conservative activist Leonard Boulware said in 1949, "Our free markets and our free persons are at stake. We don't like the proposals for further greatly enlarged government expenditures now being urged on the public by a combination of government and union officials." He elaborated on the dangers of socialism and communism: "Our real danger . . . [and] that, while we are scared to death of communism, too many of us seemingly haven't come to fear socialism at all. . . . Let's keep in mind that communism and socialism have only recently—and erroneously—come to be thought of by the public as two different things. Communism is just a slight variant of socialism, as were fascism and Nazism."[24]

Republican National Committee chair Meade Alcorn met with Dwight Eisenhower, a moderate Republican president, after Ike's reelection in 1956. Alcorn told the press that despite some tension between Eisenhower and conservative Republicans, the GOP unified in opposition to the Left's assault on free enterprise. Alcorn said that all Republicans reject the "Left-Wing, New Deal, Fair Deal philosophy of big government, government controls, deficit financing and ultimately eliminating the free enterprise system."[25]

In the 1960s, President Lyndon Johnson claimed that his Great Society programs would bolster free enterprise, which "had produced the greatest abundance in history." Conservatives cried hypocrisy. Johnson's liberal programs, they said, were killing, not protecting free enterprise. While campaigning for Goldwater in 1964, Senator John Tower (R-TX), the first southern Republican elected to the U.S. Senate since 1913, charged the Johnson administration with "smothering free enterprise" by interfering with the work of businessmen and farmers.[26]

In 1978, when Reagan was planning his third campaign for the Republican presidential nomination, he charged that Democrats had "led us down the road of collectivism." Reagan echoed Willkie's warning from 1940, saying, in the longest five minutes in history, "It is five minutes till midnight for this wonderful, unique, free enterprise system of ours."[27]

Although President Bill Clinton claimed to be a "new kind of Democrat," liberated from liberal orthodoxy, conservatives denounced his health-care plan as another socialist-style disaster that stifled markets with government controls. In an influential memo titled "The Moral Equivalent of War," Representative Dick Armey (R-TX), chair of the House Republican Conference, said that the debate over health care "is, in effect, the Battle of the Bulge of big-government liberalism." Clinton and the Democrats "are launching a final desperate gambit to win the permanent loyalty of the great middle class through dependency on a massive new government entitlement. On the outcome of this gambit hangs the future," Armey said. In the balance was whether the country would drift toward socialism or embrace Republican free enterprise ideals: "The failure of the Clinton plan will radically alter the political and policy landscapes," said Armey. "It will leave the President's agenda weakened, his plan's supporters demoralized, and the opposition emboldened. Our market-oriented ideas will suddenly become thinkable, not just on health care, but on a host of issues."[28]

Conservative commentator Cal Thomas charged that "the Clinton administration wants to take the best health care system in the world and transform it into one that will dictate who may see which doctor, and what kind of medical services will be available to you, according to what the government determines is your 'quality of life.' If that isn't characteristic of a socialist system, what is?"[29]

In the twenty-first century, conservatives derided Democratic healthcare and climate change proposals as tantamount to socialism. Michael Steele, chair of the Republican National Committee, said that with their proposed Affordable Care Act, "Obama-Pelosi want to start building a colossal, closed health care system where Washington decides." Asked if the health care plan represented socialism, Steele responded, "Yes. Next question."[30]

Senator Bill Hagerty (R-TN) said, "We need to let market forces take hold here [on climate change] rather than try to use Government dictates to produce ahead of market demand. It is happening in my State on a natural basis. I think Tennessee sets a solid model for how we can move about this. But I hate to see us come in and use the power of government to distort markets, to impose new requirements ahead of the market's arrival there."[31] Senator John Barrasso (R-WY) claimed that Democrats' proposed Green New Deal was less about climate change, more about putting government in control of every facet of our lives. "Even if it were affordable—and it is not—the proposal is so far outside of America's mainstream that it's scary. The proposal reads like an absurd socialist manifesto."[32]

Conservative Sebastian Gorka, a former advisor to President Trump, told a cheering audience at the Conservative Political Action Conference that the Democrats' proposed Green New Deal is "green on the outside, deep, deep red communist on the inside. They want to take your pickup truck, they want to rebuild your home, they want to take away your hamburgers. This is what Stalin dreamt about but never achieved."[33] In his 2019 State of the Union address, President Trump warned, "Here, in the United States, we are alarmed by new calls to adopt socialism in our country." He pledged, "Tonight, we renew our resolve that America will never be a socialist country."[34]

Although conservatives advocate free enterprise as a counter to liberal business regulations, a hands-off government does not always benefit private enterprise, severing professed principle from practice. Given a choice between free markets and pro-business interventions by the government, conservatives have consistently chosen the latter. They have put private enterprise above free enterprise through protective tariffs, business-friendly regulations, corporate loans, subsidies, special tax concessions, pro-business foreign policies, and measures to curb workers' bargaining with employers. Ironically, some of these policies have allied conservatives with such liberals as Senator Bernie Sanders (I-VT), who advocates protectionism. Conservatives have further intervened in the market to advance their social agenda.

Economists broadly agree that protective tariffs that inherently benefit certain domestic businesses over others are inconsistent with free markets. Economist Alan Blinder explains that "protectionist policies save some jobs by jeopardizing others. Why? First, protecting one American industry imposes higher costs on others." Moreover, "Efforts to protect favored industries from foreign competition may induce reciprocal actions in other countries, thereby limiting American access to foreign markets."[35]

President Woodrow Wilson, a progressive Democrat elected in 1912, persuaded Congress to slash nineteenth-century tariffs. Republicans, in their 1916 party platform, blasted Wilson's tariff reductions "as a complete failure in every respect": "The Republican party stands now, as always, in the fullest sense for the policy of tariff protection to American industries and American labor."[36] Upon regaining control of Congress and then the presidency in the elections of 1918 and 1920, conservative Republicans reversed Wilson's course. They raised tariffs, which upset the free market balance between export and import industries at home. Foreign nations responded by raising tariffs on American goods and services, clogging international free markets. In 1930, during the early stage of the Great Depression, conservative Republicans raised tariffs sharply in the Smoot–Hawley Tariff Act, which sparked another tariff war, further impeding international free markets.

President Reagan (1981–89) declared himself a free trader, claiming that protective tariffs were no longer necessary to shield U.S. private business. However, Reagan repeatedly contradicted his free trade philosophy in support of private enterprise. He established quotas on imported sugar, Japanese automobiles, and steel imports and imposed tariffs on Japanese motorcycles to benefit the domestic manufacturer Harley-Davidson. He raised tariffs on Canadian lumber and Japanese electronic goods. Reagan's protectionism prompted free market guru Milton Friedman to write that the Reagan administration had been "making Smoot-Hawley look positively benign."[37]

President Trump (2017–21) reverted to protectionism by imposing new tariffs on imported solar panels, washing machines, steel, aluminum, and Chinese imports. China retaliated with restrictions against American farmers. Trump further abandoned free market principles by providing an additional $12 billion in federal assistance to farmers. As a candidate in 2024, Trump pledged to impose additional tariffs, including a 10 percent across-the-board tariff and a 100 percent levy on cars made in Mexico by Chinese firms.[38]

President Hoover signed the Smoot–Hawley Tariff Act. However, his advocacy for business-friendly, market-busting policies began much earlier, during his eight-year tenure (1921–28) as secretary of commerce under conservative Republican presidents Harding and Coolidge. Secretary Hoover engaged with the private economy following business demands. At the urging of the struggling airline industry, Hoover pushed Congress to regulate it through the Air Commerce Act of 1926. With federal intervention, he sought to create stable and predictable competition for the industry, impede the entry of new competitors, and foster airline safety.

Hoover and the conservative Congress did not stop there. On the ground, Congress passed the Railway Act of 1926, which supervised labor-management relationships in the industry, reduced strikes, and set a pattern for federal labor policy. Congress established a Federal Radio Commission in 1927 (later the Federal Communications Commission) to impose order on the broadcast spectrum. The legislation enabled big broadcasters to keep or sell their existing frequencies and block small competitors from sharing airtime. This politically laden law required equal time for political candidates, prohibited aliens from owning radio stations, and banned indecent, obscene, or profane language. The following year, Congress extended subsidies to shipbuilders and operators on the seas in the Merchant Marine Act of 1928.[39] Business leaders welcomed the benevolent touch of government. "The commercialists stand for the policy of individualism or *laissez faire* in industry," Rinehart John Swenson observed in his 1920s political science text. Various forms of "government subsidies," however, "are not regarded as 'interference' by the industrial individualists."[40]

During the Great Depression, business leaders opposed regulations that raised costs, empowered labor, or hampered their autonomy. Even as they denounced most New Deal policies, business leaders, with the backing of conservatives, still sought and gained federal subsidies and regulations that boosted profits, limited competition, stabilized markets, and restricted labor organizing. Banks and industrial firms benefited from billions of dollars in loans and stock purchases from the Reconstruction Finance Corporation, established under President Hoover.

Then, during the New Deal era, free market conservatives pushed aside their professed ideology and joined with liberals, who also responded to business demands, to enact pro-business bills with overwhelming bipartisan majorities. In 1935, Congress passed the Motor Carrier Act, benefiting large trucking companies by limiting competition on interstate routes. The Robinson–Patman Act of 1936 amended antitrust laws to prohibit price discrimination, which aided independent grocers and other competitors of chain retailers. The following year, Congress passed the Miller–Tydings Act, which benefited brand-name producers by authorizing states to enact "fair trade" laws that set minimum prices for the resale of brand-name goods.

Congress also acted to boost oil prices and protect large-scale producers. After the Texas oil boom dropped prices to 25 cents a barrel of crude, big oil companies gained the passage of state quota laws that limited production to stabilize prices. At the federal level, in 1935, they secured the bipartisan Connally Hot Oil Act that bolstered these laws by prohibiting the interstate shipment of so-called hot oil produced in violation of state quotas. Even before the Depression, the federal government had subsidized the fossil fuel industry through special tax breaks. The intangible drilling-cost deduction enables companies to deduct much of the costs incurred from drilling new wells domestically. The depletion allowance enables extractive industries to deduct a percentage of gross income from resource extractions, allowing total deductions to exceed the project's capital investment. These tax breaks, supported by conservatives, persist despite the profitability of fossil fuel companies. In 2022, the profits reaped by Exxon, the leading fossil fuel company in the United

States, hit $55.7 billion, exceeding the GDP of ninety-two nations.[41] Yet, it still reaps the benefits of special tax breaks.

Major staple farmers secured subsidies through the Agricultural Adjustment Act of 1933 and a subsequent revision after the Supreme Court struck down the act in 1936. Lobbyists for big agriculture backed by conservatives in Congress kept agricultural subsidies alive long after their Depression-era rationale had expired. The federal government doled out about $478 billion from 2015 to 2021 in farm support for crop insurance, disasters, conservation payments, and subsidies for certain crops, including corn and soybeans, according to an analysis by the Environmental Working Group. The wealthiest 1 percent of recipients received 27 percent of this largess, and the top 10 percent got 79 percent. Senator Chuck Grassley (R-IA), a passionate defender of free markets, received more than $1.4 million in farm payments from 1995 to 2021.[42] In their 2023 budget-cutting proposals, U.S. House Republicans retained ethanol subsidies that benefited the same big corn producers that garnered other benefits from the government.

After Republicans regained control of Congress in the elections of 1946, they joined with conservative Democrats to enact, over President Truman's veto, legislation that intruded on negotiations between labor and capital. The Taft–Hartley Act of 1947 authorized the president at his discretion to halt strikes—labor's key weapon in negotiations with management—that imperiled national health or safety for a "cooling off" period of eighty days. Taft–Hartley required union officers to file an affidavit affirming that they were not supporters of the Communist Party and had no relationship with any organization seeking the "overthrow of the United States government by force or by any illegal or unconstitutional means." The Supreme Court held this provision unconstitutional in 1965.

Taft–Hartley outlawed closed shops, which required an employer to hire only union members. It prohibited wildcat strikes not authorized by union leadership and secondary boycotts of employers not included in a strike. It authorized states to pass so-called right-to-work laws that prohibit union security agreements between employers and unions that require employees who are not union members to pay union dues, thus diminishing union strength and creating free riders in union negotiations with management. It prohibited strikes by federal workers and allowed employers to fire supervisors for participating in union activities or not supporting their employer's position.

Corporations have had their hands out for benefits from the government, which violates free market principles. In July 2005, the George W. Bush administration won the passage of an energy bill that subsidized big energy companies. During the Great Recession of 2008, Bush lobbied for and signed the Emergency Economic Stabilization Act of 2008, primarily to bail out failing banks. It established a $700 billion fund for the federal government to buy out and manage toxic assets from banks.[43]

Corporate America has regularly sought and received government tax breaks and subsidies, including from governments controlled both by liberals and free-market Republicans. Among conservative-controlled states, Louisiana, in 2015, doled out public benefits worth $2.7 billion to energy companies for building liquefied natural gas plants. Wisconsin granted Foxconn Corporation a $4.8 billion incentive in 2017 for a plant to produce television screens. In 2022, West Virginia poured $1.8 billion into Nucor Corporation to build a steel plant, and Ohio doled out $2.1 billion to Intel Corporation for a computer chip factory.

From 1995 to 2023, Subsidy Tracker documented more than $200 billion distributed to individual companies by state, local, and federal governments in subsidies, loans, tax breaks and credits, venture capital, and other benefits, with many other undisclosed rewards. Recipients included some of the nation's largest and wealthiest corporations: Boeing garnered $15.7 billion, General Motors $10.1 billion, Intel $8.1 billion, and Amazon $4.1 billion.[44] These sums do not include, for example, government bailouts, air traffic control, export assistance, or the costs of statutory programs, such as agricultural benefits. The libertarian CATO Institute estimated that in 2022, the bill for "corporate welfare" hit about $100 billion.[45]

The bottom line is clear. Regardless of free market ideology, support for private enterprise has paid off politically for Republicans, who have gained the lion's share of campaign contributions from business, although companies hedge their bets. A study of corporate donations concluded that after the conservative Republican revolution of 1994 through the study's completion in 2002, "corporate groups began to give more overwhelmingly to their more favored party—the GOP." It found that corporate donors favor "the GOP by more than 2 to 1, and for challengers, the ratio is closer to 4 to 1 in favor of Republican candidates."[46] A later study of contributions by CEOs of S&P Composite 1500 companies from 2000 to 2017 found that they contributed twice as much to Republican candidates, party organizations, and committees than to their Democratic counterparts.[47]

The advent of Trump's purported conservative populism did not dry up business contributions to the GOP.[48] In the 2022 elections, the top twenty individual federal business donors contributed $499.3 million to GOP candidates compared to $368.6 million to the Democrats. Fifteen of the top twenty donors contributed exclusively or almost exclusively to Republicans. Nearly half of Democratic contributions—$178.8 million—came from a single individual—George Soros.[49] In the 2024 cycle, the partisan donation gap widened considerably. The top twenty individual federal business donors contributed $1.017 billion to the GOP compared to $199.3 million to the Democrats, a ratio of 5 to 1.[50]

A study of the top five earners from each of the leading S&P Composite 1500 public corporations found that in 2020, 69 percent were registered Republicans, compared to 31 percent for registered Democrats. For corporate CEOs, the Republican advantage expands to 71 percent. The study additionally found that registered Democratic executives devoted 35 percent of their political contributions to Republicans in 2020; registered Republican executives devoted 23 percent to Democrats. The combined Republican advantage in registration among executives and the differential in party contributions gave Republicans a hefty financial advantage.[51]

The point is not that business leaders buy conservative politicians but that they recognize how conservative core ideology on private enterprise pads their bottom line. A. Barton Hinkle wrote in the libertarian *Reason* magazine in 2011, "The only time GOP politicians stop criticizing government handouts, it seems, is to ask for them. Which happens a lot." He notes that "Republicans routinely utter shibboleths about the free market. Yet in practice, they often substitute government's hand for the invisible one."[52]

4

LIMITED GOVERNMENT

A central paradox of U.S. politics is that people crave benefits the government has doled out since the New Deal but hate their government. Franklin D. Roosevelt's New Deal was a transforming moment in American life. It challenged old structures of power, threw up new ones, and shifted the center of politics by taking on responsibility for steering the economy, promoting social welfare, regulating labor relations, and curbing business abuses. Henceforth, Americans would expect their government to assure prosperous times, good jobs, high wages, and aid to those unable to fend for themselves.

Despite expecting tangible benefits from the government, people also clung to traditions of self-help, limited government, states' rights, and fiscal responsibility. These counterimpulses have deep roots in the United States. The astute British observer James Bryce wrote in 1888, "Individualism, the love of enterprise, and the pride in personal freedom, have been deemed by Americans not only as their choicest, but their peculiar and exclusive possessions."[1]

Conservatives draw on their version of Christian teaching to justify limited government. "Government itself is composed of fallen individuals and is far from perfect," wrote conservative theologian Art Lindsley. "As a result, scripture makes clear that God has also placed limits and expectations on the government." He claimed, "New Testament passages imply that government's primary role is 'negative' not 'positive'—focused more on punishing evil and praising good behavior and less on providing goods and services."[2] Christian conservative economist Anne Bradley says, "The scriptures emphasize limited models of government in order to protect our natural, God-given rights." Thus, "Governments that extend beyond the protection of person and property into the provision of positive rights, such as medical care, education, or a job, can only do so at the expense of another."[3]

Polls from the late 1930s showed overwhelming public support for federally guaranteed health care, minimum wage laws, and government work programs. Yet, Americans opposed the trend toward government regulation and centralized power. They favored cutting back on spending for relief and the general functions of government.[4] A later compilation covering thirty years of Gallup polling had the headline "Public Firm in View Government Is Doing Too Much, Too Powerful." In polling from 1992 to 2023, Gallup found that except for the pandemic year of 2020, more Americans believed that government "is trying to do too many things that should be left to individuals and businesses" than believed "that government should do more to solve our country's problems."[5]

Unable to compete with the liberal Santa Claus of government largess, conservatives have played the other side of the paradox. They appealed to people's alienation from government and their belief in individual initiative and private action. Conservatives have promised to limit the size and scope of government in rhetoric if not in practice. They aim to foster individual freedom and autonomy and avoid the corrupt bureaucracy that big government breeds. Big government, said Senator Frederick Steiwer (R-OR) before the Republican National Convention of 1936, "inevitably seeks to build itself greater and stronger on the ruins of the people's liberties. It reaches for the control of the education of children and for the formation of thought, and finally all human rights, including religious freedom, must yield to tyranny." Steiwer foreshadowed what in modern parlance conservatives dubbed the "swamp" or the "deep state."[6] However, conservatives pled for limited government only in opposition to liberal control. When in power, conservatives advanced their versions of big government.

Conservatives and liberals differ not on the size and scope of government, but on its purposes and programs.

Conservatives have pledged allegiance to limited government since they dominated national politics in the 1920s. During his winning 1920 presidential campaign, Warren Harding (R-OH) said, "The world needs to be reminded that all human ills are not curable by legislation, and the statutory enactment and excess of government offer no substitute for quality of citizenship."[7] In anticipation of Republican victories in the elections of 1952, Senator Karl E. Mundt (R-SD) organized a "Committee to Explore Political Realignment." He hoped to realize the long-deferred conservative dream of uniting Republicans and conservative southern Democrats behind a platform of "limited government." He proposed to "join the voting strength of like-minded voters in 1952 regardless of where they live geographically or how they are registered politically."[8]

During his 1964 campaign, Barry Goldwater warned, "Our tendency to concentrate power in the hands of a few men deeply concerns me. We can be conquered by bombs or by subversion; but we can also be conquered by neglect—by ignoring the Constitution and disregarding the principles of limited government."[9] Conservative commentator M. Stanton Evans said in 1967, "What the Republican Party should in fact be 'for' is clear enough on the record. It is for 'the American Constitution, 'limited government.'"[10]

During his 1980 presidential campaign, Ronald Reagan pledged to "get the government off the backs of the great American people." Reagan famously said in his inaugural address, "Government is not the solution to our problem. Government is the problem." In his 1989 farewell address, Reagan hoped that "we once again have reminded people that man is not free unless government is limited. There's a clear cause and effect here that is as neat and predictable as a law of physics: As government expands, liberty contracts."[11]

Conservative support for limited government continued in the twenty-first century. The Republican Party Platform of 2000 claimed, "Since the election of 1860, the Republican Party has had a special calling—to advance the founding principles of freedom and limited government and the dignity and worth of every individual."[12] In 2004, Representative Mike Pence (R-IN) said, "And conservatives know that if you reject these principles of limited government and urge others to reject them you can be my ally, you can be my friend but you cannot call your-self a conservative."[13]

At the 2010 Conservative Political Action Conference (CPAC), Senate candidate Marco Rubio (R-FL) said, "When Republicans are about lim-ited government, Republicans are successful. When they are about any-thing else, Republicans are not."[14] At CPAC, a coalition of eighteen prominent conservatives led by Edwin Meese, President Reagan's former attorney general, released a manifesto—the Mount Vernon Statement: "We recommit ourselves to the ideas of the American Founding. Through the Constitution, the Founders created an enduring framework of limited government based on the rule of law." A constitutional conservatism, it said, "applies the principle of limited government based on the rule of law to every proposal." About 50,000 individuals signed the manifesto.[15] The 2016 Republican Party Platform said, "We reaffirm the Constitu-tion's fundamental principles: limited government, separation of powers, individual liberty, and the rule of law."

The second of Representative Mike Johnson's seven core conservative principles from 2018 read: "For individual liberty to be championed, government must be reduced. We believe, as our founders did, that le-gitimate government operates only by the consent of the governed and is more efficient and less corrupt when it is limited in its size and scope."[16]

In 2023, the former director of President Trump's National Economic Council and Fox Business host Larry Kudlow said, "The populist issue has been and remains limited government. For nearly 50 years, maybe even more for all I know, the majority of Americans believe that govern-ment is too large and taxes are too high." He advised that "all the Repub-lican leaders must talk about limited government. . . . The GOP does best when it sticks with first principles: limited government and economic growth."[17]

Since FDR's New Deal, conservatives have denounced liberal big government programs. In 1934, conservatives who led the Republican National Committee drafted a "Statement of Principles": "We must not see destroyed in four years a civilization which has been centuries in building." New Deal liberals, "in place of individual initiative, seek to substitute complete government control of all agricultural production, of all business activity." The drafters invoked the word "American" three times in half a sentence, advocating "American democracy, working along American lines, in accordance with the spirit of American institutions." It was a baby step from this manifesto to a one-line platform that a local activist proposed: "ONE GOD, ONE COUNTRY, ONE RELIGION, ONE LAW, ONE FINANCE, ONE PUBLIC SCHOOL. ONE LANGUAGE, ONE VOTE, ONE TICKET."[18]

Representative Charles Eaton (R-NJ) echoed these charges: "The ultimate aim of the New Deal is to place all American industry, business, and individual liberties under the control of government here in Washington."[19] Conservative House minority leader Bertrand Snell (R-NY), however, characterized the campaign against the New Deal as "between those who believe in the philosophy of Thomas Jefferson and Abraham Lincoln and those who believe in the Russian philosophy of Lenin and Trotsky."[20] In his address to the 1936 Republican National Convention, former president Herbert Hoover said, "Either we shall have a society based upon ordered liberty and the initiative of the individual, or we shall have a planned society that means dictation." Thus, "government must either release the powers of the individual for honest achievement or the very forces it creates will drive it inexorably to lay its paralyzing hand more and more heavily upon individual effort."[21]

After six years of the New Deal, Senator Robert A. Taft prophesied, "If we stop the tremendous expansion of government activity, regulation and taxation, it is not too late to resume the progress which has made this country the envy of the world; but if we continue for six years more the course which we have pursued, it is a bold man who will say that we can restore them to prosperity under a democratic form of government."[22]

Conservatives claimed that FDR was preparing the nation for war to expand executive power, squeeze industry, and keep Americans addicted to liberal big government. "What Roosevelt has in mind is to insist that money which heretofore has gone for boondoggling and political purposes is necessary for national defense," wrote conservative John Callan O'Laughlin, publisher of the *Army Navy Journal*. "Our participation in another world war," said Senator Arthur Vandenberg (R-MI), "would swiftly and necessarily force our government into the straitjacket of an American dictatorship."[23]

In response to President Harry Truman's Fair Deal, Senator Taft said in 1950, "Truman wants to bring the government into every field of individual and community and national life."[24] William E. McVey (R-IL), during his winning 1950 campaign for the U.S. House, charged the Truman administration with "the concentration of government power." He warned, "We have traveled this road farther than most of our people realize."[25] In 1952, Truman's last full year in office, the conservative American Bankers Association called for "a reduction of bureaucracy": "Big government is unmanageable and inevitably leads to corruption."[26]

During the presidency of the liberal reformer Lyndon Johnson (1963–69), Republican National Committee chair Bill Miller said, "We Republicans aren't quite convinced that the government can do more for everybody and still cut spending. We are against poverty. But we are also against impoverishment of the people by big government."[27] William Miller—no relation—the 1964 Republican nominee for vice president, declared, "Big Government has one hand in everyone's pocket, and one hand in everybody's business."[28] Senator Roman Hruska (R-NE) warned in 1966 that "for 30 years America has been marching towards a monolithic government of ever expanding scope and size. In the last 100 days legislative steps long dreamed of by the advocates of [this] type of government have been realized and the foundation has been laid for even more of them. The appetite for even more expansion seems insatiable and the march unstoppable with the one-man consensus comprising the government today." The consequence, he said, is "disaster, the outlook is dim and depressing," unless Americans choose a different path.[29]

Republicans assailed President Barack Obama's signature Affordable Care Act (ACA) of 2010 as a dangerous intrusion into people's lives. The 2008 Republican vice presidential nominee Sarah Palin (R-AK) claimed that ACA—known as Obamacare—sets up "death panels" to decide who will get lifesaving care and who will not. Palin flatly said, "The America I know and love is not one in which my parents or my baby with Down Syndrome will have to stand in front of Obama's 'death panel' so his bureaucrats can decide, based on a subjective judgment of their 'level of productivity in society.'" Other conservatives chimed in. Senator Chuck Grassley (R-IA) said, "We should not have a government program that determines you're gonna pull the plug on Grandma."[30] Three years after the passage of ACA, conservative Fox News host Sean Hannity claimed, "There is new evidence to suggest the so-called Obama Care death panels are in fact alive and well."[31]

In 2013, Representative Michelle Bachman (R-MN), a former candidate for the Republican presidential nomination, padded the warnings about an intrusive government. She charged that the IRS was gathering a database of "intimate" details about every American. "So now we find out these people are making decisions based on our politics and beliefs, and they're going to be in charge of our health care," Bachman said. "There's a huge national database that's being created right now. Your health care, my health care, all the Fox viewers health care, their personal, intimate, most close to the vest secrets will be in that database, and the IRS is in charge of that database." The grave danger is that "the IRS will have the ability potentially—will—will they?—to deny health care, to deny access, to delay health care? This is serious! Based upon our political beliefs?"[32]

In 2022, Newt Gingrich (R-GA), former Speaker of the House, mocked President Biden's legislative agenda as "the Joe Biden-big government socialists' disaster." He blamed Biden for an increased cost of living: "In the middle of this cost-of-living crisis, Biden and the big government socialists proved how out of touch with reality they are when they scheduled a White House event to celebrate the dishonestly named Inflation Reduction Act."[33] After listening to Biden's 2023 State of the Union address, Senator Tommy Tuberville (R-AL) said, "The divide between President Biden's big-government view of our country and the conservative vision for our potential has never been wider."[34]

Republicans decry the growth of government when out of power, but when in power, they revert to their brand of big government. Conservative big government controls personal behavior, enforces loyalty, regulates education, throttles unions, and builds the armed forces. During the conservative-dominated 1920s, conservatives backed Prohibition, which restricted people's choice of drinking. Prohibition created an illegal underground economy, while the prisons swelled with felons convicted of violating the dry laws and collateral crimes. Bootlegging operations culminated in organized crime; the cost of federal law enforcement quintupled.[35]

Conservatives in state and national governments in the 1920s expanded government to combat alleged left-wing subversion. From 1917 to 1921, twenty-eight states enacted criminal sedition laws, which banned disloyal advocacy that ranged from advocating the forcible overthrow of the government to any disloyal, profane, or abusive speech about the government, the military, or the American flag. Conservatives applauded as the Supreme Court broadly construed these laws. Despite agreeing that the Bill of Rights applied to the states, the conservative Court ruled in 1925 that state prosecutors need not wait "until the revolutionary utterances lead to actual disturbances of the public peace."[36]

In the federal government, J. Edgar Hoover became director of the Justice Department's Bureau of Investigation (later renamed the Federal Bureau of Investigation) in 1924. Until he died on the job forty-nine years later, Hoover pursued a central mission of countersubversion to combat communism and suspected left-wing sympathizers. He methodically expanded his bureaucratic power and molded the FBI to fit his pursuit of subversives, with the relentless zeal of *Les Misérables*' Inspector Javert pursuing Jean Valjean for stealing bread. Hoover provided legitimacy to nearly any anticommunist crusade that emanated from the political Right for decades to come.[37]

The anticommunist, big government crusade leaped forward in February 1919 when Theodore Roosevelt Jr. and other World War I veterans founded the American Legion. The Legion quickly became the nation's largest veterans' organization. It signed up more than 800,000 members in its first year, or one-fifth of all who had served in the military during the war. This predominantly conservative organization made "100 percent Americanism" its organizing principle to "wipe out every element of disloyalty in the nation," which included allegedly radical unions and political movements. A resolution passed at the Legion's organizing meeting called upon Congress to "pass a bill or immediately deport every one of those Bolsheviks or Industrial Workers of the World." The Legion backed stern government antisedition laws at the state and national level and cooperated with official antiradical efforts through a network of Legion spies and informants.[38]

In 1923, American Legion commander Alvin Owsley cited Italian fascism as a model for combating left-wing forces in the United States: "The American Legion is fighting every element that threatens our democratic government—Soviets, anarchists, I.W.W.s [Industrial Workers of the World], revolutionary socialists and every other 'red.' Should the day ever come when they menace the freedom of our representative government, the Legion would not hesitate to take things into its own hands—to fight the 'reds' as the Fascisti of Italy fought them. Do not forget that the Fascisti are to Italy what the American Legion is to the United States."[39] In 1927, a delegation of 200 Legionnaires led by their national commander marched with Mussolini's fascists in Rome.[40]

Beyond the American Legion, Italian fascism emerged as the Far Right's largest and most prestigious movement. Inspired by Mussolini, pro-fascist sentiment spread through patriotic societies such as the Sons of Italy, the Federation of Italian War Veterans, and the Dante Alighieri Society, all of which had ties to the Lictor Federation, which Mussolini's government organized to promote Italian fascism in the United States. The Italian American press overwhelmingly backed Mussolini, as did most of the Catholic Church's leadership in the United States, impressed by a dictator who had signed a concordat with the Vatican in 1929. Until Mussolini's war against Ethiopia in 1935–36, Italian fascism escaped the opprobrium of its Nazi counterpart.[41]

As early as the 1920s, conservatives leveraged government authority to control the content of history texts that allegedly focused too much on slavery and racial discrimination and too little on American patriotism. Conservatives targeted the commonly used history text by David Muzzey, *An American History* (1911). Critics objected to its highlighting the beginning of Black slavery in 1619 and the continuing slave trade. They charged that Muzzey belittled revolutionary patriots and exhibited "pro-British" bias. By the mid-1920s, nearly half the states had introduced or enacted legislation to control the content of history texts. In 1923, Oregon prohibited any book that "belittles or undervalues" the heroes of the nation's history. Wisconsin simultaneously banned "textbooks containing seditious or disloyal matter." Wisconsin prohibited using any school text that "defames our nation's founders or misrepresents the ideals and cause for which they struggled and sacrificed."[42] By the early 1930s, Muzzey's text had faded from school curricula nationwide.

Conservatives produced their own "patriotic" history as an alternative to Muzzey and other objectionable texts. The American Legion partnered with Charles F. Horne, an English professor at City College of New York, to write a heroic account of the American experience that would unite whites north and south. Horne wrote that slavery benefited Africans and primarily burdened white masters. "The blight of slavery fell less upon their race than on their masters," he claimed. However, Horne riddled his text with so many basic historical errors that it failed to gain traction in the states.[43]

In the South, North Carolina, under pressure from conservative groups, dropped the use of the Muzzey text in 1922 and conformed to the predominant Jim Crow era of a pro-Confederate version of U.S. history that endured through the late twentieth century. Southern texts and teaching blamed the North for the Civil War and glorified the South's "lost cause." They portrayed slavery in glowing terms for Blacks and condemned Reconstruction as a misguided effort to elevate unfit Black people to a status equal to whites. Textbooks and teachers left Blacks voiceless; Southern officials harassed nonconforming teachers and banned books that did not conform to this white supremacist view of history.[44]

Conservative Christians led an effort for government to ban the teaching of human evolution. In their view, evolution contradicted the book of Genesis, conflated men with beasts, and substituted theory for fact. By teaching that humanity developed without divine purpose, fundamentalists said that evolutionary theory reduced the timeless moral standards of religion into a fleeting product of human will. A few states and many local school districts responded by prohibiting the teaching of human evolution. Fundamentalists, however, lost the public relations battle with modernists in the 1925 trial of high school teacher John Scopes for violating Tennessee's law against teaching that man ascended from apes. The trial halted the momentum for new anti-Darwin laws. Still, statutes and regulations stayed on the books in parts of the South and West, stalling nationwide the teaching of evolution in many public schools.[45]

FBI director Hoover further intruded into the lives of Americans through his COINTELPRO operations that lasted from 1956 until their public exposure in 1971. Hoover initiated more than 2,000 secret surveillance and harassment measures directed mainly at the Left and civil rights groups. Hoover spied on and disrupted what he called the "Black Nationalist-Hate Group" and the "New Left Group." Unlike the "White

Hate" program, which the FBI had confined to such violent groups as the KKK and the Nazi Party, the "Black Nationalist" program swept in civil rights organizations such as Martin Luther King Jr's Southern Christian Leadership Conference and the NAACP. On November 21, 1964, soon after King won the Nobel Peace Prize, the FBI sent King an anonymous threatening letter calling him "a complete fraud and a great liability to all of us Negroes." The "New Left" program was an equally elastic politically charged effort "designed to neutralize the New Left and the Key Activists," according to a memo by Assistant Director Charles Brennan of the FBI. It swept up most groups that opposed the Vietnam War or participated in the women's rights or Native American movements.[46]

The Lavender Scare of the 1950s led to expanded government surveillance and control of homosexuality. Pressured by the influential Senator Joseph McCarthy and other conservatives, the usually moderate Dwight Eisenhower pledged during his successful 1952 election campaign to achieve a "moral uprising" and a "clean house" in government. "The first thing is to call in the heads of every investigating agency in the federal government," he said. "We will make clear to them—clear beyond any chance of misunderstanding—that the finding out and rooting out of those who practice or condone subversion or corruption is their first and their most urgent business."[47]

President Eisenhower quickly signed in early 1953 Executive Order 10450, which, for the first time, explicitly barred homosexuals from federal employment or work with federal contractors by including the categories of "immoral" behavior and "sexual perversion." The order led to the firing of at least 5,000 federal civilian employees, military personnel, and government contractors. Many others likely declined to apply for these restricted positions. Officials did not fully repeal the antihomosexual policy until presidents Bill Clinton and Barack Obama issued new executive orders.

Conservatives pursued the Lavender Scare in the states, with similar provisions to rule out homosexuals from government employment, including in public schools. Conservative Democratic governments in Florida were notably zealous in their anti-homosexual campaign. In 1956, the Florida state legislature established the Florida Legislative Investigation Committee, also known as the "Johns Committee," after its first chair, conservative Democratic state senator and former acting governor Charley Eugene Johns. The Johns Committee launched a wide-ranging investigation of alleged anti-Christian, immoral homosexuality among public college and university students and faculty.

The Johns Committee deployed state police for their investigations and relied on dubious accounts from student informants, including secretly recorded set-up conversations. It seized medical records from the institutions' health centers and probed the content of classroom instructions and the books assigned for student reading. Its activities led to the dismissal of more than fifty students and the termination of more than twenty university employees. In 1964, the committee published a handbook on the dangers of homosexuality. The publication declared that the homosexual's goal is to "bring over" the young person, to "hook him to homosexuality." Thus, "the person affected by the practicing homosexual is first a victim, then an accomplice, and finally himself a perpetrator of homosexual acts." The handbook called for a "Homosexual Practices Control Act for Florida" that would "serve to radically reduce the number of homosexuals preying on the youth of Florida."[48] When later asked if he regretted his actions, Johns said, "If we saved one boy from being made homosexual, it was justified."[49]

In the second decade of the twenty-first century, Christian conservatives renewed their big government crackdown on gays and lesbians, which they expanded to include trans persons. Florida was once more the epicenter. In 2022, the Republican-controlled legislature passed, and Republican governor Ron DeSantis signed, the "Don't Say Gay" bill. The legislation prohibited in public schools "classroom instruction by school personnel or third parties on sexual orientation or gender identity." Although the law initially covered kindergarten through third grade, a subsequent ruling by the Florida Board of Education extended the ban to all grade levels.[50]

Like the earlier Johns Committee's claims that educators were recruiting students into homosexuality, Governor DeSantis said that students "should be protected from schools using classroom instruction to sexualize their kids as young as 5-years-old."[51] DeSantis spokesperson Christine Pushaw tweeted that "the bill that liberals inaccurately call 'Don't Say Gay' would be more accurately described as an 'Anti-Grooming Bill.'"[52]

The Florida Family Policy Council, an advocacy group for the bill, said that it was "necessary because government schools in the US have become ideological, political and are more interested in shaping a child's politics and sexual inclinations than they are in teaching academics of reading, writing, math, and education."[53] In 2024, Florida settled with plaintiffs challenging the constitutionality of the law. The law stays on the statute books, but teachers and students can now talk about sexual identity and gender orientation, but not in formal classroom instruction.[54]

In 2016, North Carolina became the first state to pass legislation barring trans persons from using bathrooms consistent with their gender identity. In 2023, Florida enacted more restrictive legislation that required all state institutions with a bathroom, locker room, or changing facility "to have separate facilities for men and women based on biological sex." Additionally, Florida law now requires sex education programs in public schools to teach that only birth determines sex, which is binary and unchangeable. It authorizes parents to object to classroom or library reading list material that describes any sexual conduct, even if it is not pornographic. A complaint would trigger removal pending investigation for permanent removal. According to a compilation by the ACLU, more than 550 bills targeting the LGBTQ community were pending or enacted as of the 2014 sessions, overwhelmingly in states with Republican-controlled legislatures.

Conservatives in Florida and other Red states have used the power of government to restrict gender-affirming care. Florida prohibited gender-affirming care for minors and required adult patients "to be informed about the dangers and irreversible nature of these procedures and to give written, informed consent."[55] As of 2024, twenty-five states controlled by Republicans have enacted bans on gender-affirming care for minors. In December 2024, the Supreme Court heard oral arguments on whether such bans violated the equal protection clause of the Fourteenth Amendment.[56]

In conservative-controlled states, legislatures and governors reprised the textbook and teaching wars of the 1920s to impose a governmentally enforced conservative orthodoxy on education. Through mid-2023, eighteen predominantly Republican states banned teaching so-called critical race theory in public schools. The theory posits that discrimination is embedded in U.S. institutions and practices, an analysis sustained by the consensus of recent scholarship, as illustrated by a sample of prize-winning books.[57] Policymakers could not draw upon academic studies to justify the ban. Instead, they followed the political strategy to motivate a white political base, devised by Republican activist Christopher Rufo, neither a scholar nor an academic. Rufo envisioned a massive political payoff for Republicans from bashing critical race theory, which he labeled "the perfect villain." Rufo excerpted seemingly alarming phrases from alleged critical race theory scholarship, some decades old: "I basically took that body of criticism, I paired it with breaking news stories that were shocking and explicit and horrifying, and made it political. Turned it into a salient political issue with a clear villain." When "strung together," he wrote, "the phrase 'critical race theory' connotes hostile, academic, divisive, race-obsessed, poisonous, elitist, anti-American."[58]

Conservatives would impose upon young people their ideologically driven view that the United States is a color-blind meritocracy where everyone succeeds or fails by merit, and discrimination disappeared long ago. Conservative orthodoxy even downplays past discrimination and violence against minorities. Florida's 2023 Standards for African American History pass over Florida's long and ongoing history of discrimination against Black people. It fails to mention that Florida officials arrested and jailed civil rights protestors or that both of the state's U.S. senators and eleven of twelve representatives voted against the Civil Rights Act of 1964. The standards portray the horrific, white-perpetrated massacres of Black people in Ocoee and Rosewood, Florida, as part of "acts of violence perpetrated against and by African Americans." As with Horne's failed text from the 1920s and pro-Confederate southern texts, the standards said that "slaves developed skills which, in some instances, could be applied for their personal benefit," even though as the property of white masters, slaves could not sell their labor for a wage, accumulate wealth, buy property, start a business, or create a better life for their enslaved children. The standards fail to disclose the true horrors of slavery or how Florida perpetuated slavery and discriminated against free Black people.

State government intrusion on education also aims to scrub any meaningful discussion of racial discrimination in public schools. As of mid-2023, at least sixteen states have passed laws restricting the teaching of "divisive concepts," which include the following:

- Such virtues as merit, excellence, hard work, fairness, neutrality, objectivity, and racial colorblindness are racist or sexist.
- An individual, by virtue of the individual's race or sex, is inherently privileged, racist, sexist, or oppressive, whether consciously or subconsciously.
- An individual bears responsibility for actions committed by other members of the same race, ethnic group, or sex.
- An individual, by virtue of his or her race, color, sex, or national origin, should be discriminated against or receive adverse treatment to achieve diversity, equity, or inclusion.[59]

The government's prohibitions on educators' freedom of speech across these states are similar, even identical. These coercive government policies did not arise organically from issues unique to the states but from a concerted national campaign by the Republican Party and conservative groups such as the American Legislative Exchange Council (ALEC), Fox News, and the Heritage Foundation. ALEC began the nationwide push for laws restricting the teaching of certain concepts with which conservatives disagree. According to journalist Tyler Kingkade, who has investigated the national movement, ALEC "is one of the groups that have been hosting webinars, especially over the winter between the election and the inauguration of Biden, to talk about critical race theory. And so this predates this wave of activism we've seen confronting school boards, where they were getting together and talking about how critical race theory was infiltrating schools and what needed to be done to stop it." In December 2020, ALEC hosted the well-attended workshop "Against Critical Theory's Onslaught."[60]

Fox News furthered the nationwide movement. As of June 2021, it had mentioned critical race theory (CRT) about 1,300 times. Kingkade notes, "It is definitely something that people in conservative, in Republican circles think is going to help them in elections. This is something that aides to Republican campaigns have said is something they see as an issue they can paint all Democrats with."

The Heritage Foundation's flagship 2021 Annual Conference featured sessions titled "Restoring Confidence in Our Elections" and "Combatting Critical Race Theory in the Classroom." Heritage had prepared an e-book,

"CRT: Know It When You See It and Fighting It When You Can." In a close parallel to arguments made in Florida, Heritage claimed that "for years, critical race theory has dominated colleges and universities. But right now, the movement is growing. Critical race theory is invading our K-12 schools, workplaces, state and federal governments, and even the military." Heritage developed model legislation and a legislative tracker for state bills, which explains the parallels in bans on critical race theory and other disfavored concepts.[61] Jacob Grumbach, professor of political science at the University of California, Berkeley, explains that Red states have used the coercive force of government to become authoritarian "laboratories of democratic backsliding."[62]

The gravest threat to those who seek control over people's lives comes from informed and well-educated citizens, which explains the conservative crackdown on education. Professors Sergei Guriev and Daniel Treisman, in *Spin Dictators: The Changing Face of Tyranny in the 21st Century*, explain that "to divide the public from the informed, rulers insult the latter, question their motives, label them elitist or unpatriotic, and inflame cultural resentments."[63] This analysis explains the playbook of Republicans in Florida and other states with their dictates on education. Republicans and independent conservatives in the states have stirred up resentment against unpatriotic, left-wing "elites" in education as justification for controlling what public institutions teach citizens.

It is indicative of Republican efforts to substitute state-imposed authoritarian dogma for free speech and informed inquiry when Florida's conservative commissioner of education, Richard Corcoran, says that the state must "police" teachers "on a daily basis." "I've censored, or fired or terminated numerous teachers." "There was an entire classroom memorialized to Black Lives Matter. I made sure she was terminated," Corcoran bragged. Corcoran, a Republican, is the former speaker of the Florida State House and, until his retirement in April 2022, an appointee of Governor DeSantis. "Education is our sword, that's our weapon," Corcoran said."[64]

Many Red states extended their governmental crackdown on education by abolishing diversity, equity, and inclusion programs and authorizing the banning of books with content that clashes with conservative values. A report by the free speech organization PEN America found, "The 2022–23 school year has been marked to date by an escalation of book bans and censorship in classrooms and school libraries across the United States." "Overwhelmingly, book banners continue to target stories by and about people of color and LGBTQ+ individuals." Book bans are most prevalent in the staunchly conservative states of Texas, Florida, Missouri, Utah, and South Carolina. The most frequently banned books included Margaret Atwood's classic, *The Handmaid's Tale,* and Nobel Prize winner Toni Morrison's *The Bluest Eye.*[65]

The rise of international terrorism led conservatives to expand the government's intrusions into the private lives of Americans. After the terrorist attacks of September 11, 2001, President George W. Bush launched the most comprehensive program for surveillance in the nation's history. This authoritarian initiative bypassed the Constitution's Fourth Amendment protections against unreasonable searches and seizures and the Federal Information Surveillance Act's requirements for the authorization of electronic surveillance. Under Bush's program, known as Total Information Awareness (TIA), the government was to sweep into a central database sensitive information on Americans, including credit card purchases, magazine subscriptions, web browsing histories, phone records, school grades, bank deposits, gambling histories, passport applications, travel tickets, driver's licenses, gun licenses, toll records, judicial records, divorce records, drug prescriptions, medical records, fingerprints, and even DNA and facial recognition information.[66]

The government would then analyze this information to develop early warnings of terrorist activity, with largely cosmetic privacy protections. Without a hint of irony, Bush tapped Iran–Contra conspirator John Poindexter, President Reagan's former national security advisor, as program director. Congress terminated funding for the program, which *New York Times* columnist William Safire called "the supersnoop's dream: a Total Information Awareness about every U.S. citizen." However, the Bush administration renamed the program, dropped privacy protections, and moved it into the "invisible government" of the National Security Agency, free of public scrutiny.[67]

President Bush expanded the government's reach into private lives by pushing the USA PATRIOT Act through Congress in 2001. The act loosened restrictions on domestic surveillance and gave federal agents greater latitude to use "National Security Letters" to gain secret access to people's financial, travel, email, and phone records without a court order or a grand jury's finding of probable cause. It imposed a gag order that prohibited recipients of such letters from disclosing the demand for records.

The Bush administration narrowly gained passage of another expansive government program to subsidize prescription drug purchases by seniors, the Medicare Prescription Drug, Improvement, and Modernization Act of 2003. This seemingly liberal program undermined the Democratic advantage on health care and substantially benefited Bush's business constituency. The legislation failed to restrain prices, giving drug companies large windfall profits.[68]

The prescription drug program complemented another big government initiative under President Bush, the No Child Left Behind legislation. Despite some grousing, most conservatives in Congress backed legislation that held public schools accountable for student achievement, provided alternatives for parents in low-performing schools (but only within the public school system), and cultivated the reading, math, and science skills needed for a productive workforce. The arts, music, civics, history, and social studies did not receive equal attention. The law also benefited companies that marketed standardized tests, educational software, and for-profit educational centers.[69] Historian Gareth Davies characterized No Child Left Behind as a big government measure that "increased the federal role in elementary and secondary schooling beyond anything that Lyndon Johnson could possibly have imagined."[70]

New elements of conservative big government emerged in Bush's second term. The administration confirmed in late 2005 that the president authorized the National Security Agency to wiretap Americans without warrants, bypassing requirements of the Foreign Intelligence Surveillance Act of 1978. Members of Congress, Republicans and Democrats, seized opportunities to benefit from big government through the record $286 billion transportation bill of 2005 that earmarked more than 6,000 special projects for nearly every member's state or district. In response to its botched response to Hurricane Katrina in New Orleans in 2005, President Bush promised a massive government rebuilding program for the city.[71]

In 2006, the Bush administration gained a renewed Patriot Act and the Military Commissions Act that gave the executive branch authority to define persons, possibly including U.S. citizens, as "unlawful enemy combatants" whom the government could potentially detain indefinitely. Aliens, including legal residents of the United States whom the government defined as unlawful enemy combatants and were tried by military tribunals, could be denied protections of the Geneva Convention against torture, habeas corpus rights to challenge their imprisonment, and constitutional safeguards against coerced and secret testimony. "Have Republicans become the party of torture, secret prisons, and indefinite detention?" asked libertarian author James Bovard in *The American Conservative* magazine, which Pat Buchanan had founded in 2002.[72]

During his 2024 campaign, candidate Trump promised to erode government restraints to seek vengeance against his political enemies. In an early June interview with *Fox News*, Trump said, "Look, when this election is over, based on what they've done, I would have every right to go after them."[73] On August 28, Trump reposted on his social media network a doctored image of President Biden, Vice President Kamala Harris, and former secretary of state Hillary Clinton in orange prison jumpsuits. He threatened to haul former president Barack Obama before a military tribunal.[74]

Trump further pledged to institute what would be one of the most significant intrusions into people's lives in U.S. history: the detention in concentration camps and the mass deportation of undocumented immigrants. These immigrants do not live in isolated communities but intermingle with U.S. citizens and lawful residents. They are married to citizens and lawful residents and have millions of children who are citizens. Moreover, the government often mistakes citizens and lawful residents for undocumented immigrants. The plan would upend the lives of tens of millions.[75]

Conservative big government includes a robust military establishment. In recounting conservative principles, Senator Jesse Helms (R-NC), a leader of Senate conservatives, said in 1976, "In the field of defense the United States must never be only 'second-to-none'; we must be superior to all or tyranny will win the day and the totalitarian way of life will be imposed on us. Other nations can equivocate because they presume they can hide under our umbrella. But if we lose our preeminence we have nowhere to hide except in subjugation or extinction."[76]

Ronald Reagan promised to rebuild the military in a 1980 campaign speech at the Veterans of Foreign Wars Convention. "We must regain that margin of safety I spoke of both in conventional arms and the deployment of troops," he said. "And we must allow no weakness in our strategic deterrent."[77] In constant dollars, defense spending rose by 47 percent during Reagan's two terms (1981–89),[78] which included an arsenal of new weapons systems: missiles, tanks, and bomber and fighter planes. The administration launched the Strategic Defense Initiative, or "Star Wars," to develop a high-tech defense against a nuclear missile strike. Despite skepticism, Congress appropriated $3 billion of the $4 billion that Reagan requested.

George W. Bush pledged to bolster the military in a September 1999 speech to cadets at the Citadel. "We now are entering this period of consequences, and things don't look good," Bush said. "The armed forces have gotten older, mostly smaller, and lacking in the resources needed for the long haul in a dangerous world." He promised to "begin creating the military of the next century."[79] Defense spending rose 51 percent in constant dollars during the two Bush terms (2001–2009).

In a 2020 speech, President Trump boasted that under his watch, "our military is completely rebuilt, with its power being unmatched anywhere in the world—and it is not even close." He added, "We have purchased the finest planes, missiles, rockets, ships, and every other form of military equipment" and created "the first new armed service since 1947: the U.S. Space Force." In a single Trump term, defense spending rose by 14 percent in constant dollars.

For the twenty years of three conservative Republican presidents, Reagan, George W. Bush, and Trump, defense spending rose by an average of 21 percent in constant dollars per each four-year term. For the sixteen years of two completed Democratic presidencies—Clinton and Obama—defense spending declined by an average of 5 percent in constant dollars per four-year term.

Conservative big government policies in the states include restrictions on the autonomy of localities. After Fani Willis, district attorney for Fulton County, Georgia, began investigating Trump, Georgia enacted legislation that authorized a state-appointed commission to remove local prosecutors. Texas has prohibited cities and counties from enacting legislation beyond state law. The ban overturns progressive policies in local governments and restricts their freedom of action in the future. In April 2024, Ken Paxton, Texas's conservative Republican attorney general, sued Harris County, the home of Houston, to block a pilot program that would provide financial assistance to families in the county's poorest neighborhoods. These communities are disproportionately minority, and 75 percent of county residents approved of the aid.[80]

In Florida, Governor DeSantis suspended a local elected prosecutor from a Democratic jurisdiction, with the goal "to amass information that could help bring down [the prosecutor] not to find out how [he] actually runs the office," said the judge who reviewed the suspension. Undaunted, DeSantis suspended a second elected Democratic prosecutor. Florida also enacted antisanctuary cities legislation compelling local governments to cooperate with the detainment policies of U.S. Immigration and Customs Enforcement (ICE). Mississippi passed legislation establishing an unelected state-appointed court system in the 80 percent Black capital city of Jackson. The bill would expand the capital police force to cover majority white neighborhoods in the city.

After the U.S. Supreme Court overturned *Roe v. Wade* in 2022, Red states have expanded government to prohibit abortions. According to *New York Times* columnist Jamelle Bouie, "Of course, the crown jewel of the Republican effort to build a more intrusive, domineering government is the set of laws passed to ban or sharply limit abortion, regulate gender expression and otherwise restrict bodily autonomy. These laws, by their very nature, create a web of state surveillance that brings the government into the most private reaches of an adult's life, or a child's."[81]

Akin to Prohibition's imposition on the liquor industry, conservatives in the 2020s have used the power of government to impose their vision of Christian values on business. This effort seeks to purge "wokeness"— roughly defined as a liberal cultural influence—from American life. Conservatives targeted companies engaging in environmental, social, and governance (ESG) investing to combine profit-seeking with social responsibility.

In 2021, Republicans in Texas enacted legislation that, according to the state comptroller, "prohibits state agencies that invest funds from investing in financial companies that boycott energy companies." Republicans in Texas have said they consider ESG investing equivalent to an energy company boycott.[82] By mid-2023, seven Republican-controlled states enacted anti-ESG legislation, with many more considering such bills.[83] In Florida, Governor DeSantis launched an attack on the allegedly "woke" Disney Corporation after it criticized his "Don't Say Gay" legislation. DeSantis said that Disney had "crossed a line." In April 2022, DeSantis added legislation to a special legislative session to end Disney World's status since 1967 as an "independent special district," with exemptions from most state regulations. Republicans in the state house quickly complied with DeSantis's wishes. DeSantis also pushed through the state legislature a bill prohibiting state officials from making ESG investments or ESG bond sales.[84]

Conservatives pushed their anti-ESG campaign nationally. Former vice president Mike Pence blasted ESG investing in a 2022 op-ed, "Republicans Can Stop ESG Political Bias." "I'm old enough to remember when liberals accused big business of consistently being on the side of Republicans," Pence said. "But in 2022 the woke left is poised to conquer corporate America and has set in motion a strategy to enforce their radical environmental and social agenda on publicly traded corporations."[85] In 2023, Republicans narrowly pushed an anti-ESG bill through Congress, with support from two conservative Democrats in the Senate. House Republicans, however, fell far short of overriding President Biden's veto, his first.[86]

Since Calvin Coolidge crushed the Boston police strike in 1919, conservatives have deployed government power to favor employers in relations between businesses and unions. The Taft–Hartley Act of 1947 restricted union organizing, strikes, and other forms of pro-worker activity. In 1981, President Reagan fired the striking air traffic controllers and decertified their PATCO union. From a peak of about one-third of the workforce in the early 1950s, union membership plummeted to about 10 percent in 2023.

Conservatives have proven highly selective in their defense of limited government. *The quarrel between conservatives and liberals is not about big government but the purposes of government.* Both conservatives and liberals have advanced their versions of big government. "Both the left and the right want government involvement, but in different domains. Believing that Republicans will make good on pledges to reduce the size and scope of government makes us Charlie Brown to politicians' football-holding Lucy," noted the libertarian *Reason* magazine.[87]

5

FISCAL RESPONSIBILITY

For more than a century, conservatives have insisted that the federal government balance its books and control the deficit by cutting spending, not raising taxes. For conservatives, support for a balanced federal budget—similar to backing limited government—checks the rise of liberal welfare and regulatory programs. Fiscal responsibility resonates with Americans' belief that the government should spend within its means, much like a business or a household. Conservatives claim that restrained spending benefits the public by controlling inflation and keeping resources private. A Gallup poll from 1937, just after President Roosevelt's landslide victory in the election of 1936, found that 63 percent of respondents agreed that "it is necessary at this time to balance the budget and start reducing the national debt"; 23 percent disagreed, and 13 percent expressed no opinion.[1] This support for fiscal responsibility endured in Gallup polling from 2011 to 2023, which found at least three-quarters of respondents consistently worried a "great deal" or a "fair amount" about "federal spending and the budget deficit."[2]

Conservatives often turn to their vision of Christianity to justify a balanced government budget. Celebrity preacher Ralph Drollinger says we are "the stewards of God's creation. For those who have trusted in

Christ, an attitude of stewardship is a necessary requirement of obedience." You are "entrusted by God with a stewardship responsibility, not only in terms of your personal and familial life—but in terms of how you manage the state." Stewards of the state should heed Paul's prescription, "*Owe nothing to anyone*" (Romans 13:8). The lesson is to avoid overextensions, be they personal or national. Thus, "the first biblical principle then, is for Public Servants to balance the annual budget, lest they immediately or eventually end up *owing*." Drollinger draws a warning from Solomon (*The borrower becomes the lender's slave*; Proverbs 22:7). He adds that budget deficits risk reducing a person or nation to "if not a *slave* in the fullest sense of that word, a person or nation of much lesser status."[3]

Conservatives have a long tradition of advocating for fiscal responsibility. When President Calvin Coolidge, a conservative Republican, the successor to the deceased Warren Harding, ran for election in 1924, his party's platform declared, "We demand and the people of the United States have a right to demand rigid economy in government. A policy of strict economy enforced by the Republican administration since 1921 has made possible a reduction in taxation and has enabled the government to reduce the public debt by $2,500,000,000." After his winning campaign, Coolidge said in 1925, "I favor the policy of economy, not because I wish to save money, but because I wish to save people."[4] Coolidge was the last conservative president to uphold strict fiscal discipline. The four most conservative presidents who followed—Hoover, Reagan, George W. Bush, and Trump—oversaw substantial budget deficits during their tenures. Despite this history of fiscal excess, conservatives have continued to don the mantle of fiscal responsibility.

The Republican Party Platform of 1936 pledged to "balance the budget—not by increasing taxes but by cutting expenditures, drastically and immediately."[5] After the outbreak of world war in 1939, as polls showed the public clamoring to aid the allies resisting Hitler,[6] Republicans continued to preach fiscal responsibility. The Republican Party Platform of 1940 declared, "We solemnly pledge that public expenditures, other than those required for full national defense and relief, shall be cut to levels necessary for the essential services of government."[7]

By 1964, a Republican Party Task Force report reinforced the importance of a balanced budget, stating that "a balanced budget to support the value of our money must be the cornerstone of our fiscal policy."[8] In 1979, a report by the Republican staff of the House Budget Committee stressed that the government must achieve fiscal responsibility through spending restraint: "We believe that the vast majority of the American people who support a balanced budget (opinion polls have estimated this number at about 80 percent) expect that this balance will be achieved by cutting spending, not raising taxes."[9] In 1982, President Reagan backed a balanced budget amendment to the Constitution. Reagan said that he was leading a "people's crusade," a "mobilization of the people who live on Main Street, U.S.A. . . . to make government understand its job is to wipe out deficits and not let deficits wipe us out."[10]

As part of its strategy for recapturing Congress in 1994, Republicans unveiled their "Contract with America," which pledged sweeping reforms. "THE FISCAL RESPONSIBILITY ACT," the first of the Contract's proposals, promised, "a balanced budget/tax limitation amendment and a legislative line-item veto to restore fiscal responsibility to an out-of-control Congress, requiring them to live under the same budget constraints as families and businesses."[11] Shortly after taking over Congress in 1995, Republicans passed a resolution for a balanced budget amendment, which lacked sufficient votes for enactment.

Despite previous setbacks, the Republican Party Platform of 2016 (the party did not adopt a platform in 2020) called for a balanced budget amendment. "The Republican path to fiscal sanity and economic expansion begins with a constitutional requirement for a federal balanced budget," the platform said. "We will fight for Congress to adopt, and for the states to ratify, a Balanced Budget Amendment. . . . Only a constitutional safeguard such as this can prevent deficits from mounting to government default."[12]

In 2018, Republicans, who held the majority in the House, voted for a balanced budget amendment, not just a resolution. Despite united GOP support, it failed to gain the two-thirds vote needed for passage.[13] Representative Mike Johnson's "Seven Core Principles of Conservatism" in 2018, particularly the sixth principle on fiscal restraint, highlighted the gravity of the issue: "Because government has refused to live within its means, America is facing an unprecedented debt and spending crisis." "Federal debt now exceeds $26 trillion, and our current fiscal path is unsustainable and dangerous, jeopardizing our nation's economic growth, stability and the security of future generations. Congress has a moral and constitutional duty to resolve the crisis, bring spending under control, [and] balance the federal budget."[14]

The Heritage Foundation's "True North" compilation of essential Republican principles echoed this sentiment in 2019: "The federal deficit and debt must not place unreasonable financial burdens on future generations. Tax policies should raise only the minimum revenue necessary to fund constitutionally appropriate functions of government."[15]

After FDR took office in 1933, conservatives charged him with hypocrisy for abandoning his 1932 platform pledge of "an immediate and drastic reduction of governmental expenditures" and a "balanced budget."[16] Instead, they accused FDR of an orgy of ruinous, runaway spending and dangerous deficits. At a meeting of the Chicago Republican Roundtable in 1935, conservative activist Jacob Allen compared FDR to P. T. Barnum. He pointed to the "plain repudiation by the mighty political 'Barnum' of his own and his party's pledges to the American people," including "a balanced budget and a 25% reduction of federal spending."[17] Senator Arthur Vandenberg agreed that the Democrats' 1932 platform is "not only dead, but mangled beyond all possibility of recognition—high promises which, when contrasted with actual performance, are the modern paraphrase of Dr. Jekyll and Mr. Hyde-Park."[18]

During the 1938 midterm campaigns, former president Hoover compared the United States under FDR to the fascist nations of Europe that "all undertook new deals under some title." He warned that under continued Democratic government, we have "more budget deficits, more inflation, more increase in national debts, more taxes for the future." He called for the government to "stop this spending, inflation, and pump priming."[19] A year later, with the world plummeting toward war in 1939, Senator Robert A. Taft opposed rearming by spending on strategic materials: "The question is, Where is the cash coming from that will have to be paid out for these strategic materials? Who is going to pay for them? The taxpayers of the United States are going to pay for them. There is only one way to stop spending, and that is to stop appropriating money, and so far as I can see, the only way to stop appropriating money is to stop authorizing appropriations."[20]

After Republicans gained a majority in the U.S. House following the 1952 elections, they wasted no time attacking President Truman's final budget. Speaker Joseph W. Martin Jr. (R-MA) denounced it as a "spend-thrift budget." Representative Daniel Reed (R-NY), chair of the House Ways and Means Committee, called it "fantastic" and pledged that "there's going to be a tax cut and there's going to be a balanced budget," ignoring the contradiction. Senator Walter F. George (D-GA), a conservative Democrat, agreed, saying, "The principal duty of this Congress and the new administration is to see to it that the budget is cut."[21]

In *A Choice Not an Echo*, Phyllis Schlafly accused Democrats of bolstering Soviet communism to justify reckless government spending. "This hidden policy of perpetuating the Red Empire to perpetuate the high level of federal spending and control is revealed in secret studies made by the Kennedy administration," Schlafly said.[22] After Lyndon Johnson won a full term in 1964 and expanded his Great Society program, Representative Gerald Ford (R-MI), the House minority leader, pledged the GOP to cut "nonmilitary, nonessential spending." "I find it hard to understand how the national government can ask business and labor to avoid price and wage increases which are measured in terms of millions of dollars when it is increasing nondefense spending by many billions," said Ford.[23] William F. Buckley Jr., still the preeminent conservative journalist, said in 1968 that the national debt "is increasingly a matter of national concern, the Keynesians and their apostles, or more accurately the Keynesians' apostles to the contrary notwithstanding. And of course even now we are continuing to add to the national debt."[24]

Conservative accusations of fiscal irresponsibility through heedless spending continued through the Democratic administrations of Barack Obama and Joe Biden. Senator John Cornyn (R-TX) told the conservative Heritage Foundation in 2011, "The debt is actually a national security problem" under President Obama. "If we continue down the current path, we not only won't have the money to provide the safety net for the most vulnerable in our society, we won't have the money to provide for our national defense and keep us all safe."[25]

In 2011, Republicans, who controlled the House, approved legislation (ultimately blocked by the Democratic Senate) that tied raising the debt ceiling to Congress enacting and submitting a balanced budget amendment to the states.[26] In the Senate, Minority Leader Mitch McConnell

(R-KY) rebuked President Obama for irresponsible spending. McConnell endorsed Republican demands to cut government spending, calling the budget deficit "the nation's most serious long-term problem."[27]

During the Biden administration, Matthew Dickerson of the Heritage Foundation charged, "President Joe Biden's American Rescue Plan Act included many damaging policies that increased deficit-financed government spending by nearly $2 trillion, stoking inflation to rates not seen in four decades. . . . Reducing the growth of government spending is necessary to ensure a sustainable fiscal future and a prosperous economy."[28] Representative Vern Buchanan (R-FL) said in January 2023, "Washington's massive spending problem has led to record-high levels of inflation and soaring interest rates, which are killing the budgets of everyday Americans and small businesses across the country. Our country is on an unsustainable path and we risk losing our standing on the world stage unless Democrats work with Republicans to reduce spending and adopt real budget reform."[29]

In the spring of 2023, Republicans, who again controlled the House, demanded significant spending cuts in exchange for agreeing to raise the debt ceiling. However, they balked at slashing military budgets or the popular entitlement programs of Social Security, Medicare, and Medicaid. The final compromise included only modest cuts in discretionary programs.[30]

Conservatives advocated for fiscal responsibility with rhetoric, not policy. During the 1920s, conservative Republican administrations had managed to keep federal spending low and pile up budget surpluses. These achievements ended permanently with the advent of the Hoover administration in 1929 and the onset of the Great Depression. During Hoover's four years (1929–33) in office, federal spending rose 107 percent in constant dollars, adjusted for inflation. The deficit reached a peacetime record of $3.6 billion in constant dollars in 1932, compared to a surplus of $939 million in 1928. As a percentage of Gross Domestic Product (GDP), the federal debt rose from .7 percent in 1928 to 4.6 percent in 1932. During the first eight years of the FDR administration, the federal debt declined by 46 percent as a percentage of GDP to just 2.8 percent in 1940, despite conservative charges of runaway Democratic spending.

President Reagan, who had promised limited spending and balanced budgets, smashed all previous records for federal deficits. During Reagan's two terms, yearly deficits ranged from $191 billion to $429 billion in constant dollars. Federal spending in constant dollars increased by 21 percent, and the deficit rose by $2.5 trillion, from 32 percent to 50 percent of GDP. The fiscal strain continued during the administration of Reagan's Republican successor, George H. W. Bush. During his four years in office, federal spending increased by 12 percent, and the deficit rose by $1.5 trillion in constant dollars, from 50 percent to 61 percent of GDP.

The next Republican president, George W. Bush, presided over a surge in deficits. During Bush's two terms, federal spending rose 33 percent in constant dollars, and the federal debt climbed from 55 percent in President Clinton's last year, to 68 percent of GDP. Even before the Great Recession of 2008, the debt under Bush reached 62 percent of GDP. The military buildup and two wars contributed to rising spending under Bush, but nondefense expenditures increased by 29 percent in constant dollars during his term.

President Obama increased federal outlays more modestly than Bush. During his eight years in office, federal spending increased by 24 percent in constant dollars. Deficits did soar during the early years of his presidency due to decreased revenues from the Great Recession and its aftermath. However, by the end of Obama's eight years, the deficit in constant dollars had declined by nearly two-thirds, from $1.5 trillion in 2009 to $561 billion in 2016.

Obama's successor, Trump, campaigned on promises of reducing the national debt "big league." "We owe $19 trillion as a country," he said. "And we're gonna knock it down and we're gonna bring it down big league and quickly, we're gonna bring jobs back, we're gonna bring business back, we're gonna stop our deficits, we're gonna stop our deficits, we're gonna do it very quickly."[31] Yet federal spending and deficits rose each year of the Trump presidency, reaching $891 billion in constant dollars in 2019 before soaring to $2.8 trillion in the pandemic year of 2020. The deficit declined in President Biden's first two years, dropping in constant dollars to $1.1 trillion in 2022, but it rose in the next year.

A comprehensive study of deficit financing under Republican and Democratic administrations since World War II found that "the recent debt growth under the Trump administration is remarkable, especially since it occurred during years of economic expansion. The rhetoric of political debate might give the impression that this is an unusual behavior for a conservative government." However, "the reality is quite different. Since the end of WWII, Republican administrations have systematically been more prone to expand debt, except during times of crisis. The Trump administration is continuing in this tradition."[32]

During Trump's presidency, Republicans voted three times to raise the debt ceiling without hesitation, granting him almost unchecked freedom on spending and taxes despite the ballooning deficits. Yet, under the Biden administration, they rebranded themselves as fiscal hawks, demanding deep budget cuts in exchange for their support to raise the debt ceiling.

A study of twenty-one votes in the twenty-first century found that "in the ten debt ceiling votes under a Republican administration, an average of 65 percent of House Republicans and 74 percent of Senate Republicans voted in favor of adjusting or suspending it. But in Democratic administrations, those numbers decline to 24 percent and 20 percent, respectively." The falloff is not nearly as dramatic for Democrats: "Under Democratic presidents, an average of 86 percent of House Democrats and 98 percent of Senate Democrats voted for debt ceiling increases. Under Republican presidents, 51 percent of Democrats in the House and 58 percent in the Senate still voted to increase the debt ceiling."[33]

In 2023, after Speaker Kevin McCarthy (R-CA) reached a compromise with Democrats on spending cuts, 68 percent of his Republican House caucus voted for the McCarthy-backed bill, while a higher 78 percent of Democrats voted aye. In the Senate, only 35 percent of Republicans voted for the bill, compared to 92 percent of Democrats.

Republicans and conservative advocates have applied their fiscal responsibility mantra selectively. When in opposition, they have consistently condemned Democrats for overspending and increasing the national debt. Yet when in power, Republicans have often been less fiscally responsible than their Democratic counterparts. Michael A. Cohen, a fellow at the nonpartisan Eurasia Group Foundation, has observed, "One party preaches fiscal responsibility and never delivers. The other party delivers fiscal responsibility to avoid charges of deficit fickleness from the other, profligate party."[34]

6

STATES' RIGHTS

The U.S. Constitution established a federal republic, with authority divided between the national and state governments. The supremacy clause sets federal law as the supreme law of the land. Still, the Tenth Amendment says, "The powers not delegated to the United States by the Constitution, nor prohibited by it to the states, are reserved to the states respectively, or to the people." Controversies over national versus state prerogatives burned through the United States in the nineteenth century. During the War of 1812, antiwar Federalists held the Hartford Convention that extolled states' rights and contemplated the secession of New England states from the Union. During the Nullification Crisis of 1828–30, South Carolina, led by the champion of slavery John C. Calhoun (D-SC), sought to nullify a federal tariff law. Disputes over states' rights exploded in the secession of Southern states to protect slavery from federal encroachment.

The Southern secession of 1861 exposed the flexibility of the states' rights doctrine, which the modern conservative movement would later adapt for its own purposes. Despite their rhetoric, Confederate leaders did not enshrine states' rights in their constitution. Instead, they sacrificed states' rights to safeguard slavery. The Confederate Constitution prohibited states from interfering with slavery, declaring that "the right of property in said slaves shall not be thereby impaired," and ensuring that in any new state or territory, "the institution of negro slavery, as it now exists in the Confederate States, shall be recognized and protected by Congress."[1] "States' rights were only a means to an end. Slavery was always most important," according to historian Michael DeMarco.[2] Even before secession, southern leaders had abandoned states' rights when it came to federal initiatives, such as the Fugitive Slave Act of 1850, that bolstered the institution of slavery.

Today, conservative support for states' rights is again a Trojan horse to counter liberal antibusiness programs and to protect conservative values. Like other "outer belt" principles, states' rights are flexible, and conservatives will set the doctrine aside when more pressing priorities arise. Despite its historical associations with slavery, secession, and Jim Crow laws in the South, the concept of states' rights has an enduring appeal. For those who believe that local or state governments are better suited to address their needs than the federal government, states' rights have become a safeguard against federal overreach. A 1936 Gallup poll, at the height of FDR's New Deal, found that 56 percent of Americans preferred concentrating government power at the state level over the federal government.[3]

Later surveys continued to register the public's approval of states' rights. A 2010 Pew Research Center poll found that 77 percent of respondents had a "positive reaction" to states' rights.[4] A 2016 Gallup poll found that 56 percent of respondents favored "concentration of power in the state government" compared to 37 percent who chose "concentration of power in the federal government." Additionally, a 2022 Pew Research Center poll found "that 32% of Americans have a favorable opinion of the 'federal government in Washington,' 54% have a favorable opinion of 'your state government' and 66% a favorable opinion of 'your local government.'"

Nineteenth-century Democratic presidents Andrew Jackson and Grover Cleveland prioritized states' rights over national authority. Not until the election of Woodrow Wilson in 1912 did Democrats begin to move away from Cleveland-style politics. Although southern Democrats remained committed to states' rights, Wilson expanded federal authority through antitrust laws, labor protections, and the Federal Reserve system.

By the 1920s, the Republican Party, which had once supported a more activist federal government, shifted toward endorsing states' rights. President Coolidge articulated this shift in 1926. "States are the sheet anchors of our institutions," he said. "If the authority of the States were struck down, disorder approaching chaos would be upon us within 24 hours. No method of procedure has ever been devised by which liberty could be divorced from local self-government. No plan of centralization has ever been adopted which did not result in bureaucracy, tyranny, inflexibility, reaction, and decline."[5]

This sentiment carried into Republican campaigns and platforms. In 1936, Republican presidential nominee Alf Landon pledged his "defense of the rightful powers of the states." The Republican Party's "inheritance," he said, "is of scrupulous deference to those rights within all the amplitude provided by the Constitution."[6] During World War II, the Republican Post-War Advisory Council met on September 6, 1943 (Mackinac Conference), and reaffirmed the party's commitment "to the federal system of government by which basic rights and duties are reserved to the States, free of dictation and subject to the control of their people."[7] In 1960, Senator Barry Goldwater, the leading Republican conservative, again upheld states' rights: "The 10th Amendment is a prohibitory rule of law. . . . Nothing could so far advance the cause of freedom as for state officials throughout the land to assume their rightful claims to lost state power and for the federal government to withdraw promptly and totally from every jurisdiction which the Constitution reserves to the states."[8] In 1962, the Joint Committee on Republican Principles echoed these beliefs, arguing that "the federal system of the United States was designed to prevent excessive centralization of political power and to defend individual liberty at home." Thus, "The national government should be prepared to cooperate with the states and localities and not elbow them aside or smother them with direction and control."[9]

President Nixon echoed this sentiment in his 1971 State of the Union Address: "The time has now come in America to reverse the flow of power and resources from the States and communities to Washington, and start power and resources flowing back from Washington to the States and communities and, more important, to the people all across America." He called for "a new partnership between the Federal Government and the

States and localities—a partnership in which we entrust the States and localities with a larger share of the Nation's responsibilities."[10]

President Reagan further institutionalized this commitment to states' rights through an executive order issued during his second term reinforcing states' sovereignty in the federal system. His order proclaimed, "In most areas of governmental concern, the States uniquely possess the constitutional authority, the resources, and the competence to discern the sentiments of the people and to govern accordingly." It mandates that "in the absence of clear constitutional or statutory authority, the presumption of sovereignty should rest with the individual States. Uncertainties regarding the legitimate authority of the national government should be resolved against regulation at the national level."[11]

In his 1999 manifesto, *A Charge to Keep*, George W. Bush articulated a similar perspective, differentiating his beliefs from "a philosophy that seeks solutions from distant bureaucracies. I am a conservative because I believe government closest to the people governs best." During the 2000 campaign, an editorial in the conservative *Daily Pennsylvanian* termed "American federalism the decisive issue in [the presidential] campaign." The editorial highlighted the contrast between Vice President Al Gore's support for the "modern regulatory state" and Bush's plan to devolve significant federal authority to the states."[12]

After the 2008 election of Barack Obama ended eight years of Republican administrations, fourteen Republican-controlled states passed "state sovereignty resolutions." South Dakota's resolution called upon the federal government to "halt its practice of assuming powers and imposing mandates on the states for purposes not enumerated in the Constitution of the United States." Alaska's resolution "claims sovereignty for the state under the Tenth Amendment to the Constitution of the United States over all powers not otherwise enumerated and granted to the federal government by the Constitution of the United States." Arizona's resolution says, "The scope of power defined by the Tenth Amendment means that the federal government was created by the states specifically to be an agent of the states."[13]

In 2011, Representative Mike Pence highlighted the urgency of respecting states' rights: "If the republic is to survive, we must have a revival of federalism and state-based constitutionalism." When he was governor of Indiana, Pence asserted that his state "must take the lead in pushing back against federal mandates."[14] Virginia Republican Dave Brat, an economics professor and staunch conservative who won a congressional seat after surprisingly defeating House Majority Leader Eric Cantor in the 2014 GOP primary, said, "The 10th Amendment is the big one; the Constitution has enumerated powers belonging to the federal government. All the rest of the powers belong to the states and the people."[15] The Republican Party Platform of 2016 said, "Every violation of state sovereignty by federal officials is not merely a transgression of one unit of government against another; it is an assault on the liberties of individual Americans."

Reflecting decades of conservative GOP rhetoric, Representative Mike Johnson affirmed in 2021, "I'm a Tenth Amendment guy, I know all of you all believe in that as one of our core principles, and it certainly is. The idea of federalism is uniquely American, we perfected it, and made it really one of the core truths that were built upon, and we're losing that. You see a rising tide of members elected to Congress who openly advocate for a strong centralized federal government because that's the necessary step towards their socialist utopia."[16]

Conservative southern Democrats had their own states' rights agenda to protect Jim Crow discrimination from federal interference. In 1937, conservative Democrats joined Republicans in Congress to circulate a "Conservative Manifesto," which declared that "except where state and local control are proven definitively inadequate, we favor the vigorous maintenance of states' rights." Senator Josiah Bailey (D-NC) primarily drafted the manifesto. Senators Harry F. Byrd (D-VA), Carter Glass (D-VA), Walter F. George (D-GA), Ellison D. "Cotton Ed" Smith (D-SC), and Millard Tydings (D-MD) signed on. In 1968, George Wallace, the segregationist former and future Democratic governor of Alabama, told a joint session of the Louisiana State Legislature that he was running for president "to turn back to you and other legislatures across the Nation some voice in the affairs of your state."

During his 1932 campaign, liberal Democrat Franklin Roosevelt pledged that "every new or old problem of government must be solved . . . by each state in its own way."[17] Republicans pounced on what they saw as hypocrisy. Representative Allen Treadway (R-MA) said that contrary to FDR's "promise to protect State rights, he has ruthlessly usurped State functions in complete disregard of the Constitution." The New Deal, Treadway said, "had as its object the further centralization of power and authority in the President."[18]

Jouett Shouse, a conservative Democrat and president of the American Liberty League, America's first all-purpose conservative organization, said, "The President has renounced entirely the theory of states' rights to which the Democratic Party is traditionally committed and takes the view that all social and economic problems should be controlled by the Federal Government, regardless of the clear limitations of the Constitution."[19] Another conservative Democrat, Mrs. William Joshua Barney (the name she preferred), a leader of the Independent Coalition of American Women, said she backed Republicans in 1936 because her party had repudiated its states' rights tradition. "The essence of the Democratic Party was states' rights," she said. Yet "practically everything the New Deal has done is tending toward centralizing authority and responsibility in Washington rather than the states. . . . The president has been given so much power we are in danger of having a dictatorship in this country."[20]

Conservative southern Democrats in Congress balked at FDR's second-term Fair Labor Standards Act that threatened the South's low-wage economy and its dual-wage system for Blacks and whites. The bill would set minimum wages and maximum hours and ban child labor. Southern Democrats in Congress blasted the legislation for shredding states' rights. Representative Edgar E. "Goober" Cox (D-GA) said, "The bill proposes the greatest single step towards centralized bureaucracy yet taken in the history of the Nation, no one disputes." That it "infringes upon States' rights and local self-government, is admitted." Senator Hattie Caraway (D-TX), the first woman elected to a full Senate term, said, "Our Government was founded on the principle of States' rights, and has, because of that, achieved and maintained a leading position among nations which could have come no other way." Yet, backers of national fair labor standards "want to take away the last vestige of States' rights."[21]

Senator Josiah Bailey said, "The preservation of this 'home rule' by the States is not a cry of jealous Commonwealths seeking their own aggrandizement at the expense of sister States. It is a fundamental necessity if we are to remain a truly united country." The United States "has been a democracy where through a division of government into units called

States the rights and interests of the minority have been respected and have been given a voice in the control of our affairs."[22]

In the late summer of 1937, as Congress debated the Fair Labor Standards Bill, editorials in about a dozen southern newspapers, led by the flagship *Atlanta Constitution*, denounced FDR for abandoning "the states' rights traditions of nineteenth-century Democratic presidents Thomas Jefferson, Andrew Jackson, and Grover Cleveland." The *Atlanta Constitution* editorialized, "The South has been loyal to Democracy. It has believed with all of its political mind and strength in the Jeffersonian ideals of states' rights and the freedom of the citizen." Only "the Democratic South can lead back to the principles of Jefferson, Jackson, and the fathers of freedom."[23] "The present Democratic Party has assumed the name of the old. It has not preserved the identity of the familiar principles. States' rights have been tossed overboard by bright young men and a party head who believe in the centralization of government" (*Dallas Daily News*). The South, which has long upheld the "Jeffersonian principle of democracy—the rights of the states to self-government and freedom of action of individuals in conducting their private affairs may well decide that it has reached a crossroads and much choose the banner under which it will enlist." (*Augusta Chronicle*).[24]

President Roosevelt, frustrated with conservative states' rights southern Democrats, attempted to purge them in the Democratic primaries in 1938. His effort to distinguish between Democratic liberals and conservatives, which he termed separating the "sheep" from the "goats," ultimately failed, as every targeted senator retained their seat. The purge was "a bust," admitted Democratic Party chair James Farley. One significant outcome of this failed initiative, combined with the opposition to national fair labor standards, was the formation of a conservative coalition. This coalition, consisting of Republicans and conservative southern Democrats, would hold significant sway in Congress for decades.[25]

Conservative southern Democrats routinely invoked states' rights to justify Jim Crow racial segregation and discrimination. In 1936, Governor Eugene Talmadge (D-GA), a segregationist, and John Kirby, the former National Association of Manufacturers president, formed the Southern Committee to Uphold the Constitution. They claimed that "the Democratic Party was established on the foundation of States rights," only to be violated by FDR, who fostered "the destruction of the constitutional safeguards of the people and of the States" and embraced "theories and actions which are alien, foreign, and inimical to America and Americanism."[26] Prominent entrepreneurs funded the committee, including Alfred P. Sloan Jr., the president of General Motors, the DuPont brothers, and Edward W. Mudge, the president of Weirton Steel.[27]

To the chagrin of southern Democrats, in 1948, the Democratic Party adopted its first ambitious civil rights programs. Senator Richard Russell (D-GA), the tacit leader of southern Democrats, warned against tampering with "States' rights and white supremacy," the basis of "Southern devotion to the Democratic Party." He said a "federal Gestapo was poised to deploy "every power of the Federal Government . . . to destroy segregation and compel intermingling and miscegenation of the races in the South."[28]

The Southern Governor's Conference tapped Governor Strom Thurmond (D-SC) to run for president as the nominee of a new segregationist party in 1948. Although dubbed the "Dixiecrats" by the media, its official name was the "States' Rights Party." The Governor's Conference said, "The present leadership of the Democratic party has deserted the principles of government upon which the Democratic party was founded. As never before, the time has come for strong and effective action by the Southern states not only to save the Democratic party but to preserve the right of the states to govern themselves and preserve American democracy."[29] Thurmond won 2.5 percent of the popular vote and thirty-nine electoral votes from four Deep South states where his states' rights movement controlled the Democratic machines.

After the Supreme Court's *Brown v. Board of Education* (1954) decision outlawed legal segregation in schools, 101 southern Democratic senators and representatives responded with a states' rights "Southern Manifesto." The authors condemned the decision as an "encroachment on the rights reserved to the states and to the people, contrary to established law, and to the Constitution."[30]

Southern Democrats, who continued to dominate their states, invoked states' rights against the Voting Rights Act of 1965. "It is this dual sovereignty exercised by the States and the Federal Government that, in my opinion, has caused the United States to make such outstanding progress in world affairs and to retain local freedom and individual liberty," said Senator Allen Ellender (D-LA). "Notwithstanding all the success that has been ours in the past under dual sovereignty, an attempt is now made to take away from six sovereign States rights which were reserved for them when the Constitution was adopted many years ago."[31]

Senator James Eastland (D-MS) warned that such encroachment would topple the federal system: "The entire structure of our Federal system will inevitably come crashing down. Once you have opened this Pandora's box of congressional mischief, you will unleash a chain reaction which will finally culminate in the establishment of an all powerful, unchecked, unanswerable, supersocialist state; a new order in which the States will be reduced to mere administrative arms of a monolithic Federal bureaucracy." "When that occurs, Mr. President, the dark night of despotism will descend like a pall upon this great Nation and the rule of tyranny will pervade this land," said Eastland.[32]

As the political landscape shifted from a Democratic to a Republican South, Republicans—who had once supported the Voting Rights Act—began to echo similar sentiments. In 2021, Democrats introduced two significant federal voting rights bills. The John R. Lewis Voting Rights Enhancement Act of 2021 aimed to restore the preclearance requirement for certain jurisdictions, which the U.S. Supreme Court had invalidated in 2013. The For the People Act of 2021 proposed expanding voting rights through same-day registration, automatic registration at state offices, and independent commissions for drawing congressional district lines. The John Lewis bill, said Senate Republican leader Mitch McConnell, "grant[s] to the Justice Department almost total ability to determine the voting systems of every state in America." In dismissing the For the People Act, McConnell said, "This is not a federal issue. It oughta be left to the states. There's nothing broken around the country. The system upheld very well during intense stress in the latter part of the previous Congress. There's no rational basis for federalizing this election."[33]

Representative Debbie Lesko (R-AZ) contended that the For the People Act "weaponizes the Federal Election Commission, infringes on States' rights, and drastically limits freedom of speech. Arizona requires voter I.D. and prohibits ballot harvesting." The act "will undo Arizona laws."[34] Representative. Earl L. "Buddy" Carter (R-GA) agreed that the act "compromises States' rights and leaves Washington as the arbiter of managing elections, which runs against the Constitution. . . . This legislation compromises State voter I.D. integrity laws and moves to roll back the important work that has been done in this space."[35]

Jonathan Williams, executive vice president of the conservative lobby group American Legislative Exchange Council, charged in 2023 that President Biden's legislative agenda on matters such as climate change, gun control, federal pandemic aid, voting rights, and infrastructure "has the common thread of trying to federalize decisions in Washington, and central government versus allowing the states to compete with each other." The Biden administration is "changing the incentive structure for many states in favor of a big government agenda. [Biden's] policy agenda has been to undermine state autonomy and federalism wherever possible."[36]

Modern conservatives, much like their Confederate predecessors, have abandoned the principle of states' rights when politically expedient or aligned with their core values. The Eighteenth Amendment instituting Prohibition and its enabling legislation, supported by conservatives, imposed some of the most stringent regulations on the states since Reconstruction. The amendment nullified the "wet" laws of about a third of the states, affecting more than half the population. Senator Charles S. Thomas (D-CO) objected that the Prohibition amendment "will fundamentally alter our system of government, abolish the States, and substitute a national democracy for a representative Republic. In so doing it deprives the states of their sovereign autonomy."[37]

Conservative efforts to remedy moral and social ills through national government controls extended beyond Prohibition to a national war on drugs. A near panic over the alleged drug-induced crime wave that hit the United States during the 1920s led conservative reformers to declare the first national war on drugs. Drug use threatened the survival of American civilization and the salvation of souls. In 1929, Congress established a Federal Bureau of Narcotics to enforce the drug laws, overriding the states' enforcement.[38] In 1937, Congress enacted the Marijuana Tax Act, which effectively criminalized marijuana use nationwide, regardless of state law. Conservative evangelical Christian Harry Anslinger, whom President Hoover had appointed to head the Federal Bureau of Narcotics, drafted the law.[39] Later, President Nixon's establishment of the Office of Drug Abuse Law Enforcement in 1972 shifted the antidrug campaign from rehabilitation to criminal enforcement, with the federal government overriding state drug laws and even raiding medicinal marijuana dispensaries in California.[40]

Since the 1970s, conservatives have advocated for increased federal control over welfare programs to limit the generosity and flexibility of state-administered benefits. In 1970, when Representative John W. Byrnes (R-WI), the ranking Republican on the House Ways and Means Committee, was asked about his support for stringent federal conditions on welfare, he responded, "We can't trust the states. We can't depend upon them to carry out our program."[41] The imposition of federal controls came full circle in 2023 when more than twenty Republicans in Congress sponsored legislation to tighten state work requirements for federal food stamp programs. The proposal would end waivers for the work requirement in place for about a third of the states and increase the age limit for such requirements from forty-nine to sixty-five. Republicans inserted this proposal into the bill that raised the debt ceiling, which Congress enacted in June 2023.

Conservatives sponsored the Defense of Marriage Act of 1996, which "defines the terms 'marriage' and 'spouse,' for purposes of federal law only, to reaffirm that they refer exclusively to relationships between persons of the opposite sex." The act authorized states to deny recognition of same-sex unions from other states. It barred same-sex couples from many federal benefits, such as joint tax returns, insurance benefits for government employees, and social security survivors' payouts. The majority report of House Republicans expressed their goal of blunting developments in the states, specifically in Hawaii: "H.R. 3396 is a response to a very particular development in the State of Hawaii." Specifically, "the state courts in Hawaii appear to be on the verge of requiring that State to issue marriage licenses to same-sex couples. . . . The Defense of Marriage Act is an effort by Congress to clarify the extremely complicated situation that may result from one State's recognition of same-sex 'marriage.'"[42]

In his 2000 presidential campaign, George W. Bush reversed his previous states' rights stance. During the contentious recount in Florida, Bush successfully petitioned the U.S. Supreme Court to overrule the state courts' decisions. In contrast, Democrats championed the cause of states' rights in this instance. A brief from fourteen Democratic state attorneys general argued that overturning state court decisions would be "highly offensive to basic principles of federalism." The brief emphasized that "no power of the state is more clearly recognized in the Constitution than the power to control elections—particularly with regard to the appointment of electors for president."[43]

In one of the Bush administration's first actions, it sought to nullify Oregon's assisted suicide law that voters had overwhelmingly approved in a referendum. Bush's attorney general, John Ashcroft, claimed that assisted suicide was not a legitimate medical purpose under the federal Controlled Substances Act, despite states typically controlling medical practices. The dispute reached the U.S. Supreme Court, which upheld Oregon's law by a 6 to 3 decision in 2006. Justice Anthony Kennedy ruled in his majority opinion that the U.S. attorney general "is not authorized to make a rule declaring illegitimate a medical standard for care and treatment of patients that is specifically authorized under state law." He concluded that the attorney general does not have the power "to effect a radical shift of authority from the States to the Federal Government to define general standards of medical practice in every locality."[44]

A year before the Oregon decision, in 2005, the first year of Bush's second term, conservative consultant Craig Shirley wrote, "It is unconscionable to think that any modern Republican would aggressively or gleefully embrace the growth of government or oppose the decentralization of power in Washington."[45] President Bush and his conservative allies in Congress did not listen. A revealing moment came in March 2005. President Bush and Representative Tom DeLay (R-TX), the leader of House conservatives, pushed Congress to intervene in the case of Terri Schiavo, a brain-damaged patient in Florida who had existed in a vegetative state for fifteen years. State courts had sanctioned a decision by Schiavo's husband to remove her feeding tube and stop prolonging her life. Still, right-to-life conservatives had made her plight a national issue they hoped would put a human face on their movement. To prevent the imminent removal of the feeding tube, Congress passed an emergency bill requiring federal courts to review the case, which the U.S. Court of Appeals for the Eleventh Circuit declined. This federal intrusion into a state and family matter contradicted states' rights and other self-professed conservative principles, such as judicial restraint, the sanctity of the family, the sacred bond between husband and wife, and private decision-making without government meddling.[46]

Also, in 2005, conservatives pushed the Protection of Lawful Commerce in Arms Act through Congress. The act shields federally licensed gun manufacturers, dealers, sellers, and trade associations from civil lawsuits in federal and state courts. It lists six limited exceptions but otherwise requires that such lawsuits "be immediately dismissed by the court in which the action was brought or is currently pending." "These lawsuits impose unreasonable burdens on interstate commerce in firearms and ammunition and can have a significant economic impact on this industry," said Representative Jeb Bradley (R-NH) in a press release. "We should be focusing on the perpetrators who commit crimes with firearms, rather than lawsuits directed against gun manufacturers, which will only restrict the rights of law-abiding citizens."[47]

The Real ID Act of 2005 further exemplified the shift away from states' rights. It imposed federal standards on state-issued driver's licenses and other forms of identification, requiring states to meet specific verification, security, and data-sharing requirements. For the first time in U.S. history, the act established federally mandated national identification cards, giving the federal government access to personal information across states. Eventually, federal officials would only accept Real IDs for boarding airplanes or entering federal facilities.

Conservatives abandoned states' rights to push for nationwide restrictions on abortion. Since 1976, except for 2024, the Republican Party Platform has endorsed a constitutional amendment that would ban all abortions, overriding state laws. Although support for this amendment was largely symbolic, the U.S. Supreme Court's *Dobbs* (2022) decision overturning *Roe v. Wade* (1973) opened the door to banning abortions across the land through legislation.

Influential Senator Lindsey Graham (R-SC), who chaired the Senate Judiciary Committee when Republicans held the majority, had a stunning reversal on states' rights and abortion. In June 2022, Graham insisted that states should regulate abortion: "All of us in the conservative world have believed that there's nothing in the Constitution giving the federal government the right to regulate abortion," he said. Graham reiterated this commitment to states' rights in August. "I've been consistent—I think states should decide the issue of marriage and states should decide the issue of abortion," he flatly said.

A month later, Graham reversed course. "This is not a states' rights issue. This is a human rights issue," he said. "So, no matter what California or Maryland will do . . . I am going to advocate a national minimum standard." "Abortion is not banned in America. It's left up to elected officials in America to define the issue. States have the ability to do it at state level. And we have the ability in Washington to speak on this issue if we choose," Graham said at a press conference introducing his antiabortion bill. "I have chosen to speak."

Graham introduced a bill prohibiting abortions nationwide after fifteen weeks gestation, and Republicans introduced similar legislation in the House. Republicans have refrained from acting on these bills, not because they have abandoned their commitment to regulating abortion across the states, but to shield the party from the political damage wrought by such unpopular bills. The abortion issue stung Republicans in the midterm elections of 2022, and subsequent polls showed that more than 60 percent of Americans favored having abortions always or usually available.[48]

Former vice president Mike Pence, an apostle of states' rights, straddled the issue but still came down in favor of a national abortion ban. "I welcome any and all efforts to advance the cause of life in state capitals or in the nation's capital," said Pence. However, when asked about legislation to institute a federal abortion ban, he said, "And I have every confidence that the next Republican president, whoever that may be, will stand for the right to life. My consistent message will be to legislators and to governors around the country, and the leaders here in Washington D.C., is to by all means advance the cause of life. However long I have left in the public debate, or on this earth, I'm going to be a part of advancing the cause of life all across this nation."[49]

Donald Trump, too, muddled the abortion issue during his 2024 campaign. In March 2024, he signaled his willingness to back a national abortion ban after fifteen weeks gestation, with exceptions for rape, incest, and life-threatening emergencies. "The number of weeks, now, people are agreeing on 15, and I'm thinking in terms of that, and it'll come out to something that's very reasonable," he said. As always, Trump hedged, saying that he thought abortion should be a state issue.[50] Simultaneously, conservatives pursued a legal strategy to restrict the availability of abortions in every state. The lawsuit that conservative groups filed on limiting access to the abortion pill mifepristone sought to ban the pill or make it difficult to obtain in states without restrictive abortion laws.

The Heritage Foundation's Project 2025, a blueprint for governing, drafted primarily by former Trump staffers with Trump's blessing, according to a former cabinet member intimately involved with the project, recommends restricting state autonomy on abortion rights.[51] It calls upon the Centers for Disease Control and Prevention (CDC) to penalize states that do not submit data on the frequency of abortions within their borders. The plan would withdraw Medicaid funds for states that require abortion insurance and instruct federal officials to take legal action against local officials who refuse to bring cases against women and doctors who violate state abortion bans.[52] Although Trump tried to distance himself from the project during his campaign, he seemed to have embraced it once he was elected.[53]

Conservatives have sought to impose national legislation to override state control on issues related to sexual orientation and gender identity. In 2022, thirty-three congressional Republicans introduced the Stop the Sexualization of Children Act of 2022 to prohibit any use of federal funds in the states "to develop, implement, facilitate, or fund any sexually-oriented program, event, or literature for children under the age of 10, and for other purposes." The act broadly defines "sexually oriented material" as "any topic involving gender identity, gender dysphoria, transgenderism, sexual orientation, or related subjects." The act applies to any institution, program, or event that receives federal funding or takes place on federal property. It covers public schools, libraries, hospitals, and federal facilities in the states. It would sweep in books and sex education materials. Although the bill appears to apply only through the third grade, it includes a clause that refers to "age appropriate or developmentally appropriate," which could extend the ban.[54] Republicans modeled the national bill on a similar law in Florida that was initially limited to the third grade, but the state Board of Education extended it to all grades.[55]

Speaker Johnson, the "Tenth Amendment guy," introduced legislation to extend nationwide a ban on discussion of sexual orientation and gender identity in early public education. He co-sponsored legislation to ban gender-affirming care for minors nationally, and co-sponsored the "Life at Conception Act," which declares a fetus as a person under the Fourteenth Amendment and would, in effect, ban abortion in every state.[56]

When in power, conservatives have often sought to curtail state policies on a range of issues, including pandemic protections, LGBTQ rights, immigration, environmental regulations, and taxation. During the COVID-19 pandemic, President Trump claimed he had "total power" over the states to force them to "reopen": "When somebody's president of the United States, the authority is total. And that's the way it's got to be. It's total. It's total. And the governors know that." Charlie Sykes, a former conservative talk show host, said that this boast of total authority should have "enraged" Republican conservatives who "have pointed to the 10th Amendment as the very essence of decentralized government. . . . Instead they shrugged."[57]

In 2021, Republicans introduced the Child Welfare Provider Inclusion Act, which would prohibit states and localities from taking adverse action against adoption and foster care providers who decline to provide services based on religious beliefs. The law would authorize providers citing religious convictions to deny the placement of youth with otherwise qualified, licensed LGBTQ foster and adoptive families. If enacted, it would nullify the laws of twenty-five states plus the District of Columbia that prohibit adoption or foster care agencies from discrimination based on sexual orientation or gender identity.[58]

Early in his first administration, President Trump issued an executive order to withhold federal grant funds from "sanctuary" jurisdictions that have laws or regulations that limit cooperation with the policies for detaining alleged illegal immigrants enforced by Immigration and Customs Enforcement (ICE). The order would have covered approximately ten states and more than 150 cities until courts blocked its enforcement. President Biden rescinded the order soon after his inauguration.

The Trump administration in 2019 withdrew a waiver that authorized California to adopt stricter tailpipe emission standards for vehicles than national requirements. This order, too, became entangled in the courts until the Biden administration rescinded it. Conservatives have limited the ability of states to finance their priorities through state and local taxation. The 2017 Republican-sponsored tax cut bill capped the federal tax deduction for state and local taxes. This cap hit especially hard at Blue states that have relied on property and state income taxes to fund public services. Speaker Paul Ryan (R-WI) admitted that the cap targeted "profligate, big-government states."[59]

Conservative meddling in local prosecutions of Trump was not an exception but the rule for conservatives. Award-winning journalist Mary C. Curtis wrote in 2022 that from the time of the "Confederates who eventually went to war over the right of their states to own men, women and children," to the present, "the concept of states' rights has never been pure." It "can be quite malleable when it interferes with a desired outcome."[60]

CHAPTER

7

PERSONAL MORALITY AND RESPONSIBILITY

Conservatives argue that Christian virtues should guide politics, contending that morally responsible leaders are essential for a well-functioning nation. They believe that if the issue with politics is "bad politicians," the solution is to elect good ones. Conversely, if the problem is "bad citizenry, rather than bad legislation," leaders should steer the nation toward virtue. For conservatives, personal morality and responsibility are fundamental values that should disqualify transgressors from public office, regardless of their policy positions or party affiliation.

This moralistic stance sets conservatives apart from libertarians. Unlike conservatives, libertarians are consummate pluralists who tolerate personal choices on issues such as prostitution, pornography, adultery, same-sex marriage, drug use, and abortion—choices that conservatives often deem immoral. When libertarianism began to emerge as a political movement in 1971, William F. Buckley Jr., the leading conservative commentator of the time, publicly denounced it as a "kind of anarchy. . . . The ideological licentiousness that rages through America today makes anarchy attractive to the simple-minded."[1]

Conservatives often favorably compare their high moral standards with the relativistic ethics of libertine liberals, who reject absolute notions of right and wrong. However, this commitment to personal morality and responsibility is inconsistent. Conservatives overlook or rationalize the moral failings of their allies, shifting blame elsewhere rather than holding their leaders accountable. This pattern of excusing morally flawed conservative figures, evident since the 1920s with President Warren Harding, persists into the present. It includes officials and candidates at the highest levels of government and leaders of major Christian conservative denominations. "Most people do not really want freedom, because freedom involves responsibility, and most people are frightened of responsibility," Sigmund Freud observed.

Vice president elect Calvin Coolidge, whose rectitude set him apart from the excesses of his running mate Harding, put a conservative stamp on personal morality and responsibility in 1920. "The great lesson of economic and political experience is that people and parties and nations must observe the moral standards," Coolidge said. "The obligations assumed by our platform, our campaign, but most of all those imposed by the everlasting necessity of righteous conduct . . . are to be amply and fully discharged by the Republican Party."[2]

During his 1964 presidential campaign, Barry Goldwater positioned himself as another exemplar of personal morality. He argued that presidents are role models for the nation and must exhibit the highest personal moral standards. Americans "look up to their President and their Government and they expect to find integrity, honesty, indestructible moral fiber," he said. The nation's leadership "must show, clearly and constantly the morality and the honesty which our people have every right to expect." Goldwater promised "every effort to a reconstruction of reverence and moral strength."[3]

In 1979, Robert Grant, the founder of the conservative Christian lobby Christian Voice, celebrated the union of biblically inspired morality and conservative politics: "Biblical Christians tend to be conservative. They are oriented toward personal morality, thrift, and an aversion to the federal government as an answer to problems." Grant urged conservative Christians to flock to the polls in 1980 and judge candidates on "a scale of morality," not just policy or partisanship.[4]

For Russell Kirk, "the regeneration of spirit and character" is "conservatism at its highest." "It has been said by liberal intellectuals that the conservative believes all social questions, at heart, to be questions of private morality," Kirk said. "Properly understood, this statement is quite true. A society in which men and women are governed by belief in an enduring moral order, by a keen sense of right and wrong, by personal convictions about justice and honor, will be a good society—whatever political machinery it may utilize." In contrast, "a society in which men and women are morally adrift, ignorant of norms, and intent chiefly upon gratification of appetites, will be a bad society—no matter how many people vote and no matter how liberal its formal constitution may be."[5]

In 1998, Representative Frank Riggs (R-CA) said, "We have balanced the budget and eliminated the federal deficit. Now we need to address the moral deficit. We must teach our children that there is nothing more important than personal morality, that the truth matters and character counts."[6] In *A Charge to Keep* (1999), George W. Bush said that when he ran for governor of Texas, "Most of all I worried about changing the culture, a culture I described as saying, 'If it feels good, do it, and if you've got a problem blame somebody else.'" The cure, he said, is "to usher in an era of personal responsibility."[7]

Pat Buchanan, former Nixon advisor and 1992 candidate for the Republican presidential nomination, said in 2019, "With secularism's triumph, we Americans have no common religion, no common faith, no common font of moral truth. We disagree on what is right and wrong, moral and immoral. Without an agreed-upon higher authority, values become matters of opinion."[8]

From the 1920s through the present, conservatives have consistently privileged their moral righteousness against the alleged lax morals of liberals. The editor of the pro-Republican *Wesleyan Christian Advocate* wrote in 1928, "Its [the Democratic Party's] position indicates a distinct moral decadence, the deterioration of lofty moral ideals. It will put the political parties of this nation on notice . . . that if a political party dares to disregard the conscience of this nation . . . it may expect a rude awakening on election day."[9]

During the 1930 debates over tariffs, Senator Reed Smoot (R-UT) condemned the decadent morals of Democrats who opposed an amendment banning the importation of obscene materials. "This question is one which strikes at the morals of every young boy and girl in the United States," he said. "I did not believe that there were such books printed in the world—books that the Senator from New Mexico [Democrat Bryson Cutting] referred to and said ought to be in the libraries of the people of the United States. They are lower than the beasts!"[10] Smoot added, "Let me suggest to the Senator [Cutting] that if he will read the Bible altogether, he will never stand on this floor defending any such rotten stuff as he appears to be defending."[11]

The conservative backlash against President Clinton's consensual affair with White House intern Monica Lewinsky exemplified this ongoing moral confrontation. Clinton was arguably the most conservative Democratic president of the twentieth century, promoting a "third-way philosophy" that aimed to transcend traditional political boundaries by working cooperatively with businesses, cutting the deficit, reducing middle-class taxes, and building a strong military. He also pledged to increase police presence, uphold the death penalty, and "end welfare as we know it." He rebuked Black militancy and distanced himself from his party's special interests. "Clinton was a pretty good president for a Republican," Michael Moore said. Yet, conservatives perceived him as a moral hypocrite. Despite Clinton's efforts to present himself as a pragmatic, centrist leader, conservatives disparaged him for what they saw as his libertine lifestyle.

The right-wing animosity toward Clinton intensified following the sex scandal that led to his impeachment in 1998. Before this scandal, conservatives had already been working to undermine Clinton's credibility. From 1994 to 1997, the premier conservative financier Richard Mellon Scaife invested $2.4 million in the *American Spectator* magazine's "Arkansas Project," which aimed at exposing Clinton's alleged sexual escapades and other moral failings. Additionally, conservatives supported Paula Jones, a former Arkansas state employee who accused Clinton of sexual harassment, despite the Right's usual aversion to such litigation. Figures such as James D. Johnson, the former segregationist Arkansas state senator who regretted the end of Jim Crow and viewed Clinton as emblematic of a new South, circulated rumors of crime and scandal surrounding the president.[12]

Protestant evangelical leaders insisted that Clinton's moral transgressions disqualified him for public office. Franklin Graham, the son of legendary evangelist Billy Graham, in a *Wall Street Journal* op-ed, "Clinton's Sins Aren't Private," denied that private behavior does not affect public service, decrying "the notion that what a person does in private has little bearing on his public actions or job performance, even if he is the president of the United States."[13] Gary Bauer, head of the Family Research Council, aired a televised ad lamenting that news coverage of the Clinton scandal has "taught our children that lying is okay, that fidelity is old-fashioned and that character doesn't count." He argued that Clinton had added to a dangerous "virtue deficit" in public life. "Mr. President, it is time for you to put our country and our children first. It is time for you to resign."[14]

James Dobson, the founder of Focus on the Family, said, "As it turns out, character DOES matter. You can't run a family, let alone a country, without [character]. How foolish to believe that a person who lacks honesty and moral integrity is qualified to lead a nation and the world! . . . The American people have now heard the President's dramatic confession of adultery. There is no longer any reason to speculate, and yet, the media reports that the majority continues to believe 'it doesn't matter.'"[15] Pat Robertson told a cheering crowd at the annual convention of the Christian Coalition that Clinton has "debauched, debased, and defamed" the White House and turned it into a "playpen for the sexual freedom of the poster child of the 1960s." He said that resignation was "too easy" an escape for the president, who should be impeached and removed from office.[16]

William Bennett, a self-appointed moral guardian and President Reagan's secretary of education, published *The Book of Virtues* in 1993. He followed up with *The Death of Outrage: Bill Clinton and the Assault on American Ideals* in 1998.[17] Bennett said, "A President whose character manifests itself in patterns of reckless personal conduct, deceit, abuse of power, and contempt for the rule of law *cannot be a good president*." He scorned "the President's apologists" who "are attempting to redefine the standard of acceptable behavior for a president because they believe in Clinton's policies." "They are defining morality down, radically lowering the standards of what we expect from a president, and changing for the worse the way politics is and will be practiced." The apologists would have us commit "an unthinkable act of moral and intellectual disarmament."[18] Mike Pence insisted that "Bill Clinton must resign or be impeached."

"In a day when reckless extramarital sexual activity is manifesting itself in our staggering rates of illegitimacy and divorce, now more than ever, America needs to be able to look to her First Family as role models of all that we have been and can be again," Pence said.[19]

In 1998, the Southern Baptist Convention (SBC), the leading theologically and politically conservative denomination, passed a resolution on the "moral character of public officials." In an unmistakable reference to President Clinton, the resolution said, "Some journalists report that many Americans are willing to excuse or overlook immoral or illegal conduct by unrepentant public officials so long as economic prosperity prevails." However, "Tolerance of serious wrong by leaders sears the conscience of the culture, spawns unrestrained immorality and lawlessness in the society, and surely results in God's judgment." It "implore[d] our government leaders to live by the highest standards of morality both in their private actions and in their public duties, and thereby serve as models of moral excellence and character." It urged "all Americans to embrace and act on the conviction that character does count in public office, and to elect those officials and candidates who, although imperfect, demonstrate consistent honesty, moral purity and the highest character."[20]

After the Clinton scandal, conservatives continued to target allegedly immoral liberals. In 2003, conservative commentator Joseph Farah wrote, "The national Democratic Party is immoral to the core. Any American who would vote for Democrats is guilty of fostering the worst kind of degeneracy. The leaders of this party are severely out of touch with mainstream, traditional American values. They are crusaders for perversion, for licentiousness, for nihilism and worse."[21]

In a 60 Minutes interview on April 2, 2023, Representative Marjorie Taylor Greene (R-GA) called Democrats "the party of pedophiles." "Democrats support—even Joe Biden the president himself supports—children being sexualized, having transgender surgeries. Sexualizing children is what pedophiles do to children." When pressed by the interviewer, Greene responded, "I'm calling out the truth basically."[22]

Among the conservative rank and file, a 2022 Pew Research Center Survey found that 72 percent of Republicans regarded members of the Democratic Party as "less moral than other Americans." Amidst the polarization of recent politics, the survey found that 63 percent of Democrats leveled the same charge against Republicans.[23] The two parties differed sharply, however, in their views on morality. Democrats stressed the values of tolerance and fairness, whereas Republicans focused on personal lifestyles. Another 2022 survey found that 49 percent of Republicans and 52 percent of 2020 Trump voters agreed with Greene that Democrats were running child sex-trafficking rings.[24]

Despite this moral outrage, conservatives have typically ignored or defended their leaders' moral transgressions. As a U.S. senator and then president, Warren Harding was a known, notorious womanizer. Harding's steamy and sexually explicit letters to his mistress, Carrie Phillips, revealed that the Republican National Committee paid her thousands of dollars in hush money to conceal their affair. Harding's affairs continued while in office. One of his mistresses, Nan Britton, authored a book that luridly described their sexual encounters in the White House. Britton was thirty-one years younger than Harding. His wife, Florence, was five years older than he. "There isn't one iota of affection in my home relationship," Harding wrote of his marriage. "It is merely existence, necessary for appearance's sake."[25] Britton filed a paternity suit against the Harding estate, claiming that he had fathered her out-of-wedlock child and left no provisions for their daughter. The Harding family refused to acknowledge any responsibility for the child. DNA testing confirmed her claim in 2015.[26] Harding's womanizing sparked false rumors that his jealous wife had poisoned him to death on their Alaska cruise in August 1923. Harding's widow then burned his official and private papers.

Yet conservatives avoided Harding's moral failings or leaped to his defense despite widespread knowledge of his infidelities. "It's a good thing I'm not a woman. I would always be pregnant. I can't say no," President Harding had told reporters.[27] Representative John Tillman (D-AR), a conservative, said, "Many of us have had fraternal relationships with the dead statesman [Harding] and respected him, liked him, believed in him. We feel a grievance at this [Britton's] attack. Politics does not matter in this affair."[28]

Conservative figures dismissed criticisms and labeled his accuser, Nan Britton, not Harding, as morally deficient. The inconsistency in conservative moral outrage shows that partisanship outweighed morality. A resolution sponsored by Harding's former attorney general, Harry A.

Daugherty, who had led the effort to cover up Harding's affairs, and fifteen other "friends of Harding" said, "Now, the American people, as a people, have never been swayed by the lip of libel or the tongue of slander and their devotion to his memory and their judgment of his virtue and merit is the final answer and appropriate reward to his labors."[29] During Britton's trial against the Harding estate, former U.S. representative Grant E. Mouser (R-OH) called Harding's accuser "deranged, demented, lascivious, and obsessed to get money." He posed Harding's good character against Britton: "His only fault was his great heart which trusted all humanity."[30]

When President Hoover dedicated the Harding memorial in 1931, he extolled the late president as a man of "character," a "man of delicate sense of honor, of sympathetic heart, of transcendent gentleness of soul—who reached out for friendship, who gave of it loyally and generously in his every thought and deed. He was a man of passionate patriotism. He was a man of deep religious feeling. He was devoted to his fellow men." The transgressions of Harding's appointees in the Teapot Dome scandals "never touched the character of Warren Harding." Unfortunately, Harding "had been betrayed by a few of the men whom he had trusted, by men whom he had believed were his devoted friends."[31]

Newt Gingrich (R-GA), Speaker of the House (1995–99) and a key figure in President Clinton's impeachment, was himself guilty of multiple infidelities, including an extramarital affair during the impeachment debates. He resigned the speakership on November 6, 1998, and left Congress when his term ended in January 1999. His successor as speaker-elect, Bob Livingston (R-LA), admitted to multiple extramarital affairs following media revelations of his transgressions. Similarly, Representatives Helen Chenoweth (R-ID), Dan Burton (R-IN), and House Judiciary Committee chair Henry Hyde (R-IL)—who led Clinton's impeachment—also acknowledged affairs. Hyde dismissed his five-year affair with a married woman as a "youthful indiscretion," despite being forty-one years old and married when the affair began.[32]

Livingston retreated into private life, but Gingrich remained a prominent and influential figure in conservative politics. At one point, he led all Republican contenders in polls for the 2012 presidential nomination. Although his campaign ultimately faltered, Gingrich continued to thrive in conservative circles. He consulted with Republican candidates, authored popular books on the Right, and became a Fox News contributor. Gingrich also raised funds for Republicans and held positions as a fellow at the conservative Heritage Foundation and Hoover Institution. He chaired several conservative organizations, including American Solutions for Winning the Future, the Center for Health Transformation, and Renewing American Leadership. Gingrich supported Trump's presidential candidacies in 2016 and 2020 and was reportedly considered a potential running mate for Trump in 2016. He backed Trump's false claims of Democratic fraud in the 2020 election and advised Republicans on reclaiming the U.S. House in 2022. In 2023, following revelations of Trump's criminal indictments, Gingrich asserted, "The time has come for all Americans who believe in our core values to meet those who would destroy our children and civilization with equally firm, clear language."[33]

Representative Dennis Hastert (R-IL), an evangelical Christian with a place on the honor roll of the Christian Right Moral Majority, replaced Livingston as Speaker (1999–2007). Hastert was a serial child molester. In 2015, Hastert pled guilty to felony charges for his sexual abuse of children. Among other crimes, Hastert had obstructed justice by paying hush money to one of his victims and lying to federal investigators. U.S. District Court judge Thomas M. Durkin said, "Nothing is more stunning than having 'serial child molester' and 'Speaker of the House' in the same sentence." The judge imposed a sentence of fifteen months in prison and a $250,000 fine.

Leading conservative evangelicals largely downplayed Hastert's crimes. Hastert's alma mater, Wheaton College, the nation's flagship Christian evangelical institution, said only, "We commit ourselves to pray for all involved, including Speaker Hastert, his family, and those who may have been harmed by any inappropriate behavior." At his sentencing hearing, three board members of Wheaton College testified on Hastert's behalf.[34] Tom DeLay, former Republican majority leader in the U.S. House, the leader of conservatives in that chamber, wrote, "When Speaker Hastert became Speaker of the House and I became Majority leader, he started a bible study every Wednesday at lunch," DeLay said. "We all have our flaws, but Dennis Hastert has very few. He is a good man and loves the Lord. He gets his integrity and values from Him." He called Hastert a man of "strong faith" and "great integrity."[35]

Conservatives who condemned Clinton took a markedly different stance regarding Trump. William Bennett, who could have rewritten *The Death of Outrage* by simply substituting Trump's name for Clinton's, silenced his outrage and became one of the very "apologists" he once righteously denounced. "Our country can survive the occasional infelicities and improprieties of Donald Trump. But it cannot survive losing the Supreme Court to liberals and allowing them to wreck our sacred republic," Bennett said.[36] Without a hint of irony, he added that those who stand against Trump suffer "from a terrible case of moral superiority." After Trump's presidency, Bennett said, "He ran a great country and policy trumps personality." Bennett said that Trump should not run in 2024, not because the scales fell from the moralist's eyes, but because we "need a generational shift" and a candidate who could win.[37]

Similarly, Gary Bauer offered Trump his absolution. After the Manhattan district attorney indicted Trump for paying hush money to a porn star and concealing it as a business expense, Bauer called the case "a travesty of justice and a body blow to the survival of our constitutional republic." "Millions of Americans will see it for what it is—an attempt to remove the former president from the American political stage." Bauer asked "all Americans to pray for President Trump and his family."[38]

When a jury found Trump civilly liable for sexually assaulting, injuring, and defaming journalist E. Jean Carroll, Bauer once again rallied to the former president's defense. "The case is full of holes, and there is virtually no evidence to support her accusations," Bauer said, shifting blame from Trump to the so-called deep state—even though a private citizen brought the suit under state law. "The Deep State has targeted Donald Trump from Day One because he threatened the left's power, and he threatened the establishment that has run this country into the ground for decades," Bauer said. "They are determined to destroy him."[39]

After the New York criminal indictment, Franklin Graham defended Trump, portraying him as divinely chosen to lead the United States. Graham contended that the charges "are definitely politically motivated." He asked Christians to pray that "God's hand would be upon him, protect him, and direct him in every step he takes—and that God's will be done."[40] "It is disappointing that our legal system has become so politicized. Pray for our nation," Graham tweeted.[41]

Republican leaders who once declared Bill Clinton unfit for the presidency because of moral failings were quick to dismiss the E. Jean Carroll verdict. Former vice president Pence said, "Well, I think this is something that the media cares more about." Senator Lindsey Graham said, "I think the New York legal system is off the rails when it comes to Donald Trump." Senator Tommy Tuberville said the verdict "makes me want to vote for him twice." Senator Marco Rubio called the verdict "a joke."[42]

For Trump, the Southern Baptist Convention buried its moral hatchet. Although a few church leaders spoke out against Trump's violations of Christian morality, most SBC leaders either stayed silent or openly supported him. Southern Baptist leaders were one-third of Trump's 2016 Evangelical Executive Advisory Board, including two recent SBC presidents and the former SBC Ethics & Religious Liberty Commission president. In explaining his participation, Ronnie Floyd, the SBC president from 2014 to 2015, said nothing about personal morality but referred to a grab bag of other "evangelical concerns" about "Supreme Court appointments, abortion, religious liberty, Israel and the Middle East, poverty, crime, violence, lack of opportunity in urban areas, and racial tension."[43]

Southern Baptist leaders were even more unified in supporting Trump's reelection in 2020 and 2024. Their outrage over Clinton's moral failings had shifted to dismissing personal morality as irrelevant; now, only policy mattered. Former SBC president Jack Graham said evangelical Christians must support a pro-life president. We must back a president who has "proven a reliable partner" in "efforts to make sure unborn children have the right to live. . . . Supporting him is a no-brainer."[44]

After the 2024 election, SBC president Clint Pressley tweeted, "Thanks be to God for a decisive result in the presidential contest and for pro-life victories in Florida, Nebraska, and South Dakota. I and millions of my fellow Southern Baptists will be praying for you." "'The Lord reigns, let the earth rejoice'—Psalm 97:1." NBC News reported that evangelical leaders celebrate Trump's win as a "prophecy fulfilled," with a "divine mandate." In 2024, 82 percent of white evangelical Protestants voted for Trump, up from 76 percent in 2020. However, Trump made inroads in the Hispanic evangelical vote, winning 67 percent.[45]

Most white evangelical Protestants followed their leadership in absolving Trump of moral responsibility. Survey data revealed a significant shift in perspective: as late as 2011, 60 percent of white Protestant evangelicals nationwide agreed that a public official who "commits an immoral act in their personal life" cannot still "behave ethically and fulfill their duties in their public and professional life." In October 2016, after the release of the *Access Hollywood* tape, in which Trump bragged about sexually assaulting women, this commitment plummeted to 20 percent. In 2018, with Trump as president, concern about moral failings dropped again to 17 percent.[46]

Few political candidates embodied personal moral failings as dramatically as Herschel Walker, the 2022 Republican candidate for U.S. Senate in Georgia—a pivotal race for control of the Senate. Walker, who acknowledged fathering children out of wedlock, preached against absentee fathers despite having little contact with his children. Although he ran as a staunchly antiabortion candidate, two women credibly accused him of pressuring them to undergo abortions after pregnancies resulting from relationships with him. Revelations from his former wife, Cindy Grossman, and police records showed that he had repeatedly threatened her. Prosecutors did not charge Walker, but Grossman obtained a protective order against him in 2005, years after Walker claimed that religious conversion had changed his life. Walker's son Christian charged, "You're not a 'family man' when you left us to bang a bunch of women, threatened to kill us, and had us move over 6 times in 6 months running from your violence."[47] During the 2022 campaign, Walker also misled voters about his credentials, including his education, charitable work, experience with law enforcement, and business accomplishments.[48]

Despite these concerns, conservatives rallied around Walker, viewing him as a model conservative on policy and a potential swing vote for Senate control. They attributed his blemished character to Democratic critics. "The Democrats want to destroy this country, and they will try to destroy anyone who gets in their way. Today it's Herschel Walker, but tomorrow it's the American people," said Senator Rick Scott (R-FL), who led the national Republican senatorial campaign operation. "I'm proud to stand with Herschel Walker and make sure Georgians know that he will always fight to protect them from the forces trying to destroy Georgia values and Georgia's economy, led by Raphael Warnock."[49]

"I think we're going to stick with Walker, we're going take it all the way to the end," said Senate Minority Leader Mitch McConnell. "I think they're going to hang in there and scrap to the finish."[50] Senator Tom Cotton (R-AR) said, "Herschel Walker is going to help build a Republican majority in the United States Senate." He "will be a leader in the Senate, just like he's been a leader in sports and in business for the state of Georgia, unlike your current U.S. Senator Raphael Warnock."[51] Conservative commentator Dinesh D'Souza dismissed the allegations against Walker as "staged" by his opponents. "We know it's staged," he said. "The actors themselves know what they're doing. It's fake news!"[52] Ralph Reed, the former executive director of the Christian Coalition and the founder and president of the conservative Faith & Freedom Coalition, implored voters to ignore Walker's moral trespasses. "Voters are far more likely to vote based on inflation, the economy, high gas prices, and the failure of Biden policies," Reed said.[53] "I don't care if Herschel Walker paid to abort endangered baby eagles," said conservative radio host and former National Rifle Association spokesperson Dana Loesch. "I want control of the Senate."[54]

Even as conservatives rallied behind Walker, they attacked his Democratic opponent, Raphael Warnock, an Atlanta pastor, by reviving debunked accusations of domestic abuse and financial misconduct from his 2020 Senate campaign. These attacks, however, didn't sway voters. Exit polls revealed that 60 percent of voters prioritizing honesty and integrity voted for Warnock, compared to 38 percent for Walker.

Beyond these prominent cases, sex scandals have also engulfed numerous other conservative Republicans, including judges, governors, and members of Congress. Sexual abuse and cover-ups among conservatives are not isolated to a few bad apples but are systemic. Liberals such as former 2004 vice presidential candidate John Edwards (D-NC), former New York governors Eliot Spitzer (D) and Andrew Cuomo (D), and former U.S. representatives Barney Frank (D-MA) and Anthony Weiner (D-NY) have also become embroiled in sex scandals. Still, there is no comparable frequency of predation and cover-ups among prominent liberals. A study examining eighty Republican versus Democratic sex scandals from 2000 to 2013 found that three-quarters involved Republicans.[55]

Further studies indicate that Republicans, despite their vocal support for family values, are prone to excuse or overlook sex scandals within their ranks. A 2022 study found that "Republicans do not strongly penalize candidates facing allegations of sexual assault or harassment, especially if the candidate is identified as a Republican." In addition, "research finds that social conservatives are more prone to rape myth acceptance than liberals."[56] Another recent study found that "rank-and-file Democrats were more likely than their Republican counterparts to hold co-partisans accountable for their alleged [sexual] transgressions."[57]

Sexual predation is also widespread within conservative evangelical churches, a crucial voter base for conservative politicians. In its 2000 mission statement, "Baptist Faith and Message," the Southern Baptist Convention (SBC) stressed righteousness—personal morality—and sinners' need to seek true redemption: "The unrighteous will be consigned to Hell, the place of everlasting punishment. . . . All Christians are under obligation to seek to make the will of Christ supreme in our own lives and in human society." Thus, "Christians should oppose vice, and all forms of sexual immorality." It warned, "The unrighteous will be consigned to Hell, the place of everlasting punishment." Sinners can still take personal responsibility for transgressions and seek repentance in Christ, who "made provision for the redemption of men from sin."[58]

However, for decades, SBC staffers, volunteers, and pastors had sexually assaulted women within their congregations, while church leaders either covered up or enabled the abuse. It wasn't until media outlets exposed the scandal in 2017—decades after the abuse began—that the SBC acted. It commissioned the investigating firm Guidepost Solutions to study the charges. The 2022 Guidepost report confirmed rampant sexual abuse over decades within the SBC. The report found that church leaders, who were themselves in several cases identified as abusers, did not condemn the abuse, demand that sinners seek redemption, expel offenders, or take remedial action. Instead, the SBC leadership covered it up—keeping secret a list of 700 victims of sexual abuse—and enabled it by protecting abusers and blaming and shaming the victims. Guidepost found that "those who actually suffered at the hands of SBC clergy or SBC church staff or volunteers—who spoke out the most, and who criticized the SBC's inaction, were denigrated as "opportunistic," having a "hidden agenda of lawsuits," wanting to "burn things to the ground," and acting as a "professional victim."

D. August "Augie" Boto, general counsel to the SBC Executive Committee and at one point its interim president, maligned the victims as tools of the devil, claiming that Satan sent them to distract the SBC from its evangelical mission. "This whole thing should be seen for what it is," Boto wrote in an internal email. "It is a satanic scheme to completely distract us from evangelism. It is not the gospel. It is not even a part of the gospel. It is a misdirection play. . . . This is the devil being temporarily successful."[59]

Christa Brown, who was repeatedly raped by her minister as a child and then dismissed and vilified by church leaders, experienced firsthand "the damage done by a faith group that enables abuse and turns a blind eye to clergy-predators in their midst." "I felt powerless, unsafe, targeted, disconnected, and humiliated." Brown learned how "Bible verses, prayer, hymns, faith, God-talk and church rituals are perverted into weapons for sexual assault and then hammered into shields for church cover-ups."[60]

Conservative proponents of absolute right and wrong largely ignored or downplayed the SBC scandal. High-profile figures such as Fox News hosts Laura Ingraham, Tucker Carlson, and Sean Hannity, who typically speak out against moral transgressions, remained silent. Conservative members of Congress did not tweet in outrage, hold press conferences, or demand public hearings. State leaders who had rushed to condemn so-called grooming by restricting the mention of LGBTQ issues in schools were conspicuously quiet in the face of actual sex crimes committed in churches within their jurisdictions.

A January 2023 report, "Evidences of Concern within the Southern Baptist Convention," by the Conservative Baptist Network (CBN), an influential voice within the evangelical community, warned of dangers supposedly posed by critical race theory and homosexuality while minimizing sexual abuse in its ranks. Its discussion of the Guidepost report filled just three and a half of its forty-nine pages, in a section titled "Questions, Double Standards, and Lacking Transparency." The CBN devoted just a single passive-voice half sentence to deploring sexual abuse: "Once again, sexual misconduct, abuse, and/or violence should be grieved, and justice should be served in all cases," which it followed with a consequential "but" that exempted the SBC: "but Southern Baptists have experienced notably fewer instances of abuse than concurrent organizations" (whatever those might be). In most of its abuse section, the CBN ripped the Guidepost investigation for allegedly "an alarming number of concerns" and for including LGBTQ persons in its company.[61]

SBC leadership further outraged survivors of abuse for the amicus brief it filed in the Supreme Court of Kentucky petitioning to exclude third parties accused of covering up abuse from a law extending the statute of limitations for abuse claims. Although the SBC is not a party to the Kentucky lawsuit, it chose to submit a brief on behalf of the SBC, its Executive Committee, the Baptist Theological Seminary, and Lifeway Christian Resources, which publishes, distributes, and sells Christian books, literature, and music. The brief admits, "Amici have a strong interest in the statute of limitations issue presented in this appeal."[62] That is, in constraining the statute of limitations for third parties, such as itself, accused of covering up abuses. An editorial by three abuse survivors in the SBC claimed that it filed the brief to protect itself from pending and future lawsuits. "The duplicity of it boggles the mind," they wrote. "Their entire focus is on institutional protection, not on 'the pursuit of justice on behalf of the abused.'"[63]

Sex transgressions and cover-ups by conservative evangelical Christians extend beyond the SBC. Reverend Ted Haggard, a prominent opponent of same-sex marriage, was an informal advisor to the George W. Bush administration on family issues and president of the flagship National Association of Evangelicals from 2003 to 2006. In 2005, *Time* magazine recognized him as one of the twenty-five most influential evangelicals. After a male prostitute accused Haggard of paying him for sex and drugs over three years, prominent evangelicals initially rallied to his defense. However, the accusations were later found to be largely accurate, and Haggard resigned his presidency in November 2006. Haggard entered counseling from other ministers and declared himself cured. He reemerged in 2010 as the founder and pastor of the Saint James Church in Colorado Springs. In 2022, he sold the warehouse housing the church for $1.95 million, amidst new revelations that he had allegedly molested young boys in the church.[64]

Coy Privette, a prominent former evangelical pastor, was president of the North Carolina Christian Action League, a member of the National Consultation on Pornography, and a county commissioner. In 2007, he pleaded guilty to six charges of aiding and abetting prostitution and resigned from the Christian Action League. However, Privette has little accountability for his crimes. He served no jail time, had his record expunged, and continued to hold his position as county commissioner through the end of his term in 2010. Fellow conservatives warmly eulogized Privette upon his death in 2015.[65]

Multiple male parishioners sued Bishop Eddie Long of the New Birth Missionary Baptist Church in Georgia for pressuring them for sex while they were teenagers. Long settled out of court. A pool attendant claimed that since he was twenty, he had years of sex with Jerry Falwell Jr.'s wife, while Falwell looked on with voyeuristic glee. Falwell is the son of the founder of the Moral Majority and president of Liberty University. Tony Alamo of the Alamo Christian Foundation in California was convicted on ten counts of sexual assault and transporting minors across state lines for sexual purposes.

Josh Duggar headed a family-friendly show on The Learning Channel (TLC) and served as a lobbyist for the Family Research Council. He described his family as the "epitome of conservative values," and advocated against divorce, gay marriage, and abortion. For years, Dugger had been molesting multiple underage girls, including members of his family, and received and possessed child pornography. In March 2003, when his parents brought his crimes to the attention of church elders, they did not report them to the police and instead purportedly gave him counseling. Only many years later, in 2019, did Duggar's crimes come to police attention, and he was sentenced to twelve years in prison on charges of child pornography. The statute of limitations had expired on his crimes of child sexual abuse. Leaders of the Willow Creek megachurch in Illinois covered up allegations of sexual assault against founder Bill Hybels that a church inquiry later found were credible. Ravi Zacharias was an internationally acclaimed evangelical pastor and founder of Ravi Zacharias International Ministries (RZIM). For decades, RZIM had ignored his rampant sexual abuse of women, which they acknowledged only after Zacharias died in 2020.

Robert Morris is the lead pastor of the Dallas-area Gateway Church, a conservative evangelical church that has baselessly railed against the alleged sins of LGBTQ persons.[66] In June 2024, Morris admitted that in the 1980s, "I was involved in inappropriate sexual behavior with a young lady in a home where I was staying. It was kissing and petting and not intercourse, but it was wrong." Morris was in his twenties at the time and married with a child. He confessed to his "behavior" only after the victim finally stirred up the courage to go public. Morris's confession was fundamentally misleading. His victim was no "young lady" but a child of twelve when Morris began molesting her with sexual touching, fondling, and eventually attempted intercourse. Morris's violation of the child continued for four and a half years.

Belying the euphemism "inappropriate sexual behavior," Morris's pedophilia, the repeated sexual molestation of a child, is a serious crime punishable under current Texas law by twenty-five years to life imprisonment. Morris claimed he fully confessed his sin to church elders. They never investigated his claim or reported it to the police. Instead, church leaders covered up his abuse and ensured he would not be accountable. They claimed to have washed away his sin with counseling and restored him to the ministry with all the privileges and benefits that followed. By 2024, Morris had reportedly accumulated an estimated net worth of $117 million. When Morris's victim approached him for restitution, she said that Morris threatened her with prosecution. After the revelation of Morris's child sexual abuse, church leaders just let him resign, which one church elder said was a "difficult" decision, and defended Morris's subsequent "moral purity." They belatedly claimed to investigate his crime. The statute of limitations has likely run out on Morris's crime and on the possible criminal complicity of church officials—for concealment of a crime.[67]

Prominent church leaders such as Robert Morris are not alone among conservative, evangelical pastors embroiled in child sex scandals in his state of Texas. In 2022, a *Newsweek* study found that "at least 10 Texas pastors, former pastors and youth ministers were arrested, charged or convicted for various allegations of sexual abuse of children." Nearly all represented conservative evangelical churches. Among the more egregious offenses, authorities charged Aaron Shipman, the head pastor at Bible Baptist Church, with repeatedly sexually assaulting a teenager over two years, beginning when she was sixteen.[68]

Sexual abuse is also rampant within the Catholic Church in the United States. For decades, thousands of Catholic priests sexually abused children. Church leadership covered up their crimes until exposed by independent investigations. Leaders even moved abusive priests from one jurisdiction to another, enabling the transgressors to continue their crimes. Recent reports have found that sexual abuse proliferated under the direct authority of the Church. Native American children endured years of tolerated sexual abuse in schools run by the Catholic Church or its affiliates.[69]

Sexual abuse within conservative religious organizations and their cover-up is systematic, not random, far outstripping offenses within more liberal church groups or LGBTQ organizations. Two intertwined features explain the prevalence of sexual abuse and its cover-up by church leaders. Men control conservative religious organizations for the benefit of men, subordinating women and, by extension, children (see chapter 11). The male leaders of these organizations believe they are God's messengers on earth and are more concerned with preserving their power and authority than dealing with sexual abuse within their ranks.

Larry Eubanks, pastor of the First Baptist Church of Frederick, Maryland, observes that "the Southern Baptist Convention and the Roman Catholic Church hold little in common," except "they both believe Scripture forbids women from holding the position or performing any of the functions of pastor or priest" and "they are both struggling with clergy sex abuse crises." When you combine man's "physical power and positional authority" along "with the spiritual authority of God's calling and imprimatur, abuse is, if not inevitable, at least predictable," Eubanks said. "In insisting that a male-only clergy is ordained by God and enshrined in Scripture, both the Southern Baptist Convention and the Roman Catholic Church have institutionalized a gross imbalance of power, which makes the most vulnerable members of their communities [women and children] susceptible to abuse and harassment. They have used that power to cover up the resulting crimes, which increases both the power of the abusers and the vulnerability of the actual victims and potential victims."[70]

Christa Brown, a survivor of rape by SBC clergy, blasted SBC reforms as "image repair strategies" that failed "to reckon with the human cost of its decades-long travesty" or hold those responsible accountable. The SBC is trying "to plug the holes in a system that is *designed* to have holes. At best, that's an exercise in frustration. The holes aren't a bug; they're a feature." "In words and deeds, SBC leaders have, for years, communicated a 'You don't matter' message to survivors." "And until they earnestly reckon with the harms of the past, all their talk about doing better in the future merits *skepticism*."[71] Sheila Wray Gregoire, an authority on women's issues from a Christian, biblical perspective, explains that "in their churches and at their men's ministry retreats," conservative evangelical men "will be told objectification is just a natural, unavoidable part of being male."[72]

This pattern of sexual abuse, moral failure, and institutional cover-up highlights the contradiction between conservative evangelical rhetoric on family values and the reality within many of their organizations. The willingness to protect abusers while condemning external moral failings suggests that political and institutional interests often outweigh genuine moral accountability.

A study of sexual abuse by the Catholic Church concludes that "a full explanation of sexual abuse of children by Catholic priests must go beyond the sexually deviant behavior of the few 'rotten apples.' Rather, child sexual abuse by Catholic priests should be examined in the context of a social organization. The analysis must go beyond an examination of individual offenders and victims and view the phenomenon in the universe of the organization as a breakdown of the institution, disregarded or facilitated by the underlying organizational structure in which the harm occurred."[73] Maryland attorney general Anthony Brown, who investigated about 600 cases of sexual abuse by Catholic priests in the Archdiocese of Baltimore, said, "It is clear that the church valued the denials of the abusers over the claims, the complaints, and the credibility of the abused."[74]

Justice Clarence Thomas of the U.S. Supreme Court, now at the center of one of the most significant personal scandals in the Court's history, illustrates a troubling case of conservative disregard for personal morality and responsibility. Unlike previous controversies, Thomas's misconduct does not involve sexual impropriety but rather severe conflicts of interest and attempts at concealment. Between 1998 and 2003, Thomas failed to disclose hundreds of thousands of dollars in income earned by his wife from the Heritage Foundation, a conservative think tank. His excuse? He claimed not to understand the straightforward disclosure forms—yet he continues adjudicating complex constitutional matters. It wasn't until the media exposed the omission that Thomas amended his disclosures.

More troubling still is Thomas's financial entanglement with billionaire conservative and Republican megadonor Harlan Crow, who has a profound interest in Supreme Court rulings. Over the past two decades, Crow has lavished Thomas with unreported gifts, including at least six trips on Crow's private jet, stays at his Adirondacks resort, cruises on his superyacht, and numerous luxury vacations, altogether valued in the millions. Crow also paid for the private school tuition of Thomas's nephew, whom Thomas was raising. Crow even bought property from Thomas, including his mother's home, for $133,000. Afterward, Crow invested $30,000 into the property and allowed Thomas's mother to live rent-free. Thomas defended his nondisclosure of these perks by claiming they fell under a "hospitality" exemption, even though the law explicitly excludes travel from such exemptions. He also failed to disclose the real estate transaction with Crow, alleging he took a monetary loss on the deal—a justification entirely irrelevant under the regulation that required reporting transactions of more than $1,000 regardless of profit or loss.[75]

Additionally, Thomas omitted details about other financial benefits from Crow and other Republican megadonors with vested interests in Supreme Court decisions. Adding to the mire, Anthony Welters, a wealthy conservative businessman, lent Thomas $267,239 to buy a luxury recreational vehicle. According to the U.S. Senate Committee on Finance report, Thomas paid interest briefly on the loan but "never repaid a substantial portion of the loan." Thomas again failed to report this transaction.[76]

In 2012, Conservative activist Leonard Leo paid $25,000 to Ginni Thomas for purported polling services, although she is not a pollster, and instructed there be "no mention of Ginni." He channeled the payments through a conservative nonprofit group, the Judicial Education Project (JEP), run by former Trump spokesperson Kellyanne Conway. That same year, the JEP filed a brief in the landmark Supreme Court voting rights suit on the preclearance of voting law changes under the Voting Rights Act.[77] Leo also helped finance a multiyear laudatory public relations campaign on Justice Thomas's behalf.[78]

As the head of the conservative Federalist Society, Leo played a key role in guiding the judicial appointments of conservative federal judges under Presidents George W. Bush and Donald Trump. His network of advocacy groups supported judicial confirmations and promoted conservative interpretations of the law. A 2019 *Washington Post* investigation revealed that Leo had helped raise $250 million from largely undisclosed donors to advance these aims. "Judicial confirmations these days are more like political campaigns," Leo remarked at a 2019 Council for National Policy meeting. "We stand at the threshold. No one in this room has probably experienced the kind of transformation that I think we are beginning to see."[79]

In 2024, after media revelations of Crow's largess, Thomas retroactively disclosed lavish trips from 2019 financed by Crow, valued at several million dollars. However, Senator Richard Durbin (D-IL), chair of the Senate Judiciary Committee, found that according to documents that Crow provided the committee, Thomas failed to report at least three other lavish trips that Crow financed. Durbin also found that even Thomas's 2019 disclosures contained serious omissions.[80]

Rather than admonish Thomas or demand that he assume responsibility for his undisclosed conflicts of interest, conservatives again blamed his critics. Senator Lindsey Graham framed the revelations as a political attack. "This assault on Justice Thomas is well beyond ethics. It's about trying to delegitimize a conservative court that was appointed through the traditional process," Graham said. "This is an unseemly effort by the Democratic left to destroy the legitimacy of the Roberts Court, it's put people at risk, it's put their personal safety at risk." Senator Mike Lee (R-UT) said that the Left "obviously can't persuade the American people to adopt their radical policies through legislation, so they're attempting to destroy the court's credibility and intimidate the Republican appointed justices and their families, starting with Justice Thomas. They're making clear that justices who disagree with them will pay a price, and it's a price that the radical left is determined to ensure is extremely high. This is all just a thuggish shakedown."[81] Virtually every Republican in the Senate and House opposed legislation establishing a code of ethics for the Court.

This selective outrage highlights a fundamental contradiction within the conservative movement. When Bill Clinton's infidelities became known, conservatives argued vehemently that his moral failings disqualified him from the presidency. Yet, in the face of similar or more egregious behavior by their leaders—whether Trump's infamous *Access Hollywood* tape or the systemic abuse within the SBC—conservatives have either rallied to the defense of the accused or remained silent. This willingness to overlook moral failings for political power reveals a troubling double standard.

The double standard becomes especially apparent when one considers the vast conservative infrastructure that promotes family values and moral integrity, particularly among evangelical Christians. These groups, which wield significant political influence, have remained loyal to figures such as Trump, Herschel Walker, and other morally compromised politicians because they align with conservative policies on issues like abortion, religious liberty, and gun rights.

Thomas Paine's words from *Common Sense* ring especially true in this context: "A long habit of not thinking a thing WRONG, gives it the superficial appearance of being RIGHT." Over time, the repeated dismissal of moral transgressions within conservative ranks has created a dangerous precedent in which the pursuit of political gain supersedes personal accountability. This pragmatic approach to politics may have short-term benefits, but it erodes the moral authority that conservatives claim to champion. By excusing their misdeeds while condemning those of their opponents, conservative leaders risk being seen not as champions of morality but as just another political faction willing to compromise principles for power.

8

LAW AND ORDER

It didn't start with Richard Nixon. Commentators often credit Nixon for embedding the conservative focus on "law and order" in his victorious 1968 presidential campaign. Upon accepting the Republican nomination, Nixon said, "As we look at America, we see cities enveloped in smoke and flame. We hear sirens in the night. . . . We see Americans hating each other; fighting each other; killing each other at home." "The greatest tradition of the rule of law is plagued by unprecedented lawlessness." And under his administration, "The wave of crime is not going to be the wave of the future in the United States of America."[1] Nixon tapped into the public's widespread fear of rising crime. A 1968 Gallup poll found that Americans worried about "crime and lawlessness" as the "top domestic problem."[2]

However, conservatives had long fashioned themselves as defenders of law and order before Nixon's campaign. Like Nixon, they capitalized on public fears about crime to advance their core values, often using a heavy-handed approach toward strikes and left-leaning protests. Their messaging frequently contained veiled or explicit appeals to concerns about minority and immigrant crime, a tactic aimed at energizing their white voter base. Gallup polling demonstrates that law and order remains a potent political issue. From 2001 to 2024, Gallup found that a plurality and usually a majority of respondents were "very dissatisfied" or "somewhat dissatisfied" with "the nation's policies to reduce or control crime." In early 2024, the "dissatisfied" percentage reached 69 percent despite falling crime rates.[3]

Governor Calvin Coolidge gained fame as "the apostle of law and order" and the 1920 Republican nomination for vice president by quashing a Boston police strike in 1919. "This is not a strike," Coolidge said. "There is nothing to compromise, nothing to arbitrate, because there can be no arbitration of the law." He asserted that "there is no right to strike against the public safety by anybody, anywhere, any time."[4] Coolidge railed against the crime and looting that erupted during the strike. He blamed the strikers, whom he scorned as "deserters," and called the State Guards to restore order. Nine Bostonians died during the disorders, eight of them shot by guardsmen. In reflection, Coolidge said, "Disobedience to the law is disobedience to the people." Coolidge won a landslide re-election as governor with his self-proclaimed "law and order" campaign.[5] Former president William Howard Taft (R-OH) praised Coolidge as "the protagonist of the cause of the supremacy of law and order."[6]

In the 1920 election, General Leonard Wood, a leading contender for the Republican presidential nomination, echoed Coolidge's sentiment: "We can best honor Lincoln by doing things which are necessary to maintain this country, which Lincoln saved by standing firm for law and order."[7] Warren Harding, who defeated Wood for the nomination, said in his acceptance address, "I believe in law enforcement . . . that security and the majesty of the law are the first essentials of liberty. He who threatens destruction of the Government by force or flaunts his contempt for lawful authority, ceases to be a loyal citizen and forfeits his rights to the freedom of the Republic."[8] Together, Harding and Coolidge represented a robust law-and-order ticket. "Best of all, the nominees represent law and order, which the Republican Party has always and, I trust, always will stand for," said Justice Robert von Moschzisker of the Supreme Court of Pennsylvania.[9]

This commitment to law and order became a defining feature of the Republican Party. In 1928, Senator Frank B. Willis (R-OH) proudly declared, "The Republican Party has never wavered in the matter of law enforcement. . . . The history of the party leaves no doubt. It will and ought to speak in no uncertain terms in favor of the maintenance of law and order."[10] House Minority Leader Bertrand Snell, chair of the 1936 Republican National Convention, told the gathering that Republicans had "a great heritage—a political force which personifies the deeply rooted American instinct for law and order."[11]

The far-right John Birch Society (JBS), founded by candy magnate Robert Welch in 1958, combined anticommunism with strong law-and-order appeals to build a conservative base. Welch, who was also a leader in the National Association of Manufacturers, claimed that a vast communist conspiracy had infiltrated a quarter of the U.S. government and was undermining law and order. More mainstream conservatives, such as William F. Buckley Jr., eventually distanced themselves from the JBS, but Welch's rhetoric motivated conservatives. By 1960, the JBS had established as many as 100 chapters in 34 states. Northeastern University professor Edward H. Miller observed that the JBS was "never excommunicated" from conservatism and that "his [Welch's] style of politics remained extremely potent after his death."[12]

In 1963, the JBS initiated the "Support Your Local Police and Keep Them Independent" project (SYLP): "We urged members to create ad hoc SYLP committees to pull together members and supportive nonmembers to protect local police and the communities they serve."[13] The SYLP campaign bundled together fears of communist agitation and Negro lawlessness. Welch explained, "The darkening storm of activated hatred between white people and colored people . . . has been carefully planned, subtly fomented, cleverly nourished, and raised to tremendous forces of disruption by the Communist conspirators and the misguided dupes and allies. . . . It is not desegregation as an end in which they are interested, but the bitterness, strife, and terrors of mob action which can be instigated while that end is supposedly being sought."[14]

In a pamphlet denouncing independent review boards for hampering the police, the JBS warned, "Communist-inspired racial riots are getting to be a regular part of the American scene." It said that in responding to civil rights demonstrators, the Birmingham, Alabama, police "was doing a superb job of maintaining law and order" until provoked by "hotheads and dupes among the Negroes."[15] A JBS ad in the *Birmingham News* claimed that the civil rights movement "is not influenced by Communists, as you frequently hear. It has been deliberately and almost wholly created by the Communists."[16]

During his 1964 campaign, Republican presidential candidate Barry Goldwater criticized a morally compromised, lawless society: "The moral fiber of the American people is beset by rot and decay." "It is on our streets that we see the final, terrible proof of a sickness which not all the social theories of a thousand social experiments has even begun to touch. Crime grows faster than population, while those who break the law are accorded more consideration than those who try to enforce the law."[17] Goldwater's rhetoric echoed broader conservative anxieties about crime and moral decline, setting the stage for future law-and-order campaigns.

In 1953, Ronald Reagan embodied the archetypal tough sheriff as Frame Johnson in the film *Law and Order*, a persona he would later embrace in his political career. Reagan channeled this image into his policies as a presidential candidate and president. The Republican Party Platform at the 1980 convention that nominated Reagan declared, "Republicans will address the real problems that face Americans in their neighborhoods day by day—deterioration and urban blight, dangerous streets and violent crime that make millions of Americans, especially senior citizens, fearful in their own neighborhoods and prisoners in their own homes."[18]

Reagan's emphasis on law and order became central to his presidency. In a speech to police chiefs during his first year in office, he lamented, "The frightening reality" is that "crime has advanced and advanced steadily in its upward climb, and our citizens have grown more and more frustrated, frightened, and angry." "When we took our oaths of office, you and I, we made certain promises. We said we would uphold the law, whether those who violate it are common criminals or misguided members of a public employees' union." He added, "It may be old-fashioned, but nothing sums up this personal commitment more than the simple word, 'honor.'" Reagan called for the preventive detention of accused criminals, a relaxing of the rule that excludes illegally obtained evidence, and a "war on drugs."[19]

Vice President George H. W. Bush (R-TX) followed a similar path when running for president in 1988, presenting himself as the "law and order candidate," much like Coolidge had decades earlier. He expressed frustration with the justice system: "There's something wrong with the system when the modern day version of a prison break is crawling through some loophole." "The rights accorded to criminals should never overshadow the wrongs done to the victims." At one rally, Bush dramatically showcased a bulletproof vest with three stopped slugs, advocating for police protection in the fight against crime.[20]

After the deadly and destructive Los Angeles riots of 1992, President Bush doubled down on his law-and-order message. "The primary duty of government is to protect the safety of lives and property," Bush said, playing defense against accusations of racism. "There is nothing racist, there is nothing divisive about protecting decent people from crime. Some say it's playing politics. Well, they're wrong. Playgrounds overrun by gangs, senior citizens locked behind triple-bolted doors, or mothers shot through open kitchen windows—this isn't the America we want." Bush kept critics away from his event.[21]

George W. Bush, as Republican governor of Texas, upheld this tough-on-crime approach, preparing for his presidential campaign by affirming the need for "tough laws and long sentences to keep criminals off the streets."[22] Bush ran in 2000 on a law-and-order Republican Party Platform, as his father did. "We can go forward, step by difficult step, to recreate respect for law—and law that is worthy of respect," the Platform said. It lauded "our Republican governors, legislators, and local leaders [who] have taken a zero tolerance approach to crime that has led to the lowest crime and murder rates in a generation." Still, "At the same time, we recognize the crucial leadership role the president and the Congress should play in restoring public safety."[23]

Donald Trump, the next successful Republican presidential candidate, leaned heavily into the law-and-order narrative during his 2016 campaign. On November 22, 2015, a day after his supporters roughed up a Black protestor at a rally in Alabama, Trump tweeted an image of a dark-skinned masked figure pointing a gun at alarming murder statistics. The image claimed, without verification from official data, that Black perpetrators killed 81 percent of white Americans murdered in 2015.

At a March 2016 rally in St. Louis, Trump harped on his commitment to law and order. "There has to be some decorum," he said. "There has to be some law and order in our country."[24] In his speech accepting the Republican presidential nomination, Trump reiterated, "We will be a country of generosity and warmth, but we will also be a country of law and order."[25] After Trump's election, his attorney general, Jeff Sessions, said in 2018, "Under President Trump, we are determined to advance President Reagan's work of restoring the rule of law. President Trump sent us an order to support our men and women in blue and to 'reduce' crime in America."[26]

During demonstrations in the spring of 2020 that demanded racial justice after police in Minneapolis killed George Floyd, Trump branded demonstrators as "thugs." He warned that if states or cities refused to act forcefully, "I will deploy the U.S. military and quickly solve the problem for them." He told the governors, "You have to dominate—if you don't dominate, you're wasting your time."[27]

Conservatives have historically framed their commitment to law and order as a counterpoint to allegedly negligent, "soft-on-crime" liberals. In a 1929 address, President Herbert Hoover chastised his liberal opponents for their lack of commitment to enforcing the law. "A surprising number of our people, otherwise of responsibility in the community, have drifted into the extraordinary notion that laws are made for those who choose to obey them," Hoover said. We face "the possibility that respect for the law as law is fading from the sensibilities of our people. . . . Law should be observed and enforced until it is repealed by the proper processes of our democracy."[28]

Arthur T. McGonigle, the 1958 Republican nominee for governor of Pennsylvania, implored voters to help him fight crime. He charged that the current Democratic governor, George M. Leader, and David L. Lawrence, the Democratic mayor of Pittsburgh and his gubernatorial opponent, "are soft on crime and the record proves it."[29]

By the 1960s, the conservative campaign against permissive liberals tapped into white fear of Black crime to fuel their campaign against 'permissive' liberals. In 1964, Barry Goldwater blasted the Johnson administration for failing to uphold law and order. According to a confidential campaign memo, "Johnson has failed to exert leadership or to take action in curbing the increase in crime (occurring throughout the country), arresting the trend toward riots, looting, and vandalism as a way of life, halting the widespread breakdown in law and order, or reversing the decline in morality and increase in disrespect for the value of human life." Conservatives attributed the dissolution of an orderly society to liberal permissiveness, the expulsion of God from public life, and social programs that battered the family and rewarded bad habits. They used carefully coded language to rally whites fearful of Black crime and sexuality without directly stirring racial antagonism. "Every element of the breakdown of public order," the memo urged, should "be treated as a prong of a single fork—a fork labeled 'moral crisis' [and] jabbed relentlessly from now until election day."[30]

In the speech that formally opened his presidential campaign, Goldwater charged, "The shadow of scandal falls, unlighted yet by full answers, across the White House itself." This lack of morality, he charged, feeds the crime problem. "It is a responsibility of the national leadership . . . to encourage every community in this nation to enforce the law, not let it be abused and ignored," Goldwater said.[31]

On the campaign trail four years later, Republican candidate Nixon warned that crime would double within a year if the "soft-on-criminals" Democrats retained the presidency. The liberal U.S. Supreme Court, he said, favors "the criminal forces over the peace forces."[32] Nixon's running mate, Maryland governor Spiro Agnew, blasted the Democrats as "soft on inflation, soft on Communism, and soft on law on order." He ripped the "self-appointed elitists" who thought their "educations give them the right to decide which laws to obey and which to disregard." "The fact we have a law and order issue at all is a searing indictment of the present administration. It demonstrates an inability to maintain order and a failure to make law meaningful."[33] Nixon responded, "I share his [Agnew's] views that we should hit hard on the issue of law and order."[34]

Independent presidential candidate George C. Wallace (a Democrat until 1995), the former and future segregationist governor of Alabama, sought to outflank Nixon on law and order. Wallace's campaign materials highlighted his unwavering stance compared to the irresolution of Nixon and the Democratic nominee, Vice President Hubert Humphrey. Wallace supported "law and order" while Nixon gave political "lip service" to crime, and Humphrey "weakly" blamed crime on poverty. Wallace would "crush riots with a swift blow," while Nixon stood silent and Humphrey supported "anarchy and riots." Wallace opposed "supreme court dictatorship." Nixon offered "apologies for Earl Warren," and Humphrey, the "criminal lover," defended "LBJ-crony Justice Abe 'Fixer' Fortas."[35]

During his 1984 reelection campaign, President Reagan said he had dealt with the recent recession and Soviet "expansionism" and would now overcome "the crisis of crime in America." Congressmen blocking his anticrime program are "the same liberal leadership that has done nothing but stand in the way" of economic recovery initiatives.[36] Reagan's vice president, George H. W. Bush, in his 1988 campaign for president, reprimanded his Democratic opponent, Massachusetts governor Michael Dukakis, for backing a furlough program that put dangerous criminals back on the streets. "Some people need to be taken off the streets, and kept off the streets," Bush said. "That's why I think it's disgraceful that my opponent supported the only furlough program in 50 states, and throw the federal program in too, that furloughed murderers who had not served enough time to be eligible for parole."[37]

The Bush campaign unabashedly exploited white fears of dangerous Black men. An ad run by the National Security Political Action Committee, a conservative organization that spent $8.5 million supporting Bush, made Willie Horton—a convicted Black felon who raped a white Maryland woman and beat her husband while on leave from a Massachusetts prison—a familiar face of the campaign. The PAC did not randomly produce the Willie Horton ad. It followed a two-track deliberate Republican strategy. Let a little-known organization run the racist ad, and then Bush could deflect responsibility. Bush's campaign director, the hard-ball strategist Lee Atwater, had said, "If I can make Willie Horton a household name, we'll win the election." He later said they had made Willie Horton "look like Dukakis' running mate."[38]

During the controversy over President Bill Clinton's affair with White House intern Monica Lewinsky, law-and-order Republicans insisted that even a sitting president was not above the law. In justifying Clinton's impeachment in December 1998, they vowed to hold Clinton accountable for any crimes committed in covering up the affair. Representative Henry Hyde, the chair of the House Judiciary Committee, said, "No man or woman, no matter how highly placed, no matter how effective a communicator, no matter how gifted a manipulator of opinion or winner of votes, can be above the law in a democracy. That is not a counsel of perfection. That is a rock-bottom, irreducible principle of our public life." He stressed, "We cannot have one law for the ruler and another law for the ruled." Representative Thomas Bliley (R-VA) agreed that "either we are a nation of laws or we are a nation of men. If we are a nation of laws, then the highest and the lowest are subject to the same law. There is no preferential treatment and we and our Constitution grant none."[39] Senator Lindsey Graham said of Clinton, "Somebody that plays the games to the bitter end, tries to have it both ways, dances on the head of a pin, in my opinion, has forfeited their right to lead this country."[40]

During the 2016 presidential election campaign, law-and-order Republicans targeted another Democrat, Hillary Clinton, whom they charged with criminally jeopardizing national security by using a private email server for official business. Cries of "lock her up" reverberated in Trump rallies throughout the campaign. Trump echoed other conservative Republicans, saying on August 18, 2016, "In my administration, I'm going to enforce all laws concerning the protection of classified information. No one will be above the law." On September 6, he reiterated, "We can't have someone in the Oval Office who doesn't understand the meaning of the word confidential or classified." A day later he added, "One of the first things we must do is to enforce all classification rules and to enforce all laws relating to the handling of classified information." Clinton's mishandling of classified information, he charged, disqualified her from serving as president.[41] In 2018, President Trump backed and signed a law that elevated the "unauthorized removal and retention of classified documents or material" from a misdemeanor to a felony.[42]

Following the killing of George Floyd in Minneapolis on May 25, 2020, and the ensuing demonstrations, Republicans charged Democrats with fomenting violent crime, rioting, and looting. These accusations were steeped in racism, framing people of color—allegedly coddled by liberals—as inherent threats to law and order. A 2020 Trump ad shows Joe Biden kneeling before a Black church, followed by horrific scenes of violent rioting. The ad closed with the punchline, "Stop Joe Biden and His Rioters."[43] Trump tweeted during the 2020 campaign: "Why would Suburban Women vote for Biden and the Democrats when Democrat-run cities are now rampant with crime (and they aren't asking the Federal Government for help) which could easily spread to the suburbs, and they will reconstitute, on steroids, their low income suburbs plan!"[44]

Another Trump ad featured Biden's image imposed over violent riot scenes while claiming, "You Won't Be Safe in Joe Biden's America." It accused Biden of defunding the police, "letting criminals back on the streets," allowing criminals to "take over our cities," and standing by while "innocent children are shot."[45] Other recent Republican candidates followed Trump's lead. In another effort to associate Democrats with violent crime, a 2022 Wisconsin ad shows a redheaded, fair-skinned white woman attacked by a dark figure. The ad draws a red circle around the crime scene, juxtaposed with the name Mandela Barnes, who is Black, the Democratic candidate for U.S. Senate that year.[46] In 2020, Senator Kelly Loeffler (R-GA) posted an ad showing her conferring with uniformed police officers. She charged that her Democratic opponent, Doug Collins, a criminal defense lawyer, had "helped violent criminals and gang murderers get out of jail. Some struck again."[47] In the 2020 campaign for the Twenty-Fourth Congressional District, the Republican Leadership Fund ran an ad against Democratic candidate Candace Valenzuela, who would be the first Afro-Latina to serve in the Texas congressional delegation. The ad juxtaposed her image against scenes of violence and accused her of wanting to "defund the police" and allowing "dangerous criminals to flood into Texas" by "weakening our borders." We "can't trust Candace Valenzuela to keep us safe," the ad concludes.[48]

A televised ad from Tom Reed, the Republican candidate for Congress in New York's Twenty-Third Congressional District, accused his Democratic opponent, Tracy Mitrano, of being "extreme and dangerous." The ad charged her with "letting violent criminals back into our community." It said that she "refused to condemn [Black] rioters" (pictured with Mitrano in the foreground) and "supported defunding the police."[49]

Republican candidate Karen Handel in 2020 accused Black Democratic incumbent, Representative Lucy McBath, in Georgia's Sixth Congressional District of being as soft on crime, associated with violent Black protesters, and disdainful of law enforcement. The Handel campaign juxtaposed pictures of McBath against scenes of mostly Black rioters, looters, and arsonists burning police cars.[50] Ironically, McBath's son was a victim of white violence. A jury convicted Michael Dunn of murdering him.[51]

The Republican State Leadership Committee launched an attack in 2020 against Democratic state senator Bob Trammel of Georgia. Its ad superimposed the headlines, "LIBERAL BOB TRAMMEL LOVES

PROTESTING" and "LIBERAL BOB TRAMMEL WON'T DE-FEND OUR POLICE," over photos of Black Lives Matter protests, violent riots, lootings, and burning buildings.[52]

These attacks on lawless, dangerous Democrats continued in the 2022 and 2024 elections. In 2022, the Republican Party of New Mexico circulated a flyer in several congressional districts showing a black hand looming atop the head of a terrified-looking white child. It asks, "Do you want a sex offender cutting your child's hair?" The flyer accused unspecified Democrats with voting "to allow convicted sex offenders to receive licenses for professional services such as cutting hair . . . leaving unsuspecting women and children vulnerable to predators."[53] Senator Tommy Tuberville accused Democrats in 2022 of being in favor of crime. "They're not soft on crime," Tuberville said. "They're pro-crime. They want crime. They want crime because they want to take over what you got. They want to control what you have. They want reparation [for Black people] because they think the people that do the crime are owed that."[54]

A 2022 televised ad by the National Republican Senatorial Committee against Democratic Senate candidate Cheri Beasley in North Carolina charged, "We can't trust Cheri Beasley to protect our families." It said she had failed to protect victims of murder and other violent crimes. It accused her of putting murderers and sexual predators back on the streets when she was chief justice of the North Carolina Supreme Court.[55] A 2022 ad by the Republican Congressional Committee charged that Laura Gillen, the Democratic candidate in New York's Fourth Congressional District, wants to "defund the police and end cash bail. . . . Nassau families can't trust Laura Gillen with their safety." The committee played the ad against a background of a violent assault by a man with an ambiguous racial identity.[56]

In a September 2024 address to the Fraternal Order of Police, Trump charged that "American cities, suburbs and towns are totally under siege. Kamala Harris and the communist left have unleashed a brutal plague of bloodshed, crime, chaos, misery and death upon their land." He claimed that police "are not allowed to do your jobs" and "we have to get back to power and respect."[57]

In the aftermath of Trump's defeat in 2020, conservatives, not just Trump, routinely charged Democrats with stealing the election as part of a larger pattern of perpetrating election fraud. "Well, I think it's probably almost impossible under current law to ensure an accurate election," Newt Gingrich said in June 2023. "And I think the only Republican strategy in the long run is to pick issues and win by margins so big that they can't steal it. If you have a very close election, Democrats have a passion for stealing them."[58] In a September 2024 Truth Social post, Trump said he would closely monitor the upcoming election because of "rampant Cheating and Skullduggery that has taken place by the Democrats in the 2020 Presidential Election." He promised "long-term prison sentences" for "Lawyers, Political Operatives, Donors, Illegal Voters, & Corrupt Election Officials. Those involved in unscrupulous behavior will be sought out, caught, and prosecuted at levels, unfortunately, never seen before in our Country."[59]

For conservatives, these century-long professions of law and order and disparagement of liberals routinely gave way to the illicit pursuit of money, power, and ideology. Four conservative Republican administrations, Harding, Nixon, Reagan, and Trump, wove webs of illegality that entangled officials at the highest levels of the federal government.

Historians recognize Harding's administration for its significant appointments and the scandals that plagued it. Harding made several outstanding appointments on the positive side, including naming Charles Evans Hughes as secretary of state and Herbert Hoover as secretary of commerce. However, Harding also appointed close friends and political allies to high-level positions, many of whom became embroiled in scandal. Harding named his friend, Senator Albert Fall (R-NM), as interior secretary despite opposition from conservationists who rejected his philosophy of uncontrolled capitalism. Harding appointed his campaign manager and confidant, Harry Daugherty, as attorney general, dismissing the concerns of Republican senators about Daugherty's dubious character. "I have told [Daugherty] that he can have any place in my Cabinet he wants, outside of Secretary of State," Harding said. "He tells me that he wants to be Attorney General, and by God, he will be Attorney General!" Harding made his political ally Charles Forbes head of the Veterans Bureau. He put in Albert D. Lasker, a donor and 1920 campaign official, as chair of the United States Shipping Board and another crony, Thomas W. Miller, as alien property custodian. Miller's office controlled "all money and property in the United States due or belonging to an enemy, or ally of an enemy."

Private oil magnates bribed Fall for access to petroleum held in government reserves at Elk Hills, California, and Teapot Dome, Wyoming. Fall became the first cabinet member to serve a prison term, lending the name "Teapot Dome" to multiple Harding scandals. Federal prosecutors charged Daugherty with bribery in selling assets confiscated during World War I. He twice escaped conviction through hung juries. Only one juror held out for acquittal in the second trial. A public outcry eventually forced President Coolidge to dismiss Daugherty in 1924. Forbes served a year and eight months in prison for conspiracy to defraud the U.S. government. Congressional critics accused Lasker of "throwing our ships away" by selling surplus vessels at the bargain-basement price of $30 per ton, but prosecutors did not charge him criminally. Miller spent eighteen months in prison for plotting to defraud the government.

Members of both parties in the Senate voted to authorize investigations into Teapot Dome, but Republicans accused Democrats of weaponizing the investigations for political gain. In his keynote address to the Republican National Convention of 1924, Senator George Pepper (R-PA) said, "The Democrats have aimed at us and hit America" in their pursuit of investigations. Their tactics serve "to block constructive legislation, and to limit the capacity of both parties to serve the people. . . . The Democratic Party has recently forfeited whatever claim to public confidence it may have possessed." He added, "When sensible people are waiting to be told about President Coolidge's position on public questions and what the party is attempting to accomplish for good government, somebody is sure to shout: 'How about Forbes?' 'How about Fall?' and 'How about Daugherty?' Thereupon the air resounds with discordant cries and we find ourselves showered with threats and accusations in which a modicum of truth is obscured by a mass of fiction."[60]

The Republican Party Platform of 1924 blamed "both parties" for law violations. It said that although "our public life should have harbored some dishonest men, we assert that these undesirables do not represent the standard of our national integrity." It accused Democrats of exploiting the Harding scandals for political advantage: "It is a grave wrong against these patriotic men and women to strive indiscriminately to besmirch the names of the innocent and undermine the confidence of the people in the government. It is even a greater wrong when this is done for partisan purposes or for selfish exploitation."[61]

President Nixon and the leading officials of his administration and reelection campaign committed a spree of crimes not for financial gain but to retain political power. The Nixon Committee to Reelect the President (CREEP) collected a record $61 million, about double the amount raised by its Democratic opposition. It accepted illegal corporate and cash donations and sometimes arranged government favors in return. It put more pressure on the IRS than previous presidents to investigate his "enemies." CREEP subjected opponents to espionage, harassment, surveillance, and "dirty tricks," such as forging letters on an opponent's letterhead, planting false stories in the media, and spreading rumors about candidates' personal lives. The IRS probed such mainstream left-to-center groups as Americans for Democratic Action, the Urban League, and the National Council of Churches.

After Defense Department analyst Daniel Ellsberg released to the *New York Times* "The Pentagon Papers," the CIA's critical analysis of the war in Vietnam, Nixon set up a covert "plumbers" unit to plug leaks. He ordered the wiretapping of newspaper reporters and federal employees and a break-in at the office of Ellsberg's psychiatrist to find dirt on this hated enemy. CREEP operatives bugged the Democratic National Headquarters in the Watergate Building in Washington, DC. On June 17, 1972, police arrested five men employed by the campaign after they broke into the Watergate DNC headquarters allegedly to replace a defective listening device. Federal authorities later arrested two former White House aides—G. Gordon Liddy and E. Howard Hunt—for complicity in the break-in.

In a press conference on August 29, 1972, President Nixon fabricated an investigation by White House Counsel John Dean that supposedly cleared everyone in his administration and campaign of involvement "in this very bizarre incident" of the Watergate break-in. "We are doing everything we can to take this incident [seriously] and not to cover it up," he said. Nixon ironically added, "What really hurts is if you try to cover it up."[62]

Revelations that top administration and campaign officials had directed the Watergate break-in and pressured defendants for silence engulfed Nixon's second term in scandal. On August 7, 1974, Senator Goldwater joined other GOP leaders in warning the president of an unstoppable impeachment by the House and conviction in the Senate: Goldwater told Nixon that he could count on no more than fifteen votes for acquittal in the Senate. Bowing to the inevitable, Nixon resigned on August 9, 1974. In all, prosecutors secured convictions or guilty pleas from forty-eight persons for Watergate-related crimes. These felons included Nixon's three top White House officials—John Dean, H. R. "Bob" Haldeman, and John Ehrlichman—former commerce secretary Maurice Stans, and former attorney general John Mitchell, who had resigned to chair CREEP. The irony of Watergate is that its crimes were unnecessary; Nixon already had a lock on reelection. He ultimately prevailed with 61 percent of the popular vote, with 520 electoral votes to 17 for Senator George McGovern (D-SD). Both the Harding and Nixon administrations represent moments in our political history where scandals involving corruption and cover-ups threatened to undermine public trust in government, with significant consequences for the individuals and institutions involved.

Nixon took no responsibility for his actions and deflected blame on the liberal media, left-wing Democrats, and overzealous prosecutors. Watergate "would have been a blip," Nixon said in a May 1974 interview, if not for those in the news media "who hate my guts with a passion." He claimed that the "eager beavers" on the Watergate special prosecutor's staff subjected members of his administration and campaign team to an "abusive process" by "hours of grilling and questioning and all the rest. If these tactics had been used in the day of Joe McCarthy, he [the special prosecutor] would have been ridden out of town on a rail."[63]

The Watergate scandal, though a profound shock to the country's political system, saw most conservative Republicans remain loyal to President Nixon until his resignation became unavoidable. When the House Judiciary Committee passed three articles of impeachment in 1974—obstruction of justice, abuse of power, and defiance of subpoenas—voting split along ideological lines. All Democrats voted for the first two articles, but only a small minority of moderate and conservative Republicans supported impeachment. Regarding Article 3, "Defiance of Subpoenas," most Republicans voted against it, including all conservatives.[64]

During the Watergate investigations, Spiro Agnew became the first vice president to resign since John C. Calhoun in 1832. Agnew had no part in the high crimes of Watergate, but as governor of Maryland, he had committed the low crimes of pocketing bribes and kickbacks from contractors doing business with the state. The president let an expendable and guilty vice president avoid jail by pleading no contest to a single count of income tax evasion. Agnew resigned on October 10, 1973, and disappeared from public life. His resignation deepened the administration's crisis, as it faced investigations into widespread misconduct at the time.

Beyond Watergate, Nixon violated his law-and-order pledge in other ways. Upon taking office, Nixon intensified the bombing of Cambodia that President Johnson had initiated. "I want everything that can fly to go in there and crack the hell out of them," Nixon said to his national security advisor, Henry Kissinger. The president covered up this illicit bombing. The bombing of Cambodia is "the best-kept secret of the war!" Nixon told Senate hawk John Stennis (D-MS) in April 1970. Days later, in a speech, Nixon falsely said that his policy "has been to scrupulously respect the neutrality of the Cambodian people."[65]

Years later, another scandal unfolded when President Reagan's CIA director, William J. Casey, through "Project Democracy," launched a flagrant attempt at lawless governing in the dark, without accountability. Through this sustainable, self-funded "government within the government," Casey and his associates would illicitly sway public opinion, manipulate government officials, and conduct covert operations abroad. The point man for Project Democracy, U.S. Marine lieutenant colonel Oliver North of the National Security Council, said that the conspirators had built an "off-the-shelf, self-sustaining, stand-alone entity that could perform certain activities on behalf of the United States"—the ultimate version of an invisible "deep state."

No federal authority controlled this secret criminal enterprise, not the president, the Congress, or the Departments of Defense, State, or Justice. The conspirators most notoriously sold arms to Iran, a terrorist state, and funneled the profits to support the Contra rebels in Nicaragua against congressional prohibitions.[66] Right-wing donors helped keep Project Democracy afloat by contributing $10 million. Widow Ellen Garwood, a member of the conservative leadership group, the Council on National Policy, contributed $2,546,598; the equally conservative widow Barbara Newington contributed $1,148,470; and Nelson Bunker Hunt, president of the Council on National Policy, contributed $475,000. Other conservatives donated six figures to the operation, including $921,500 from Republican fundraiser May Dougherty King. The donors met with Colonel North and administration officials, including President Reagan.[67]

Despite the Contras' record of lawlessness and brutality, aid to them followed the model of the "Reagan Doctrine" to support anti-leftist forces, with no requirement that they respect democracy, the rule of law, or human rights. After seven years of investigation, Independent Counsel Lawrence Walsh could not pinpoint what Reagan knew about Project Democracy. Still, he found that the president "created the conditions which made possible the crimes committed by others."[68]

Eleven participants in the Iran–Contra scandal were found guilty or pleaded guilty to a crime. A jury convicted former national security advisor John Poindexter of lying to Congress, and Judge Harold H. Greene, for the U.S. District Court for DC, sentenced him to six months in prison. No incarceration "would be tantamount to a statement that to lie to and to obstruct Congress was of no great moment," Judge Greene said.[69] However, the U.S. Court of Appeals for DC overturned his conviction on a technicality. Similarly, it annulled the conviction of Colonel North for obstructing Congress, altering and destroying government documents, and taking an illegal gratuity. Another former national security advisor, Robert McFarlane, pleaded guilty to withholding information from Congress. Investigators found that Attorney General Edwin Meese II and Chief of Staff Don Regan participated in covering up the scandal, but the statute of limitations had passed for prosecution. In 1992, Prosecutor Walsh indicted Caspar Weinberger, Reagan's secretary of defense, but President George H. W. Bush pardoned him before trial.

Conservatives lamented the Iran–Contra scandals not for illegality but for tarnishing the president and threatening future aid to the Contras. Richard Viguerie, the Right's premier fundraiser, said, "Many conservatives are recognizing . . . that we must not lose sight of the big picture. Our opponents are not pursuing truth and beauty—they are trying to undo the 1984 election results; they are going after Ronald Reagan; they are after us."[70]

In full uniform adorned with Vietnam War medals at hearings before a joint congressional committee in July 1987, North cast the Iran–Contra matter as a patriotic effort to protect freedom of the United States from communists in our backyard. He was vindicating the lost war in Vietnam, which North said was not lost on the battlefield but by politicians "right here in this city." Conservatives cheered. "North," said Representative Newt Gingrich, a leader of conservative Republicans in Congress, "is carrying the notion that the flag is the symbol of the country you risk your life for, not the symbol of the government that was willing to kill you [in Vietnam]—the American government." "The country, for the first time in my lifetime, saw the left wing of Congress face-to-face. . . . This is the battle line."

"Oliver North is the Great Communicator, our briefer of choice," raved conservative activist Morton Blackwell, who served as an aide to President Reagan from 1981 to 1984. "Oliver North is a supporter of the conservative philosophy across the board. He's in favor of the free market and traditional values," Blackwell asserted. "The larger issue is that they've [Democrats] lost power in the country, and the only way they can destroy what we have is through these hearings in collaboration with the liberal press," said Patrick Buchanan, Reagan's former White House communications director. "It's the permanent government's way of administering a coup d'etat." The deep state at work.[71] This episode left a lasting effect on the perception of executive power, covert operations, and the conservative movement's resistance to what they saw as liberal efforts to undermine their gains.

In 2019, Representative Chris Collins (R-NY), the first member of Congress to endorse Trump for president in 2016, pleaded guilty to orchestrating a scheme to commit insider trading and making false statements to federal law enforcement agents. Judge Vernon S. Broderick of the U.S. District Court for the Southern District of New York sentenced Collins to twenty-six months in prison.[72] Representative Duncan Hunter (R-CA), another early Trump supporter, pleaded guilty to misusing $250,000 in campaign funds to finance a lavish lifestyle while drowning in debt. Judge Thomas J. Whelan of the U.S. District Court for the Southern District of California sentenced Hunter to eleven months in prison.[73] President Trump pardoned these felons in December 2020.

Trump also pardoned campaign officials and advisors convicted of, or who had pleaded guilty to, felonies: Paul Manafort (campaign chair), George Papadopoulos (foreign policy advisor), Michael Flynn (foreign policy advisor and later national security advisor), and Roger Stone (strategic advisor). Trump also pardoned before trial Steve Bannon (former

White House strategist), whom prosecutors accused of fraudulently pock-eting funds that donors contributed to build a border wall. Bannon's three associates were convicted or pleaded guilty to the scam. Bannon pleaded guilty to New York State charges for the scheme, and prosecutors convicted him in 2022 for criminal contempt in defying a congressional subpoena.

Representative George Santos (R-NY), elected in 2022 with the backing of Trump, admitted to having committed check fraud in Brazil in 2008. He revealed that he had failed to pay thousands of dollars in court judgments against him from the 2010s. In May 2023, a federal grand jury indicted Santos on thirteen criminal charges, including wire fraud and aggravated identity theft.[74] After a scathing report by the usu-ally moribund House Ethics Committee, the House invoked a rarely used procedure to expel Santos. Although the Republican leadership opposed the expulsion, given the GOP's narrow majority, 105 Republicans joined nearly all Democrats to clear the two-thirds needed for expulsion; 112 Republicans voted no.[75] A Democrat then easily won a special election by eight percentage points to fill the vacated seat.[76] After his expulsion, Santos pleaded guilty to criminal charges.[77]

In March 2019, Special Counsel Robert S. Mueller III released his report on Russian interference in the 2016 presidential election and any related crimes. Mueller did not uncover a conspiracy between candidate Trump and the Russians, but he did document nine acts of obstruction of justice by Trump. Mueller did not believe he had the authority to recommend Trump's indictment, but said he could not exonerate Trump of obstruction. Attorney General William Barr, Trump's conservative ally, spun the Mueller findings to absolve the president of wrongdoing. Even before Mueller issued his report, Barr said the special counsel had found no evidence of collusion between the Trump campaign and the Russians. However, Mueller did not investigate collusion but only criminal con-spiracy. Barr dismissed the obstruction finding, saying Trump was not guilty of that crime.

Mueller objected in writing to Barr's spin on his report, which he said, "did not fully capture the context, nature, and substance of this Office's work and conclusions." "There is now public confusion about critical aspects of the results of our investigation. This threatens to un-dermine a central purpose for which the Department appointed the Special Counsel: to assure full public confidence in the outcome of the investigations."[78] No matter. Barr had chimed a bell that Mueller could not silence.

In matters unrelated to the Mueller investigation, Trump made history when he became the only president to be impeached twice by the U.S. House (December 18, 2019, and January 13, 2021), but the Senate acquitted him both times. Trump's clashes with the law did not end with his presidency. In August 2022, Allen Weisselberg, who had served as the Trump organization's chief financial officer for decades, pleaded guilty to tax fraud and did a brief stretch in New York's Riker's Island prison. Four months later, a Manhattan grand jury convicted two Trump organizations of running a fifteen-year criminal enterprise to evade taxes and falsify business records. In March 2023, Manhattan district attorney Alvin Bragg indicted Trump on thirty-four felony counts for making hush money payments to silence women from claiming an affair with him and then falsifying business records to cover up the payments. Trump became the only criminally indicted former president and the only criminally convicted former president after a jury found him guilty of thirty-four felony counts in May 2024.

Earlier, a New York City jury had found Trump civilly liable for sexually abusing, hurting, and willfully and maliciously defaming journalist E. Jean Carroll. The jury of six men and three women deliberated for almost three hours before finding Trump liable and awarding Carroll $5 million in damages. No former president had ever been found liable by a jury for sexual abuse or defamation. In September 2024, a New York State judge in a civil lawsuit brought by Letitia James, the state's AG, found Trump liable for fraudulently inflating his assets to gain favorable loans and insurance policies. Two days before the turn of the New Year 2025, a federal appeals court upheld the E. Jean Carroll verdict.

In 2023, federal prosecutors indicted Trump for violating the Espionage Act by dangerously mishandling national security documents. The federal prosecutors further indicted Trump for his role in attempting to overturn the results of the 2020 election. Fani Willis, the district attorney in Fulton County, Georgia, indicted Trump and eighteen alleged co-conspirators for violating Georgia's antiracketeering law as part of a widespread scheme to steal the presidential election. In all, Trump faced ninety-one felony counts in four separate indictments, but all except the

New York trial were delayed until after the 2024 elections. Prosecutors dismissed the two federal indictments after Trump won in 2024.

Conservative guardians of law and order who loudly proclaimed, on solemn principle, that President Clinton was not above the law turned about face for Trump. They have ignored the substance of court findings of illegality and felony indictments, defended the former president, and deflected blame on the law enforcement system they otherwise championed.

After Manhattan DA Bragg indicted Trump, former vice president Mike Pence said, "The unprecedented indictment of a former president of the United States on a campaign finance issue is an outrage." "The weaponization of the legal system to advance a political agenda turns the rule of law on its head," said Governor Ron DeSantis (R-FL). Conservative commentator Tucker Carlson said the indictment shows it was "probably not the best time to give up your AR-15s." "The rule of law appears to be suspended tonight—not just for Trump, but for anyone who would consider voting for him."[79]

After Trump's conviction, Republicans similarly sought to deflect blame onto their opponents without delving into the details of the case. Senator John Thune (R-SD) said the case was "politically motivated from the beginning, and today's verdict does nothing to absolve the partisan nature of this prosecution." Speaker Mike Johnson said it was a "shameful day in American history" and the charges were "purely political." Senator J. D. Vance (R-OH), Trump's future vice presidential choice, called the verdict a "disgrace to the judicial system."[80]

Following the Espionage Act indictment, a few moderate Republicans criticized the former president for threatening national security. Still, conservatives attacked Special Counsel Jack Smith, whom Trump called "deranged," a "psycho," and someone who "looks like a crackhead," and deflected the focus to unsubstantiated charges against Democrats. Governor DeSantis called the indictment a "weaponization of federal law enforcement." "Why so zealous in pursuing Trump yet so passive about Hillary or Hunter?" Representative Jim Jordan called it a "sad day for America." "God Bless President Trump." Representative Marjorie Taylor Greene said, "The FBI and DOJ are so corrupt and they don't even hide it anymore." Representative Matt Gaetz (R-FL) said, "Imagine being

naive enough to believe that the Biden Bribe evidence and Trump indictment happening the same day was a coincidence." Representative Chip
Roy (R-TX) blamed Biden for the "politization of the DOJ," which indicted Trump, "even as the Biden family corruption has long been ignored."[81] Representative Elise Stefanic (R-NY) said, "It's never been more
important that we unite behind President Trump's historic campaign to
win the White House, to restore the rule of law, and save our Republic.
God bless America, President Trump, and all those targeted by Biden's
regime as we continue our efforts to end this corrupt political weaponization and stop the deep state."[82]

Across the country, Republican outrage over violations of law and
order is selective, focused on Democratic cities while ignoring Republican-
led jurisdictions. After Bragg indicted Trump, House Judiciary Committee chair Jim Jordan held a hearing on crime in Bragg's jurisdiction of
Manhattan. "Manhattan District Attorney Alvin Bragg's pro-crime, anti-
victim policies have led to an increase in violent crime and a dangerous
community for New York City residents," charged a release from Jordan's
committee. Yet, after a nationwide COVID-19 spike in 2020, crime fell
in Manhattan for the first quarter of 2023.[83] Manhattan is one of the
safest municipalities in the nation, much safer, for example, than Colum-
bus, Ohio, just south of Jordan's congressional district.

At an August 2022 roundtable on crime in New York City, Speaker
Kevin McCarthy said, "Safety and security, it's a very big issue here but
it's a big issue in every single city across America because of this progressive movement of defunding the police, electing these prosecutors who
will not uphold the law."[84] Yet the 2021 violent crime rate in Bakersfield,
California, which he represents, was more than double the rate for New
York City.

Since the Ku Klux Klan called for the violent suppression of Blacks,
Jews, and Catholics, law-and-order conservatives have threatened politically driven lawless violence. In 1968, Independent presidential candidate George Wallace said that anyone who tried to riot in Alabama would
"get a bullet in the brain." In the 1990s, conservative activists and talk
show hosts spread violent rhetoric. Pat Robertson, president of the Christian Coalition, said conservatives should use the same tactics deployed by
General Douglas MacArthur against the Japanese to fight radical leftists:
"Surround them, isolate them, bombard them, then blast the individuals

out of their power bunkers with hand-to-hand combat."[85] Former Watergate felon G. Gordy Liddy, on his popular radio broadcast, advised any listener who encountered an Alcohol Tobacco and Firearms agent to take "head shots, head shots, because they've got a vest underneath."[86] Cincinnati talk radio host Bill Cunningham blasted liberals as "loathsome dogs to be exterminated."[87] Talk radio king Rush Limbaugh warned of an imminent "second violent American revolution" because "people are sick and tired of a bunch of bureaucrats in Washington driving into town and telling them what they can and can't do with their land."[88]

After his father lost the 2020 election, Donald Trump Jr. called for "total war." "The best thing for America's future is for Donald Trump to go to total war over this election to expose all of the fraud, cheating, dead/ no longer in-state voters, that has been going on for far too long," Trump Jr. said.[89] Steve Bannon, Trump's former White House strategist, said that if Trump wins again, he should eliminate Dr. Anthony Fauci, former director of the National Institute of Allergy and Infectious Diseases and medical advisor to President Trump, and FBI director Christopher Wray, the old fashioned way, by execution. "I'd actually like to go back to the old times of Tudor England. I'd put the heads on pikes," Bannon said, "at the two corners of the White House as a warning to federal bureaucrats: You either get with the program or you're gone." Facebook removed two of Bannon's videos "for violating our policy against violence and incitement." Twitter suspended his account, citing its prohibition on "the glorification of violence," and Spotify and YouTube removed recordings with Bannon's remarks.[90] After Trump lost his legal challenges to the 2020 election, Representative Louie Gohmert (R-TX) said, "You have no remedy. Basically, in effect, the ruling would be that you gotta go to the streets and be as violent as Antifa and BLM."

The day after the January 6, 2021, insurrection, Rush Limbaugh said on his radio show, "There's a lot of people calling for the end of violence. There's a lot of conservatives, social media, who say that any violence or aggression at all is unacceptable. Regardless of the circumstances. I am glad Sam Adams, Thomas Paine, the actual Tea Party guys, the men at Lexington and Concord didn't feel that way."[91]

Trump's personal lawyer, Rudy Giuliani, who later admitted to spreading false claims about voter fraud in the 2020 election, called for "trial by combat" on the day of the January 6 insurrection. "Over the next

10 days, we get to see the machines that are crooked," Giuliani told the crowd gathered near the Capitol, "the ballots that are fraudulent, and if we're wrong, we will be made fools of, but if we're right, a lot of them will go to jail." Pounding on the podium, Giuliani shouted, "So, let's have trial by combat. I'm willing to stake my reputation, the president is willing to stake his reputation on the fact that we will find criminality there."[92]

In August 2022, after the FBI recovered about 100 classified documents at Trump's Mar-a-Lago home, Lindsey Graham warned of riots in the streets if the Department of Justice prosecutes Trump for mishandling national security documents. "There is a double standard when it comes to Trump," Graham said. "And I'll say this: If there is a prosecution of Donald Trump for mishandling classified information after the Clinton debacle . . . there will be riots in the street." Graham claimed to be making a prediction, not a threat.[93]

Two weeks before the 2022 midterm elections, Representative Tom Emmer (R-MN), the chair of the National Republican Congressional Committee, posted a video of himself firing a weapon at a range, with the comment: "Enjoyed exercising my Second Amendment rights with @KellyCooperAZ & General @JackBergman_MI1. 13 days to make history. Let's #FirePelosi." Two days later, an attacker shouting, "Where is Nancy," broke into her home and smashed the skull of her husband, Paul Pelosi, with a hammer. Speaker Nancy Pelosi was not home.[94] After the attack, Donald Trump Jr. posted an image on social media showing a hammer and a pair of underwear with the caption, "Got my Paul Pelosi Halloween costume ready."

After the first criminal indictment of Trump, Representative Andrew Biggs (R-AZ) tweeted, "We have now reached a war phase. Eye for an Eye." Kari Lake, the losing 2022 Republican candidate for governor in Arizona, warned, "I have a message tonight for Merrick Garland and Jack Smith and Joe Biden—and the guys back there in the fake news media. . . . If you want to get to President Trump, you're going to have to go through me, and 75 million Americans just like me. And most of us are card-carrying members of the NRA. That's not a threat, that's a public service announcement."[95]

Trump has frequently advocated for lawless violence, directly or indirectly, but always unmistakably. After protestors interrupted him at a rally on October 23, 2015, Trump said, "See, the first group, I was nice. 'Oh, take your time.' The second group, I was pretty nice. The third group, I'll be a little more violent. And the fourth group, I'll say get the hell out of here!" At a rally on February 1, 2016, Trump said, "If you see somebody getting ready to throw a tomato, knock the crap out of them, would you? Seriously. Just knock the hell out of them. I promise you, I will pay for the legal fees. I promise."

In October 2018, President Trump lauded Representative Greg Gianforte (R-MT) for violently body-slamming a reporter to the ground. "Any guy who can do a body-slam . . . he's my guy," said Trump. In the wake of demonstrations that demanded racial justice nationwide in the spring of 2020, Trump warned that if states or cities refused to act forcefully against demonstrators, "then I will deploy the U.S. military and quickly solve the problem for them." He resurrected a racist slogan from the 1960s: "When the looting starts, the shooting starts." At the first 2020 presidential debate, Trump addressed the violent hate group Proud Boys, telling them to "stand down and stand by." "But I'll tell you what, I'll tell you what, somebody's got to do something about [leftist movement] antifa and the left because this is not a right-wing problem." A former Proud Boys leader said that interest and membership surged after Trump's comments.

After Trump lost the 2020 election, he repeatedly called upon followers to "stop the steal" and fight to take back the country. Trump called for supporters to rally in Washington, DC, on January 6, the day a joint session of Congress met to count the electoral votes, which would declare Joe Biden the winner. "Will be wild!" Trump said. On January 6, the day his supporters stormed the U.S. Capitol, Trump said again in an incendiary rally about a stolen election, "We're going to have to fight much harder. . . . We're going to walk down to the Capitol, and . . . you have to show strength, and you have to be strong." He called on the crowd to "demand that Congress do the right thing . . . fight like hell . . . you'll never take back our country with weakness."

During his more than an hour-long harangue, Trump typically created an escape hatch, saying in a half-sentence, "peacefully and patriotically make your voices heard." Trump delayed for more than three hours in calling his followers to leave the Capitol while watching the mayhem raging on television. He did not call for assistance from law enforcement, the National Guard, or the U.S. military. During the violence that injured 140 police officers and led to several deaths, Trump incited the crowd by tweeting an attack on Vice President Pence, a target of the rioters' wrath.[96] "Kill Mike Pence," they chanted. Trump's incitement of the insurrection led to his second impeachment, with an unprecedented seven Republicans voting for conviction in the Senate.

In 2023, Trump threatened the retiring chair of the Joint Chiefs of Staff, General Mark Milley, with deadly violence. After the January 6, 2021, insurrection, Milley spoke with Chinese counterparts to assure them about the stability of the United States. He told members of Congress that Trump administration officials were aware of the call. Nonetheless, Trump wrote on his social media platform that Milley had committed "an act so egregious that, in times gone by, the punishment would have been DEATH!"[97] After a hearing on Trump's claim of presidential immunity from prosecution, he warned of "bedlam in the country" if criminal charges thwarted his reelection.[98] In a rally near Dayton, Ohio, on March 16, 2024, Trump proclaimed there would be a "bloodbath" if Biden won the general election. "Now, if I don't get elected, it's gonna be a bloodbath." "It's going to be a bloodbath for the country." Typically, Trump left himself an out. His supporters claimed he referred to the collapse of the auto industry. Yet, the term "bloodbath" is usually associated with violence, and unmistakably for his loyal followers, Trump added, "That's going to be the least of it," extending his remarks beyond the auto industry.[99] In March 2024, Trump posted an image of President Biden hog-tied on the bumper of a truck.[100]

On the campaign trail in 2024, Trump called Republican critic Liz Cheney, former U.S. representative from Wyoming, a "radical war hawk." He added, "Let's put her with a rifle standing there with nine barrels shooting at her, OK?" "And let's see how she feels about it, you know, when the guns are trained on her face."[101] At a rally on the eve of the 2024 election, Trump referred to bulletproof glass protecting him from another assassination attempt. He said, "And to get me somebody would have to shoot through the fake news. And I don't mind that so much. I don't mind that."[102]

A comparison of criminality across presidential administrations challenges the Republican narrative of being the party of law and order, in contrast to supposedly lax Democrats. Between 1953 and 2025, Republicans held the presidency for forty of those years, Democrats for thirty-two. During this period, fifty-nine officials from Republican administrations were convicted or pleaded guilty to crimes, compared to just five officials from Democratic administrations.

9

STRICT CONSTRUCTION

In response to the liberal decisions of the U.S. Supreme Court under Chief Justice Earl Warren (1953–69), Richard Nixon firmly embedded a commitment to the "strict construction" of the U.S. Constitution and laws into conservative appeals during his 1968 presidential campaign. "The offense of the Court in the Warren area was to warp the Constitution and the laws enacted by Congress, around what the 'liberal' majority thought they ought to say or mean," said editors of the conservative *Chicago Tribune*.[1] Warren Court decisions that challenged their core values and political priorities dismayed conservatives. The Court ended legal segregation in schools, expanded the rights of accused criminals, and struck down prayer in schools and anticontraception laws. It limited the reach of antiradical laws, shifted political power from white rural districts to heavily minority cities, limited business autonomy, and protected the media from defamation lawsuits.

Nixon and other conservatives argued that judges should stick to the literal meaning of legal texts and avoid considering modern social or economic conditions, scientific advances, or politics. For conservatives, the doctrine of "originalism" became closely aligned with strict constructionism. Originalism mandates interpreting the Constitution's text according to its plain meaning at the time of enactment, a principle they hoped would prevent the Court from advancing liberal causes, such as civil rights, law enforcement reform, redistricting, privacy rights, separation of church and state, and antigovernment protests.

Nixon's criticism of the Warren Court struck a chord with many Americans. A Gallup poll from the summer of 1968 found that only 36 percent rated the Court as "excellent" or "good," compared with 53 percent who rated the Court as "poor" or "fair," and 11 percent declined to express an opinion. Nixon claimed to address what he saw as the missteps of an overly politicized Court by appointing justices aligned with his stated philosophy of strict construction. He nominated Warren Burger, who had criticized liberal court decisions and defended strict construction, as chief justice to replace the retiring Warren. Nixon nominated first Clement Haynsworth and then G. Harrold Carswell for a vacant associate justice position. After the Senate rejected both nominees for lack of qualifications and unacceptable racial views, Nixon lamented, "When you strip away all the hypocrisy, the real reason for their rejection was their legal philosophy—a philosophy that I share—of strict construction of the Constitution."[2]

Future conservative leaders continued to promote strict constructionism. The "original intent" of the framers "is the only legitimate basis for constitutional decision-making," said Robert Bork, a Reagan appointee to the U.S. Court of Appeals for DC, in a 1986 law review article. It stated, "the only way in which the Constitution can constrain judges is if the judges interpret the document's words according to the intentions of those who drafted, proposed, and ratified its provisions and its various amendments." Bork concludes that "only by limiting themselves to the historic intentions underlying each clause of the Constitution can judges avoid becoming legislators, avoid enforcing their own moral predilections, and ensure that the Constitution is law."[3] Bork's views earned him a Supreme Court nomination from President Reagan the following year, which the Senate rejected.

Senator Phil Gramm (R-TX) remarked in 1987 that the philosophy of strict construction had broad public support, as evidenced by Reagan's landslide victories. Senator John McCain (R-AZ) echoed this sentiment: "The only sound course for the courts is to apply the law as it is written, not create it as they might wish it to be."[4]

A year later, President Reagan assured the conservative legal group the Federalist Society, "The principal errors of recent times had nothing to do with the shortcomings of the Founding Fathers. They had to do with courts that played fast and loose with the instrument the Founding Fathers devised. Yes, some law professors and judges said the courts should save the country from the Constitution. We said it was time to save the Constitution from them."[5]

During the 2004 presidential debates, President George W. Bush reinforced this commitment to strict construction, pledging to "pick [judges] who would not allow their personal opinion to get in the way of the law" but "would strictly interpret the Constitution of the US." In 2008, he elaborated, "One group said that judges ought to look at the Constitution as 'a document that grows with our country and our history.'" He challenged "this concept of a 'living Constitution'" because it "gives unelected judges wide latitude in creating new laws and policies without accountability to the people. And then there was another side, which I happened to be a part of, that said we needed judges who believed that the Constitution means what it says."[6] Republican presidential nominee McCain reiterated these views during his 2008 campaign, affirming his belief in strict construction and the role of courts in commanding respect for the law, not obedience to judges' political views.[7]

Premier conservative broadcaster Rush Limbaugh quipped, "What is the difference between a liberal and a conservative? A liberal will interpret the Constitution, a conservative will quote it."[8] Vice president elect Mike Pence told Republican lawmakers just before Trump's inauguration in 2017, "President Trump has been reviewing that list" of potential judicial nominees. "I can already tip you off: President Trump's going to keep his promise to the American people and he's going to nominate a strict constructionist to the Supreme Court," Pence said to applause.[9]

When nominating Brett Kavanaugh to the Supreme Court in 2018, Trump said, "In keeping with President Reagan's legacy, I do not ask about a nominee's personal opinions. What matters is not a judge's political views but whether they can set aside those views to do what the law and the Constitution require." Kavanaugh responded, "My judicial philosophy is straightforward: A judge must be independent and must interpret the law, not make the law. A judge must interpret statutes as written, and a judge must interpret the Constitution as written, informed by history and tradition and precedent."[10]

In his 2019 inaugural address, Governor Ron DeSantis said, "To my fellow Floridians, I say to you: judicial activism ends, right here and right now. I will only appoint judges who understand the proper role of the courts is to apply the law and Constitution as written, not to legislate from the bench. The Constitution, not the judiciary, is supreme."[11]

Nixon's commitment to strict constructionism came after years of conservative frustration over liberal U.S. Supreme Court justices perceived to have overstepped their bounds by injecting politics into constitutional interpretation. In 1953, President Eisenhower nominated Earl Warren, a moderate Republican, as chief justice. Warren had a distinguished career as state Republican party chair, attorney general, and governor of California, and even ran for vice president on Thomas Dewey's (R-NY) 1948 ticket. As California's attorney general, he had advocated for FDR's executive order that led to the internment of Japanese Americans.

However, as chief justice, Warren steered the Court in a surprisingly liberal direction on racial integration, civil liberties, criminal justice, privacy rights, separation of church and state, and redistricting. In 1954, Warren, backed by the other eight justices, all nominated by Democratic presidents, wrote the landmark opinion for a unanimous Court in *Brown v. Board of Education*. The decision prompted conservative southern white Democrats to decry the Court for dishonoring strict construction and instead legislating from the bench.

A day after the *Brown* ruling, Senator Richard Russell (D-GA), the de facto leader of southern Democrats, charged that *Brown* and other Warren Court decisions "are laid down in accord with the theory of the expanding Constitution brought forward in recent years—the theory which asserts that if the written word of the Constitution and its prior construction does not meet the requirements of this Court, that instead of suggesting that the Congress propose an amendment to the Constitution it will undertake, by construction of that document, to change the conditions of which they might disapprove." Russell concluded, "I deplore what I regard as being a flagrant abuse of the judicial power by the Supreme Court, as it moves to impose the purposes of the executive branch of the Government upon the sovereign States of the Nation."[12]

Governor Eugene Talmadge (D-GA) said that the Court "ignored all law and precedent and usurped from Congress and the people the power to amend the Constitution." "The only task left for the justices" was to decide "whether to cut off our heads with a sharp knife or a dull one."[13]

The "Southern Manifesto," which Russell and other Southern conservatives (ninety-seven Democrats and four Republicans) signed, blasted the Court for abandoning states' rights and dishonoring strict construction. The southerners accused the Court of exercising "naked judicial power," which "climaxes a trend in the Federal judiciary undertaking to legislate. . . . The original Constitution does not mention education. Neither does the Fourteenth Amendment nor any other amendment. The debates preceding the submission of the Fourteenth Amendment clearly show that there was no intent that it should affect the systems of education maintained by the states."[14]

Representative William McDonald Wheeler (D-GA), a conservative, responded to *Brown* by introducing legislation requiring at least six years of service as a federal or state judge for a Supreme Court appointment.[15] Wheeler targeted Chief Justice Warren and seven other Democratic-nominated justices who had signed on to *Brown* but lacked such service. In justification, Wheeler cited a letter from M. L. Powell, a public school principal from his district: "I firmly believe that this unwise decision [*Brown*] is primarily due to the lack of judicial experience of the men who now comprise the Supreme Court."[16]

In 1957, the rising conservative star William F. Buckley Jr. defended segregation in an editorial titled "Why the South Must Prevail" in his *National Review*. He posed the question as: "Is the White community in the South entitled to take such measures as are necessary to prevail, politically and culturally, in areas in which it does not predominate numerically?" His sobering answer was "Yes—the White community is so entitled because, for the time being, it is the advanced race." Buckley argued that southern whites had the right to impose their "superior mores" to achieve "genuine cultural equality between the races."[17]

Following *Brown*, the Warren Court continued to frustrate conservatives with decisions that weakened federal and state antiradical laws. By a vote of 36 to 8 in 1958, the Conference of State Chief Justices, a conservative but not extremist organization, chastised the Warren Court for abandoning "judicial self-restraint" and acting as a policymaker. In a thirty-one-page report, the Conference concluded, "Recent decisions raise considerable doubt as to the validity of the American boast that we have a government of laws and not of men."[18]

Conservative frustration spilled over into Congress. Representative George Andrews (D-AL) denounced the Court's decisions, asking, "How much longer will Congress continue to permit the Supreme Court to usurp the power of Congress, write the laws of the land, destroy States' rights and protect the Communist Party?" In response, conservative lawmakers introduced a series of legislative proposals to curb the Court's power. Senators John Butler (R-MD) and John Marshall Jenner (R-IN) sponsored a bill to prevent the Supreme Court from reviewing cases involving congressional committees, federal employee security regulations, state antisubversion laws, and state bar admissions. Senator Butler, who had initially supported a resolution to protect the Court's independence, admitted his about-face, stating that the Court had departed from its judicial role and was now pursuing a "liberal" agenda. "Our pseudo-liberals and liberal newspapers . . . evidence no concern over the invasion of the legislative field by this judicial body and appear to accept this invasion in the name of 'liberalism,'" Butler said.[19]

The Senate Judiciary Committee endorsed the bill, but the full Senate defeated it, 41 to 49. Nearly all conservative Democrats and most Republicans, all from the party's conservative wing, supported the bill.[20] Disputes over the Court's authority "is the hottest issue today before the American people," said Senator John A. Carroll (D-CO).[21]

Despite four additional appointments by Eisenhower that gave his nominees a 5-to-4 majority, the Warren Court continued to issue rulings that infuriated conservatives. The Court ruled against revoking citizenship as a punishment for a crime and creating legislative districts with boundaries that disenfranchised African Americans. In a series of decisions beginning with *Baker v. Carr* (1962), the Court required state legislatures to draw congressional and state legislative districts with roughly equal populations. These decisions reallocated power from primarily white conservative rural districts to more diverse and liberal urban districts. The Court forbade state officials from requiring or encouraging prayer in public schools. It ruled that states must provide attorneys to criminal defendants who cannot afford representation. In *Brown Shoe Co. v. United States* (1962), the Court made corporate mergers more difficult. In *New York Times v. Sullivan* (1964), the justices limited the ability of public figures to sue the press for defamation. In *Griswold v. Connecticut* (1965), the Court established the "right to marital privacy," enabling married couples to buy and use contraceptives without government restriction. In *Miranda v. Arizona* (1966), the Court required law enforcement officials to inform persons in police custody of their rights before eliciting testimony usable in prosecutions.

A movement to impeach Warren was but the deepest end of an ocean of right-wing discontent. Senator Barry Goldwater, the Republican presidential candidate in 1964, made excesses of the Warren Court a central theme of his campaign: "The Constitution is now widely held to mean only what those who hold power for the moment choose to say it means,"[22] Goldwater said. "Of all three branches of government, today's Supreme Court is the least faithful to the constitutional tradition of limited government, and to the principle of legitimacy in the exercise of power." The Warren Court, he charged, wielded "raw and naked power" by departing from the wise practice of "judicial restraint." He pledged, if elected, to appoint justices who will "support the Constitution, not scoff at it."[23] Conservative leaders hatched new plans for taming judges, including a proposed constitutional amendment that would authorize Congress to overturn Supreme Court rulings by a two-thirds vote. However, Senate Minority Leader Everett Dirksen (R-IL) failed to hold a vote on the proposed amendment.[24]

The platform for George Wallace's 1968 independent presidential campaign also embraced strict construction and condemned the Supreme Court for overstepping its boundaries: "We have seen the Federal judiciary, primarily the Supreme Court, transgress repeatedly upon the prerogatives of the Congress and exceed its authority by enacting judicial legislation, in the form of decisions based upon political and sociological considerations, which would never have been enacted by the Congress."[25]

After Warren retired in 1969, Nixon's attorney general, John Mitchell —later a Watergate felon—told the 1971 conference of the American Bar Association that the Warren Court had been "too preoccupied in the exhilarating adventure of making new law and public policy from the bench."[26] Also in 1971, law professor Robert Bork said that the Warren Court's "one person, one vote" decision invented new rights. Justice Warren's opinions are "remarkable for their inability to muster a single respectable supporting argument," Bork wrote. "The principle of one man, one vote was not neutrally derived: it runs counter to the text of the fourteenth amendment, the history surrounding its adoption and ratification and the political practice of Americans from colonial times up to the day the Court invented the new formula."[27]

With Republican-nominated justices dominating the Court since 1969, conservatives rarely raised the issue of judicial overreach, with a few glaring exceptions. *Roe v. Wade* (1973), an opinion written by Nixon nominee Harry Blackmun, drew upon the privacy rights precedent of *Griswold* to establish a woman's constitutional right to an abortion. Conservative columnist James J. Kilpatrick charged that, once again, the Court had abandoned strict construction to conjure up a right unknown to the Constitution. "This bizarre holding, in my view, was a shocking throwback to the judicial ailment known as the Lochner syndrome," Kilpatrick wrote. "This aberration dates from 1905 when the high court embarked on a series of cases in which the justices wrote their own social and economic prejudices into the Fourteenth Amendment."[28]

Justice William Rehnquist, later chief justice, wrote in his *Roe* dissenting opinion that "the asserted right to an abortion is not 'so rooted in the traditions and conscience of our people as to be ranked as fundamental.'" Instead, "To reach its result, the Court necessarily had to find within the scope of the Fourteenth Amendment a right that was apparently completely unknown to the drafters of the Amendment."[29]

In a rarely used maneuver, President Reagan asked his Justice Department in 1985 to petition the Supreme Court to overturn *Roe*, asserting that it was a product of judicial activism, not constitutional law. "The textual, doctrinal, and historical basis for *Roe v. Wade* is so far flawed," the brief said; it "is a source of such instability in the law that this court should reconsider that decision and . . . abandon it."[30]

Conservatives condemned the Court's decision in *Obergefell v. Hodges* (2015), which legalized same-sex marriage, as an example of judicial activism. In his majority opinion, Justice Anthony Kennedy, a Reagan nominee, ruled that the fundamental right to marry is guaranteed to same-

sex couples by the due process and equal protection clauses of the Fourteenth Amendment. In dissent, Chief Justice John Roberts reiterated the
familiar conservative critique of a Court that he perceived as legislating
from the bench. "But this Court is not a legislature," Roberts wrote.
"Whether same-sex marriage is a good idea should be of no concern to
us. Under the Constitution, judges have power to say what the law is, not
what it should be. . . . The majority's decision is an act of will, not legal
judgment. The right it announces has no basis in the Constitution or this
Court's precedent."[31]

Travis Weber, director of the Center for Religious Liberty at the
conservative Family Research Council, concurred, saying that "in reading
the right to same-sex marriage into the Constitution, the Court played
social policy maker instead of judge." "This decision and others like it
are enabled primarily by an understanding which fails to take a realistic
view of the Court's limited power based on the text of the Constitution."[32]
Mike Huckabee, former Arkansas governor and 2016 candidate for the
Republican presidential nomination, accused the Court of "implement-
ing judicial tyranny," not unlike King George III.[33]

Despite conservatives invoking literalism and originalism against
court decisions they find objectionable, neither doctrine offers a straightforward solution for interpreting the Constitution, allowing both liberals
and conservatives flexibility in their judicial rulings. Literalism proves
inadequate for interpreting many phrases in the Constitution that lack
clear, literal meaning, such as "general welfare," "declare war," "regulate
commerce," "necessary and proper," "high Crimes and Misdemeanors,"
"Privileges and Immunities of Citizens," "Republican Form of Government," "free exercise" of religion, "right of the people to keep and bear
Arms," "unreasonable searches and seizures," "due process of law," and
"equal protection of the laws."

"Conservatives like to insist that their judges are strict construction-
ists, giving the Constitution and statutes their precise meaning and no
more, while judges like Ms. Sotomayor are activists," said lawyer and
journalist Adam Cohen. "But there is no magic right way to interpret
terms like 'free speech' or 'due process'"—or satirically "potato chip."[34]
The invocation of originalism offers no help in giving judges a neutral,
objective basis for decision-making. Evidence of original intent is scanty,

murky, and contradictory. Historical evidence does not speak for itself without contemporary analysis and interpretation. According to Edward Hallett Carr, the eminent historian and philosopher of history, "The belief in a hard core of historical facts existing objectively and independently of the interpretation of the historian is a preposterous fallacy."[35]

The malleability of strict construction based on literalism and originalism creates the space for conservatives to imprint their values and priorities on the Constitution. In turn, liberals have assailed conservative judges for legislating from the bench. During the 1930s, liberals invoked strict construction to oppose conservative Court decisions that toppled pillars of FDR's New Deal reforms.

During FDR's first term, a conservative Court dismantled the New Deal's leading industrial and agricultural recovery engines, the National Industrial Recovery Act (NIRA) and the Agricultural Adjustment Act (AAA). It seemed poised to invalidate the Social Security Act and the Wagner National Labor Relations Act, the New Deal's crown jewels. "The conservative Supreme Court," Roosevelt said, was functioning "not as a judicial body, but as a policymaking body . . . reading into the Constitution words and implications which are not there, and which were never intended to be there."[36] Most Americans agreed. A November 1936 Gallup poll found that 59 percent of respondents agreed that "the Supreme Court should be more liberal in reviewing New Deal measures."[37]

After winning reelection by a landslide in 1936 without yet appointing a single Supreme Court justice, FDR proposed legislation to remake the Court. His proposal would expand the size of the Supreme Court by authorizing the president to nominate an additional justice for every justice older than seventy years and six months who declined to retire, which covered six sitting justices in 1937. Conservative opponents rallied to defend their vision of conservative principles embedded in the Constitution. However, conservatives, notably in the South, disregarded the protection of minority rights in the Fourteenth and Fifteenth Amendments. A constituent wrote to conservative U.S. senator James Byrnes (D-SC), "If I got up tomorrow and advocated rigid adherence to the 14th and 15th [Amendments] of the Constitution, the same folks who are yelling 'Constitution' loudly now would fight among themselves for priority in applying the tar and feathers."[38]

FDR lost the battle over "court-packing" but won the war over his proposals in the Court. In 1937, the Supreme Court upheld the Wagner Act and the Social Security Act, leveling constitutional barriers to federal welfare and regulatory laws. Ultimately, FDR put his stamp on the Court in an old-fashioned way by nominating a total of nine justices, second only to George Washington. Conservative support for the Supreme Court declined, and liberal support increased with each decision upholding a liberal program, establishing fair redistricting, or expanding the rights of minorities, the accused, and left-wing radicals.

Despite professing strict construction in 1968 and beyond, Nixon had taken the opposite position earlier. He had criticized Supreme Court justices for adhering to a strict construction of the Constitution in their 1962 decision that banned school prayer in public schools. "The Supreme Court has followed its usual practice of interpreting the Constitution rigidly," Nixon said. "It now needs guidance from Congress."[39]

As the Court moved to the right in the late twentieth and twenty-first centuries, liberals again charged conservative justices with judicial activism and overreach, particularly concerning campaign finance, voting rights, and abortion. In *Buckley v. Valeo* (1976), the Court struck down key provisions of federal campaign finance laws as unconstitutional. It invalidated limits on campaign spending by candidates and their committees, independent expenditures, and expenditures from a candidate's personal funds. The ruling also struck down statutes in twenty-six states limiting state election campaign spending. To justify overriding statute law, the Court, in effect, placed campaign spending under First Amendment protections, equating spending money with free speech.

The *Buckley* decision grounded two other rulings that outraged liberals for favoring wealthy and corporate donors. In *Citizens United v. FEC* (2010), the Court authorized unlimited spending by corporations and other outside groups. "Political speech cannot be limited based on a speaker's wealth," the Court ruled. In *McCutcheon v. FEC* (2014), the Court struck down aggregate contributions to candidates, parties, and political action committees.

Liberals challenged these decisions as politically motivated rulings that disproportionately benefited Republicans by enabling substantial funding from corporate and wealthy donors. They argued that activist conservative judges had read their political biases into the Constitution and infringed on Congress's prerogatives. Liberals contended that the Court had warped the Constitution to equate money with speech and hindered efforts to control the corruption inherent in big-money politics. They asserted that conservative justices had effectively created new rights that are neither specified in the Constitution nor reflective of the framers' original intent.[40]

"The Supreme Court's 5-to-4 decision [in *Citizens United*] last week giving American corporations the right to unlimited political spending was an astonishing display of judicial arrogance, overreach, and unjustified activism," said liberal journalist E. J. Dionne Jr. "Turning its back on a century of practice and decades of precedent, a narrow right-wing majority on the court decided to change the American political system by tilting it decisively in favor of corporate interests." "Defenders of this vast expansion of corporate influence piously claim it's about 'free speech,'" Dionne said. "But since when is a corporation, a creation of laws passed by governments, entitled to the same rights as an individual citizen?"[41]

With nearly one voice in the aftermath of *Citizens United*, Democrats denounced the conservative court of Chief Justice John Roberts for judicial overreach. Senator Dianne Feinstein (D-CA) said, "He's [Roberts] not somebody who just measures balls and strikes. It's been the most activist court that I've seen in my 17 years in the committee." Senate Judiciary Committee Chairman Patrick Leahy (D-VT) said, "[Justice Samuel] Alito and the other justices substituted their preferences for the will of Congress."[42] In a retrospective on the Supreme Court's campaign finance decisions, Representative John Sarbanes (D-MD) noted, "It's where this arrogance began on the part of Super PACs and the super wealthy armed with this idea somehow that corporations are people, money is speech. They decided that they were going to take over American politics."[43]

"Look at the evidence: there is virtually perfect concordance between the major departures by the activist bloc from conservative judicial tenets—such as judicial restraint, original intent, States rights—and the result in those cases of achieving current Republican political goals," said Senator Sheldon Whitehouse (D-RI). "One could probably call this practice 'situational judicial restraint.' A rational person could conclude, based on the evidence of the Court's behavior, the observable results that this and other decisions by the five-man conservative bloc would more properly be characterized as political prize-taking than judicial lawmaking."[44]

Liberals claimed that the Court extended its judicial activism in decisions that weakened voting rights. In *Shelby v. Holder* (2013), the Court struck down the provision of the Voting Rights Act that required jurisdictions with a history of voting discrimination to preclear any changes in voting laws and regulations with the U.S. Department of Justice. "The Court, arrogating to itself the quintessentially congressional power to decide what facts are relevant and what constitutes an appropriate remedy, struck down the formula in Section 4, eviscerating and rendering a nearly dead letter the preclearance provisions of Section 5," said Representative Jerrold Nadler. "The value of Section 5 has been its ability to respond in real time to constantly changing efforts to disenfranchise voters."[45]

Liberals further claimed that the Court had overlooked Congress's intent. In his opinion in *Shelby*, Chief Justice Roberts had focused on changes in the voting rights landscape since the 1960s. Liberal lawyer Ian Millhiser, the author of two books on the Supreme Court, noted that "Congress also chose to extend this [preclearance] requirement again in 1975, in 1982, and in 2006." In each case, a Republican president signed the reauthorization: Gerald Ford, Ronald Reagan, and George W. Bush. "Maybe Roberts was right that our nation had made enough racial progress to escape preclearance. But Congress disagreed with him. And the Constitution's text suggests that Congress has the final word," said Millhiser.[46]

In *Rucho v. Common Cause* (2019), the Court barred the federal judiciary from adjudicating political gerrymandering cases. The Court wiped out a three-judge federal district court finding that North Carolina's congressional redistricting plan violated the U.S. Constitution. In 2016, Republicans received 53 percent of the statewide congressional votes but won 10 of 13 seats. For liberal attorney Emmet J. Bondurant, a National Governing Board of Common Cause member, "No case is a better illustration of the partisan trend in the Supreme Court's election law decisions than *Rucho v. Common Cause*. In a 5 to 4 party-line vote, the Court disregarded thirty years of Supreme Court precedent. It held for the first time that partisan gerrymandering is a political question beyond both the competence and the jurisdiction of the federal courts." The ruling "was based on a misrepresentation of the constitutional basis of the plaintiffs' claims." It "also misrepresented the Court's prior precedents and disregarded the factual findings and undisputed evidence of the effectiveness of partisan gerrymandering in favoring candidates and dictating electoral outcomes."[47]

In *Brnovich v. Democratic National Committee* (2021), Justice Samuel Alito's majority opinion ruled that in evaluating voting rights challenges, federal courts should weigh the size of the burden of a challenged law, the magnitude of racial disparities, the state's interest in enacting the law, and how far the challenged law departs from standard practice at the time Congress adopted the relevant provisions of the Voting Rights Act. Further, courts must consider the accessibility of a state's entire electoral system, not just the challenged law. Alito also ruled that states could use voter fraud to justify new laws, even without proving fraud's presence or its likely future occurrence.[48] "Justice Alito was trying to turn back the clock on voting rights for many decades," said Richard Hasen, a University of California Irvine law professor. The activist Court, in "ignoring the text of the statute, its comparative focus on lessened opportunity for minority voters, and the history that showed Congress intended to alter the status quo and give new protections to minority voters, essentially offered a new and impossible test for plaintiffs to meet to show a Section 2 vote denial claim," said Hasen.[49]

Regarding the Court's campaign finance and voting rights decisions, Harvard Law professor Nicholas Stephanopoulos said, "Across the right to vote, redistricting, the Voting Rights Act and campaign finance, the court's decisions have benefited Republicans. And partisan advantage explains these decisions better than rival hypotheses like originalism, precedent, or judicial nonintervention."[50]

On gun control, the Supreme Court ruled in *Heller v. DC* (2008) for the first time that the Second Amendment guaranteed an individual right to bear arms, unconnected to maintaining a well-regulated militia. In 2010, the Court extended its ruling to the states. Critics charged that Justice Antonin Scalia, the foremost exponent of originalism, could not apply this doctrine to the Second Amendment. Not a single individual involved in voting for or ratifying the amendment had indicated that it protected the right of individuals to keep and bear arms. The critics said that Scalia's opinion for the five-justice majority read history backward from his present-day views rather than reading history forward impartially. Originalist scholar Enrique Schaerer charged that Scalia "failed to abide by his originalist principles." "To subject the Second Amendment right to a present-day popularity contest, as Justice Scalia appears to do, is to put this right on ground that is forever uncertain, unstable, and ultimately nonoriginalist," Schaerer said.[51]

Liberals blasted the decision in *Dobbs v. Jackson Women's Health Organization* (2022), which overturned *Roe v. Wade*, for following an ideological and political agenda again. Liberals argued that the Court contradicted its previous decisions on campaign finance and firearms, which had created new rights. Instead, the Court eliminated a long-standing right, asserting that it was not explicitly protected by the Constitution. "Reversing *Roe*'s long-settled protections is the shameful end result of a decades-long conservative campaign to construct a Supreme Court that would gut the right to choose," said Senator Chris Coons (D-DE). "It's the definition of conservative judicial activism: overthrowing a 50 year-old settled legal precedent without regard and laying the groundwork for extremists to go after even more long-held fundamental rights."[52]

George Washington University law professor Alan B. Morrison observed that "reading Justice Alito's [*Dobbs*] opinion, one would believe that he and others on the Roberts Court believe strongly in allowing controversial policy judgments to be made by our elected representatives, instead of by judicial activists." However, "The current majority of the Roberts Court has a very selective approach to judicial activism. Repeatedly, in a wide variety of subject areas, when the constitutional claim at issue aligns with the policy position of the political party of the president that nominated these Justices (i.e., the Republican Party), they are every bit as activist as the *Roe* majority," Morrison said. He noted that Alito criticized *Roe* for interpreting words in the Constitution "at a 'high level of generality,' which he concluded led to a vast expansion of rights protected by the Constitution." Yet, the "Roberts Court has often latched on to a word or phrase "mentioned" in the Constitution, examined its meaning at a "high level of generality," and reached a result that took the decision away from "the people's elected representatives," according to Morrison. It has, however, "done so only when the outcome supports the positions of the party of the Republican president who appointed those Justices."[53]

In *Trump v. Anderson* (2024), liberals charged that the Court majority discarded the strict wording of section 3 of the Fourteenth Amendment that disqualified insurrectionists from public office. Instead of hewing to the contemporary understanding of the amendment, liberals said, the Court protected Trump from disqualification by ruling that only an act of Congress could disqualify federal officeholders. Yet, liberals noted that section 3 does not include such a requirement. The amendment explicitly states that an act of Congress is needed only to grant amnesty to those already disqualified. Although the Court unanimously overturned Colorado's disqualification of Trump's presidential candidacy, the three liberal justices, joined by Justice Amy Coney Barrett, questioned the finding that disqualification required an act of Congress.[54]

Legal scholar Garret Epps explained that strict construction through originalism is not a constitutional doctrine but a political strategy sustained by an iron triangle of conservative academics, judges, and politicians. On two points of the triangle, as elaborated in hundreds of academic publications, originalism provides conservative judges scholarly justification for "their decisions, particularly those that overturn established precedent or further anti-democratic goals." Finally, on the triangle's third point, conservative politicians promote originalism "as the only legitimate way to divine the meaning of constitutional text." Thus, "You who criticize do not oppose us . . . you oppose James Madison, Thomas Jefferson, Alexander Hamilton, and all the secular gods of our civic religion."[55]

Although congressional Republicans had sponsored legislation to shift the membership of the Warren Court and restrict its jurisdiction, after *Dobbs*, Republicans rebuked Democrats for threatening the same response. "Judicial independence is as fragile as it is important. . . . It would be beyond reckless for Democrats to smash this centuries-old safeguard in a fit of partisan pique," said Senate Minority Leader Mitch McConnell. "If the justices fell into Democrats' trap and let political threats change legal outcomes, they would not be shoring up their institution, but undermining it. It would poison the actual source of the court's legitimacy—its impartiality."[56]

The most blatant contradiction of conservative professions of fidelity to the Constitution comes not from a Court decision but from former president Trump. In a Truth Social post on December 4, 2022, Trump said, "Do you throw the Presidential Election Results of 2020 OUT AND DECLARE THE RIGHTFUL WINNER, or do you have a NEW ELECTION? A Massive Fraud of this type and magnitude allows for the termination of all rules, regulations, and articles, even those found in the Constitution."[57] Yet few Republicans or independent conservatives arose in defense of the Constitution.[58]

In May 2023, Trump announced on Twitter that if reelected in 2024, he would issue an executive order "ENDING automatic citizenship for the children of illegal aliens."[59] This plan would, by decree, repeal the section of the Fourteenth Amendment that grants citizenship to all persons "born or naturalized in the United States," including formerly enslaved people. The U.S. Supreme Court has interpreted this clause to apply whether or not parents were legally in the country. If implemented, Trump's proposed order would require a national biological police force to check the parentage of every child born in the United States. During the 2024 campaign, Trump defied the Constitution to proclaim that he would be a dictator, if only "for day one," because "I want to drill, drill, drill."[60] No dictator on day one has ever ceased being a dictator on subsequent days.

Strict construction is a convenient political slogan for conservatives but does not influence jurisprudence, which courts inevitably infuse with ideology and politics. There is no moral high ground for conservatives or liberals on construing the U.S. Constitution. Judicial activism and overreach history are in the eye of the beholder and do not fall along political lines. The supposed neutral principle of strict construction, based on literalism and originalism, gives way to political expediency and ideology. "Nor is either ideological camp wholly strict or wholly activist," said lawyer Adam Cohen. "Liberal judges tend to be expansive about things like equal protection, while conservatives read more into ones like 'the right to bear arms.'"[61]

10

U.S. SOVEREIGNTY

Since the end of World War I, when conservatives defeated U.S. participation in the League of Nations—the Senate voted against U.S. participation in November 1919 and again in March 1920—they have claimed to stand uniquely in defense of U.S. sovereignty, defined as freedom to determine the nation's destiny free of foreign interference. For conservatives, this commitment to sovereignty is rooted in American exceptionalism, linked to the Christian values of the nation's founding pioneers. In a remarkable speech delivered in 1930 at King's Mountain, North Carolina, a Revolutionary War battlefield, President Herbert Hoover said that the "principles and ideals" of the country's exceptional civilization "grew largely out of the [Christian] religious origins and spiritual aspirations of our people." Outside contagions, such as "Socialism, or its violent brother, Bolshevism," would destroy "the nation's spiritual heritage" and "deny religion and seek to expel it. I cannot conceive of a wholesome social order or a sound economic system that does not have its roots in religious faith." Hoover lauded the country's religious ideals for "150 years of growth that have brought to us the richness of life which spreads through this great Nation. . . . Compared with even the most advanced other country in Europe, we shall find an incomparably greater diffusion of material well-being."[1]

For conservatives, U.S. sovereignty is a bulwark against foreign influences threatening core values. They fear that international agreements might impose protections for LGBTQ+ individuals, abortion rights, special privileges for women, immigrants and racial minorities, business regulations, welfare programs, high taxes, and restrictions on gun ownership. Ultimately, they worry that foreign pressures could send the United States down a slippery slope toward global governance. Social psychologist Richard A. Koenigsberg explains that conservatives' defense of sovereignty is primal. For America First stalwarts, "nations are defined by boundaries," and "the idea of being penetrated by other nations evokes anxiety and rage." Thus, "'Enemies' and statehood are two sides of the same coin. A nation defines itself by defining its enemies—those who cannot be allowed to penetrate," says Koenigsberg. "The idea of the nation is internalized into our bodies. Threats to the nation are experienced as penetration of one's body," inciting pain and anxiety at the most primal level.[2]

Conservative opposition to international agreements in the name of sovereignty remains strong. In 2024, conservatives opposed the World Health Organization's (WHO) proposed pandemic treaty, which aspired to a legally binding framework for preventing future pandemics. Tony Perkins, president of the conservative Family Research Council, called the proposed treaty "a global power grab" that puts at "risk national sovereignty" by imposing liberal social policies on the United States, including the right to abortion. "I consider this agreement not simply to be the greatest threat to freedom in human history—this package of agreements . . . is the greatest single threat to the sovereignty of our constitutional republic in its history," said Frank J Gaffney Jr, executive chairman of the conservative Center for Security Policy. "Down this road leads a global governance arrangement that is designed to crush—not restrict, not suppress—crush the sovereignty of the United States." Republican Representative Brad Wenstrup (R-OH), the chair of the House Select Subcommittee on the Coronavirus Pandemic, agreed that "the WHO wants to infringe upon our national sovereignty with their proposed 'pandemic treaty.'"[3]

This narrative against international agreements would sound familiar to Warren Harding, the Republican president elected at the dawn of modern conservatism in 1920. Under Harding, the Senate rejected the idea of U.S. participation in the League of Nations for the second time by linking American exceptionalism and sovereignty. "The American example has been the model of every republic which glorifies the progress of liberty, and is everywhere the leaven of representative democracy which has expanded human freedom," Harding said. "It is better to be the free and disinterested agent of international justice and advancing civilization, with the covenant of conscience, than be shackled by a written compact which surrenders our freedom of action and gives a military alliance the right to proclaim America's duty to the world." He condemned the League of Nations treaty as a precursor to "world super-government."[4] In his 1921 inaugural address, Harding warned that the nation "can enter into no political commitments, nor assume any economic obligations which will subject our decisions to any other than our own authority. . . . Every commitment must be made in the exercise of our national sovereignty."[5]

Senator Philander Knox (R-PA) decried Wilson's League as "a world state" and "a great catalogue of unnatural self-restraints" that would doom U.S. independence. He preferred "a new American doctrine" that "entangles us in no way." Knox invoked his evangelical Christian faith in opposition, saying the League "was seeking to usurp the function almost of Almighty Providence" and "was of well-nigh blasphemous presumption."[6] Representative John P. Hill (R-MD) said Article X, on mutual defense of League members, "would mean a super sovereignty to which America would have to sacrifice her own sovereignty."[7] President Calvin Coolidge, in his first State of the Union address in December 1923, said, "The League exists as a foreign agency. We hope it will be helpful. But the United States sees no reason to limit its own freedom and independence of action by joining it. We shall do well to recognize this basic fact in all national affairs and govern ourselves accordingly."[8]

After the outbreak of World War II in 1939, most Republican officeholders and independent conservatives criticized President Roosevelt for involving the United States in the "wrong war, at the wrong time, against the wrong enemy." The America First Committee and its celebrity spokesperson, the aviator hero Charles Lindbergh, were not strict isolationists but disengaged nationalists. They rejected U.S. responsibility for the security of foreign peoples and insisted that the Nazis posed no serious threat to U.S. sovereignty. The United States, they argued, must stay out of the war and avoid aiding either side. In 1941, Lindbergh, who had accepted honors from Hitler's government in 1938, spoke for the America First Committee. "But we in this country have a right to think of the welfare of America first," he said, "just as the people in England thought first of their own country when they encouraged the smaller nations of Europe to fight against hopeless odds. When England asks us to enter this war, she is considering her own future and that of her Empire. In making our reply, I believe we should consider the future of the United States and that of the Western Hemisphere." Lindbergh blamed not just Germany, England, France, but also the United States for provoking the European war. Like Lindbergh, Senator Robert Taft believed that the country must consider its own interests. He, too, called for "a policy of America first." For Taft, "the threat of an attack by Hitler is, and always has been, a bugaboo to scare the American people into war."[9]

During the early Cold War, America First Republicans opposed institutions and treaties that compromised U.S. sovereignty, including the International Monetary Fund, the World Bank, trade pacts, loans to foreign allies, military and economic aid, and international troop commitments. Taft, for instance, denounced NATO for resurrecting the binding commitments of Wilson's League of Nations. "As set up, it is a step backward," he said, "a military alliance of the old type where we have to come to each others' assistance no matter who is to blame." Taft and his allies were not soft on communism but believed the United States should be free to decide if and when its interests demanded involvement abroad.[10]

Other conservatives echoed Taft's sentiments. In a 1952 address, the conservative J. Reuben Clark, a leader of the Mormon Church who worked in four previous Republican administrations, charged that the United States forfeited its sovereign treaty-making powers under the UN charter. "All treaties we make must conform to the provisions of the United Nations," he said. The UN Security Council is so powerful that "the Security Council not the State Department, becomes, in the last analysis, the agency to direct our foreign relations." The Security Council deprives the United States of the right "upon which the very existence of sovereignty depends: The power to declare war." Clark further claimed that the mutual defense commitment under the NATO treaty "impairs our sovereignty in the matter of all North Atlantic problems, because they cease to be adjustable according to our interests and desires." NATO demands that the United States must maintain "a minimum on our Military Establishment. We could hardly reduce that Establishment, under the treaty, to our old, prewar size," said Clark. "It thus far impairs the exercise of our free sovereignty in this matter of purely domestic concern."[11]

Senator John Bricker targeted a proposed UN covenant on human rights. He charged that under the covenant "basic rights of the American people would be sacrificed to achieve an international bill of rights which debases the standard of freedom fashioned by our forefathers"—code words for conservative priorities. He said the covenant "subordinates national interests to the nonexistent unity of one world." It is a step on the road to "one-world government."[12]

By the Truman administration's waning days in 1952, a rift had opened within the Republican Party between the conservative America First Republicans and moderates who backed Truman's collective security arrangements. This conflict exploded in the 1952 presidential nomination battle between Senator Taft and retired general Dwight Eisenhower. Taft's disengagement from the world, Eisenhower believed, would lead to communist domination or World War III. Before the 1952 campaign, Senator Henry Cabot Lodge (R-MA)—later Eisenhower's campaign chair—warned Ike, "The neutralist and defeatist influence in the Republican Party might get so strong that it would be your duty to enter politics in order to prevent one of our great two Parties from adopting a course which could lead to national suicide." An Eisenhower campaign memo, "Demolish the Enemy," stated, "If Taft had been president, we wouldn't have to worry about bringing Gen. Eisenhower back from Europe—Europe would have fallen long ago to the Communists without Marshall Plan, etc."[13] Eisenhower barely prevailed at the deeply divided Republican National Convention and then easily defeated the Democratic nominee, Illinois governor Adlai Stevenson, in the general election of 1952.

Efforts by conservatives to protect U.S. sovereignty intensified during Eisenhower's presidency. Senator Bricker introduced an amendment restricting the nation's treaty powers. In various forms, the Bricker Amendment would require an act of Congress to implement treaties ratified by the Senate and executive agreements negotiated by presidents. The amendment eventually gained sixty-four Senate sponsors from southern Democrats and Republicans, including Senator Taft. Although Taft, chair of the Senate Judiciary Committee, backed the amendment at the request of President Eisenhower, he delayed its consideration. After Taft's illness forced him to step down as chair, the amendment finally reached the Senate floor. The original version lost overwhelmingly, but a revised, more moderate proposal narrowly failed by a single vote. Taft had passed away before the Senate cast its final vote.

During Eisenhower's first term, leading conservatives shifted from disengagement to an active nationalism to safeguard U.S. sovereignty and security. In the wake of the Korean War, conservatives adopted a Manichaean worldview, perceiving the communist Soviet Union as the true existential threat, unlike their earlier ambivalence toward Nazi Germany before Pearl Harbor. Lindbergh famously expressed this sentiment, saying, "I would a hundred times rather see my country ally herself with England, or even with Germany, with all her faults, than the cruelty, the godlessness, and the barbarism that exists in Soviet Russia." William F. Knowland (R-CA), the Senate majority leader who succeeded Taft in 1953, argued that the United States should make clear that military aggression or subversion by the Soviets would result in a nuclear response. He called for a blockade of Communist China and urged free nations in Asia to reclaim the mainland. By late 1954, engaged nationalism had swept through conservative Republican ranks so rapidly that influential journalist William S. White noted that Knowland's "Cold War views command, at least in an academic sense, a greater degree of support among Senate Republicans than do those of the Presidents."[14]

Despite this shift, elements of Brickerism survived among conservative engaged nationalists. During the 1950s, conservatives resolutely opposed UN covenants, particularly the Genocide Convention (1948) and the Universal Declaration of Human Rights (1948). They again argued that these and similar international agreements would subject the United States to foreign control, ultimately leading to the risk of ensnaring the nation in a one-world government. A resolution from the conservative Daughters of the American Revolution called for rejecting UN initiatives "which would have the effect of superseding our Constitution." The resolution opposed "any attempt to bring about through the United Nations, or any other medium, a world government or partial world government."[15] "Should such treaties as the human rights covenants or the draft statute for an international criminal court be adopted by U.N. members, we would have world government in fact if not in name," said Senator Bricker.[16]

Conservative southern Democrats joined the opposition to these conventions, fearing they would undermine Jim Crow laws and practices. Senator Walter F. George charged that the Genocide Convention was "filled with subtle and obscure and doublemeaning things that really aim to attack the constitutional setup that we have under our dual system." Leander Perez, a Democrat district attorney and the de facto political boss of Louisiana, said the UN conventions would "at one fell swoop" eliminate "a large part of the municipal sovereignty reserved to all the States of the Union over the domestic affairs of their citizens."[17]

In *A Choice Not an Echo*, Schlafly fed into the Right's conspiratorial thinking by posing Goldwater as the heroic opponent of a corrupt establishment controlled by elites and their allies abroad. For Schlafly, these conspirators were a "shadow government" that co-opted President Lyndon Johnson to sell out U.S. sovereignty by abolishing "our Army, our Navy, our Air Force and our nuclear weapons, and make us subject to a United Nations Peace Force."[18] Another more spectacularly popular self-published book from 1964, John A. Stormer's *None Dare Call It Treason*, sold 7 million copies and further bolstered Goldwater's campaign. Stormer claimed that radical elites had subverted U.S. churches, schools, and government, conditioning U.S. surrender to international communism.[19] Although Stormer is largely forgotten today, prominent conservative commentator Daniel Pipes remarked that Stormer "may be the most popular U.S. backstairs author of all time."[20]

Subsequently, conservatives successfully blocked ratification of the United Nations Convention on the Elimination of All Forms of Racial Discrimination (1965); the International Covenant on Civil and Political Rights (1966); the International Covenant on Economic, Social, and Cultural Rights (1966); the Convention on the Elimination of All Forms of Discrimination against Women (1979); the UN Convention against Torture and Other Cruel, Inhuman, or Degrading Treatment or Punishment (1984); the Convention on the Rights of the Child (1989);

the International Convention on the Protection of the Rights of All Migrant Workers and Members of their Families (1990); and the Convention on the Rights of Persons with Disabilities (2006). In each instance, they charged that the agreements would impose liberal policies on the United States.

Conservatives also opposed the Arms Trade Treaty (ATT) (2013), which covered only the export of arms to drug cartels and perpetrators of genocide or war crimes and explicitly exempted domestic gun policy. Nonetheless, Wayne LaPierre, the conservative CEO of the National Rifle Association, condemned the ATT for subverting U.S. sovereignty. "The cornerstone of our freedom is the Second Amendment," he said. "Neither the United Nations, nor any other foreign influence, has the authority to meddle with the freedoms guaranteed by our Bill of Rights, endowed by our Creator, and due to all humankind."[21] Donald Trump subsequently withdrew the United States as a signatory to the ATT. "Under my administration, we will never surrender American sovereignty to anyone," he said. "We will never allow foreign bureaucrats to trample on your Second Amendment freedom."[22]

When President George H. W. Bush spoke of a "new world order" of international cooperation among nations, he opened another rift between moderate Republican internationalists and conservative defenders of U.S. sovereignty. "Today, that new world is struggling to be born, a world quite different from the one we've known," Bush said. He envisioned "a world where the rule of law supplants the rule of the jungle. A world in which nations recognize the shared responsibility for freedom and justice." Conservative commentator Pat Buchanan, a former aide to President Nixon, challenged Bush for the 1992 presidential nomination on a platform of "America, First, Second, and Third." "We have been able to help the world when we are ourselves and retain our own independence and freedom of action," Buchanan said. "And I'll tell you the idea of subsuming American sovereignty in some globalist new world order is something that ought to be resisted and not just with words." Unlike those in the GOP who are "Wilsonians in quest for global democracy. Conservatives favor limited government and foreign policy based on the interests of the American people."[23]

Buchanan swamped Bush in the straw poll of conservatives attending the annual Conservative Political Action Conference (CPAC) and won the endorsement of the American Conservative Union. The conservative journal *Human Events* and radio host Rush Limbaugh endorsed Buchanan for president and advised listeners to cast a protest vote for him in the New Hampshire primary. Bush handily defeated Buchanan for the nomination, but his plans for a new world order faded when he lost the presidency to Bill Clinton in 1992.

In 2000, with the United States on the verge of a presidential transition, Senator Jesse Helms (R-NC), a leader of Senate conservatives, distanced the United States from the UN. "The sovereignty of nations must, of course, be respected," he said. "But, properly understood, nations derive their sovereignty—their legitimacy—from the consent of the governed." Thus, "The American people will never accept the secretary-general's claim that the United Nations is the "sole source of legitimacy on the use of force" in the world. "If the United Nations does not respect American sovereignty, if it seeks to impose its presumed authority over the American people without their consent, then it begs for confrontation and, more important, eventual U.S. withdrawal," Helms said.[24]

George H. W. Bush's son George W. Bush, channeled Senator Knowland from the Cold War days in aggressively advancing his vision of U.S. interests abroad. Bush launched wars in Afghanistan and Iraq to eradicate foreign-based terrorism. His policies followed an America-first, unilateralist strategy to preserve the nation's sovereignty, avoiding deference to any version of international law or obligations to foreign countries. Political scientists Eric Patterson and Kendra Puryear explained, "President Bush's view of the so-called 'international community' is that it has frequently failed." The "US, by default, must work to promote its own interests and security."[25]

Beginning in the late twentieth century, far-right organizations warned of invading international military forces seeking to imprison the United States in a world government. Black helicopters laden with invading UN troops would fill the American sky.[26] Books such as by Jim Keith, *Black Helicopters over America: Strike Force for the New World Order* (1994), and by Dick Morris and Eileen McGann, *Here Come the Black Helicopters!* (2012) kept the black helicopter myth flickering on the extreme Right until reignited by President Trump.

Trump dubbed himself an "America First" leader who chose "independence and cooperation over global governance, control and domination." "I promised that my Administration would put the safety, interests, and well-being of our citizens first," Trump said at the start of his term in office. "I pledged that we would revitalize the American economy, rebuild our military, defend our borders, protect our sovereignty, and advance our values. During my first year in office, you have witnessed my America First foreign policy in action. We are prioritizing the interests of our citizens and protecting our sovereign rights as a nation."

Trump withdrew the United States from ATT and the Paris Climate Accords (2016), leaving the United States isolated as the only nonparticipant. "It is time to put Youngstown, Ohio; Detroit, Mich.; and Pittsburgh, Pa., along with many, many other locations within our great country, before Paris, France," Trump said.[27] Trump withdrew the United States from the Iran nuclear agreement, the only nation to do so. "The fact is, this was a horrible, one-sided deal that should have never, ever been made," Trump said. "America will not be held hostage to nuclear blackmail. We will not allow American cities to be threatened with destruction."[28]

During his reelection campaign in 2020, Trump replayed a version of the foreign invasion myth, with invaders on planes, not black helicopters. In an August 2020 interview, Trump told Fox News host Laura Ingraham, "People that you've never heard of, people that are in the dark shadows" were pulling the strings for his Democratic opponent, Joe Biden. This tale was too much even for Trump loyalist Ingraham, who asked, "What does that mean? That sounds like conspiracy theory. Dark shadow, what is that?" Trump plowed ahead. "No. People that you haven't heard of," he said. "They're people that are on the streets. They're people that are controlling the streets. We had somebody get on a plane from a certain city this weekend, and in the plane it was almost completely loaded with thugs wearing these dark uniforms, black uniforms with gear and this and that. They're on a plane."[29]

President Hoover, in 1930, had linked American exceptionalism with Christianity in words. Nearly a century later, Trump did so symbolically. He began hawking $60 "God Bless the USA" Bibles during the 2024 campaign. An American flag adorns the Bible package, which includes the chorus of Lee Greenwood's song "God Bless the U.S.A." and copies of the Constitution, the Bill of Rights, the Declaration of Independence, and the Pledge of Allegiance. In his sales pitch, Trump said that right now "religion and Christianity are the biggest things missing from this country." "We must make America pray again."[30]

In a November 2022 article on conservative foreign policy, Nadia Schadlow, a senior fellow at the conservative Hudson Institute, reaffirmed the importance of defending U.S. sovereignty: "Sovereignty is worth protecting, particularly against infringement by global multilateral institutions." The United States "should not bestow on unaccountable organizations what is within the proper authority of elected governments."[31]

Since the League of Nations debates, conservatives have slammed Democrats and liberals for sacrificing U.S. sovereignty. In a September 1941 speech at Des Moines, Iowa, Lindbergh, speaking for the America First Committee, warned of a nation heedlessly "on the verge of war." "Who is responsible for changing our national policy from one of neutrality and independence to one of entanglement in European affairs?" Lindbergh answered: "The British, the Jewish, and the Roosevelt administration." For Lindbergh, "the danger of the Roosevelt administration lies in its subterfuge. While its members have promised us peace, they have led us to war heedless of the platform upon which they were elected."[32]

After Richard Nixon lost the presidential election of 1960, conservatives opposed the UN's election of diplomat and law professor Phillip C. Jessup to the International World Court as a threat to U.S. sovereignty. "Jessup, now a professor of international law at Columbia University," the conservative journal *Human Events* charged, "was part and parcel of the Truman–Acheson policy of appeasement in the Far East and today is a bosom pal of the internationalist clique bent on gutting American sovereignty."[33] The conservative *Chicago Tribune* called Jessup "a strange choice" for the World Court. It claimed that Bethuel Webster, former New York City Bar Association president, "an unrestricted internationalist" had pulled the strings on Jessup's election.[34] Representative John R. Pillon (R-NY) petitioned President Eisenhower and President-elect Kennedy to veto Jessup's election to protect U.S. sovereignty.[35] Despite this, Jessup took his position in early 1961.

As Ronald Reagan prepared to run for governor of California, he strongly criticized the Johnson administration's globalist tendencies. "Freedom comes but once to a nation and when it is lost it never returns," Reagan said in 1965. "We must be opposed to an administration that encroaches on our freedoms and to organizations that would cost us our national sovereignty."[36] Conservatives, including Reagan, later attacked President Jimmy Carter for negotiating the Panama Canal treaties, which would transfer control of the Canal and Canal Zone to Panama. "The proposed treaty would eliminate the rights of sovereignty we acquired in the original treaty," said Reagan. "Without these rights we must ask, What is to prevent a Panamanian regime one day from simply national-izing the Canal and demanding our immediate withdrawal?"[37] Robert M. Bleiberg, the conservative editor of the business journal *Barron's*, warned, "The US is prepared to accept a much earlier surrender of sovereignty in the Canal Zone, and to share with the Torrijos [president of Panama] regime the responsibility for the operation and defense of the vital water-way."[38] A resolution of the American Legion said in capitals: "The Ameri-can Legion Stands Staunchly against Any Proposal That Will Surrender or Subordinate American Rights or Sovereignty or the Rights of United States Citizens in the Panama Canal and the Canal Zone."

Conservatives in the Senate shared these concerns. "There is only one basic issue on the Panama Canal, and that is whether the United States will continue to control the Canal under our present sovereign rights," said Senator Strom Thurmond (R-SC). He insisted that "'sover-eignty' lies right at the heart of the Panama Canal controversy." If we sacrifice our sovereignty "we will end up with a result which will be ex-tremely detrimental, if not disastrous, to the United States."[39] A resolution on the Canal treaties by thirty-seven conservative senators stated, "The Government of the United States should maintain and protect its sover-eign rights and jurisdiction over the canal and zone, and should in no way cede, dilute, forfeit, negotiate, or transfer any of these sovereign rights, power, authority, jurisdiction, territory, or property that are indispensably necessary for the protection and security of the United States and the entire Western Hemisphere."[40]

In 2011, conservative John Bolton condemned President Barack Obama "for endangering our national sovereignty" through his globalist policies. Obama had engaged in "the internationalization of domestic issues," Bolton said. He decried globalist accords on the arms trade, cli-mate change, the death penalty, and the rights of children, women, and racial minorities. "The importance of threats to American sovereignty needs more attention from our political leaders and our media," Bolton concluded. "But most important it needs more attention from us, the citizenry. After all, it's our sovereignty that's at stake. If we don't take it seriously, no one else will."[41] Bolton was formerly George W. Bush's UN ambassador and later Trump's national security advisor.

The conservative Center for Immigration Studies (CIS) raised concerns over President Biden's 2023 executive agreement with Mexico and Canada, claiming the Declaration of North America violated U.S. sovereignty. CIS alleged that "U.S. border security and national sovereignty aren't afterthoughts in the 'Declaration of North America'—they're not considered at all." "To Biden," the "'United States' isn't a sovereign nation—just a destination. That would be fine if that were what the law allowed; it's not."[42]

As president-elect in late 2024, Donald Trump revisited concerns about the loss of U.S. sovereignty through the Panama Canal Treaty: "We foolishly gave it [the Canal] away" under President Carter. He threatened to take the Canal back under the pretext of Panama "ripping us off." Trump posted on his social media site a picture of a U.S. flag planted in the Canal Zone, with the caption, "Welcome to the United States Canal!"

In pursuit of political advantage and core values, conservatives have routinely forfeited the moral high ground on sovereignty. In the 1920s, conservatives opposed strategic or military commitments but sacrificed U.S. sovereignty to multinational corporations. Post–World War I conservatives were not isolationists intent on keeping the country sealed off from the world. Policymakers leveraged the United States' position as a creditor nation with the world's largest economy to profitably engage with the world economically. Republican-majority Congresses authorized the incorporation of investment trusts for international trade and suspended antitrust laws for exporting associations. The government assisted private interests in gaining access to oil and other raw materials and developed plans for easing the burdens of Germany's reparation payments to the allies. Congress raised tariffs on behalf of domestic producers and resisted formal financial agreements among nations. These policies created an opening for emerging multinational corporations, which established more than 1,300 foreign subsidiaries by 1929, and for private banks, which sent more capital abroad in the 1920s than lenders from all other nations combined.[43]

These multinational corporations had economic and political power beyond the control of any sovereign nation. During the 1940s, dozens of major multinational firms, including General Motors, IBM, DuPont, Ford, Alcoa, and Standard Oil, undercut U.S. security and sovereignty through contractual and other business arrangements with German companies and cartels. Most contracts predated Hitler's rise to power but continued under his rule. In some cases, deals survived Pearl Harbor. Business arrangements with the Nazis helped Hitler build his war machine and impeded United States' access to materials and technology. Alfred Sloan, president of General Motors, justified the actions by stating that multinational corporations focus solely on profit rather than prioritizing U.S. security or sovereignty. "An international business operating throughout the world," he said, "should conduct its operations in strictly business terms, without regard to the political beliefs of its management, or the political beliefs of the country in which it is operating."[44]

Before Pearl Harbor, debates on U.S. disengagement from World War II, championed by Charles Lindbergh and his conservative allies, focused on U.S. sovereignty and survival at the mercy of a hostile foreign power bent on world domination. Lindbergh openly accepted the prospect of a Nazi victory and advocated for U.S. cooperation with the regime, likening Nazi Germany to prewar France and Britain. He professed to be "perfectly neutral" regarding a Nazi or Allied victory, asserting that the United States could collaborate with either side after the war. "In the past we have dealt with a Europe dominated by England and France," Lindbergh said. "In the future we may have to deal with a Europe dominated by Germany. But whether England or Germany wins this war, Western civilization will still depend on two great centers, one in each hemisphere," as though the Nazis represented any manner of civilization.[45]

Senator Robert Taft, leader of the America First bloc in Congress, also believed that a Nazi victory would have minimal effect on the United States, despite his tepid preference for a German defeat. Taft expressed confidence that American private enterprise could flourish even after a Nazi triumph, arguing there was "no reason why Hitler should pick a quarrel with the most powerful nation in the world when he has nothing to gain by such a course." Taft derided the presumption "that the world cannot be half democratic and half autocratic." "Why not?" Taft said. Taft saw not "the slightest reason" to believe that a German victory over Britain would stop the United States from remaining "a great and prosperous democracy."[46]

Taft contended that U.S. involvement in the war would cause greater harm to American democracy than a German victory would. "Our going to war would be more likely to destroy American democracy than to destroy German dictatorship," Taft said. "Congress would be flooded by a large number of measures designed to have the Government take over business and regulate every detail of private and commercial life."[47] Clarence "Pat" Manion, conservative Democrat and Notre Dame Law School dean, agreed. Shortly before Pearl Harbor, he said, "If we conserved instead of spending the three hundred billion necessary to defeat Hitler, we will have established a complete insurance against any conceivable postwar economic problem, and at the same time, we will have saved the lives of several million American boys."[48] In 1954, Manion founded the first conservative radio talk show in the United States, the Manion Forum.

The Japanese attack on Pearl Harbor finished off the America First Committee but elicited no remorse from its leaders. "Our principles were right," said retired general Leonard Wood, the president of the America First Committee. "Had they been followed, war could have been avoided." According to Lindbergh, "The final judgment of our policies must be left to the future and to more objective times; but in this final judgment, I have complete confidence." In the four days between Pearl Harbor and Germany's declaration of war against the United States, the American First crowd still hoped that the country could avoid war with Hitler. Former president Hoover said, "We can even yet limit the area of the war." Some within America First considered supporting the war against Japan while continuing their opposition to entering the European conflict, a hope that ended when Germany declared war on the United States.[49]

During his 1968 presidential campaign, Nixon, then a private citizen, undermined U.S. sovereignty and security by covertly colluding with a foreign nation. In an effort to secure the election, Nixon sought to sabotage official U.S. policy aimed at negotiating peace to end the Vietnam War. Through his emissary, Anna Chennault—widow of Claire Lee Chennault, leader of the Flying Tigers in World War II—Nixon urged the South Vietnamese leadership to delay peace talks until after the election. Though a successful deal was uncertain even without Nixon's interference, his actions likely obstructed peace efforts in Vietnam, undermining U.S. sovereignty and potentially prolonging the war at the cost of thousands of American and Vietnamese lives.

President Lyndon Johnson, who had wiretapped Nixon's communications, overheard Nixon proclaim, "We're going to say to Hanoi, 'I [Nixon] can make a better deal than he [Johnson] has, because I'm fresh and new, and I don't have to demand as much as he does in the light of past positions,'" and heard Anna Chennault "warning them to not get pulled in on this Johnson [peace] move." In a conversation with Senate Minority Leader Everett Dirksen, Johnson said, "This is treason . . . that they're contacting a foreign power in the middle of a war." Johnson never revealed Nixon's alleged betrayal, perhaps because he believed Nixon would win anyway and did not want to risk a national crisis.

During the Reagan administration, in the Iran–Contra scandal, conservatives organized a clandestine government within the government to conduct foreign operations that contradicted the sovereign authority of the elected U.S. government. The report of Independent Counsel Lawrence Walsh concluded that the operation "was the first known criminal assault on the post-Watergate rules governing the activities of national security officials. Reagan Administration officials rendered these rules ineffective by creating private operations, supported with privately generated funds that successfully evaded executive and legislative oversight and control. Walsh found that "Congress had been defrauded." Walsh explained that this clandestine structure "did not arise primarily out of ordinary venality or greed. . . . Instead, the crimes committed in Iran/Contra were motivated by the desire of persons in high office to pursue controversial policies and goals even when the pursuit of those policies and goals was inhibited or restricted by executive orders, statutes or the constitutional system of checks and balances."[50]

Similarly, President Trump disregarded his oath to protect U.S. sovereignty. As both a candidate and president, Trump, along with his associates, engaged with foreign nations in ways that compromised U.S. democracy. On July 27, 2016, candidate Trump said, "Russia, if you're listening, I hope you're able to find the 30,000 emails [of Hillary Clinton] that are missing. I think you will probably be rewarded mightily by our press. Let's see if that happens." This marked the first instance in history where a presidential candidate solicited a foreign power to interfere in an election by hacking a private email server—a felony. Russia responded swiftly, with its agents sending malicious links to email accounts linked to Hillary Clinton's campaign. Although Trump later claimed he was "joking," Russian president Vladimir Putin was anything but amused.

Special Counsel Robert Mueller's report on Russian meddling in the 2016 campaign did not find evidence of a criminal conspiracy between Trump and Russia, partly because of destroyed evidence and uncooperative key witnesses, including Trump himself. However, Mueller concluded that Trump's campaign welcomed and exploited Russian interference. Russia's "information war" faithfully followed Trump's strategy. The Russians gleaned information and guidance from "unwitting" local Republican activists and wittingly from the Trump campaign chair, Paul Manafort. He provided inside information about the campaign to Ukrainian Konstantin Kilimnik, Manafort's associate when they both worked for pro-Russian interests in Ukraine. Kilimnik, who served as a Russian agent, passed this information on to the Russian Intelligence Services.

Mueller and other investigators uncovered at least 140 undisclosed contacts between Trump campaign associates and Russia-linked operatives, compared to zero for Clinton's campaign. Contacts continued after August 17, 2016, when the FBI informed Trump about Russian efforts to infiltrate his campaign and asked him to report any Russian openings to the Bureau. Russian hackers disseminated their dirt on the Clinton campaign through the outlet WikiLeaks, including a massive release of stolen emails just after the disclosure of the *Access Hollywood* tape rocked the Trump campaign. The Senate report contradicted Trump in finding that "Trump did, in fact, speak with his confidant Roger Stone about WikiLeaks and with members of his Campaign about Stone's access to WikiLeaks on multiple occasions." Trump mentioned WikiLeaks an average of more than five times per day during the final month of the 2016 campaign. Trump said, "I love WikiLeaks," even though in 2010 Trump had called WikiLeaks "disgraceful" and said there should be a "death penalty" for its leaking of classified documents.

No reports from the Trump campaign reached the FBI. When confronted with media coverage of Russian contacts, Trump associates followed Nixon's Watergate playbook by lying. On June 9, 2016, at Trump Tower, Donald Trump Jr., Paul Manafort, and Trump's son-in-law Jared Kushner met with Kremlin-connected Russians on behalf of the Trump campaign. According to email evidence, a Russian contact set the meeting up "to provide the Trump campaign with some official documents and information that would incriminate Hillary." This "is part of Russia and its government's support for Mr. Trump," the Russian said. Trump Jr. responded, "I love it," and the meeting occurred in June 2016. The Trump team participants claimed they learned nothing useful from the Russians, which does not exonerate them from seeking information from a foreign adversary to influence the election's outcome.

In March 2017, nine months after the Trump Tower meeting, Donald Trump Jr. lied. He disingenuously told the *New York Times*, "Did I meet with people that were Russian? I'm sure, I'm sure I did. But none that were set up. None that I can think of at the moment. And certainly none that I was representing the campaign in any way, shape or form." After the release of the Mueller report, Ellen Weintraub, chair of the Federal Election Commission, said, "It is illegal for any person to solicit, accept, or receive anything of value from a foreign national in connection with a U.S. election." Jessica Levinson, a law professor at Loyola Law School, noted that anything of value includes opposition research. "There's a reason campaigns pay for opposition research: We literally value it," Levinson said. "It can be much more useful and valuable than walking in with a check."[51]

Russia had a history of attempting to undermine U.S. sovereignty by offering candidates help to win the presidency. However, unlike the Trump team, previous candidates had swiftly rebuffed the Kremlin's advances. In January 1960, Soviet ambassador Mikhail A. Menshikov told Adlai Stevenson, a candidate for the Democratic nomination for president, that "we believe that Mr. Stevenson is more of a realist than others and is likely to understand Soviet anxieties and purposes." He offered to have the Soviet press assist Stevenson through praise or criticism at the candidate's discretion. An appalled Stevenson bluntly told the ambassador that such meddling was "highly improper, indiscreet, and dangerous." He later informed James Reston, a prominent *New York Times* columnist, about the Soviet overture, warning against foreign interference in U.S. elections. Reston wrote that the Russians displayed "both a keen interest in the United States election and appalling ignorance of the dangers in commenting on it." He warned that Americans would not tolerate any foreign interference in their sovereign democracy.[52]

In 1968, fearing the potential victory of anticommunist candidate Richard Nixon, the Soviets again attempted to intervene, this time by offering financial assistance to Nixon's opponent, Vice President Hubert Humphrey. Under orders from Moscow, Soviet ambassador Anatoly Dobrynin approached Humphrey, who immediately recognized the offer for what it was and rejected it outright. Dobrynin later recounted that Humphrey "knew at once what was going on."[53]

As president, Trump took unprecedented steps to pressure a foreign nation into meddling in a U.S. election. By withholding vital military aid to Ukraine, Trump attempted to coerce newly elected Ukrainian president Volodymyr Zelensky into launching two politically advantageous investigations ahead of Trump's 2020 reelection campaign. The first was aimed at casting doubt on Russian interference in the 2016 election, instead falsely claiming that Ukraine had interfered on behalf of Hillary Clinton. Fiona Hill, Trump's former national security advisor on Russia and Eastern Europe, testified before Congress that this claim was a false narrative "propagated by the Russian security services themselves."

The second called for Zelensky to investigate allegedly corrupt dealings by Trump's political opponent, Joe Biden. Trump bypassed official channels and delegated authority over the Ukraine operation to his personal attorney, Rudy Giuliani. The scheme backfired only when a whistleblower disclosed details of a telephone conversation in which Trump pressured Zelensky to conduct the investigations. Trump's pressure campaign led him to become only the third U.S. president to be impeached.

Trump put his disdain for the United States' sovereign decision-making on full display before the world at his 2018 summit meeting with Putin. At a joint press conference, Trump privileged Kremlin propagandists above U.S. intelligence and national security teams. A journalist asked Trump if he would denounce Russia's interference in the 2016 presidential election. Trump responded, "My people came to me, [director of national intelligence] Dan Coats came to me and some others, they said they think it's Russia. I have President Putin. He just said it's not Russia. I will say this: I don't see any reason why it would be." Trump then praised Putin for an offer to investigate the Kremlin's own interference in U.S. politics.

Conservative Republicans in Congress and their allies in the media further compromised U.S. sovereignty in their impeachment investigation of President Biden by relying on disinformation from Russian intelligence. Their smoking-gun evidence was a claim by FBI informant Alexander Smirnov that a Ukrainian energy company had paid $5 million in bribes to President Biden and his son Hunter. They breezed through warnings from the FBI that Smirnov's claims and credibility were unverified. "The F.B.I. regularly receives information from sources with significant potential biases," the warning said. Conservative journalists amplified Smirnov's dubious claim as fact. Fox News host Sean Hannity repeatedly referred to the Smirnov allegation, calling it "the biggest story of the year." The U.S. Justice Department then indicted Smirnov for perjury and revealed that his fabrications came from the Russian intelligence services.[54] In December 2024, after the election, Smirnov pleaded guilty.[55]

Even after Smirnov's indictment, conservatives showed little remorse. Former federal prosecutor Gregory J. Wallance observed that they continued to push corruption allegations against President Biden, unperturbed by the exposure of Russian propaganda. Wallance further remarked that conservatives had become more complicit in serving Russian interests than the Far Left ever was during the Cold War. "The right wing, through Republican Party control of the House and journalists like Tucker Carlson, has given Russia a foothold in the U.S. for propaganda and influence unlike anything the Soviets were able to build in their time," Wallance said. "The old Kremlin masters of the American Communist Party never dreamed they could accomplish anything like this."[56]

Conservative support for U.S. sovereignty has proven selective. Although they frequently invoke sovereignty to oppose international agreements that conflict with their core values, they have sacrificed it when political power, private enterprise, or traditional Christian values are at stake. Stewart Patrick, a senior fellow at the Council on Foreign Relations, pointed out in 2019 that "sovereignty is also one of the most frequently invoked, polemical, and misunderstood concepts in politics—particularly American politics. The concept wields symbolic power, implying something sacred and inalienable: the right of the people to control their fate without subordination to outside authorities. Given its emotional pull, however, the concept is easily high-jacked by political opportunists."[57]

RELIGION, RACE, IMMIGRANTS, AND SEX

In 1919, Reverend George A. Simons, a Christian missionary in Russia during the Bolshevik Revolution, spun an alarming tale to the U.S. Senate Subcommittee on the Judiciary. Simons claimed that Jews from the United States had incited the Bolshevik Revolution in Russia. "I have a firm conviction that this thing [the Bolshevik Revolution] is Yiddish, and that one of its bases is found in the East Side of New York," said Simons. He added that "more than half the agitators in the so-called Bolshevik movement were Yiddish" and that "I do not think the Bolshevik movement in Russia would have been a success if it had not been for the support it got from certain elements in New York, the so-called East Side." When asked how he knew that most of the Bolsheviki were Jewish, Simons responded, "I usually know a Jew when I see one."[1]

The danger of Jewish radicalism, Simons said, spread to the United States and beyond as part of a secret Jewish conspiracy to control the world and destroy Christianity. Citing alleged Jewish anti-Christian propaganda, Simons warned, "It shows what this secret Jewish society has been doing in order to make a conquest of the world and to make Christianity as ineffective as possible, and finally to have the whole world, if you please, in their grip." The Jews who had incited Bolshevism in Russia had returned to incite revolution here. "I have no doubt in my mind that the predominant element in this Bolsheviki movement in America is, you may call it, the Yiddish of the East Side," Simons said.[2] Republican senators responded positively to Simons's testimony. None challenged the link between Jews and the destruction of Christianity across the world.

Since Simons's time, conservatives have consistently stoked animosities against Jews, African Americans, immigrants, defiant women, and nonheterosexuals. Conservatives leverage emotionally charged issues to distinguish themselves from liberals and energize their political base in ways that policy debates cannot. These explosive social issues also serve as a distraction, allowing conservatives to advance their pro-business agendas with little backlash.

In the years following Simons's testimony, conservatives continued to echo his warnings of Jewish conspirators subverting the United States. Henry Ford, the iconic industrialist of the 1920s, became obsessed with the "Jewish question." He published a four-volume set of books collectively titled The *International Jew: The World's Foremost Problem*. Ford drew on articles published from 1920 to 1922 in his *Dearborn Independent*, which his dealers distributed to 600,000 readers. Ford and other conspiracy-minded conservatives relied heavily on a purported Jewish plot to dominate the world described in the *Protocols of the Elders of Zion*, a forged document that the Russian czar's secret police circulated to justify pogroms against Jews. The *Protocols* purportedly proved that Jews were the destructors of Christian civilization, preying on virtuous producers of real wealth and feeding on chaos, such as the turmoil that followed World War I. Though Ford later retracted his false claims, he could not undo his damaging accusations.

In 1931, a Republican-led U.S. House investigation validated these fears, claiming Jews led the American Communist Party: "The district organizers are responsible for communist activities throughout their districts such as forming nuclei among factory workers, contacting political campaigns, arranging mass demonstrations, circulating, communist literature, and raising funds. A large percentage of all the known communist district organizers are of Jewish origin."[3]

During Franklin Roosevelt's presidency, conservatives again conjured up fears of radical Jews controlling the government, this time led by presidential advisor Felix Frankfurter. Ruly Carpenter, a DuPont in-law and a director of the family's corporation, warned of a president ruled by "Frankfurter and his thirty-eight hot dogs—a gang of fanatical and communistic Jew professors." Outspoken conservative Henry Joy, president of Packard Motors, said, "There is decidedly too much Jewish influence in power in our government by presidential appointment and approval." In a front-page editorial in his *New York American* newspaper, conservative publishing magnate William Randolph Hearst wrote, "Mr. Roosevelt says HE IS NOT a Communist; but what about the Marxian professor Frankfurter, Communistic counselor of the Administration, and personal confidant of Mr. Roosevelt?"[4] Fears that radical Jews wielded excessive power in Washington spread widely among conservative men of business. Frank W. Buxton, editor of the *Boston Herald*, wrote privately about "substantial men who sympathized with anti-Semitism. . . . I was amazed at the intensity with which highly intelligent men argued that the Jews were controlling the President."[5]

In the 1930s, Father Charles Coughlin, known as the "Radio Priest," emerged as a militant social conservative and anti-Semite, broadcasting to about 30 million weekly listeners—nearly a third of the nation's adult population. During FDR's second term, Coughlin founded the Christian Front, a right-wing, paramilitary, anti-Semitic group that urged Americans to "act, buy and vote Christian." His magazine, *Social Justice*, and radio sermons became overtly pro-Nazi, reprinting the *Protocols of the Elders of Zion*. He revived Simons's accusation that Jews had incited the Bolshevik Revolution, calling Nazism "a defensive front against Bolshevism" and labeling censorship attempts as "a typical case of Jewish terrorism of American public opinion."[6]

Conspiracy theories had enduring power by exploiting anti-Semitism in the United States and forcing opponents to prove a negative in refutation. "Who can prove that such a conspiracy does not exist?" asked journalist and science professor Edwin Slosson in a December 1920 analysis of Ford's anti-Semitism. He answered, "No one. A secret can never be disproved. Once you get a conspiracy complex on the brain and not even a psychoanalyst can dislodge it," Slosson said. "The conspiracy phobia is one of the worst forms of crowd madness, easy to start, hard to eradicate, and leading to persecution and pogroms, riot and revolution."[7]

The Ku Klux Klan, a grassroots manifestation of 1920s conservatism, issued warnings about "unassimilable" Jews. Although it declined in the second half of the decade, the Klan elected thousands of endorsed candidates to school boards and local governments and extended its reach to state and national offices. In 1924, Klan-backed conservative Republican candidates—none of whom were incumbents—won governor's positions in Indiana, Kansas, Maine, and Colorado, as many as seventy-five U.S. House seats, and U.S. Senate seats in Oklahoma, Colorado, and Kansas. "Victories by Klan Feature Election" announced a front-page headline of the *New York Times* on November 6, 1924.

Grand Wizard Hiram Wesley Evans articulated the Klan's ideology as one of "loyalty to the white race, to the traditions of America, and to the spirit of Protestantism," or briefly, "native, white, Protestant supremacy." It supported the "plain people" and the country's "pioneer stock Nordic race" against a "liberalism" that "has undermined their Constitution and their national customs and institutions" and "tried to destroy their God." "Eastern Jews of recent immigration," Evans charged, "are not true Jews, but only Judaized Mongols—Chazars," who, "unlike the true Hebrew," could not be assimilated. "The most menacing and most difficult problem facing America today is this of the permanently unassimilable alien."[8] For Jews, he argued, "patriotism, as the Anglo-Saxon feels it, is impossible."[9]

Charles Lindbergh, in his antiwar speeches, tapped into religious prejudice by blaming Jews for pushing the United States toward war for "reasons which are not American." He warned, "We cannot allow the natural passions and prejudices of other peoples to lead our country to destruction." Lindbergh exploited the anti-Semitic myth that Jews controlled much of American life. "Their greatest danger to this country lies in their large ownership and influence in our motion pictures, our press, our radio and our government," he said. Conservatives had blundered into controversies over the "Jewish question" before Lindbergh and would do so again, but never on so large a stage with so much at stake. For Lindbergh and Jews, it was always us versus the other.[10]

Like Lindbergh in 1941, Pat Buchanan, who would later challenge George H. W. Bush for the 1992 Republican presidential nomination, singled out Jews for pushing the United States into war—this time in the Middle East. In a 1990 television appearance, Buchanan claimed, "There are only two groups that are beating the drums . . . for war in the Middle East, the Israeli Defense Ministry and its amen corner in the United States." He named prominent Jewish figures, such as A. M. Rosenthal of the *New York Times*, former assistant secretary of defense Richard Perle, the columnist Charles Krauthammer, and former secretary of state Henry Kissinger. These Jewish names clashed with those who would fight the war, "Kids with names like McAllister, Murphy, Gonzales, and Leroy Brown," Buchanan said. Despite a media uproar over Buchanan's remarks, he said, "I don't retract a single word."[11] In 1998, Buchanan lamented that there were too few "non-Jewish whites" at Harvard. "Talk about under-representation!" he wrote. "Now we know who really gets the shaft at Harvard—white Christians."[12]

Donald Trump capitalized on anti-Semitism as a candidate and president. In July 2016, Trump posted a graphic of Hillary Clinton with a six-pointed star, similar to the Jewish Star of David, amid piles of cash. The video called her the "most corrupt candidate ever."[13] In October 2016, he charged that "Hillary Clinton meets in secret with international banks to plot the destruction of U.S. sovereignty in order to enrich these global financial powers, her special interest friends and her donors," reprising Ford's anti-Semitic attack on international Jewish bankers. "Mr. Trump focused on the very issues and themes that obsess conspiratorial anti-Semites," said Jonathan Greenblatt, the chief executive of the Anti-Defamation League. "They believe that there is an elite group of Jews who control the media, the government, and banking, and who are trying to destroy white America. They also believe that most of Hillary Clinton's donors are Jewish." After a backlash from Jewish leaders, Trump implausibly claimed, despite the context, that the six-pointed star was a sheriff's badge, not a star of David. There were no law enforcement marks on the image, and earlier, in 2015, Trump had linked Jewish money with efforts to control public life in the United Stated. "You're not going to support me because I don't want your money," Trump told a Jewish group. "But that's okay. You want to control your own politician."[14]

President Trump said that Charlottesville, Virginia, protestors in 2017 shouting, "Jews will not replace us," included some "very fine people." As a former president, Trump cheered anti-Semites when he invited two notorious anti-Semites, Kanye West and Nick Fuentes, to a rare private dinner at Mar-a-Lago. West had said on Twitter, "go death con 3 ON JEWISH PEOPLE." Fuentes had charged that the nation's problems result from the "bastardized Jewish subversion of the American creed. The Founders never intended for America to be a refugee camp for nonwhite people." "The level of antisemitism being expressed, antisemitic acts at a very elevated level, and the acceptability of antisemitism—it is all creating an environment which is, thank God, unusual for the United States, and it has to be nipped in the bud," said Rabbi Moshe Hauer, executive vice president of the Orthodox Union, one of the few Jewish groups that had supported Donald Trump.[15]

Trump has reprised the anti-Semitic trope that Jews have dual loyalties and cannot be trusted. He disparaged Jews who voted Democratic in a 2019 statement as "very, very disloyal to Israel and to the Jewish people."[16] Then, in an interview on March 18, 2024, Trump said, "the Democrats hate Israel" and "every Jewish person who votes for the Democrats hates their religion. They hate Israel and they should be ashamed of themselves."[17] Later, on September 16, 2024, Trump preemptively blamed Jews if he were to lose the election: "The Jewish people would have a lot to do with" such a loss.[18] Trump reprised the ancient libel that scapegoated the Jews for misfortunes: stolen cattle, poisoned wells, kidnapped children, famines, and setbacks in war.

In 2018, Marjorie Taylor Greene won a congressional seat, and reanimated anti-Semitic conspiracy theories about Jewish plots to take over the world. She shared a video claiming that "Zionist conspirators" are planning to flood Europe with nonwhite migrants to replace the population there, echoing the "Great Replacement" myth. Amid frightening images of dark-skinned migrant "invaders" rioting and assaulting innocent white people, the video claims that "leftists, capitalists and Zionist supremacists" have a "deliberate aim of breeding us out of existence in our own homelands." The conspirators are using "immigrant pawns" to commit "the biggest genocide in human history." In response to the video, Greene wrote on Facebook, "This is what the UN wants all over the world."[19] She also claimed that Jewish masterminds had installed lasers in space, which she blamed for starting the California wildfires.

George Santos, a Republican who won a U.S. House seat from New York in 2022, similarly exploited anti-Semitic rhetoric. Among many fabrications about his background, Santos falsely claimed that his grand-parents were Jewish survivors of the Holocaust and had fled from Hitler. He had previously made anti-Semitic jokes on Facebook, including a post where he wrote, "hight hitler" and "sombody kill her!! The jews and black mostly lolllolol!!!" [all *sic*][20]

Recently, anti-Semitism has also emerged among left-wing college students. Representative Elise Stefanik (R-NY) attempted to exploit this trend by trapping college presidents with questions about their campus speech codes and how they addressed anti-Semitic speech, including advocacy of genocide. Although the presidents struggled to respond adequately during the hearing, Stefanik's record on anti-Semitism was questionable. She had not condemned Trump for his praise of neo-Nazis at the 2017 Charlottesville demonstrations, nor had she spoken out against other anti-Semitic actions by Trump, Santos, or Greene. She remained silent after Trump's dinner with notorious anti-Semites West and Fuentes. She did not express outrage when an anti-Semite gunned down eleven wor-shippers at the Tree of Life Synagogue in Pittsburgh.

Conservative agitation on race extends to the 1920s Klan, which viewed Black people as a double threat to white Christian America through interbreeding and disloyalty. William Joseph Simmons, the founder of the 1920s Klan, warned that "Negroes" are "now ready to vote, and that these apes are going to line up at the polls, mixed up there with white men and white women." We must "keep the Negro . . . where he belongs. They have no part in our political and social life."[21] "The low mentality of savage ancestors is inherent in the bloodstream of the colored race in America," Hiram Wesley Evans said. "No new environment can more than super-ficially overcome this age-old heredity handicap."[22] Like anti-Semitism, denigration of Black people appealed to the widespread racism of the time. A former Klan member said, "Much of the opposition against the Klan was not so much based upon the Klan's activity against the Negro as it was against the Klan's assumption that it superseded the law."[23]

The American Legion further shaped conservative views on race. The Legion led the spirit of reconciliation and reunion between Union and Confederate Civil War forces that developed through veterans' organi-zations in the North and South. By emphasizing the common bond of Union and Confederate service and sacrifice during the Civil War and de-emphasizing divisiveness, especially over issues of race, "reunionist" nationalism legitimized white supremacy, demonized Reconstruction, and fed into romantic images of an idealized southern past of racial harmony and goodwill during slavery. Although many thousands of Black soldiers served in World War I, Legion policy allowed southern members to create white-only posts.[24]

Within the government, the antiradical campaign after World War I linked the Red scare and the Black scare, with Black Americans purportedly succumbing to radical propaganda and recruitment. The *New York Times* reported in July 1919, "Evidence is accumulating in the files of the Government" that radicals are seeking "to stir up discontent among the Negroes, particularly the uneducated class in the Southern States. . . . The radical organizations active in this propaganda are the I.W.W., certain factions of radical Socialist elements, and Bolsheviki."[25] A. Mitchell Palmer, President Wilson's attorney general, the architect of the "Red raids" that swept up thousands of mostly foreign-born suspected radicals between November 1919 and January 1920, said, "Practically all the radical organizations in this country have looked upon the negroes as particularly fertile grounds for the spreading of their doctrines. The radical organizations have endeavored to enlist negroes on their side, and in many respects have been successful."[26] Although a Wilsonian progressive on many domestic issues, Palmer shared and foreshadowed conservatives' militant response to the alleged threat of African American subversion in the United States.

The more conservative and militant J. Edgar Hoover equated African American demands for racial justice with subversion. Through surveillance, informants, phone taps, break-ins, and intimidation, his FBI targeted the NAACP and Black newspaper editors. It also pursued those relatively few Black leaders who participated in leftist or militant Black politics, notably Jamaican immigrant Marcus Garvey, head of the Universal Negro Improvement Association, which claimed about 2 million dues-paying members worldwide. Garvey's paper, the *Negro World*, had a circulation of 50,000. Garvey preached race pride and power, unity of the Black race across the world, collective self-help, racial separation, and self-defense, and a back to Africa "Zionism." Garvey's views antagonized fearful whites, conventional Black leaders, and the FBI, which hired its lone Black agent to infiltrate Garvey's movement. Federal prosecutors convicted Garvey of mail fraud in 1923. President Coolidge eventually commuted his sentence and deported the race leader to Jamaica.[27]

Lindbergh inserted race into his America First advocacy. He asserted that only his policy of absolute neutrality would preserve white Christian civilization. Two weeks after Germany invaded Poland on September 1, 1939, Lindbergh said the wars in Europe are "not wars in which our civilization is defending itself against some Asiatic intruder [but] simply one more of those age-old struggles within our own family of nations." A month later, he said, "Our bond with Europe is a bond of race. . . . If the white race is ever seriously threatened, it may be our time to take our part in its protection to fight side by side with the English, French, and Germans, but not with one against the other for our mutual destruction."[28]

In the 1960s, conservative Republicans pursued a deliberate strategy to win the white supremacist South, riding the wave of white resistance to the civil rights gains for Blacks. Segregationist leaders such as state Republican Party chair Wirt Yerger of Mississippi, gubernatorial candidate Charlton H. Lyons of Louisiana, and Senate candidate William Workman of South Carolina refurbished lily-white Republican Party organizations in the South. The Republican National Committee urged southerners to replace Democrats with "MORE conservative" Republicans. The Republican Party scrapped its minority-outreach division and launched an organizing drive among white southerners, ironically called "Operation Dixie." The South Carolina Republican state party reported, "In 1962 and 1964 not a single Negro showed any interest in participating in the statutory party reorganization or its activities." "This was welcomed by new Party leaders as victory in the South at any level could never be achieved by a Negro dominated party."[29]

In the North, Republicans sought to exploit the "white backlash" against Black demands for jobs, housing, and government assistance, anticipating political benefits in the 1964 elections. In a column titled "The White Man's Party," Rowland Evans and Robert Novak said that after listening to "backroom chats" at a 1963 meeting of the Republican National Committee, "substantial numbers of Republican Party leaders from both North and South see rich political dividends flowing from the Negrophobia of many white Americans."[30]

Senator Barry Goldwater, the 1964 Republican presidential nominee, had joined an Arizona branch of the NAACP and worked to integrate the Arizona National Guard. But he knew that his future as a conservative Republican depended upon uniting northern conservatives with white Protestant defenders of Jim Crow in the South. On November 18, 1961, Goldwater told a Republican meeting in Atlanta that he opposed measures "to enforce integration of the schools." The Republicans, he said, could not "out-promise the Democrats" in competition for Black votes. The party needed to "go hunting where the ducks are." He voted against the Civil Rights Act of 1964, upheld the rights of states to decide their own affairs, and opposed "forced integration."[31] His allies purged African American leaders from the Republican Party.[32]

Journalist Robert J. Donovan reported that "Goldwater spoke directly to the [white] southerner audiences that turned out to hear him. And what he said, to judge by their responses, was music to their ears."[33] Goldwater's political strategy helped him defeat the Republicans' Eastern establishment candidate, Nelson Rockefeller, and win the Republican presidential nomination in 1964 with support from 97 percent of southern delegates at the national convention.

Once nominated, Goldwater avoided overt racist appeals, but civil rights advocates and southern segregationists knew where he stood. Goldwater continued indirect appeals to white supremacists, promising to curb the excesses of the hated Warren Court and uphold states' rights. He derided LBJ's antipoverty program, which white southerners believed favored Black people.[34] Martin Luther King Jr. said that although Goldwater is not personally bigoted, the senator "articulates a philosophy which gives aid and comfort to the racists." Whitney M. Young, director of the National Urban League, said that Goldwater has made "an attempt to appeal to all of the fearful, the insecure, prejudiced people in our society." Three southern Democratic segregationist governors who had resisted integration in their states broke with their party to endorse Goldwater: George C. Wallace of Alabama, Orville Faubus of Arkansas, and Paul B. Johnson of Mississippi.[35] In South Carolina, former Dixiecrat presidential candidate Senator Strom Thurmond turned Republican to back Goldwater. So did former South Carolina governor James F. Byrnes, who called Goldwater's vote against the Civil Rights Act his "finest hour."[36] Goldwater won three of these four states, Louisiana, and Georgia for a sweep of the Deep South in the general election, which was the first for any Republican candidate since Reconstruction. Elsewhere, Goldwater only won his home state of Arizona.[37]

In subsequent elections, Richard Nixon and Ronald Reagan followed a similar strategy of indirect racial appeals, to the extent that "no matter how much deniability any coded language may have provided, were still crystal-clear to many southern whites" and not lost on African Americans, concluded political scientists Angie Maxwell and Todd Shields.[38] Nixon promised a restoration of law and order and denounced Black protests and riots. He derided the Warren Court for favoring "the criminal forces over the peace forces." He promised "benign neglect" on the enforcement of civil rights laws. "If Nixon becomes president, he has promised that he won't enforce either the Civil Rights or the Voting Rights Acts. Stick with him," said Senator Thurmond.[39]

Republican vice presidential candidate in 1968, Maryland governor Spiro Agnew, pandered to race more explicitly than Nixon. He said that Black people "should not engage in civil disobedience even against unjust laws" because "civil disobedience often leads to violence," implicitly blaming peaceful Black protestors for white attacks on them. Agnew opposed "all busing" of school children because "it was very difficult to uproot children from the limits of their world and transport them to another world."[40] When asked why he hadn't visited residents of Black neighborhoods supposedly victimized by criminals, Agnew responded, "If you've seen one city slum, you've seen them all."[41]

Conservative former and future governor George Wallace, running as an independent candidate in 1968, sought to outflank Nixon on racial issues. Though he no longer proclaimed "Segregation now! Segregation tomorrow! Segregation forever!" Wallace continued to oppose civil rights legislation, defend "states' rights," and attack Black welfare recipients and federal judges. Wallace attacked "the so-called civil rights laws" as "really an attack on the property rights of this country." To uphold "states' rights," he would avoid "telling you how to run your schools."[42] Wallace said he would "crush riots with a swift blow," adding that "proper use of the police power is the only thing left now to try to curtail anarchy in this country." He would crack down on "welfare cheaters" and the "select elite group" of bureaucrats and judges who looked "down their noses at the average man in the street." He decried "reverse discrimination" against whites and said, "The biggest bigots in the world are—they're the ones who call others bigots."[43]

For Wallace and his southern white followers, intruding federal bureaucrats had replaced the punishing carpetbaggers of Reconstruction. Wallace told a cheering capacity crowd at Madison Square Garden, "We don't have riots in Alabama. They start a riot down there, first one of 'em to pick up a brick gets a bullet in the brain, that's all." He ignored a demonstrator who shouted, "Wallace talks about law-and-order! Ask him what state has the highest murder rate! The most rapes! The most armed robberies!"[44]

Wallace was not strategically naïve. Aware that he could not win the presidency, Wallace still hoped to win enough states to deny either Nixon or Humphrey an Electoral College majority and throw the election into the U.S. House. With each state having one vote and southern states holding the balance of power, Wallace sought to become the kingmaker, dictating that the next president must stop enforcing all civil rights laws and let the South govern its race relations. Wallace came close. He won five southern states, including four Goldwater had carried, but Nixon narrowly prevailed, winning 301 electoral votes to Humphrey's 191 and Wallace's 46.

Although Nixon avoided overt racial slurs during his campaign, he was more candid in private. The country's problems, he said in 1968, are "all about law and order and the damn Negro-Puerto Rican groups out there." After winning the election, he complained about needing to "keep some incompetent blacks" in the administration. "I have the greatest affection for them, but I know they ain't gonna make it for 500 years." Like Theodore Roosevelt, he brooded over the "suicide" of the white race: "When births decline, nations decline." In twenty years, the United States would be "40 percent Black, Mexican, etc. Those who have fewest [children] should have the most."[45]

In 1988, the George H. W. Bush presidential campaign played overtly on anti-Black racism with the Willie Horton ad that disparaged their Democratic opponent, Michael Dukakis. When Barack Obama began campaigning for president in 2007, Rush Limbaugh repeatedly aired a parody song, "Barack, the Magic Negro," about Obama's popularity with white voters. Limbaugh's clip featured a comedian mimicking the singing voice of the Black celebrity Reverend Al Sharpton, bemoaning that whites will "vote for him and not for me 'cause he's not from da hood."[46] After Obama's election, Limbaugh said, "If any race of people should not have guilt about slavery, it's Caucasians," who only played a small role historically in the world wide phenomenon of slavery. During the election campaign of 2016, Limbaugh read excerpts from an essay by white nationalist Samuel Francis.[47]

Donald Trump engineered his political rise on what is perhaps the most egregious racist falsehood in modern U.S. politics: the "birther" conspiracy. In 2011, Trump falsely claimed that President Obama, the nation's first Black president, was not born in the United States and had illegitimately assumed the presidency Despite overwhelming evidence disproving this claim—including Obama's birth certificate, birth announcements in Hawaiian newspapers, and official records—Trump continued to push the baseless lie for years. In 2016, under mounting pressure, Trump reluctantly retracted his birther claims but offered no apology.

Trump continued to exploit race as president. In 2019, Trump tweeted that four women of color in the U.S. Congress, Alexandria Ocasio-Cortez (D-NY), Ayanna Pressley (D-MA), Ilhan Omar (D-MN), and Rashida Tlaib (D-MI)—are "from countries whose governments are a complete and total catastrophe" and that they should "go back" to those countries. Three of these four representatives were born in the United States. During his 2020 reelection campaign, Trump propagated another birther-style myth, suggesting that Joe Biden's running mate, Kamala Harris, who is of African American and East Asian descent, lacks the requirements to be next in line for the presidency. "I heard it today that she doesn't meet the requirements," said Trump. "And by the way, the lawyer that wrote that piece is a very highly qualified, very talented lawyer." After doing the damage by claiming that the charge is credible, Trump typically left himself an escape hatch: "I have no idea if that's right."[48] Harris was born in California and has lived continuously in the United States throughout her adult life. She served as California's attorney general and then as U.S. senator, and vice president, far more impressive qualifications than Trump brought to his candidacy in 2016.

Later in the campaign, Trump falsely claimed that Harris "happened to turn Black" a few years earlier when "all of a sudden, she made a turn" in her identity, presumably for political purposes.[49] Harris had always identified as both Black and Asian. She attended Howard University, a historically Black institution, pledged with an all-Black sorority, and joined the Black Caucus as a U.S. senator. Trump had reprised the racist practice of the Jim Crow South, when white supremacists defined the racial identity of people of color, most notoriously in Virginia, where the law defined anyone with a single drop of Black blood as Black and subject to segregation and other forms of discrimination.

Trump and his running mate, Senator J. D. Vance, disparaged Black Haitian immigrants as barbarians who were stealing and eating pets, cats and dogs. "In Springfield, they are eating the dogs," Trump said in the September 10, 2024, presidential debate. "The people that came in, they are eating the cats. They're eating—they are eating the pets of the people that live there." Vance reiterated this charge on X. "It's possible, of course, that all of these rumors will turn out to be false," Vance later admitted. But he added, "keep the cat memes flowing."[50]

From the onset of the Cold War through the present, conservatives have brewed together racism and anti-Semitism. In the 1950s and 1960s, they claimed that cunning and manipulative Jews were using gullible Black people to incite rebellion against white Christians and destroy race relations in the South. Shortly after the *Brown v. Board of Education* (1954) decision, the right-wing publication *Common Sense* charged, "The Jewish Communist Party of America has always envisioned arming the 15,000,000 American Negroes as an army with which to enslave the white population of America." It added "that the wholesale slaughter of ministers, schoolteachers, and independent businessmen in the South has already been planned by the Yiddish revolutionaries, in the process of setting up a Black Republic under the leadership of the notorious Negro Communist Paul Robeson." *Common Sense* vilified Justice Felix Frankfurter of the Supreme Court as "one of the most sinister men in America" who directed the "World Jewish conspiracy."[51]

State Senator Edward O. McCue (D-VA), a conservative Democrat, charged in 1956 that integration "is being aided and abetted by the Communists and the Jews. The Communists want to mongrelize the race—weaken and conquer; and the Jews they're so clannish, they want it so they'll end up being the only pure white race left, and have it all over everybody."[52] Louisiana's political boss, Leander Perez, claimed that "Zionist Jews" were the "main driving force behind forced racial integration. He charged that "the Jews are leading the Negroes." "I do resent any goddam Jew trying to destroy our country and they are using the Negroes for it!" Perez said.[53]

The Liberty Lobby, founded by publicist Willis Carto in 1957, pledged to liberate Washington, DC, from occupation by "an aggressive coalition of minority special interest pressure groups." By the late 1960s, the lobby claimed 200,000 subscribers to its monthly *Liberty Letter*, far surpassing all other political publications from the Right or Left. Carto's ideology combined anti-Semitism, extreme anticommunism, and white supremacy. He warned of a grinding struggle between "the white and the colored races of the world, of which Russia is lord." His demonology blamed Jews for instigating World War II and deceiving Americans into fighting the Nazis, who were "the only real anti-communists forces which have ever existed and perhaps doomed the entire West." In the postwar era, he argued that a "ruling elite in Washington," under Jewish influence, was retreating "before an aroused, armed Russian-Asiatic threat." In 1969, Carto published the pivotal work on Holocaust denial, *The Myth of the Six Million*, and in 1979 launched the Institute for Historical Review as the epicenter of Holocaust denial.[54]

Although Willis Carto, like fellow conspiracy theorist John Stormer, is scarcely remembered today, his influence on the right was substantial. John P. Jackson Jr., a historian of anti-Semitism, termed Carto "the most important organizer of the antisemitic right."[55] Despite their obscurity today, conspiracy theorists such as Stormer and Carto have influenced the contemporary conservative movement arguably more than "respectable" figures such as William F. Buckley Jr. and Russell Kirk. Buckley and his erudite *National Review* team futilely hoped to control the "'know-nothing' leaders while maintaining connections and potential influence over their followers," who were the passionate mass base of conservatism.[56]

With the advent of the Black Lives Matter movement in the twenty-first century, conservatives recycled theories about Jews, now led by billionaire George Soros, duping Blacks into wrecking Christian civilization in the United States. A 2018 congressional election ad in Minnesota by the National Republican Campaign Committee shows Soros looming over piles of cash with violent images of Black people in the background. The ad labels Soros as the "connoisseur of chaos" and "the funder of the left."[57]

In Texas during the 2020 election, several Republican county chairs circulated a fake flier linking Soros, Black Americans, and Democrats with rampant violence. The flier depicted a masked man beside a Black power symbol: "Get paid to be a . . . Professional Anarchist! Get paid up to $200/Direct Action! Remember, Direct Action Gets The Goods. Contact your local Open Society Foundation Branch." It says, "funded by George Soros" and lists the Thurston County Democrats as contacts.[58]

Other 2020 ads in Texas directly blamed Soros and, by implication, liberals for inciting and funding Black violence. Agriculture Commissioner Sid Miller posted a picture of Soros under the caption: "This man is pure evil." Miller then fabricates a statement that he implies came from Soros. It read, in all capitals: "CLIMATE CHANGE DIDN'T WORK. IMPEACHMENT DIDN'T WORK. THE VIRUS DIDN'T WORK. START THE RACE WAR."[59] Sue Piner, chair of the Comal County Republican Party, posted a harsh picture of Soros with a similar caption, also in capitals: "I PAY WHITE COPS TO MURDER BLACK PEOPLE. AND THEN I PAY BLACK PEOPLE TO RIOT BECAUSE RACE WARS KEEP THE SHEEP IN LINE."

In May 2020, following demonstrations in Minneapolis, influential conservative commentator Candace Owens tweeted, "The Minneapolis chief of police just confirmed that many of the protesters that are burning down the city are NOT FROM MINNEAPOLIS. My guess: As he did with Antifa, Democrat George Soros has these thugs on payroll. He is funding the chaos via his Open Society Foundation." One of her followers responded, "Great time to charge George Soros with terrorism."[60]

After the indictment of Trump by Alvin Bragg, the Black district attorney for New York County, Trump and his allies once again attacked Soros, accusing him of using Black people for political gain. They claimed, as they had with violent Black rioters, that Soros had funded and controlled Bragg. Trump referred to Bragg as "Soros-backed," "Soros-funded," and "Soros-controlled." J. D. Vance tweeted that the prosecutor was "bought by George Soros." Governor Ron DeSantis called the case a "manufactured circus by some Soros-DA." Never mind that Bragg is a graduate of Harvard Law School and a former assistant U.S. attorney. Trump has called him an "animal."

Not surprisingly, white supremacist and anti-Semitic groups have backed Trump. In 2016, the Ku Klux Klan supported Trump for president. Under the banner headline "Make America Great Again," the official Klan newspaper *Crusader* lauded Trump's policies and goals.[61] In November 2016, hundreds of white Christian nationalists gathered to celebrate Trump's victory. In a speech opening the gathering, white supremacist Richard Spencer said, "Hail Trump" and "hail our people," "hail victory!" prompting Nazi-style salutes from the crowd. White supremacist groups such as the Proud Boys and the Oath Keepers would later help organize the January 6 insurrection to keep Trump in power.

This pattern of scapegoating is not new. After World War I, conservatives sounded the alarm about "new" immigrants from Southern and Eastern Europe. They spun an immigration threat narrative that these heavily Jewish and Catholic newcomers, though here legally, brought crime, disease, and radical politics. The immigrants, conservatives charged, threatened traditional culture and the racial purity of the "Anglo-Saxon" or Nordic pioneer stock. John H. Pelletier, the executive secretary of the Morals Efficiency Association of Southern California, warned in 1921 of admitting "aliens from the slums of the cities of the world. They are not of the Nordic race; their love of liberty is not balanced by respect for the law, which is characteristic of Anglo-Saxons. Their religious beliefs, moral principles, and standards of living are far below those of the average American; they are not capable of self-government nor of assimilation." He added that "we have been admitting carriers of venereal disease, potential insane cases, epileptics, criminals, prostitutes, and feeble-minded individuals generally."[62] In 1922, Clinton Stoddard Burr, a frequently cited anti-immigrant conservative, warned that immigration "threatens not alone ourselves, but in an insidious racial degree menaces the blood and character of our descendants to infinite generations; and thus imminently threatens the stability, genius and promise of achievement of the American Commonwealth."[63]

Representative Bertrand Snell (R-NY), chair of the House Rules Committee, said in 1924 that Congress's vote on a proposed immigration restriction bill "will decide the very nature and character of future

America." Congress should act immediately, Snell said, to avoid "being deluged by this threatened migration." Representative Albert Henry Vestal (R-IN) said that "among those who have entered our country are immigrants whose mental, moral, and physical make-up constitute a menace to the political, economic, and social life of the Republic."[64] Representative Grant M. Hudson (R-MI) called the effort to restrict immigration an "epoch-making struggle." The United States, he said, was admitting "innumerable" immigrants "who have had no training or race inheritance in self-government and with ideals far below ours." In a foreshadowing of "Great Replacement Theory," Hudson added, "our American race, the race that made the Nation what it is, is now almost swamped. The present battle will decide whether Americanism shall be effaced from our land or whether it shall be permitted to expand and develop to the freedom and blessing of the human race."[65]

Conservatives drew upon the pseudo-scientific disciplines of racial science and eugenics—selective breeding to improve the race—to amplify their immigrant threat narrative. This extreme variant of Darwinian theory presumed that inherited traits determined the capacities of individuals and races. Conservatives might believe that every soul could be saved, but not that every person or race had the capacity for civilized achievement. Racial science and eugenics backed claims about the superiority of white "Anglo-Saxon" or "Nordic" Protestants from Western Europe as compared to Blacks, other colored peoples, and whites from Southern and Eastern Europe. Japanese and Chinese had a special status as inassimilable competitors to America's "Great Race."

For conservatives, racial science justified their privileges and politics. It replaced social with biological explanations for the prevalence of crime, poverty, and immorality among certain racial groups. It provided a rationale for shutting the country's doors to less fit peoples, strictly punishing crime, legally separating the races, relegating Black people to menial jobs, and barring interracial marriage. It discredited social welfare measures, minimum wages, and rehabilitation programs. It complemented conservative maternalism by elevating motherhood as the duty of racially superior women. The fear of what Theodore Roosevelt had called "race suicide" again raised the specter of defeminized women, too independent and educated for motherly duties. "This contemplation of a career better than motherhood is merely a delusion," Charles W. Eliot, the conservative president emeritus of Harvard, warned the Harvard Dames in 1924.[66]

At the 1921 International Eugenics Congress at the American Museum of Natural History, the *New York Times* reported that participants unanimously agreed that "immigration restriction is essential to prevent the tainting of the race" and "the deterioration of American civilization." Columbia University professor Henry Fairfield Osborn, the president of the Congress and the Museum, said, "We are slowly awakening to the consciousness that education and environment do not fundamentally alter racial values. We are engaged in a serious struggle to maintain our historic republican institutions by barring the entrance of those who are unfit." "There is a new appreciation of the spiritual, intellectual, moral, and physical value of the Nordic race, and that a warning is being given that it must not be too severely depleted by emigration," Osborn said.[67]

Genetics researcher Harry Laughlin, a consultant to the Republican-controlled U.S. House Committee on Immigration, asked rhetorically in a 1924 congressional hearing on immigration restriction if the nation "decides that we have national ideals worth saving, not only in national tradition and individual quality, but also by racial ingredients, the Nation must exercise stricter control over immigration." "We can continue to be American, to recruit to and to develop our racial qualities, or we can allow ourselves to be supplanted by other racial stocks," Laughlin said.[68] Laughlin presented data purportedly showing the intelligence level of various racial and nationality groups. At the bottom was the Russian-born, with 60.4 percent of supposed inferior intelligence, the Italian-born at 63.4 percent, the Polish-born at 69.9 percent, and lastly "U.S. southern Negroes" at 86.2 percent.[69]

In 1924, Congress passed the Johnson–Reed Act, sponsored by two conservative, anti-immigrant Republican lawmakers: Representative Albert Johnson (R-WA) and Senator David Reed (R-PA). The law capped European immigration at about 150,000 per year, with nationality quotas based on the origins of the U.S. population in 1890. This quota system favored Western and Northern Europe at the expense of the heavily Jewish and Catholic countries of Eastern and Southern Europe. The quota for immigrants from Great Britain, for example, with a total population of 43 million, exceeded the combined quotas for Bulgaria, Czechoslovakia,

Estonia, Hungary, Italy, Latvia, Lithuania, Poland, Russia, Romania, and Yugoslavia, with a total population of 257 million.[70] In defense of his quotas, Representative Johnson, a prominent exponent of racial science and eugenics, condemned recent Jewish immigrants as "filthy, un-American, and often dangerous in their habits."[71] Senator Reed said that the new wave of immigrants brings "men of alien speech, thoughts, and habits." Unless policymakers stanch this flow, Reed said, the United States would collapse "the way Rome went."[72]

The Johnson–Reed Act imposed additional controls, requiring entry visas with photographs, and explicitly excluding Japanese and other Asians. In one crucial concession to business, the act exempted most of the Western Hemisphere so that Mexico could continue supplying Western farmers with cheap labor. Unlike Eastern and Southern Europeans, policymakers considered Mexicans to be migrant workers who shuttled between the United States and their homeland according to demands for their labor.

By excluding Blacks, Asians, Latinos, and Native Americans from calculations of U.S. national origins for immigration quotas, the Johnson–Reed Act enshrined whites as a privileged category, legally and culturally. Court decisions that strictly interpreted U.S. law that limited naturalization to "free white persons" and those of African descent reinforced racial standards. The Supreme Court ruled in *U.S. v. Thind* (1923) that an immigrant from India, "a high caste Hindu, although of the Caucasian or Aryan race, is not a white person within the meaning of the naturalization laws," which "were to be interpreted in accordance with the understanding of the common man." The Court recognized that unlike Asians, "immigrants from Eastern, Southern and Middle Europe, among them the Slavs and the dark-eyed, swarthy people of Alpine and Mediterranean stock" merged into the white population "and lose the distinctive hallmarks of their European origin." U.S. society moved toward a polarity between whites and nonwhites as the new immigrants' "distinctive hallmarks" faded after the 1920s. As the *Thind* Court anticipated, however, race continued to be constructed and reconstructed, with opportunities for a decent life turning on both legal and de facto distinctions between whites and nonwhites.[73]

Opponents of these restrictive measures included liberal intellectuals, Jewish and Catholic members of Congress, and Black leaders who objected to reinforcing discrimination. A coalition of prominent opponents led by Louis Marshall, the president of the American Jewish Committee and counsel for the NAACP, futilely urged President Coolidge to veto a bill that "stimulates racial, national and religious hatreds and jealousies" and "encourages one part of our population to arrogate to itself a sense of superiority and to classify another as one of inferiority."[74]

Twenty-first-century conservatives raised another immigration threat narrative against Latinos and Muslims. The culprits had changed, but the charges had not. Conservatives warned of an immigrant invasion by dangerous and diseased persons, a Third World capture of the United States, and the decline of the white race with its traditional culture and values. The conservative Tea Party of the Obama era warned in 2014 that "Washington is not only failing to protect our borders—it's failing to protect our citizens from dangerous, communicable diseases." It claimed that under the Obama administration "sick children and adults flooding our borders . . . are not only allowed to stay, but are being sent to undisclosed locations throughout the United States."[75] A year later, in announcing his 2016 presidential campaign, Donald Trump said, "When Mexico sends its people, they're not sending their best. . . . They're bringing drugs. They're bringing crime. They're rapists." As usual, Trump left himself an escape hatch: "And some, I assume, are good people." Trump broadened his indictment of Mexicans: "It's coming from more than Mexico. It's coming from all over South and Latin America, and it's coming probably—probably—from the Middle East. But we don't know. . . . And it's got to stop and it's got to stop fast."

John Tanton, a latter-day exponent of racial science and eugenics, founded the country's premier conservative anti-immigrant organization, the Federation for American Immigration Reform (FAIR) in 1977. "One of my prime concerns," Tanton wrote to a donor, "is about the decline of folks who look like you and me."[76] "I've come to the point of view that for European-American society and culture to persist requires a European-American majority, and a clear one at that," Tanton said.[77] In 2011, Linda Chavez, the former director of the Office of Public Liaison in the Reagan administration, called Tanton "the most influential unknown man in America."[78] FAIR denigrated nonwhite immigrants as "low IQ" and dangerously prolific "breeders" and warned against "Latino ethic tribalism."[79] FAIR compared an immigration entry center to "a Tenth circle of hell."

It warned that "the American way of life" is at stake in the battle to control undocumented immigration.[80] In a November 2022 fundraising email, FAIR's longtime president, Dan Stein, wrote, "We can't allow the invasion of our borders to destroy our communities."[81]

Tanton initially sought support from both Republicans and Democrats, but he ultimately concluded that Republicans were more likely to benefit from the immigrant threat narrative. FAIR collaborated closely with Republican legislators in Florida to facilitate the enactment of the state's antisanctuary cities law in 2019. FAIR's policies closely mirror priorities of the second Trump administration.

In a 2012 address to a Texas Republican group, Stephen Steinlight, the spokesperson for the Center for Immigration Studies, the "think tank" offshoot of FAIR, said immigration is "about Mexicans." Steinlight interweaved "Mexican" with "illegal" and "criminal" as though they were all equivalent. "Current levels of immigration are much too high" and will "radically transform who and what we are," said Steinlight. "We cannot fix the entire Third World or even Mexico by bringing them all here." He warned that illegal aliens had overflowed our prisons. Mirroring Tanton's political strategy, he claimed that because of Democratic welfare handouts, "Mexicans register Democrat 4 to 1 or [correcting himself] 5 to 1." Thus, the Republican future must be in solidarity with anti-immigrant groups.[82] At an April 2019 Republican-sponsored press conference in Florida, Amapola Hansberger, head of the conservative Legal Immigrants for America (LIFA), warned of "the consequences of permitting open borders and allowing people that have never been vetted to come in—they will kill you."[83]

At a 2022 rally for Republicans, Representative Marjorie Taylor Greene explicitly evoked the "Great Replacement Theory," accusing nonwhite immigrants of "replacing" white Christian Americans. "Joe Biden's five million illegal aliens are on the verge of replacing you, replacing your jobs and replacing your kids in school and, coming from all over the world, they're also replacing your culture," Greene said. "And that's not great for America."[84]

Trump and his allies similarly framed Latino immigration as an invasion. In 2018, Trump tweeted, "Many Gang Members and some very bad people are mixed into the Caravan heading to our Southern Border.

Please go back, you will not be admitted into the United States unless you go through the legal process. This is an invasion of our Country and our Military is waiting for you!"[85] In late September 2024, Trump warned of an American apocalypse from the immigrant invasion. Like Hansberger, he pilloried the supposed immigrant invaders as "stone-cold killers," "worse than any of our criminals," "monsters," and people who "have no heart" and "don't care who they kill."[86]

During his first presidential campaign, Trump warned that Muslims, not just Latino immigrants, threatened the United States. On December 17, 2015, he announced, "Donald J. Trump is calling for a total and complete shutdown of Muslims entering the United States until our country's representatives can figure out what is going on." On March 9, 2016, Trump said, "I think Islam hates us. There's something there that—there's a tremendous hatred there. There's tremendous hatred. We have to get to the bottom of it. There's an unbelievable hatred of us." "This all happened because, frankly, there's no assimilation," Trump later elaborated. "They [Muslims] are not assimilating. . . . They want to go by sharia law. They want sharia law. They don't want the laws that we have. They want sharia law."[87]

FAIR celebrated Trump's proposed Muslim ban: "Both here and in other Western democracies, we are witnessing the radicalization of immigrants and their children in mosques that spread ideologies that are antithetical to those societies," FAIR said in an official statement. "The fact that these domestic incubators of Islamic radicalism are having a greater influence on recently arrived immigrants and their children than the values on which this country was founded is worrisome."[88]

Recent Republican political campaigns in the United States have frequently used immigration, particularly the threat of illegal immigrants, as a core narrative to galvanize their voter base. Over the years, various campaigns have utilized exaggerated or fear-based imagery, often involving Hispanic and Muslim populations, to link immigration with crime, economic strain, and national security risks. These ads and messages consistently play on racial, cultural, and religious fears, using emotionally charged imagery and misinformation to shape public opinion on immigration, positioning nonwhite immigrants, especially those from Hispanic and Muslim communities, as threats to the security and values of naïve-stock Americans.

In his 2010 U.S. senatorial campaign in Louisiana against Democrat Charlie Melancon, David Vitter, the Republican incumbent, ran an ad that showed Hispanic alleged "illegal aliens" sneaking through a hole in a fence and then welcomed by persons wielding a Melancon banner and a giant check made out to "all illegal aliens," signed by Timothy Geithner, Obama's treasury secretary. A band playing "America the Beautiful" celebrates the illegals, who drive away in a limo while they hang their check out of a window, jeering all the way. After the *New Orleans Times-Picayune* slammed Vitter for a racist ad, an edited version included a still photo of three menacing-looking, dark-skinned young Hispanic men staring at the viewer. The image has the caption, "Melancon voted for Benefits for Illegals."[89]

In 2018, the Republican Governors Association aired an ad targeting David Garcia, the Democratic nominee for governor of Arizona. The ad accused Garcia of wanting to abolish Immigration and Customs Enforcement (ICE) and claimed he "won't protect the border. He can't be trusted to keep #Arizona safe." A white woman says that Garcia's policies would increase crime, including sex and drug trafficking, followed by images of police officers making arrests, including a man who appears to have gang tattoos. It depicts a man in a hoodie walking down a dark street while brandishing a knife and a fair-skinned white woman who supposedly represents sex trafficking victims.[90]

During the 2018 Republican primary for governor in Florida, Richard Corcoran, then speaker of the state House of Representatives, released an anti-immigration ad showing a terrified, innocent-looking white girl being gunned down by a fierce-looking Hispanic male. "This could have happened to any family, anywhere," Corcoran narrates. The ad references the shooting of Kate Steinle by an undocumented immigrant, Garcia Zarate, not recently in Florida but three years earlier in San Francisco. Corcoran doesn't mention that Zarate was acquitted of murder and manslaughter charges because, unlike the fictional video, the jury found the shooting to be accidental.[91] Ron DeSantis, who ultimately won the governor's race in Florida, also disseminated an ad that showed him teaching his young daughter how to build a wall with toy blocks to protect against dangerous immigrants.[92] After his victory, DeSantis appointed Corcoran as Florida's commissioner of education and later as president of the newly restructured conservative New College of Florida.

A 2024 ad by the Trump campaign claims President Biden made Vice President Harris the "Border Czar" "to fix immigration," but "she ignored it" and "lied." It showed dark, menacing figures attacking prostrate police officers and immigrants pouring over the border. The ad claimed that the Biden administration had opened the border to "ten million illegal immigrants" leading to "70,000+ deaths annually" from illegal drugs and to migrant "crime out of control." Kamala Harris, the ad warned, is "failed, weak, and dangerously liberal."[93]

Georgia lieutenant governor Casey Cagle, in his 2018 campaign for the Republican gubernatorial nomination, ran an ad featuring several young, tattooed Hispanic men—allegedly members of the violent MS-13 gang—accompanied by the charge that "liberal politicians across the country are shielding criminal illegal aliens and making it possible for them to terrorize us on our streets." The ad shows fearsome men wielding weapons allegedly aimed at law-abiding citizens. These "criminal illegal aliens are spreading across the country," Cagle proclaims.[94] Republicans in other states, including Georgia, New York, and Texas, ran comparable ads with nearly identical stock photos of grim, tattooed young Hispanic men, also supposedly MS-13 members.

In 2022, former Trump aides, now part of Citizens for Sanity, aired an ad during the first game of the World Series blaming President Biden for letting illegal immigrants overrun the United States: "This giant flood of illegal immigration is draining your paychecks, wrecking your schools, ruining your hospitals, threatening your family. Mixed among the masses are drug dealers, sex traffickers and violent predators."[95] A series of Republican ads for the 2022 congressional elections accused President Biden of complicity in the alleged mass murder of Americans by illegal immigrants: "The latest mass murder in America didn't involve guns. It was a direct result of Joe Biden's open-border policy." A 2022 ad by the Republican Party of Texas said, "The Biden administration's failure to secure our southern border has led to a record influx of illegal aliens and illicit drugs. The ads blasted Biden for "allowing illegal immigrants to invade" the United States with "terrorists, drugs, and crime."[96]

Republican ads did not spare the immigrant threat from Muslims. In October 2016, the Kansas Republican Party circulated a mailer that asked, "Have you met the new neighbors? ISIS is not going away anytime soon." It featured a rural landscape with a windmill punctuated by an

ISIS flag and a dangerous-looking figure holding an assault rifle with his face covered by a keffiyeh. The flier said, "Let's keep terrorists out of Kansas!"[97]

Similarly, in 2016, the conservative group Save American Now ran an ad titled "Welcome to the Islamic State of America." It said that "weak leaders have allowed unsecured borders" and let "radical Islamists" infiltrate the county. It warned that these invaders would "practice Jihad" and impose "Sharia law" on the United States. It claimed that "from the Hollywood Hills to the Statue of Liberty, radical Islamic culture has transformed everything." The ad shows Muslims celebrating in front of the White House and the names of Hollywood stars written in Arabic. The Statue of Liberty is dressed in a burqa, holding a star and crescent. The ad concludes with an American flag transformed into an ISIS flag, with voices pledging allegiance to "the Islamic State of America."[98]

During Minnesota's 2016 race in the Eighth Congressional District, Republican candidate Stewart Mills accused his Democratic opponent, Rick Nolan, of facilitating ISIS terrorism in the United States. Mills's ad began: "Minnesota leads the nation in the number of recruits for ISIS. ISIS wants to infiltrate America and they're using Syrians to do it." Nolan, the ad charged, supports bringing "100,000 unvetted Syrians to America before the end of the year and Nolan voted for Hillary Clinton's Iran nuclear deal that gave over $100 billion to the leading sponsor of terrorism." "Rick Nolan is weak and dangerous," the ad warned.[99]

In November 2017, President Trump retweeted three misleading videos produced by Britain's white nationalist group, Britain First, showing Muslims supposedly committing acts of violence and smashing a statue of the Virgin Mary. The most inflammatory video showed an alleged "Muslim migrant" attacking a young boy on crutches. The Dutch attorney general's office, which prosecuted the case, said the suspect was born and raised in the Netherlands. The office does not release data on the religion of suspects.

Trump spokesperson Sarah Huckabee Sanders, now the Republican governor of Arkansas, refused to disavow the videos. The president, she said, "is dealing with those real threats, and those are real no matter how you look at it." A spokesperson for Theresa May, the Conservative Party's prime minister of the UK, said Trump was "wrong" to share the videos.

"Britain First seeks to divide communities through their use of hateful narratives which peddle lies and stoke tensions," May said. The former grand wizard of the Ku Klux Klan enthusiastically endorsed the release of the videos. "Thank God for Trump!" he tweeted. "That's why we love him!"[100]

In Minnesota's 2018 attorney general race, Republican candidate Doug Wardlow sent out a mailer labeling his Muslim opponent Keith Ellison as "one of the most dangerous men in America." Ellison, Wardlow charged, "associated with known terrorists and radical Islamic groups dedicated to destroying America and has sworn to take down our president." "It isn't just that Ellison hangs around with radicals and terrorists. Ellison himself is a radical," said the mailer.[101]

In 2019, conservative commentator Laura Loomer, who won the Republican nomination for Florida's Twenty-First Congressional District in 2020, posted an anti-Muslim video. "But the truth is, is that Islam is a cancer on society," Loomer said. "Islam is a cancer on humanity, and Muslims should not be allowed to seek positions of political office in this country. It should be illegal." In support of Loomer's primary candidacy, President Trump retweeted in all caps, "PLZ $$$ LAURA LOOMER FOR CONGRESS."[102] Loomer lost the general election to her Democratic opponent. Loomer later joined the Trump campaign for its stretch run in 2024.[103]

During the 2020 campaign, a full-page ad created by the far-right Christian organization Ministry for the Future of America appeared in the *Tennessean* newspaper, featuring pictures of President Trump and the pope. The ad warned that "Islam" would detonate a "nuclear device" in the city of Nashville on July 18, demonstrating "the escalating warfare brought by the Islamic religion."[104]

As the presidential campaign started to pick up in December 2023, Trump escalated his denigration of immigrants by channeling the racial determinism of Laughlin, Tanton, and even Adolf Hitler, who had accused Jews of poisoning the German people. During a speech in New Hampshire, he said, "Immigrants are poisoning the blood of our country." Lest there be any confusion, Trump blamed the poisoning on immigrants of color. "They poison mental institutions and prisons all over the world, not just in South America, not just to three or four countries that we think about, but all over the world," Trump said. "They're coming into our country from Africa, from Asia, all over the world." Despite criticism for his Hitlerian rhetoric, Trump doubled down on his claim, saying at a later rally that migrants crossing the southern border "are destroying the blood of our country." Trump's conservative Republican allies did not defend his comments; instead, they blamed them on the Biden administration's border policies. "Unfortunately, that type of rhetoric is what happens when you don't have a border policy that works," said Senator Mike Rounds (R-SD).[105]

At a fundraiser on April 6, 2024, Trump said that he wanted immigrants only from "nice" predominantly white countries. "And when I said, you know, Why can't we allow people to come in from nice countries, I'm trying to be nice," Trump said as the crowd chuckled. "Nice countries, you know like Denmark, Switzerland? Do we have any people coming in from Denmark? How about Switzerland? How about Norway?"[106]

Issues related to sexuality—encompassing women's roles within family and society, nonheterosexuality, and nonbinary identities—intensified the Right's emotionally charged appeals. In the 1920s, historian Kathleen Blee explained, the Ku Klux Klan was "deeply misogynistic despite any kind of rhetoric they have about 'enlisting our sisters in the struggle.'"[107] Men controlled the Klan and excluded women from membership. Women formed an auxiliary, the Women's Ku Klux Klan (WKKK). Although some WKKK leaders advocated for women's (white, native-born Protestants only) equality, the WKKK followed its mission of perpetrating the Klan's racist, anti-Semitic, anti-Catholic, and anti-immigrant ethos.

Klan propaganda asserted that Christianity justified the subordination of women and the male control of their sexuality. The Klan tome *Christ and Other Klansmen* censured "women [who] blasphemed God by disobeying their husbands." Klan leader E. Y. Clarke said there must be a "strong organization constantly preaching that woman's place is in the home." Klan spokesman Samuel Saloman warned that free love "was running wild among the enlightened and emancipated and sex-conscious women of America and Europe." Such liberation, he said, would reduce women to "a harlot," a "clandestine prostitute."[108]

For anti-vice crusaders, censorship laws guarded against the lascivious display of women's bodies. They argued that access to obscene materials, contraception, and abortion led to promiscuity, perversion, broken marriages and families, and women liberated from the control of men. Conservatives cautioned against radicals who would tear children from their homes and raise them in state-run nurseries, claiming these radicals would dismantle sexual restraint and manly competition. They feared a reversal of sex roles that feminized men and coerced women into "unnatural" masculine roles through forced labor and conscription. Conservative women perceived a threat in those who embraced the era's unisex hedonism, characterized by short skirts, bobbed hair, drinking, smoking, vigorous sports, and sensual music. The music director of the General Federation of Women's Clubs described jazz as "the accompaniment of the voodoo dancer, stimulating the half-crazed barbarian to the vilest deeds." It was an "expression of protest against law and order, that Bolshevik element of license striving for expression in music."[109]

In the 1920s, conservatives mounted campaigns against what they termed "smut." The prewar trend of increased sexual experience before or outside of marriage accelerated. Skirts and bathing suits rose above the knee, and popularized Freudian psychology touted sex as healthy and repression harmful. Sexuality became increasingly visible in popular culture, while risqué materials fueled an underground market for pulp novels, lurid memoirs, and pornographic magazines. Conservative journalist Frank Kent warned that the "great bumper American smut crop" posed "a greater menace to the future than any communistic, socialistic, or Bolshevistic propaganda."[110] Society was "assailed on all sides by a million erotic stimuli—in literature, in the theatre, and in life," wrote popular philosopher and historian Will Durant in 1929. "The sexual instinct escaped from the jail in which Puritanism had imprisoned it and ran amuck in the streets."[111]

Moral reformers intertwined their anti-smut campaign with conservative opposition to immigration, claiming that smut thrived symbiotically with subversion, feminism, and the perceived low morals of new immigrants from Southern and Eastern Europe. "The parlor Bolshevists in literary and art circles," wrote John S. Sumner, head of the New York Society for the Suppression of Vice, "are just as great a menace" as political agitators. "While the governmental authorities are struggling against foreign ideas and their advocates regarding political attack," he said, "we have had the same conflict with foreign ideas calculated and intended *to break down American standards of decency and morality*." Sumner warned that "sex antagonism" brought on by "radical feminists" will "eventually break down the moral fiber of the nation."[112]

Conservatives won the biggest cultural battle of the early twentieth century through the self-censorship of an immoral, unconstrained movie industry, the public's predominant form of entertainment. Conservatives pushed hard for the censorship of movies, which they viewed as dominated by shameless Jewish entrepreneurs. The United States needed to rescue the film industry "from the devil and the hands of 500 un-Christians," said Reverend Wilbur Fiske Crafts, one of the country's first professional religious lobbyists.[113] Conservatives failed to gain federal regulation of the movies but won self-censorship by the movie industry and the strengthening of regulation by the states. Hollywood adopted self-regulation to avert federal regulation and ease pressure from religious leaders and the movies' financiers. Presbyterian elder and former Republican Party chair Will H. Hays headed a new professional association, the Motion Picture Producers and Distributors of America, which adopted a voluntary production code in 1930.

The Code, which became mandatory in 1934, reinforced right-wing views on race, religion, sexual expression, obscenity, homosexuality, and the family. It said, "No picture shall be produced that will lower the moral standards of those who see it." The Code banned the depiction of "*Miscegenation* (sex relationships between the white and black races)." Movies must not mention Jesus Christ, "except in reverence." They must not ridicule "good, innocence, morality or justice," "law, natural or divine," and "*ministers of religion*." There could be no showing of "excessive and lustful kissing, lustful embraces, suggestive postures and gestures" or any inference "that low forms of sex relationship are the accepted or common thing." Movies must not depict "*sex perversion* or any inference to it," or include "obscenity in word, gesture, reference, song, joke, or by suggestion." Always, "The sanctity of the institution of marriage and the home shall be upheld."[114]

Conservative Catholics, organized into a Legion of Decency, joined evangelical Protestants in a rare collaboration to censor the movies. Catholic journalist Joseph Breen headed the new Code Administration. Not just anti-Semitism but anti-Catholicism pervaded evangelical Protestantism in the early twentieth century. It would be many decades before evangelical Protestant conservatism reconciled with a politically conservative Catholicism that put anticommunism, defense of private enterprise property, and Victorian morals above church teachings on poverty, labor, war and peace, and the death penalty.

Conservatives grew increasingly alarmed in the 1960s and 70s as sexual activity escalated, and the women's movement demanded sexual freedom and challenged traditional family dynamics as a tool of male control. In 1960, the U.S. Food and Drug Administration approved the birth control pill. A feature in *U.S. News* asked, "Is the Pill regarded as a license for promiscuity? Can its availability to all women of childbearing age lead to sexual anarchy?" Renowned author Pearl Buck warned the pill's "potential effect upon our society may be even more devastating than the nuclear bomb."[115]

Other disturbing trends followed: in 1968, Hollywood replaced the production code with a new film-rating system. Divorce rates and out-of-wedlock births soared, with more single parents or unmarried partners raising children. By the 1970s, the traditional nuclear family—consisting of husbands, wives, and children—made up only about a third of families. The feminist movement became more prominent and assertive. In response, Pat Buchanan, in 1971, called for a return to authority, advocating conservative interpretations of white Christian values. "It has been elitist assaults on traditional morality and traditional patriotism that have helped to weaken and destroy the ties between the young and the Church, and the young and the government," Buchanan said. "To the central crisis—the crisis of authority—they offer less than nothing."[116]

The situation darkened further for conservative moralists in the early 1970s when Congress sent the Equal Rights Amendment (ERA) to the states for ratification, and the Supreme Court established abortion as a constitutional right. These events prompted conservatives to retool their rhetoric, if not the substance of their defense of women's traditional roles in society. They recast themselves as positive and forward-looking "pro-family" champions of "family values," portraying liberals as adversaries of these virtuous ideals. For Christian conservatives, the feminist revolution, the ERA, and *Roe v. Wade* threatened the divinely ordained, hierarchical nuclear family. In her bestseller *The Total Woman* (1973),

Marabel Morgan argued for a subordinate role for women, claiming men would richly reward such a stance. "God ordained man to be the head of the family, its president," Morgan said. She advised her female readers, "Your husband is what he is. Accept him as that." Thus, "a Total Woman caters to her man's special quirks, whether it be in salads, sex, or sports." This subordination, she claimed, was a good deal for the "Total Woman" who would win love, sex, physical protection, and financial support from their men.

Phyllis Schlafly, who organized the campaign that halted ratification of the ERA, took the lead in rallying conservatives behind a passionate pro-family agenda, also with a distinctly subordinate but allegedly rewarding role for women. The family, she said, is "the basic unit of society, which is ingrained in the laws and customs of our Judeo-Christian civilization," with men at the head and women deriving the benefits claimed by the "Total Woman." In 1975, Schlafly founded her pro-family Eagle Forum as a membership organization that strived to preserve "the family as the basic unit of society, with certain rights and responsibilities, including the right to insist that the schools permit voluntary prayer and teach the fourth 'R' (right and wrong) according to the precepts of the Holy Scriptures." Two years later, Schlafly founded the Pro-Family Coalition, published *The Power of the Positive Woman* (1977), and organized a well-attended "Pro-Family Rally" that upstaged the feminist "International Year of the Woman" gathering in Houston, Texas, and inspired other women activists. She warned that feminists were "going to drive the homemaker out of the home. . . . They want to relieve mothers of the menial task of taking care of their babies. They want to put them in the coal mines and have them digging ditches." The bottom line for Schlafly and other pro-family conservatives is to confine women's sexuality to marriage and their lives to the home, with men in control and women dependent on male goodwill and generosity.[117]

Schlafly helped revive grassroots conservatism, gaining right-wing acclaim as the unmovable force that halted the seemingly unstoppable momentum of the ERA just three states shy of ratification. Although she claimed to represent ordinary people opposed to liberal elites, Schlafly mobilized an antipluralist minority to block an amendment supported by Congress, state legislatures representing three-quarters of Americans, and two-thirds or more of nationwide survey respondents.

The broader conservative movement aligned with Schlafly's warnings on unchecked female sexuality, perceived threats to the traditional male-headed family, and the quest for gender equality. This ideology reinforced male dominance and maintained women's subordinate role in society. In his "cultural war" speech at the 1992 Republican National Convention, Pat Buchanan mocked Hillary Clinton to a cheering response. "Hillary believes that 12-year-olds should have a right to sue their parents, and she has compared marriage as an institution to slavery," Buchanan said. "Friends, this is radical feminism . . . abortion on demand, a litmus test for the Supreme Court, homosexual rights, discrimination against religious schools, women in combat—that's change, all right," but "not the kind of change we can tolerate in a nation that we still call God's country."[118]

When Hillary Clinton joined the debates over welfare reform, Governor Tommy Thompson (R-WI) responded, "We've finally got the chance to move people off welfare, and we really don't need the tender loving care of Hillary Clinton to mess it up."[119] It was not just the men belittling Clinton. Conservative commentator Laura Ingraham said in 2000, "Certainly she is not a good role model for women. Her personal life has turned into a bizarre, sad relationship where both husband and wife depend in desperate and unhealthy ways on each other at different times of their lives. . . . Hillary is a road map on how not to lead your life as a young woman today." Ingraham concluded that "Hillary is mostly the product of her marriage, and her main work has been to prop up her husband's political career."[120]

In March 2007, with Clinton preparing to run for president, conservative host Glenn Beck said on his radio show, "She's the stereotypical bitch. You know what I mean? She's that stereotypical nagging—[screeching]. You know what I mean?"[121] In December 2007, after Clinton had declared for the presidency, Rush Limbaugh asked, "Will Americans want to watch a woman get older before their eyes on a daily basis?"[122] In 2013, looking ahead to a Clinton campaign in 2016, the seventy-four-year-old Senate leader Mitch McConnell said in a speech at the Conservative Political Action Conference, "Don't tell me Democrats are the party of the future when their presidential ticket for 2016 is shaping up to look like a rerun of the 'Golden Girls.'"[123]

In 2012, after Congress enacted the Affordable Care Act (2010), Georgetown University law student Sandra Fluke testified before Congress about the excessive cost of contraception and argued against religious exceptions for contraceptives under insurance plans. Limbaugh responded by calling her a "slut" and a "prostitute." "Who goes before a congressional committee and essentially says that she must be paid to have sex, what does that make her?" Limbaugh asked. "It makes her a slut, right? It makes her a prostitute. She wants to be paid to have sex." "She wants you and me and the taxpayers to pay her to have sex. What does that make us? We're the pimps. (interruption) The johns? We would be the johns? No! We're not the johns."[124] "So, Ms. Fluke and the rest of you feminazis, here's the deal," Limbaugh later said. "If we are going to pay for your contraceptives, and thus pay for you to have sex, we want something for it, and I'll tell you what it is. We want you to post the videos online so we can all watch."[125]

During the 2016 campaign, Trump said, "the only card she [Clinton] has is the woman's card. She's got nothing else going on. And frankly, if Hillary Clinton were a man, I don't think she'd get 5 percent of the vote. The only thing she's got going is the women's vote. And the beautiful thing is that women don't like her, OK?" He later emphasized, "If she didn't play the woman's card she would have no chance, I mean zero, of winning." Trump added, "I just don't think she has a presidential look. And you need a presidential look. You have to get the job done." During the last presidential debate, when Clinton began talking about Trump's taxes, he interrupted: "Such a nasty woman."[126]

A Trump ad during the campaign showed selected footage of Hillary Clinton stumbling and coughing. The narrative said Clinton lacked the "fortitude, strength, or stamina to lead in our world."[127] Newt Gingrich joined in, telling Fox News host Sean Hannity, "This coughing stuff, I hope [Hillary's] all right. It's a little disturbing." During this warning, Gingrich began coughing. "Now you sound like Hillary," Hannity joked. "By the way, yours didn't last four minutes and 20 seconds, thank God." Gingrich responded, "No, I'm in good shape. At least I'm in better shape than Hillary."[128] During the 1990s debates about women in the military, Gingrich had questioned women's fitness for combat. "Females have biological problems staying in a ditch for 30 days because they get infections, and they don't have upper body strength," Gingrich said.[129]

In late September 2024, Trump claimed that if elected, he and other men would take care of women. They would not have to worry or think for themselves about anything, including decisions about their reproductive lives. "You will no longer be abandoned, lonely or scared," Trump said. "You will no longer be in danger. You will no longer have anxiety from all of the problems our country has today. You will be protected, and I will be your protector." And yes, "You will no longer be thinking about abortion."[130]

Trump's 2024 running mate, Senator Vance, had disparaged women by denouncing the Democratic Party as being run by "childless cat ladies." In a 2021 interview, Vance said that the Democrats and corporate elites are run by "a bunch of childless cat ladies who are miserable at their own lives and the choices that they've made and so they want to make the rest of the country miserable, too." "And how does it make any sense that we've turned our country over to people who don't really have a direct stake in it?" Vance later tried to walk back this insult, saying he had directed his criticism not at people without children but at the Democratic Party for being "anti-family and anti-child."[131]

In 1998, the Southern Baptist Association revised its "Baptist Faith and Message" to explicitly subordinate women to men. "A wife is to submit herself graciously to the servant leadership of her husband even as the church willingly submits to the headship of Christ," the new message said. The husband, in turn, "has the God-given responsibility to provide for, to protect, and to lead his family."[132] In June 2023, 12,737 members of the Southern Baptist Convention (SBC), still the largest Protestant denomination, though with a slightly shrinking membership, attended the church's annual convention in New Orleans. The convention reaffirmed its doctrine of wifely submission and issued dire warnings about our failing culture. Speakers told of a "teetering" nation, "sexual insanity," threats to "real men," "all this trans stuff," and a "culture" that "descends into a spiritual abyss."[133]

The perils faced by Christianity in the United States figured prominently at the gathering. "Things have changed in America," said pastor Tom Wilder to a reporter. "I believe we're in an anti-Christian nation." Ryan Helfenbein, executive director of Liberty University's Standing for Freedom Center, told the convention that a "biblical world view" was on the decline. "The nation certainly was formed and founded by Christians.

It was shaped by the pulpit, and I think it's going to take the pulpit to save the nation."[134]

The delegates, known as "messengers," overwhelmingly voted to prohibit women from serving as pastors in affiliated churches and expelled two congregations with women pastors. Control remains firmly in male hands across nearly 50,000 SBC affiliated churches. At a breakfast hosted by the Conservative Baptist Network, evangelist Tim Lee said that we need women "working in our churches. We just don't need you to be the pastors of our churches."[135] As in the family, the church should benefit from women's labor while keeping men in control.

Church leader Albert Mohler defended the ban on women pastors by appealing to divine authority: "It's a matter of biblical commitment, a commitment to the scripture that unequivocally, we believe, limits the office of pastor to men. It is an issue of biblical authority." The exclusion of women is "high on the list of contemporary concerns precisely because it's one of the issues that has been a sign of creeping liberalism." Pastor Linda Barnes-Popham, an equally devout evangelical who had ministered to the expelled Fern Creek Baptist Church for thirty years, disagreed: "I believe every word in the Bible, but there are passages such as those in 1st Timothy, in Corinthians that our church would interpret differently than Albert Mohler interprets them." She denounced church leaders as hypocrites who have construed scripture for their self-serving ends. "The Bible has been used like a weapon of some of these folks," she said, "a weapon against those of us who believe it as strongly as they do. We just interpret it differently."[136]

Only the more conservative Protestant denominations in the United States prohibit the ordination of women. Most agree with Barnes-Popham and ordain women pastors, including the United Methodist Church, Presbyterian Church USA, Salvation Army, Evangelical Lutheran Church in America, Unitarian Universalist Church, Society of Friends (Quakers), Disciples of Christ, United Church of Christ, Episcopal Church in the USA, Assemblies of God, Brethren, and the Mennonite Church USA.[137] Unlike the SBC, other less conservative Baptist groups ordain women pastors, including the Cooperative Baptist Fellowship and the Alliance of Baptists; as of 2017, 174 women had served as pastors in these two Baptist groups.[138]

The experience of women in the SBC challenges the conservative claim that women gain love and protection from their subordination to men. Church messengers in New Orleans voted to ban women pastors just a year after the Guidepost report found rampant sexual abuse of women within the SBC. The same executive committee of the SBC that covered up and enabled this abuse orchestrated the vote to limit the ministry to men. The conservative evangelical journal *Christianity Today* noted that the issue of "sexual abuse in churches—almost receded into the background at this year's [2023] gathering, which was overrun by debates around women serving as pastors." Efforts to address the abuse, the journal reported, "have been slow, complicated, and not without controversy."[139]

Abuse survivor Christa Brown blasted the SBC's reforms as "image repair strategies" that failed "to reckon with the human cost of its decades-long travesty." She insisted that abuse within the SBC was systematic, not random. "I do not believe people within the SBC have even begun to reckon with the depth and scope of the harm they have done—individually, collectively and institutionally."[140]

In the Catholic Church, women have remained under male control, with the Church's socially conservative male leadership resisting all calls to expand the role of women in the Church. In his 1994 apostolic letter, "On Reserving Priestly Ordination to Men Alone," the socially conservative Pope John Paul II quotes Pope Paul VI saying that the exclusion of women is found in "the example recorded in the Sacred Scriptures of Christ choosing his Apostles only from among men; the constant practice of the Church, which has imitated Christ in choosing only men; and her living teaching authority which has consistently held that the exclusion of women from the priesthood is in accordance with God's plan for his Church."[141] Advocates for the ordination of women, such as Jane Via, ordained as a priest in an unsanctioned ceremony, disagree. "There are no scriptural barriers to the ordination of women," Via said, "and in the first 300–400 years of the early church I believe the evidence shows clearly included the ordination of women as deacons, the ordination of women as priests, and the ordination of women as bishops."[142]

In a 2022 interview, Pope Francis reiterated that the biblical foundations of the Church forbid the ordination of women, suggesting they should contribute to the Church "the administrative way." He said women do a "better job" than men at managing things.[143] Thus, men remain in control while women do their busy work. As in the SBC, male control has not prevented but facilitated horrific sexual abuse among the all-male priesthood, likewise covered up by Church officials.

On abortion, conservative Catholics first led the campaign against the *Roe* decision, then were joined by evangelical Protestants. Joint opposition to what they called aborted babies contributed to a rapprochement between conservative Catholics and Protestants. *Roe*'s opponents marched in the streets and advocated for a constitutional amendment to protect the unborn, which became an enduring plank of the Republican Party platform starting in 1976, until excluded for political reasons in 2024.

Adherents of the movement they dubbed "right to life" filed lawsuits challenging *Roe*, which ultimately succeeded in the *Dobbs* case when a 6 to 3 conservative Court overturned the decision in June 2022. Chief Justice John Roberts said, "The hardest decision I had to make was whether to erect fences and barricades around the Supreme Court,"[144] after the leaking of the *Dobbs* decision—harder, apparently, than denying countless women the right to control their reproduction—a right that had existed for fifty years. After the *Dobbs* ruling, twenty-one Red states banned abortions, with most lacking exceptions for rape or incest. In these states, antiabortion advocates claimed to be protecting innocent lives, even if in the womb.

Since the erotically charged society of the 1920s, conservatives have stirred fears that Americans, especially the young, were falling victim to deviant sexuality, such as prostitution, oral sex, and homosexuality, the perpetrators of venereal disease. After World War I, efforts to prevent venereal disease through education and the administration of chemical prophylaxis that had been effective for U.S. soldiers gave way to moral uplift and law enforcement. For moral reformers of the 1920s, preventative measures only encouraged prostitution and promiscuity. Their solution was to restore the moral integrity of society and rigorously prosecute prostitutes and other sex offenders. Congress failed to renew wartime appropriations for controlling venereal disease, and state censorship boards banned as obscene films and other forms of antivenereal propaganda.[145]

Widespread prejudice against homosexuality led many LGBTQ persons to conceal their sexual preference through "lavender marriages," heterosexual unions for show. Though theaters and speakeasies of the 1920s occasionally showcased homosexual displays, such expressions dwindled as the end of Prohibition and the onset of the Great Depression prompted a crackdown on homosexuals. The Hays Code further eradicated homosexual characters from films.

During the Cold War, conservatives exploited the Lavender Scare of homosexuals for political gain. Conservatives targeted homosexuals to galvanize their voter base with minimal risk. They accused homosexuals of disrupting traditional values, weakening the family, and aiding communist agendas. Senator Kenneth Wherry (R-NE), exploited the widespread homophobia and anticommunist sentiment of the 1950s when he accused the Truman administration of "dereliction to duty in the executive branch in permitting these moral perverts to obtain reemployment." He said there were "holes in the system" that enabled homosexuals to slip through. Guy George Gabrielson, the chair of the Republican National Committee, distributed a newsletter warning that "the sexual perverts" who had "infiltrated our Government" were "perhaps as dangerous as the actual Communists." Representative Cliff Clevenger (R-OH) told of "a cell of perverts hiding around Government," protected by "the sob sisters and thumb-sucking liberals."[146]

The coordinated campaign against homosexuals and communists worked politically for conservatives. In 1952, Republicans won the White House and both chambers of Congress for the first time since 1928. Although several factors contributed to this Republican triumph, the historian Randolph W. Baxter concluded that Senator Wherry, in pursuit of "extreme partisanship" had "managed to turn the single issue of closing the homosexual security gap from a six-week 'preliminary investigation' into a five-month full-Senate-subcommittee inquiry." The well-publicized inquiry "further discredited the Truman administration at a time when it was already drawing blistering fire from McCarthyite anti-Communists."[147] The first scientific national survey on homosexuals by Louis Harris and Associates in 1965 found that 70 percent of respondents said that homosexuals were more harmful than helpful to American life, only 1 percent said they were more helpful, and 29 percent said it didn't matter.

In the 1970s, the Right reignited its politically motivated antihomosexual campaign. A 1978 survey by Yankelovich, Skelly, and Wright found that 59 percent of respondents deemed homosexual relationships unacceptable for anyone, 35 percent said such relationships were only acceptable for others, and 6 percent found them acceptable for both others and themselves. As gays and lesbians began to demand the same rights as racial minorities, conservatives spotlighted the perceived threat to traditional family life posed by the "homosexual lifestyle" and concerns over the recruitment of children.

Pop singer and Florida orange juice spokesperson Anita Bryant brought the Right's vision of a gay menace to a national spotlight when she formed Save Our Children in 1977 to oppose a Dade County gay rights ordinance. She accused gay and lesbian activists of launching a "disguised attack on God" and "recruiting children" to their immoral way of life: "What's happening is that, in the name of human rights, vice is becoming virtuous." Bryant complained of reverse discrimination against straight parents and defended "the civil rights of parents to save their children from homosexual influence." With conservatives from across the country rallying to her aid, Bryant secured the signatures needed to submit the ordinance to a referendum of voters, the first of its kind in the nation. Voters rejected the ordinance by a two-to-one margin, but the battle over gay and lesbian rights continued.[148]

The protection of marriage, children, and the family from the "gay lifestyle" became a driving force for recruitment and fundraising on the right. Reverend Robert Billings, an advocate for private Christian schools who became Reagan's "religious coordinator" for the 1980 campaign, said, "We need an emotionally charged issue to stir up people and get them mad enough to get them up from watching TV and do something. I believe that the homosexual issue is the issue we should use." Even the National Conservative Political Action Committee (NCPAC), headed by closeted homosexual Terry Dolan, warned in a fund-raising letter, "Our nation's moral fiber is being weakened by the growing homosexual movement and the fanatical ERA pushers (many of whom publicly brag they are lesbians)." Some libertarians, such as David Brudnoy, a Boston-based talk show host, questioned a campaign that said such things as "Kill a Queer for Christ" and charged "that the drought in California is God's punishment because of liberalized sex laws there. . . . Good Lord!" He wondered how the Right could "forget all the conservative great men and women of our time who are, or were, homosexuals." However, most conservatives, including *National Review* and *Human Events* editors, fell in line.[149]

In the second decade of the twenty-first century, conservatives reignited their crusade against nonheterosexuals, adding transgender and nonbinary persons. The U.S. Supreme Court legalized same-sex marriage in 2015, and the percentage of young Americans identifying as lesbian, gay, bisexual, or transgender was on the rise. Conservatives raised the alarm over these events to rally their base, demonize the opposition, and drive fundraising. Future Speaker Mike Johnson said of the same-sex marriage decision, "If activist judges can reject thousands of years of history and legitimize homosexual marriage, then transsexual and group marriages of every sort follow. Experts project that homosexual marriage is the dark harbinger of chaos and sexual anarchy that could doom even the strongest Republic."[150] The new Lavender Scare took hold among Republicans. A Gallup survey found that in just one year, the percentage of Republicans believing that same-sex relationships are morally acceptable tumbled from 56 percent in 2022 to 41 percent in 2023.

After Florida enacted its "Don't Say Gay" bill, Governor DeSantis resurrected inflammatory claims, reminiscent of the Johns Committee, saying that students "should be protected from schools using classroom instruction to sexualize their kids as young as 5 years-old."[151] The Florida Family Policy Council, an advocacy group for the bill, said that it was "necessary because government schools in the US have become ideological, political and are more interested in shaping a child's politics and sexual inclinations than they are in teaching academics of reading, writing, math, and education."[152] Even Representative Marjorie Taylor Greene's claim that pedophiles run the Democratic Party resonated with conservatives, 49 percent of whom say that "top Democrats are involved in elite child sex-trafficking rings," according to a 2022 poll.[153]

Conservatives again stirred fear and disgust by conjuring images of predatory gay men posing as trans women invading women's bathrooms. In 2014, the city of Houston was considering an ordinance to forbid discrimination based on sexual orientation, which would bring it in line with almost every other big city. Dr. Ed Young, pastor of a conservative Houston megachurch, charged that the ordinance would open "ladies' restrooms . . . to men who feel or claim to feel that they are women. As a result, restrooms, showers, and locker rooms throughout Houston will be open to sexual predators who can use this proposed ordinance as cover of protection to violate women and children."[154] This bathroom panic harkens back to arguments against the ERA and claims by white supremacists during Jim Crow that integration would give Black male predators access to white female victims. [155]

In recent years, Republicans have capitalized on emotionally charged issues surrounding LGBTQ and transgender rights for fundraising purposes. The *New York Times* reported in 2023 that opposition to transgender care "has reinvigorated a network of conservative groups, increased fund-raising, and set the agenda in school boards and state legislatures." Matt Sharp, the senior counsel for the Christian conservative Alliance Defending Freedom, said that issues revolving around transgender orientation have created "a sense of urgency." He reported that these issues had driven thousands of new donors to the Alliance.[156] The American Principles Project, another Christian conservative group that recently focused on transgender care, spent less than $1 million in the 2020 elections but upped its spending to $7 million in the 2022 contests.[157]

Ron DeSantis, a candidate for the 2024 Republican presidential nomination, issued an appeal for donations with the headline, "Do not tell my children that men can get pregnant." The email asked, "Why do Joe Biden and the Left think it's common sense to salute the Pride Flag? Or fly it equal to our American Flag? Why does the Left find it appropriate to applaud a group of topless transgender women on the White House lawn at a 'family-friendly event' where children were present?"[158]

During his campaign for the 2024 presidential nomination, Trump said, if reelected president, he would ask Congress "to pass a bill establishing that the only genders recognized by the United States government are male and female, and they are assigned at birth," and that he will "sign a new executive order instructing every federal agency to cease all programs that promote the concept of sex and gender transition at any age."[159]

In April 2024, the Vatican starkly condemned gender-affirming surgery. Pope Francis's *Dignitas infinita* railed against any effort to obscure "the sexual difference between man and woman." It linked this condemnation to its affirmation that life begins at conception: "It follows that any sex-change intervention, as a rule, risks threatening the unique dignity the person has received from the moment of conception." It adds that gender-affirming surgery "intends to deny the greatest possible difference that exists between living beings: sexual difference," which is "the most beautiful and most powerful of them." The document opposed surrogate births, but it also condemned criminal penalties for homosexuality.[160]

Since the 1920s, conservatives have effectively mobilized their base while marginalizing opposition by emphasizing an "us versus them" narrative: Christians versus Jews, whites versus Blacks, immigrants versus natives, men versus women, straight versus gay, and binary versus non-binary gender. Beyond policy matters such as spending, taxation, regulation, infrastructure, health care, or welfare, cultural challenges have posed an existential threat to conservatives' vision of right and wrong and the country they hold dear.

Cultural warfare matters most at a time when the white and Christian share of the electorate is declining, and the nonreligious vote is ascending. From the election of Ronald Reagan in 1980 to the defeat of Trump in 2020, the percentage of non-Hispanic whites in the electorate has tumbled from 88 percent to 67 percent, and the percentage of Christians from 90 percent to 68 percent. The percentage of voters without a religious affiliation soared from 5 percent to 22 percent. Senator Lindsey Graham had a point when he admitted in 2012 that the challenge for Republicans is that "we're not generating enough angry white guys to stay in business for the long term."[161]

Since then, the priority for Republicans has been to mobilize as much of their shrinking voter base as possible and to capitalize on the cultural conservativism, antifeminism, anti-Semitism, and opposition to undocumented immigrants that characterize a segment of minority voters. A 2023 NBC News poll asked respondents to choose between the objectives of "promoting greater respect for traditional social and moral values" and "encouraging greater tolerance of people with different lifestyles and backgrounds." The poll found that 51 percent of whites, 48 percent of Blacks, and 51 percent of Hispanics chose "traditional values," whereas 40 percent of whites, 47 percent of Blacks, and 44 percent of Hispanics chose "tolerance of different lifestyles."[162]

For conservatives, culture wars packed an emotional wallop that policy issues lacked. "Everything Is the Culture War Now," the *National Review* observed in a 2023 headline. Republican "candidates have all kinds of policy proposals, but it's the culture-war stuff that gets the crowds jazzed," the editors observed. "What kind of gender-change procedures should be legal for those under age 18, if any; whether schools should inform parents about the pronouns their child prefers; whether those born men should compete in women's sports; whether the Disney Corporation is attempting to indoctrinate the young fans of its pop-culture offerings." They noted that, unlike attacks on LGBTQ or transgender persons, "arguments about economics and foreign policy do not get the blood pumping."[163]

12

DONALD TRUMP AND CONSERVATISM

Much conventional wisdom contends that Donald Trump has betrayed conservatism. "Don't dare call [Trumpism] conservative—Republicans who follow Trump have betrayed their philosophy," political commentator S. E. Cupp said. "Conservatism, rightly understood and not misappropriated by a president who couldn't spell it if he had to, is a set of principles espousing free enterprise, limited government, fiscal austerity, deregulation, a strong national defense and free trade. Social conservatism supports Judeo-Christian values, including a respect for life."[1] Political analyst Brian Stewart said that Trump has "stripped his party and American politics of its high purpose and nobility. The hundred-year war for American conservatism has taken a mighty long time to be so lavishly betrayed, and so decisively lost."[2]

Conservative radio host Charles J. Sykes said in 2018, "As a conservative, I despair at Republicans' support for Trump. His vision is not conservatism. It's hard to refute those who say Trump is the product of conservatism but refute them we must. We are better than this."[3] Renowned conservative columnist George Will said in 2021 that Trump "made me realize that conservatism was a label that could be hijacked."[4] Bill Kristol, the former editor of the conservative *Weekly Standard*, said in 2022, "It would be foolish to watch Trump take over the Republican Party—to watch so many conservative elites rationalize and acquiesce and enable Trump—and then say, 'Conservatism is totally healthy.' You can't say that with a straight face."[5]

If Trump has betrayed conservatism, why have rank-and-file and elite conservatives lined up behind him for nearly a decade? Trump's conservative support lasted and grew through two impeachments, devastating civil verdicts against him, and ninety-one state and federal felony counts, after which "Watergate looks downright quaint," said journalist Linda Feldman.[6] His conservative support persisted through thirty-four felony convictions for defrauding the electorate and government by falsifying hush money payments to a porn star as legal work. Political scientist Hans Noel of Georgetown University noted that for Trump, "You can say, 'That's not real conservatism.'" However, "at the end of the day, you're wrong if no one agrees with you."[7]

In the 2016 presidential election, Trump secured 81 percent of the conservative vote, which increased to 85 percent in 2020, and 90 percent in 2024, surpassing all Republican candidates since exit polling began in the 1970s, including Ronald Reagan. An average of 86 percent of Republicans approved of his performance as president, starkly contrasting to just 6 percent of Democrats. Interestingly, Republicans rated Trump as significantly more conservative in 2022 than in 2016, with his ranking rising from 6.5 to 8.0 on a scale of 1 to 10.[8] Polling from primary elections through Super Tuesday 2024 found that approximately 90 percent of very conservative voters backed Trump, compared to a minority of moderates. Trump's sweep of the Super Tuesday primaries guaranteed him the delegates needed for his renomination.

Trump has maintained near unanimous support among Republicans in Congress. In the House, no Republican voted for the articles in Trump's first impeachment in December 2019; only 10 of 211 voted for his second impeachment in January 2021. Of the ten who voted for impeachment, four lost their seats in Republican primaries to Trump-backed opponents, and four chose to retire, leaving only two in office after the 2022 election.[9] The two most outspoken Trump critics in the House, Liz

Cheney (R-WY) and Adam Kinzinger (R-IL), joined the Democratic-led January 6 Committee and were censured by the Republican National Committee. Cheney lost her seat in the 2022 Republican primary, and Kinzinger retired from Congress.

In the Senate, Mitt Romney (R-UT) was the only Republican to vote for conviction in Trump's first trial. Seven Republicans, including Romney, voted for conviction in Trump's second trial. Only one of the seven faced the voters in 2022, Lisa Murkowski of Alaska, who won reelection and is considering leaving the Republican Party.[10] The Republican Party in Louisiana censured Senator Bill Cassidy, but he will not face reelection until 2026. Similarly, Senator Susan Collins (R-ME), a rare Republican moderate, is not up for reelection until 2026. Senator Romney chose not to seek reelection in 2024. Richard Burr (R-NC), Pat Toomey (R-PA), and Ben Sasse (R-NE) have since left the Senate. Of Congress's most vocal critics of Trump, only Romney remained in office through 2023 but will depart in 2025.[11]

In October 2023, the U.S. House Republicans unanimously elected the pro-Trump Mike Johnson as Speaker. Johnson had enthusiastically enlisted in Trump's crusade to overturn Biden's victory in the 2020 election. He stands with Trump on every major domestic issue and shares Trump's reluctance to back NATO or provide military assistance to Ukraine. Trump had torpedoed Tom Emmer's (R-MN) candidacy, which had won a majority vote in the GOP caucus. Trump derided Emmer as "totally out-of-touch with Republican Voters" and a "Globalist RINO."[12]

However, not only Trump but also his conservative predecessor, George W. Bush, has faced accusations of betraying conservatism from self-proclaimed guardians of the conservative cause. In 2006, conservative fundraiser Richard Viguerie said that "George W. Bush and other big government Republicans hijacked the conservative cause." Bruce Bartlett, a White House aide to Ronald Reagan, called Bush a "pretend conservative" who "betrayed the Reagan Legacy." In the unkindest cut of all, patriarch William F. Buckley Jr. said, "If you had a European prime minister who experienced what we've experienced it would be expected that he would retire or resign."[13]

Business executives mostly counted their money from the Bush tax cuts and prescription drug legislation and held their tongues. So did

Christian Right leaders who had their eye on Bush's establishment of the Office of Faith-Based and Community Initiatives and his conservative Supreme Court appointments. Like Trump, George W. Bush and other conservative presidents discarded the conventionally accepted litany of "outer belt" propositions while faithfully pursuing the hard-core principles of preserving private enterprise and the Right's version of traditional Christian principles. Like Trump, Bush still garnered overwhelming support from conservative political leaders and voters. In 2004, 84 percent of conservatives voted for Bush's reelection.

Trump is not an anomaly but the logical heir to the modern conservative movement. Trump won the Republican presidential nomination in 2016 not because he challenged conservative orthodoxy but because he articulated core principles more forthrightly and forcefully than any other candidate. The anti-immigrant movement of the 1920s that led to draconian quota laws for Europe and the exclusion of Asians prefigured Trump's campaign against dangerous immigrants from Latin American and Muslim countries. In a brick-and-mortar vision of the paper walls erected in 1924, Trump promised to build a physical wall on the U.S.-Mexican border. The racially tinged and antielite appeal of the 1920s Klan, the assault on "elites," and conspiracy theories of Phyllis Schlafly, John Stormer, and Willis Carto, Richard Nixon's law-and-order appeal to a "silent majority," and George Wallace's presidential campaigns foreshadowed Trump's campaign style and appeal. Trump's Christian nationalism traces its roots to the Klan, the pre–World War II America First movement, and Christian Right organizations such as Spiritual Mobilization, founded in 1934. His commitment to cutting taxes and regulations aligns with conservative priorities spanning from Calvin Coolidge to George W. Bush.

Trump's invocation of a culture war recalls the crusading moralists of the 1920s and beyond, including J. Howard Pew's 1964 declaration of war against those who deny "the faith of our fathers," and Buchanan's declaration at the 1992 Republican National Convention that "there is a religious war going on in our country for the soul of America. It is a cultural war, as critical to the kind of nation we will one day be as was the Cold War itself."[14] Analysts derided this divisive message, but Republican candidate George H. W. Bush enjoyed a respectable postconvention bounce of about eight points in the polls.

Dick Armey, a member of the Republican House leadership, declared a war against Democrats during the Clinton administration, equivalent to the Battle of the Bulge that pivotally secured an Allied victory in Europe during World War II. Fundraising appeals of the influential Christian Coalition in the 1990s pilloried opponents as "abortionists," "militant homosexuals," and "ultra-feminists" intent upon "destroying marriage," "harvesting babies," and achieving "the wholesale destruction of parental authority." Coalition president Pat Robertson warned that liberals "who are working for the dissolution of our society, also want to destroy Christianity and Bible-based religion."

The secret to Trump's unshakable support from devout conservative Christians emerged in one of the most consequential speeches of his political career. In a January 2016 address at Dordt College, a small Christian institution in Sioux City, Iowa, Trump told his nearly all-white audience that he would make Christianity great again in America. As a "true believer" in Christianity, Trump said, he recognized that Christians "don't exert the power that we should have. But you know the fact is that there is nothing the politicians can do to you if you band together. You have too much power. But the Christians don't use their power." "We have to strengthen."

If he's elected, Trump said, "we're going to be saying 'merry Christmas' again. Just remember that. And by the way, Christianity will have power." Trump alone, he assured his audience, will restore Christianity to preeminence in the country: "Because if I'm there, you're going to have plenty of power. You don't need anybody else. You're going to have somebody representing you very, very well. Remember that."[15] "We started out as a Christian nation," said evangelical Christian Rob Drieson after listening to Trump's talk. "I guess the biggest concern for me is trying to keep our country the way it was. Conservative."[16]

New York Times religious reporter Elizabeth Dias noted that this speech explains that "evangelicals did not support Mr. Trump in spite of who he is. They supported him because of who he is, and because of who they are." Trump is a bully and a brawler without constraints. But for devout conservative Christians, he is their bully and brawler, battling for their religion and culture. "In many ways," said Robert Jeffress, pastor of a megachurch in Dallas, "Christians feel like they are in an existential cultural war between good and evil, and they want a warrior like Donald Trump who can win."[17]

Conservative Christians have not seen such a brawler since Joe McCarthy took on the commies and homosexuals in the 1950s. Unlike Trump, former vice president Mike Pence lives an exemplary Christian life. However, evangelical Christians recognize that neither Pence nor any other Trump rival would defend their way of life with Trump's intensity and unyielding determination. Trump is "the bad man who makes good things possible," said theologian Robert Franklin of Emory University, but "unfortunately, under this narrative, Trump can literally do no wrong. His wrong is right. No other politician gets that kind of pass."[18]

A study of the 2016 election by sociologists David Norman Smith and Eric Hanley found that financial worries did not account for the Trump vote. Instead, voters looked for "a domineering leader who would 'crush evil' and 'get rid of rotten apples' and stand up 'against feminists, liberals, immigrants, and minorities.'"[19] In the Dordt speech, Trump delivered his most controversial and oft-quoted line, "I could stand in the middle of Fifth Avenue and shoot somebody, and I wouldn't lose any voters, OK?" which overshadowed his pledge to uphold Christianity. With this remark, Trump signaled the solidity of his base support and the unstoppable force of his campaign. The Dordt audience cheered in response.

As president, Trump continued to represent the American conservative tradition faithfully. He appointed federal judges who upheld the agenda of protecting private enterprise and the Right's version of white Christian values. His singular legislative accomplishment was a tax cut that benefited the rich and corporations. He used his executive powers to crack down on immigration from the Middle East, Africa, and Latin America and to dismantle regulations on the environment, transportation safety, banking safeguards, and civil rights. Nothing that Trump said or did as president would have shocked or surprised a conservative of the 1920s.

Tellingly, Trump's rivals for the 2024 Republican presidential nomination did not dissent significantly from his domestic or border policies, but some questioned his character, criminal culpability, and electability. On foreign policy, former governor Nikki Haley (R-SC) proposed an engaged nationalism that actively promotes U.S. interests abroad. Yet, both forms of nationalism draw from a long-standing precedent in Republican politics.

Trump's relentless pursuit of power, irrespective of the means or implications for democracy, is rooted in a conservative belief that liberal opponents are not simply wrong on issues, but fundamentally sinful, un-American, and detrimental to the values that have historically made the nation great. This "us versus them" mentality, viewing opponents as alien and illegitimate, is not unique to Trump. As explained by Joanne Freeman, a professor of American history and American studies at Yale University, "The [Republican] party's unity is the problem, its shared focus on ends (uncontested rule) over means (democratic practices). Norms and rules be damned, they feel entitled to maintaining power. This isn't democracy. It's the heartbeat of authoritarianism."[20]

Virtually everything that liberals and a few maverick conservatives find objectionable about Trump is consistent with the precedents set within modern American conservatism since the 1920s, as illustrated by the non-exhaustive examples below:

— **Lawlessness**: Interior Secretary Albert Fall, Charles Forbes, Thomas W. Miller, Speaker Dennis Hastert, President Richard Nixon, Vice President Spiro Agnew, Attorney General John Mitchell, Commerce Secretary Maurice Stans, H. R. Haldeman, John Ehrlichman, National Security Advisor John Poindexter, National Security Advisor Robert McFarlane, National Security aide Oliver North, Paul Manafort, Roger Stone, National Security Advisor Michael Flynn, Steve Bannon, Rudy Giuliani, Representative Chris Collins, Representative Duncan Hunter, Macrae Dowless, Representative George Santos.

— **Personal Moral Failings**: President Warren Harding, Speaker Newt Gingrich, Speaker Bob Livingston, Speaker Dennis Hastert, Representative Henry Hyde, the Southern Baptist Convention Executive Committee, Herschel Walker, Jerry Falwell Jr., Justice Clarence Thomas, Representative George Santos.

— **Anti-Semitism**: Reverend George A. Simons, the Ku Klux Klan, Henry Ford, Charles Lindbergh, Ruly Carpenter, William Randolph

Hearst, Reverend Wilbur Fiske Crafts, Father Charles Coughlin, Common Sense, Henry Joy, State Senator Edward O. McCue, Leander Perez, Willis Carto, Pat Buchanan, Agriculture Commissioner Sid Miller, Representative Marjorie Taylor Greene, Representative George Santos.

— **Racism**: Ku Klux Klan, the Hays Code, American Legion, Charles Lindbergh, Governor Eugene Talmadge, Senator Strom Thurmond, State's Rights Party, Senator Richard Russell, J. E. Earle Ellis, Leander Perez, Bob Jones Sr., White Citizen's Councils, Willis Carto, William F. Buckley Jr., Senator Barry Goldwater, Governor George Wallace, President Richard Nixon, Vice President Spiro Agnew, Lee Atwater, Willie Horton ad, J. Edgar Hoover, Rush Limbaugh, Agriculture Commissioner Sid Miller, Christopher Rufo, Representative George Santos.

— **Xenophobia:** Ku Klux Klan, President Calvin Coolidge, Henry Laughlin, Henry Fairfield Osborn, Representative Bertrand Snell, Representative Albert Henry Vestal, Senator David A. Reed, Representative Albert Johnson, Representative Grant M. Hudson, Pat Buchanan, John Tanton, Federation for American Immigration Reform, Center for Immigration Studies, Governor Ron DeSantis, Steven Steinlight, Education Commissioner Richard Corcoran, Representative Marjorie Taylor Greene, Senator J. D. Vance.

— **Homophobia**: Senator Joseph McCarthy, State Senator Charley Eugene Johns, Senator Kenneth Wherry, Guy George Gabrielson, Representative Cliff Clevenger, Anita Bryant, Senator Jesse Helms, Phyllis Schlafly, Jerry Falwell Sr., Moral Majority, Christian Coalition, Southern Baptist Convention, Governor Ron DeSantis, House Speaker Mike Johnson.

— **Sexism**: Ku Klux Klan, John S. Sumner, Governor Tommy Thompson, Speaker Newt Gingrich, Southern Baptist Convention, Jerry Falwell Sr., Rush Limbaugh, Ralph Drollinger, Laura Ingraham, Glenn Beck, Senate Leader Mitch McConnell, Senator J. D. Vance.

— **Lying**: Henry Ford, President Richard Nixon, Attorney General John Mitchell, Speaker Dennis Hastert, National Security Advisor John Poindexter, Governor Sarah Palin, Sean Hannity, Steven Steinlight, Representative Michelle Bachman, Herschel Walker, Representative George Santos.

— **Authoritarianism**: Charles Lindbergh, Senator Joseph McCarthy, President Richard Nixon, Pat Buchanan, President George W. Bush, Governor Ron DeSantis, Education Commissioner Richard Corcoran.

— **Conspiracy Theories**: Reverend George A. Simons, Henry Ford, Senator Thomas David Schall, Charles Lindbergh, Common Sense, Senator John Bricker, Willis Carto, Phyllis Schlafly, John Stormer, John Birch Society, Black Helicopter Myth, Representative Marjorie Taylor Greene.

— **Demonizing Opponents**: Ku Klux Klan, Governor Eugene Talmadge, Senator Thomas David Schall, Senator Simeon Fess, Senator Joseph McCarthy, Speaker Newt Gingrich, Interior Secretary James Watt, Glenn Ellmers, Sebastian Gorka, Representative Marjorie Taylor Greene.

— **Inciting Violence**: Ku Klux Klan, Governor George Wallace, Pat Robertson, G. Gordon Liddy, Rush Limbaugh, Bill Cunningham, Rudy Giuliani, Donald Trump Jr., Steve Bannon, Representative Louie Gohmert, Rudy Giuliani, Representative Tom Emmer, Representative Andy Biggs, Kari Lake.

Consistent with this analysis, veteran political columnist Jonathan Chait dubbed Trump "the most pure conservative president ever." He wrote in 2018 that "the conservative movement's willingness to embrace Trump is not an accident. The traits that endeared him to the movement have clear historical antecedents. He follows in the path of other right-wing heroes in American history: Charles Coughlin, Joseph McCarthy, Rush Limbaugh." Thus, "Trump's base within the party lies on its right, not its left. The Republicans who most adore him are the most conservative ones, and those most alienated from him are the most moderate."[21] Anthea Butler, chair of the Department of Religious Studies at the University of Pennsylvania, agrees that "Trump is not an aberration." Rather, he represents "the eventual end of all evangelical political action: electing a white male candidate who reinforces biblical sexual and gender norms, is suspicious about immigrants and Islam, and, most importantly, believes in white America."[22]

Under Trump—and long before—conservatives have engaged in a struggle for control over public life in the United States against a liberal tradition they have seen as evil, un-American, and corrosive of the institutions and traditions that made the nation great. The Left, too, has scorned the opposition as a danger to the United States, particularly in the Trump era. However, since the 1930s, conservatives have done so with particular force and conviction. Conservatives have conjured up the phantasma of liberals who threaten the traditions that sustained our civilization with their pluralistic values, their program of social engineering, and their trampling on the moral teachings of religion. Conservatives had to stay disciplined, mobilize their resources, and wage total war against liberals by any means available, with unconditional surrender as the only acceptable result. Hamlet told Rosencrantz and Guildenstern, "There is nothing either good or bad, but thinking makes it so." President Herbert Hoover set the tone for conservative's total war against liberals when he declared during his unsuccessful reelection campaign in 1932 that his opponent Franklin Roosevelt and the Democrats "bring forth a philosophy of government which would destroy the whole American system on which we have built the greatest nation of one-hundred and fifty years."[23] John Mitchell, President Nixon's former attorney general and campaign chair, justified to a Senate committee that the dangers of electing a Democratic president in 1972 justified the crimes of Watergate: "The reelection of Richard Nixon as compared to what was available on the other side, was so much more important" than anything done by the Nixon administration and reelection campaign. In 1975, prosecutors convicted Mitchell of conspiracy, obstruction of justice, and perjury.

Representative Newt Gingrich, the architect of the conservative revolution of 1994, branded Democrats as the "enemies of normal Americans" and the Clintons as "counterculture McGovernicks" presiding over a White House of "left-wing elitists." Gingrich expanded this critique, saying in 2010, "The America in which we grew up is vastly different from the America the secular-socialist Left want to create. And that's why saving America is the fundamental challenge of our time. The secular-socialist machine represents as great a threat to America as Nazi Germany or the Soviet Union once did."[24]

After Trump lost his legal battles to overturn the presidential election in 2020, the premier conservative commentator Rush Limbaugh said, "I actually think we're trending toward secession. There cannot be a peaceful coexistence of two completely different theories of life, theories of government, theories of how we manage our affairs. We can't be in this dire a conflict without something giving somewhere along the way."[25]

In 2021, after Trump lost the presidency, conservative commentator Glenn Ellmers wrote in the respected conservative Claremont Institute's *The American Mind* that Trump's opponents "are not Americans in any meaningful sense of the term." Critically, "They do not believe in, live by, or even like the principles, traditions, and ideals that until recently defined America as a nation and as a people." The true Americans, he said, the Trump supporters, must mount a "counter revolution" to save "*the* one, authentic America."[26]

Conservative Notre Dame professor Patrick Deneen, in *Regime Change: Toward a Postliberal Future* (2023), strikes similar themes. Liberalism, he claims, has decayed and degraded the United States, with its denigration of tradition, faith, authority, and community. He attributes liberalism's "totalitarian undertaking" as "the consequence of the most fateful and fundamental 'separation'—the so-called separation of church and state." This separation must be reversed so the country can again become integrated with conservative Christianity. He calls for the urgent toppling of the liberal order not through democratic processes but by "the raw assertion of political power," including "extralegal and almost bestial" forms of resistance, such as "mobs running through the streets." Senator J. D. Vance praised the book: "Deneen does more than show how our present ruling class has declared war on beauty, tradition, and the social institutions that make life worth living; he articulates a vision for a populist politics that can rebuild what has been torn down."[27]

President Trump slammed Democrats who didn't stand and applaud during his 2018 State of the Union speech as "un-American" and "treasonous." In his November 2023 Veteran's Day speech and social media post, Trump channeled the Nazi dehumanization of "vermin" Jews that justified their persecution and eventual mass murder. He promised to "root out" the "vermin" among his political enemies. He pledged "that we will root out the communists, Marxists, fascists and the radical left thugs that live like vermin within the confines of our country, that lie and steal and cheat on elections, and will do anything possible—they'll do anything—whether legally or illegally, to destroy America, and to destroy the American dream." "The threat from outside forces is far less sinister, dangerous, and grave than the threat from within."[28] Ruth Ben-Ghiat, a New York University scholar of fascism, authoritarianism, and propaganda, warned that "calling people 'vermin' was used effectively by Hitler and Mussolini to dehumanize people and encourage their followers to engage in violence." Pulitzer Prize-winning historian Jon Meacham agreed that "to call your opponents vermin and to dehumanize them is to not only open the door but to walk through the door toward the most ghastly kinds of crimes."[29]

Since the 1930s, conservatives have not sought to maintain stability, which would have meant acquiescing in the liberal state. Instead, they have pursued the revolutionary objective of overturning the liberal order and challenging our pluralist civilization. Elcott and his coauthors noted that political movements of the Right "seek to permanently win, end the game with total victory, and, in essence, shut down the game."[30]

Throughout the last century, winning for conservatives meant advancing without wavering, their unshakable core values of protecting private enterprise and their version of traditional Christian values. "The basic fault lines," said the renowned sociologist Peter L. Berger, "are not between people with different beliefs but between people who hold these beliefs with an element of uncertainty and people who hold these beliefs with a pretense of certitude."[31]

EPILOGUE

In the 2024 presidential election, Donald Trump became only the second former president elected to a nonconsecutive term after Grover Cleveland won another term in 1892, serving as president from 1885 to 1889 and 1893 to 1897. Trump secured victory in every swing state, giving him a decisive Electoral College victory, 312 to 226, against his Democratic opponent, Kamala Harris. He narrowly won the popular vote by about 1.5 percent, becoming only the second Republican, after George W. Bush in 2004, to win the popular vote since 1992.

Trump's victory came with consolidated conservative support. Exit polls revealed that he garnered 90 percent of votes from self-identified conservatives, compared to 40 percent of moderates and just 7 percent of liberals. Among white, born-again evangelical Christians, Trump captured 82 percent of the vote, compared to 40 percent from all other groups combined. Nearly every prominent conservative federal and state officeholder endorsed his candidacy, reinforcing his role as a unifying conservative figure.

Trump's win follows the trajectory of the American Right since the 1920s. He repudiated virtually all the professed, malleable outer-belt claims of conservatives while adhering to conservatism's core values of protecting private enterprise and its version of traditional Christian values. As did past conservatives, he exploited the emotional issues of xenophobia, racism, misogyny, and anti-Semitism.

— **Free Enterprise**. Trump has proposed instituting the most draconian tariffs in U.S. history.[1] These tariffs would stifle free markets at home and clog the free flow of goods and services across international borders. Contrary to Trump's claims, foreign nations will not pay for the tariffs. American consumers will pay through artificially imposed price increases on goods and services, whereas favored businesses will profit through protection from foreign competition.

— **Limited Government**. Trump's proposals also challenge the principle of limited government, a cornerstone of professed Republican ideology, through two unprecedented measures. First, he has called for the deportation of approximately 11.5 million undocumented immigrants, beginning with those with criminal records and expanding to a sweeping removal of all undocumented individuals. This plan would massively expand immigration enforcement, intruding into the lives of millions of Americans. Many undocumented immigrants are deeply integrated into our society—married to U.S. citizens or raising children who are citizens—making deportation a significant government overreach into private lives.

Trump has proposed eliminating the Fourteenth Amendment provision that grants U.S. citizenship to children of undocumented immigrants born on U.S. soil, affirmed by a 6–2 decision of the conservative U.S. Supreme Court in 1868. This proposal would require a biological police force, hauntingly similar to the Nazi police that probed the ancestry of Germans to check for Jewish heritage. Trump's police would have to determine the parentage of every child born in the United States to establish their parents' immigration status. His proposal would also require U.S. citizens to provide documentary proof of citizenship—the "show us your papers" hallmark of dictatorial regimes.

— **Fiscal Responsibility**. Trump has proposed sweeping tax cuts for individuals and corporations that would significantly increase the federal deficit. According to the nonpartisan Congressional Budget Office, merely extending the tax cuts from Trump's first term for an additional decade would add $4.6 trillion to the deficit. To offset the effect of these cuts, Trump has suggested eliminating waste and inefficiency in government programs through a commission led by billionaires Elon Musk and Vivek Ramaswamy. However, past attempts at similar initiatives have primarily failed because meaningful spending reductions inevitably affect core government benefit programs—cuts that Congress is unlikely to approve. For instance, in 1982, President Ronald Reagan created the Grace Commission, headed by magnate J. Peter Grace, to address waste and offset the effects of his tax cuts. Despite these efforts, the federal debt tripled during Reagan's two terms (1981–89), illustrating the limitations of such approaches.

— **States' Rights**. Trump's proposals on voting and other state-regulated matters would override many existing state laws and practices, significantly curtailing states' autonomy. He has called for restricting voting to Election Day only, overriding forty-seven states that currently offer early voting, thirty-six that allow no-excuse absentee voting, and eight that conduct elections entirely by mail. His proposed ID requirements for voting, likely mandating photo identification, would conflict with the policies of fourteen states that currently have no documentation requirements and fifteen states that do not require photo IDs. Additionally, he seeks to mandate documentary proof of citizenship for voter registration, a policy currently enforced only in Arizona.

Beyond voting, Trump's agenda would impose federal authority over issues traditionally left to states. He has proposed limiting diversity, equity, and inclusion (DEI) programs, LGBTQ protections, and gender-affirming care at the state level. Despite waffling on abortion rights for political purposes during the 2024 campaign, Trump would likely support abortion restrictions in as many as thirty states where abortion remains legal. Moreover, Trump has vowed to cut federal funding for schools and programs that teach critical race theory, gender ideology, or other content he deems politically or socially inappropriate, further encroaching on state and local education policies.

— **Personal Morality and Responsibility**. Trump's moral transgressions include a history of adultery and accusations of sexual abuse from more than twenty-five women. A civil jury found Trump liable for sexually assaulting, harming, and defaming E. Jean Carroll. In another case, a jury determined that he committed extensive financial fraud in his business dealings. Additionally, a criminal jury convicted him on thirty-four felony counts for falsifying business records to evade campaign finance and tax laws. A special prosecutor also indicted Trump—the cases were later dismissed—for attempting to overturn the 2020 election and illegally retaining hundreds of national security documents.

Trump burst into prominence among conservatives through the worst, most protracted lie in the history of U.S. politics. He claimed, contrary to evidence, that Barack Obama, the country's first Black president, was born in Africa, not Hawaii, and therefore ineligible for the presidency. Fact-checkers have since established that Trump was by far the biggest liar in the history of the presidency. Trump assumes no responsibility for his actions but invariably blames others: lying women, the deep state, biased media, rigged judges and juries, and his liberal opponents.

— **Law and Order**. Trump's approach to law and order raises significant concerns about the rule of law. He has threatened to prosecute political opponents without evidence of wrongdoing, undermining the principle of impartial justice. His proposals include using the military for domestic law enforcement, a clear violation of the Posse Comitatus Act, which restricts such actions. Trump has advocated rolling back protections against police misconduct and expanding the militarization of police forces. Additionally, he has suggested ending the political independence of the FBI, turning it into a partisan police force. Perhaps most concerning, Trump pardoned more than a thousand individuals convicted for their roles in the violent January 6, 2021, attack on the U.S. Capitol.

— **Strict Construction**. Trump's pledge to abolish birthright citizenship contradicts the plain meaning of the Fourteenth Amendment as affirmed by Supreme Court precedent. Trump's three Supreme Court nominees have often abandoned the principles of strict constructionism, instead interpreting the Constitution in ways that align with their ideological values. This shift has been evident in decisions affecting abortion rights, gun control, presidential immunity from prosecution, and the disqualification clause of the Fourteenth Amendment, section 3. Contrary to the separation of powers enshrined in the Constitution and the Impoundment Control Act, he has claimed the power to impound—not spend—money appropriated by Congress.

— **American Sovereignty**. Trump's "America First" foreign policy ostensibly aims to preserve U.S. sovereignty but often undermines it in practice. He has shown deference to foreign dictators seeking to destabilize U.S. democracy and disrupt its institutions. His policies threaten the collective security framework that has safeguarded the nation since World War II. Domestically, Trump's vision of governance involves expanding presidential power to near-authoritarian levels, bypassing the people's sovereignty. "A majority, held in restraint by constitutional checks and limitations, and always changing easily with deliberate changes of popular opinions and sentiments, is the only true sovereign of a free people," said Abraham Lincoln.

Although he has discarded certain outwardly professed conservative principles, Trump has remained steadfast in promoting the Right's core agenda of advancing private enterprise and its interpretation of traditional Christian values. In a second term, he will lack the constraints of a re-election campaign and have no advisors who might moderate his right-wing impulses. Trump's second term proposed nominations are stacked with loyalists and lack restraining figures of the first Trump administration, such as former chief of staff John Kelly, former secretary of defense James Mattis, or former director of national intelligence Dan Coats.

Although Trump's proposed market-busting tariffs will help some industries while potentially hurting others, his other initiatives broadly advance the interests of private enterprise. Trump has pledged to reduce business taxes and eliminate federal regulations governing environmental protections, civil rights, financial fraud, and consumer health and safety. Trump has also vowed to weaken federal agencies that oversee businesses, appointing business-friendly leaders to key positions. His appointees to the Supreme Court have already curtailed federal regulatory authority, a trend likely to continue under the second Trump administration. Trump's Department of Justice will likely side with corporate interests, and he will likely appoint pro-business leaders to the National Labor Relations Board (NLRB), thereby hampering union-organizing efforts and producing rulings favorable to businesses. He also plans to open federal lands and waterways to increased drilling and mining, creating new profit opportunities for energy companies.

Although not religious himself, Trump has followed a cultural agenda set by the Right's perspective on traditional Christian values. He backs prayer in schools and religious symbols, such as the Ten Commandments, in the public square. His school choice proposals would allow parents to access public money for the religious education of their children. He opposes rights for LGBTQ persons and for transgender care. He supports business owners' right to refuse services to potential customers on religious grounds. Trump would create a task force to oppose alleged anti-Christian bias. Despite politically hedging on abortion during the campaign, Trump would likely back efforts to restrict access to abortion, including the defunding of Planned Parenthood. He could ban most abortions without new legislation by reviving the Comstock Act and ordering the FDA to rescind approval of abortion pills. He would likely expand reproductive restrictions beyond abortion by seeking to withdraw coverage for contraceptive services under the Affordable Care Act.

Trump's alignment with the Christian Right reflects their broader ambition of establishing a government rooted in their interpretation of biblical values. Talia Lavin, author of *Wild Faith: How the Christian Right Is Taking Over America*, observed, "What they want is a kingdom of Christ on Earth, and they want it now."[2] Trump's proposed nominations reflect this influence. For example, he has nominated Russell Vought, a self-identified Christian nationalist and architect of Project 2025, as head of the Office of Management and Budget. Other key nominations include Pete Hegseth as secretary of defense, John Ratcliffe as CIA director, Mike Huckabee as ambassador to Israel, Kristi Noem as secretary of homeland security, and Kari Lake as head of the Voice of America (VOA). These figures are deeply tied to the Christian Right, suggesting a continued effort to advance its agenda within the second Trump administration.

Since the 1920s, conservative leaders have often relied on rhetoric that stirs up the base through appeals to anti-Semitism, xenophobia, racism, and misogyny. Trump followed this playbook, targeting specific groups to galvanize his supporters. He repeatedly attacked Jewish billionaire and Holocaust survivor George Soros, accusing him of manipulating the legal system by influencing Black Manhattan district attorney Alvin Bragg to indict him. Trump falsely claimed that Soros controlled a vast network of district attorneys and state attorneys general across the country. After his indictment in Georgia, Trump posted his booking mugshot with guns pointed at his face, labeled as "Soros" and "pedophile." He suggested that Jews, the perennial scapegoats in history, would be to blame if he lost in 2024, and accused Jews who supported the Democratic Party of betraying their religion.

In a manner reminiscent of the restrictionists of the 1920s, Trump painted immigrants as dangerous "others" who would "poison the blood" of the nation and pass on "bad genes." In the 1920s, anti-immigrant activists aimed their rhetoric at Eastern and Southern European immigrants. For Trump, however, the target is nonwhite immigrants, with a particular focus on undocumented individuals. He has demonized these predominantly law-abiding, industrious immigrants, portraying them as violent criminals who would invade homes, harm families, and even eat pets. Among voters who supported the deportation of undocumented immigrants, 87 percent backed Trump. Following the election, Trump nominated hardline anti-immigrant advocate Tom Homan as his "border czar."

Trump's attacks on Kamala Harris, his Democratic opponent with mixed Asian and African heritage, echoed the racial slurs of the Jim Crow era. He labeled Harris as "dumb" and "mentally deficient," suggesting that such traits would disqualify her from the presidency. Yet, Trump implied, these very characteristics would not prevent her from holding "Black jobs," a term he used to refer to positions allegedly "taken" by undocumented immigrants. Trump also mocked Harris's racial identity, claiming she had only recently "turned Black" for political gain. This rhetoric drew from the racial categories established by white supremacists during the Jim Crow era, where a single drop of Black blood could define someone as Black, as in the case of Virginia's racial classifications. Among Trump's proposed nominees to head fifteen cabinet-level departments, twelve are non-Hispanic whites; one is Black (Scott Turner, Housing), and two are Hispanic (Marco Rubio, State Department, and Lori Chavez-DeRemer, Labor).

Trump has pledged to be the protector of women, whether they like it or not, thus depriving women of agency and, like his evangelical Christian allies, subordinating women to men. He claimed that Harris would be "overwhelmed" and "melt down" when facing authoritarian male leaders worldwide. At his final campaign rally, Trump called former Speaker Nancy Pelosi "evil, sick, crazy." He said unmistakably that he wanted to but would not use another word that began "bi—." Trump's running mate, Senator J. D. Vance, called liberal women "a bunch of childless cat ladies who are miserable at their own lives and the choices that they've made." This paternalism appealed not only to men but also to conservative women who, like the preeminent antifeminist Phyllis Schlafly, believed that women benefited from the shielding of men, who should lead the family, the church, and the broader society.

Trump's ability to consolidate support from his white, evangelical base was necessary but not sufficient to explain his comeback from defeat in 2020 to victory in 2024. Beyond this core constituency, Trump made modest gains among Black voters, increasing his share by 2 percent compared to 2020, and more substantial gains among Hispanic voters, with a 13 percent swing. His strongest support among Hispanics came from men, some of whom may have found his brash, hypermasculine rhetoric appealing. Additionally, many Hispanic voters, who tend to lean culturally conservative, felt alienated by being broadly associated with migrants and undocumented immigrants, which they perceived as unfair stereotyping.

The 2024 election, however, was shaped by more than shifting demographics. Voters evinced widespread anti-incumbent sentiment and significant economic grievances, amplified by an unprecedented disinformation campaign from the Right. This campaign, powered by such conservative media outlets as Fox News, right-wing podcasters with millions of followers, and Elon Musk's extraordinary $250 million effort to support Trump, reached billions of viewers. Musk, the owner of X (formerly Twitter) and the world's richest person with a fortune exceeding $300 billion—greater than the GDP of most nations—played a particularly outsize role in disseminating disinformation.

This pervasive disinformation skewed public perceptions across the board. Inflation poses a genuine challenge for many Americans. Still, false claims circulated widely that it was spiraling out of control, that jobs were disappearing, unemployment was soaring, real wages were plummeting, and the stock market was collapsing. Paradoxically, surveys conducted shortly after the election revealed that voters' perceptions of the economy improved substantially, even though no real economic changes had occurred. This stark shift underscored the influence of disinformation on voter beliefs.

Similarly, disinformation about undocumented immigrants influenced voter attitudes. Many came to believe that undocumented residents were dangerous criminals despite data showing they commit crimes, including violent crimes, at less than half the rate of native-born Americans. Others blamed these workers for undermining the economy and draining taxpayer resources despite their essential contributions to such industries as construction, agriculture, hospitality, and personal services. Undocumented workers pay more in taxes than they receive in public benefits. According to estimates, mass deportation of undocumented immigrants could push the U.S. economy into a recession. Misinformation has also fueled fears about crime, with claims of surging violence during the Biden administration contradicting FBI data showing that crime rates had fallen.

Disinformation was singularly effective in denying Democrats the benefit of the abortion issue. In the wake of the Supreme Court's overturning of the protections of *Roe v. Wade*, abortion had the potential to power Harris to victory. More than 60 percent of Americans, per several surveys, disapproved of the Court's ruling. Exit polls showed that 66 percent of voters believed that abortion should always or usually be legal, compared to 30 percent who thought it should usually or always be illegal, for a pro-choice lead of 36 percent. Yet disinformation by Trump and his allies, notably Musk, so thoroughly diffused the abortion issue that it provided no consequential advantage to Harris in the final voting.

No disinformation campaign was more telling than the $20.5 million that Musk poured into a super PAC during the last month of the election. Its sole objective was to neutralize the abortion issue by equating Trump's stance on abortion with the late liberal icon, Supreme Court Justice Ruth Bader Ginsburg.[3] Harris's lead on who voters trusted more on abortion did not reach a 36 percent pro-choice gap or even 5 percent. It collapsed to a de minimis 3 percent, 49 percent to 46 percent. Harris won 93 percent of voters who trusted her more on abortion, and Trump won 96 percent of voters who trusted him more; based on the 152.3 million votes cast for Harris and Trump in 2024, Harris's lead on abortion netted her only 2 million votes. If, however, her lead on the issue had reached just one-third of the pro-choice, anti-choice margin (12 percent), she would have gained a net of 15 million votes, more than enough to turn the election in her favor.[4]

The swing states of Arizona and Nevada provide instructive examples. In Arizona, a right-to-abortion amendment won a smashing victory by 23 percent, 61.6 percent to 38.4 percent. In Nevada, voters backed a right-to-abortion measure by a yet larger 29 percent, 64.4 percent. Yet Trump prevailed in the state by 3 percent, 50.6 percent to 47.5 percent.

Even before Musk launched his abortion-focused super PAC, Republicans had muddled the abortion issue. Astonishingly, polls of six battleground states—Arizona, Georgia, Michigan, Nevada, Pennsylvania, and Wisconsin—found that 17 percent of voters said that Biden, not Trump, was "most responsible" for overturning *Roe v. Wade*; 13 percent were not sure, and 14 percent said "neither" or "both." Just 56 percent named Trump, who had boasted about appointing the Justices responsible for ending *Roe.*, as most responsible.[5] As a reflection of the muddled abortion issue and other considerations, Biden's 15 percent lead among women in 2020 shriveled to just 8 percent for Harris in 2024.

The Russian government contributed significantly to the pro-Right disinformation campaign, leveraging its advanced AI and digital capabilities. News Guard's Election Misinformation Tracker linked nearly a hundred disinformation sites to foreign governments, with all but two (from Iran) originating from the pro-Trump Putin regime in Russia.[6]

Darrell M. West, a senior scholar at the Brookings Institution specializing in research into disinformation, observed that false and pejorative claims reached unprecedented levels during the 2024 election cycle: "We can't ignore the ways in which disinformation shaped views about the candidates, affected how voters saw leader performance, and generated widespread media attention." According to West, purveyors of disinformation were remarkably effective in shaping the campaign narrative because of their extensive reach. "False claims were broadly disseminated on social media, amplified through humorous memes, picked up and legitimized by mainstream media outlets, and further circulated by internet mega-influencers," said West. "Leading candidates bolstered this disinformation during rallies, debates, and interviews, embedding it into the core of the campaign." "Polling data revealed that these false narratives significantly influenced public perceptions of the candidates, key issues like the economy, immigration, and crime, and the overall tone of media coverage," West concluded.[7]

Journalist Sarah Steffen highlighted the stark political imbalance in disinformation: "The volume of disinformation targeting Harris far exceeded that directed at Trump, experts said well before November 5." This asymmetry created an uneven playing field, shaping voter attitudes and media discussions in ways that heavily favored Trump's campaign.[8] When it comes to controlling human beings, there is no better instrument than lies. "Humans live by beliefs," said the novelist Michael Ende. "And beliefs can be manipulated. The power to manipulate beliefs is the only thing that counts."[9]

Conservative ideology and politics persist beyond any single figure. Donald Trump may stand out for his dishonesty, self-interest, and divisive, violent rhetoric, but his departure from the political stage would likely leave the conservative agenda unchanged. Other leaders would undoubtedly step forward to champion the same core values that conservatives have promoted since the end of World War I. The unwavering loyalty of the conservative base to what they believe Trump represents ensures continuity because the movement's rank and file remain unshaken in their loyalty. The social philosopher Hannah Arendt wrote, "Total loyalty is possible only when fidelity is emptied of all concrete content, from which changes of mind might naturally arise."[10]

NOTES

CHAPTER 1. Dispensable versus Core Conservative Values

1. "House Judiciary Subcommittee on Constitution, Civil Rights and Civil Liberties Holds Hearing on Voting Rights," *CQ Transcriptions*, 16 August 2021.

2. David Sivak, "GOP Balances Election Integrity and States' Rights in House Election Bill," *Washington Examiner*, 16 July 2023, https://www.washingtonexaminer.com/news/1152739/gop-balances-election-integrity-and-states-rights-in-house-voting-bill.

3. *National Federation of Independent Business, et al. v. Department of Labor, et al.*, U.S. Supreme Court, Members of Congress, *Amicus Curiae in Support of Applicants*, December 2021, https://www.cassidy.senate.gov/wp-content/uploads/media/doc/MOC%20Amicus%20FINAL_0.pdf.

4. U.S. House of Representatives, Judiciary Committee, "Jordan, Comer, Steil Demand Communications, Documents, and Testimony from Manhattan DA Alvin Bragg," Press Release, March 20, 2023, https://judiciary.house.gov/media/press-releases/jordan-comer-steil-demand-communications-documents-and-testimony-manhattan-da.

5. Brief, *Alvin Bragg Jr. v. Jim Jordan*, U.S. District Court, Southern District of New York, Case No. 23-cv-3032, 4 November 2023, https://int.nyt.com/data/documenttools/bragg-v-jordan-complaint-23-cv-3032/b7f1a0e43619867d/full.pdf.

6. Kevin Breuninger, "Trump Georgia DA Rejects House GOP Demand for Records as 'Unjustified and Illegal,'" CNBC, 7 September 2023, https://www.cnbc.com/2023/09/07/trump-georgia-da-rejects-house-gop-demand-for-records-as-illegal.html.

7. "U.S. Must Mirror Vermont, Aiken Says, or Perish," *Washington Post*, 24 July 1938, M11.

8. Lakatos's original work is complex and obscure, but the *Stanford Encyclopedia of Philosophy* provides a readable summary, https://plato.stanford.edu/entries/lakatos/.

9. Other works include, for example, Michael Oakeshott, "On Being Conservative," in *Rationalism in Politics and Other Essays* (London: Methuen, 1962), 168–96; Roger Scruton, *The Meaning of Conservatism* (New York: Macmillan, 1980); Robert A. Nisbet, *Conservatism: Dream and Reality* (Minneapolis: University of Minnesota Press, 1986); Ted Honderich, *Conservatism* (Boulder, CO: Westview Press, 1991); Kieron O'Hara, *Conservatism* (London: Reaktion Books, 2011), and Edmund Neill, *Conservatism* (Boston: Polity, 2021). See also James Alexander, "The Contradictions of Conservatism," *Government and Opposition* 48 (2013): 594–615.

10. U.S. Congressman Mike Johnson, "7 Core Principles of Conservatism," 2018, https://mikejohnson.house.gov/7-core-principles-of-conservatism/. See also Johnson's first press conference as Speaker, "House Republican Leadership News Conference," 2 November 2023, C-Span, https://www.c-span.org/program/public-affairs-event/house-republican-leadership-news-conference/634583; David Corn, "Mike Johnson Urged a Religious Test for Politicians," *Mother Jones*, 31 October 2023, https://www.motherjones.com/politics/2023/10/mike-johnson-urged-a-religious-test-for-politicians/.

11. Rachel del Guidice, "'True North' Outlines 14 Conservative Principles," *The Daily Signal*, 21 October 2019, https://www.dailysignal.com/2019/10/21/true-north-outlines-14-conservative-principles/.

12. Yascha Mounk, "Responsibility Redefined," *Democracy: A Journal of Ideas*, Winter 2017, https://democracyjournal.org/magazine/43/responsibility-redefined; Jim DeMint, *Falling in Love with America Again* (Washington, DC: Heritage Foundation, 2014), 1.

13. Arabella Kenealy, *Feminism and Sex-Extinction* (London: T. Fisher Unwin, 1922), 96.

14. Stephen Wolfe, *The Case for Christian Nationalism* (Moscow, ID: Canon Press, 2022), 289, 448.

15. Lawrence Glickman, "Donald Trump and the Anti-New Deal Tradition," *Organization of American Historians: Progress, A Blog for American History*, n.d., https://www.oah.org/process-blog/trump-anti-new-deal/. See also George Wolfskill, *The Revolt of the Conservatives: A History of the American Liberty League, 1934–1940* (Boston: Houghton Mifflin, 1962); George Wolfskill and John A. Hudson, *All but the People: FDR and His Critics, 1933–1939* (New York: Macmillan, 1969).

16. David M. Elcott, with C. Colt Anderson, Tobias Cremer, and Volker Haarmann, *Faith, Nationalism, and the Future of Liberal Democracy* (Notre Dame, IN: University of Notre Dame Press, 2021), 13–15.

17. Jonathan Haidt, "Why Working-Class People Vote Conservative," *The Guardian*, 5 June 2012, https://www.theguardian.com/society/2012/jun/05/why-working-class-people-vote-conservative. On the appeal of conservative social issues, see also the bestseller by Thomas Frank, *What's the Matter with Kansas?* (New York: Henry Holt, 2004), and the scholarly commentary: Larry M. Bartels, "What's the Matter with *What's the Matter with Kansas?*," *Quarterly Journal of Political Science* 1 (2006): 201–26; Frank W. Young, "'What's the Matter with Kansas,' A Sociological Answer," *Sociological Forum* 28 (2013): 864–72.

18. Scott Atran, "Sacred Values," *Library of Social Science*, 13 March 2018, https://www.libraryofsocialscience.com/newsletter/posts/2018/2018-03-13-atran2.html.

19. For an analysis of this turnabout in the correlation between party and race, see Allan J. Lichtman, *The Embattled Vote in America: From the Founding to the Present* (Cambridge, MA: Harvard University Press, 2018).

20. Matthew Levendusky, *The Partisan Sort: How Liberals Became Democrats and Conservatives Became Republicans* (Chicago: University of Chicago Press, 2009).

21. Lydia Saad, "U.S. Political Ideology Steady; Conservatives, Moderates Tie," Gallup, 1992–2021, https://news.gallup.com/poll/388988/political-ideology-steady-conservatives-moderates-tie.aspx.

22. Drew DeSilva, "The Polarization in Today's Congress Has Roots That Go Back Decades," Pew Research Center, 10 March 2022, https://www.pewresearch.org/short-reads/2022/03/10/the-polarization-in-todays-congress-has-roots-that-go-back-decades/; Katharina Bucholz, "How Diverse Is Congress," Statista, 27 February 2023, https://www.statista.com/chart/18905/us-congress-by-race-ethnicity/.

23. Lydia Saad, "Democrats' Identification as Liberal Now 54%, a New High," Gallup, 17 January 2023, https://news.gallup.com/poll/467888/democrats-identification-liberal-new-high.aspx.

24. American Conservative Union Foundation, 2021 Ratings of Congress, http://ratings.conservative.org/congress.

25. DeSilva, "The Polarization in Today's Congress."

CHAPTER 2. Traditional Christian Values

1. Martin Pengelly, "'Go Pick Up a Bible,' Speaker Mike Johnson Defends Anti-LGBTQ+ Views," *The Guardian*, 25 October 2023, https://www.theguardian.com/us-news/2023/oct/27/mike-johnson-christian-bible-lgbtq-abortion-rights. Ashton Pittman, Twitter (X) post on Mike Johnson, https://twitter.com/ashtonpittman/status/1717342823572259075.

2. Russell Contreras, "Most Americans Cool to Christian Nationalism as Its Influence Grows," *Axios*, 28 February 2024, https://www.axios.com/2024/02/28/poll-christian-nationalism-americans-reject.

3. Gregory A. Smith, Michael Rotolo, and Patricia Tevington, "45% of Americans Say US Should be a 'Christian Nation,'" Pew Research Center, 27 October 2022, https://www.pewresearch.org/religion/2022/10/27/45-of-americans-say-u-s-should-be-a-christian-nation.

4. PRRI Staff, "Support for Christian Nationalism in All 50 States: Findings From PRRI's 2023 American Values Atlas," PRRI, 28 February 2024, https://www.prri.org/research/support-for-christian-nationalism-in-all-50-states/.

5. Peter Wehner, "The Polite Zealotry of Mike Johnson," *The Atlantic*, 31 October 2023, https://www.theatlantic.com/ideas/archive/2023/10/polite-zealotry-mike-johnson/675845/.

6. Shailer Mathews, "Ten Years of American Protestantism," *The North American Review*, May 1923, 592; George M. Marsden, *Fundamentalism and American Culture* (New York: Oxford University Press, 1982), 92, 193–95. See also Mark A. Noll, *American Evangelical Christianity: An Introduction* (Malden, MA: Blackwell, 2001); Andrew Athelstone and David Ceri Jones, *The Oxford Handbook of Christian Fundamentalism* (New York: Oxford University Press, 2024); and for comparative perspectives, Martin E. Marty and R. Scott Appleby, eds., *The Fundamentalism Project*, Vols. 1 to 5 (Chicago: University of Chicago Press, 1991–1995).

7. Marsden, *Fundamentalism and American Culture*, 92.

8. Minutes, *Christianity Today*, Board of Directors, 6 January 1959, *Christianity Today* Papers, Box 1, Billy Graham Resources, Wheaton, IL.

9. Pew to John Young, 18 June 1957; Pew to Graham, 1 October 1956; Graham to Pew, 27 September 1956, J. Howard Pew Papers, Boxes 48, 53, Hagley Library and Museum, Wilmington, DE.

10. CNN, "Exit Polls" (2020, National Results), https://www.cnn.com/election/2020/exit-polls/president/national-results; CNN, "Exit Polls" (2024, National Results), https://www.cnn.com/election/2024/exit-polls/national-results/general/president/0.

11. Michele F. Margolis, *From Politics to the Pews: How Partisanship and the Political Environment Shape Religious Identity* (Chicago: University of Chicago Press, 2018). On the relationship between Trump and white evangelical Christians, see Anand Edward Sokhey and Paul A. Djupe, *Trump, White Evangelical Christians, and American Politics: Change and Continuity* (Philadelphia: University of Pennsylvania Press, 2024).

12. Paul Froese, "Religion and American Politics from a Global Perspective," *Religions* 5 (2014): 648–62.

13. "Beverly Hills New Pastor Arrives," *Los Angeles Times*, 29 October 1948, A1.

14. The Editors of Fortune and Russell Davenport, *USA: The Permanent Revolution* (Saddle River, NJ: Prentice-Hall, 1951), 34.

15. Russell Kirk, *The Conservative Mind* (London: Faber and Faber, 1954), 26.

16. Andrew L. Whitehead, Samuel L. Perry, and Joseph O. Baker, "Make America Christian Again: Christian Nationalism and Voting for Donald Trump in the 2016 Presidential Election," *Sociology of Religion* 79 (2018): 151–52.

17. Emma Green, "The Conservatives Are Dreading—and Preparing—for Civil War," *The Atlantic*, 1 October 2021, https://www.theatlantic.com/politics/archive/2021/10/claremont-ryan-williams-trump/620252/.

18. Jim Daly, "Freedom in Christ," Focus on the Family, n.d., https://www.focusonthefamily.com/parenting/freedom-in-christ/.

19. "Our First, Most Cherished Liberty: A Statement on Religious Liberty by the United States Conference of Catholic Bishops Ad Hoc Committee on Religious Liberty," United States Conference of Catholics Bishops, March 2012, https://www.usccb.org/committees/religious-liberty/our-first-most-cherished-liberty.

20. See also, PPRI Staff, "Understanding Partisanship Among Catholic Voters Prior to the 2024 Presidential Election," PPRI Research, 1 November 2024, https://www.prri.org/spotlight/understanding-partisanship-among-catholic-voters-ahead-of-the-2024-presidential-election/.

21. Office of Public Affairs, U.S. Department of Justice, "Attorney General William P. Barr Delivers Remarks to the Law School and the de Nicola Center for Ethics and Culture at the University of Notre Dame," 11 October 2019, https://www.justice.gov/opa/speech/attorney-general-william-p-barr-delivers-remarks-law-school-and-de-nicola-center-ethics.

22. Onalee McGraw, *Secular Humanism and the Schools: The Issue Whose Time Has Come* (Washington, DC: Heritage Foundation, 1976), 11, 12, 14.

23. Katherine Stewart, "'Religious Liberty' Used to Uphold Conservative Privileges," *American Bar Association*, 5 July 2022, https://www.americanbar.org/groups/crsj/publications/human_rights_magazine_home/intersection-of-lgbtq-rights-and-religious-freedom/religious-liberty-used-to-uphold-conservative-religious-privileges/.

24. Mary Sennholz, *Faith and Freedom: The Journal of a Great American J. Howard Pew, Compiled by Mary Sennholz* (Grove City, PA: Grove City College, 1975), 57.

25. Ken Ham, "Christianity Is Under Attack," Answers in Genesis, https://answersingenesis.org/christianity/christianity-is-under-attack/.

26. Tomi Lahren, "Christians Are under Attack from Shows Like 'The View' and Evil Far-Leftists," OutKick, 20 April 2023, https://www.outkick.com/christians-are-under-attack-from-shows-like-the-view-and-evil-far-leftists-tomi-lahren/.

27. Brian Tashman, "Mike Huckabee Defends Ex-Gay Therapy," Right Wing Watch, 23 April 2015, https://www.rightwingwatch.org/post/mike-huckabee-defends-ex-gay-therapy-warns-gay-rights-will-outlaw-christianity-god-help-us-all/.

28. Annie Karni, Ruth Graham, and Steve Eder, "For Mike Johnson Religion Is at the Forefront of Politics and Policy," *New York Times*, 27 October 2023, https://www.nytimes.com/2023/10/27/us/politics/mike-johnson-speaker-religion.html.

29. Elizabeth Dias, "'Christianity Will Have Power,'" *New York Times*, 9 August 2020, https://www.nytimes.com/2020/08/09/us/evangelicals-trump-christianity.html.

30. Sarah Fortinsky, "Cheney Trolls Trump over Bible Sale, Suggests He Read Verse on Adultery," *The Hill*, 26 March 2024, https://thehill.com/home news/campaign/4558230-cheney-trolls-trump-over-bible-sale-suggests-he-read-verse-on-adultery/.

31. Tim Reid, "Trump Tells Christians They Won't Have to Vote after This Election," Reuters, 28 July 2024, https://www.reuters.com/world/us/trump-tells-christians-they-wont-have-vote-after-this-election-2024-07-27/.

32. "Calls for Drug War Aid," *Los Angeles Times*, 20 March 1924, A3; "Snatched by Dealers in Human Souls!," *Washington Post*, 22 June 1924, SM1; David F. Musto, *The American Disease: Origins of Narcotic Control* (New Haven, CT: Yale University Press, 1973), 91–229; Joseph F. Spillane, "Building a Drug Control Regime, 1919–1930," in *Federal Drug Control: The Evolution of Policy and Practice*, ed. Jonathon Erlen and Joseph F. Spillane (New York: Pharmaceutical Products, 2004), 25–59.

33. A. F. Pollard, *Factors in American History* (New York: Macmillan, 1925), 83.

34. U.S. Senate, 71st Cong., 2nd Sess., "Obscene Literature: Digest of the Laws Enacted in the Various States," 1 November 1929.

35. 46 Stat. 688 (1930) 19 U.S.C. 1305.

36. Joel Allan Carpenter, ed., *Biblical Prophecy in an Apocalyptic Age: Selected Writing of Louis S. Bauman* (New York: Garland, 1988), 6.

37. "Is Man Bound to Win," *Sunday School Times*, 26 March 1933, 208; *The Teacher*, August 1935, 27, 39; Congdon, "Christian Patriotism," *Moody Monthly*, November 1936, 112. See, generally, Joel A. Carpenter, *Revive Us Again:*

The Reawakening of American Fundamentalism (New York: Oxford University Press, 1997).

38. *The Teacher*, September 1934, 51, and July 1935, 57; Kent L. Johnson, *War, Depression, Prohibition and Racism: The Response of the Sunday School to an Era of Crisis, 1933–1941* (Lanham, MD: University Press of America, 1992), 26; see *The Christian Advocate*, 2 January 1936, 21; Elzoe Prindle Stead, "Consummating Programs," typescript, 1933, Gerald L. K. Smith Papers, Box 1, Bentley Library, Ann Arbor, MI; "Faith Alone Seen as Light of World," *New York Times*, 25 November 1935, 10.

39. "New Deal's Reign Called Anti-Bible and Anti-Christian," *Los Angeles Times*, 1 July 1939, A3.

40. Sennholz, *Faith and Freedom*, 105–6.

41. J. Howard Pew to Henry S. Brown, 30 April 1945, J. Howard Pew to Robert Lund, 31 January 1950, J. Howard Pew to James I. Wendell, 27 October 1950, Pew Papers, Boxes 8 and 26.

42. "Roosevelt Notes Backed by Hoover," *New York Times*, 29 September 1938, 22.

43. "Bricker Again Flays New Deal in Relief Crisis," *Washington Post*, 17 December 1939, 2.

44. Kevin M. Kruse, "How Corporate America Invented Christian America," *Politico*, 15 April 2015, https://www.politico.com/magazine/story/2015/04/corporate-america-invented-religious-right-conservative-roosevelt-princeton-117030/.

45. "Spiritual Mobilization: Early History," *Truth in Action*, 15 January 1943, Iowa Right-Wing Collection, Microfilm, Reel 133.

46. "National Association of Evangelicals: What It Is and How Does It Function," Report of the NAE Field Secretary, 21 September 1943, Papers of the National Association of Evangelicals, Graham Resources, Box 65; "Resolutions Adopted by the 8th Annual Convention," 21 April 1950, Papers of Herbert John Taylor, Graham Resources, Box 67; Bernard Kruse, "An Organization Which Stands Fast," *Chicago Tribune*, 14 May 1950, 14.

47. Carpenter, *Revive Us Again*, 161–76.

48. Thomas E. Bergler, "Winning America: Christian Youth Groups and the Middle-Class Culture of Crisis, 1930–1965" (PhD diss., University of Notre Dame, 2000), 110.

49. John C. Turner, *Bill Bright and the Campus Crusade for Christ: The Renewal of Evangelicalism in Postwar America* (Chapel Hill: University of North Carolina Press, 2009).

50. "Records of the Fellowship Foundation: Historical Background, Christian Anti-Communism Crusade, https://archives.wheaton.edu/repositories/4

/archival_objects/2465220020; "The Christian Answer to Communism," n.d., Radical Right Papers, Box 25, Hoover Institution, Palo Alto, CA; Fred Schwarz, "Will the Kremlin Conquer America by 1973?," Herbert Philbrick Papers, Box 65, Library of Congress, Washington, DC.

51. Billy Graham, "My Answer," n.d., J. Howard Pew Papers, Box 55; Billy Graham to J. Howard Pew, 27 September 1956, Pew Papers, Box 48.

52. Graham to Pew, 26 March 1955, Pew Papers, Box 42.

53. David K. Johnson, *Lavender Scare* (Chicago: University of Chicago Press, 2004).

54. David W. Reinhard, *The Republican Right since 1945* (Lexington: University of Kentucky Press, 1983), 63; Edwin R. Bayley, *Joe McCarthy and the Press* (Madison: University of Wisconsin Press, 1981), 73.

55. Ellis, "Segregation and the Kingdom of God," *Christianity Today*, 18 March 1957, 6–9.

56. Justin Taylor, "Is Segregation Scriptural? A Radio Address from Bob Jones on Easter of 1960," TGC (The Gospel Coalition), 26 July 2016, https://www.thegospelcoalition.org/blogs/evangelical-history/is-segregation-scriptural-a-radio-address-from-bob-jones-on-easter-of-1960/.

57. "Records of the Fellowship Foundation, Historical Background," Billy Graham Resources, https://archives.wheaton.edu/repositories/4/resources/987; "Church Group Votes, Elects 17 From Congress, *Washington Post*, 17 January 1946, 8; "Christian Leadership Group Told of Meetings at The Hague," *Washington Post*, 5 July 1952, 12; Jeffrey Sharlet, "Jesus Plus Nothing: Undercover among America's Secret Theocrats," *Harper's*, March 2003, 53–64; Lisa Getter, "Showing Faith in Discretion," *Los Angeles Times*, 27 September 2002, https://www.latimes.com/archives/la-xpm-2002-sep-27-na-prayer27-story.html.

58. Randall Balmer, "The Real Origins of the Religious Right," *Politico Magazine*, May 2014, https://www.politico.com/magazine/story/2014/05/religious-right-real-origins-107133/.

59. "Proposed IRS Regulations Threaten Private Schools," *Human Events*, 7 October 1978, 1; Muriel Dobbin, "Evangelical Lobby Gears Up to Shepard Its Extensive Flock to the Polls," *Baltimore Sun*, 21 October 1979, A3; Joseph Crespino, "Civil Rights and the Religious Right," in *Rightward Bound*, ed. Bruce J. Schulman and Julian E. Zelizer (Cambridge, MA: Harvard University Press, 2008), 91.

60. Lawrence Hurley, "Chief Justice Roberts Says Building a Fence around the Supreme Court Was the 'Hardest Decision' of His Tenure," NBC News, 24 May 2023, https://www.nbcnews.com/politics/supreme-court/roberts-calls-building-fence-supreme-court-hardest-decision-tenure-rcna85956; Allison Mc-

Cann and Amy Schoenfeld Walker, "Tracking Abortion Bans across the Country," *New York Times*, 25 September 2024, https://www.nytimes.com/interactive/2024/us/abortion-laws-roe-v-wade.html.

61. Jacques Billeaud and Morgan Lee, "What to Know about Abortion in Arizona under the Near-Total 1864 Ban," Associated Press, 10 April 2024, https://apnews.com/article/arizona-abortion-ban-what-to-know-797a4bbbc738497fe2284d6870c5be24.

62. Ivana Saric, "Why a 19th-Century Law Matters in the Supreme Court Abortion Pill Fight, *Axios*, 16 March 2024, https://www.axios.com/2024/03/26/supreme-court-abortion-pill-case-comstock-act.

63. *Food and Drug Administration, et al. v. Alliance for Hippocratic Medicine, et al.*, U.S. Supreme Court, No. 23–235, 13 June 2024.

64. "History of Abortion Ballot Measures," Ballotpedia, November 2024, https://ballotpedia.org/History_of_abortion_ballot_measures.

65. Jerry Falwell, *Listen America* (New York: Doubleday: 1980), 128.

66. Kenneth A. Briggs, "The Electronic Church," *New York Times*, 10 February 1980, E10; David Snowball, *Continuity and Change in the Rhetoric of the Moral Majority* (Westport, CT: Praeger, 1991), 67-71; Susan Friend Harding, *The Book of Jerry Falwell: Fundamentalist Language and Politics* (Princeton. NJ: Princeton University Press, 2000), 3–29.

67. Christian Voice, *Congressional Report Card: How Your Congressman Voted on 14 Key Moral Issues* (Washington, DC: Christian Voice, 1980).

68. "Fellowship Foundation Contributors," 1977, and "Leadership (Fellowship) Council Chart," n.d., Fellowship Foundation Papers, Boxes 574 and 381, Billy Graham Resources.

69. Stella Rouse and Shibley Telhami, "Most Republicans Support Declaring the United States a Christian Nation," *Politico*, 12 September 2022, https://www.politico.com/news/magazine/2022/09/21/most-republicans-support-declaring-the-united-states-a-christian-nation-00057736.

70. Owen Amos, "Inside the White House Bible Study Group," BBC, 8 April 2018, https://www.bbc.com/news/world-us-canada-43534724; Matthias Schwartz, "How the Trump's Cabinet Bible Teacher Became a Shadow Diplomat," *New York Times Magazine*, 29 October 2020, https://www.nytimes.com/2019/10/29/magazine/ralph-drollinger-white-house-evangelical.html.

71. Sarah Pulliam Bailey, "Televangelist: Christians Who Don't Vote Are 'Going to be Guilty of Murder,'" *Washington Post*, 11 October 2016, https://www.washingtonpost.com/news/acts-of-faith/wp/2016/10/11/televangelist-christians-who-dont-vote-are-going-to-be-guilty-of-murder/.

72. Bailey, "Televangelist."

73. Susan B. Ridgley, "Conservative Christianity and the Creation of Alternative News: An Analysis of Focus on the Family's Multimedia Empire," *Religion and American Culture* 30 (2020): 1; Dan Gilgoff, *The Jesus Machine: How James Dobson, Focus on the Family, and Evangelical America Are Winning the Culture War* (New York: St. Martin's, 2007), 18–42.

74. Concerned Women of America, "Beverley LaHaye—CWA Founder," https://concernedwomen.org/cwa-founder-beverly-lahaye/.

75. Robin Toner, "Thinkers on the Right," *New York Times*, 22 November 1994, B7.

76. "Mapping Attacks on LGBTQ Rights in State Legislatures," ACLU, 26 May 2023, https://www.aclu.org/legislative-attacks-on-lgbtq-rights.

77. Allison Sherry, "Post Supreme Court Ruling, Colo. Anti-Discrimination Law Will be Tested in New Ways," NPR, 6 July 2023, https://www.npr.org/2023/07/06/1186154264/post-supreme-court-ruling-colo-anti-discrimination-law-will-be-tested-in-new-way.

78. Ruth Graham, "The Court Delivers Another Reassuring Decision for Religious Conservatives," *New York Times*, 30 June 2023, https://www.nytimes.com/2023/06/30/us/politics/religious-conservatives-supreme-court.html.

79. On the Social Gospel, see Robert T. Handy, ed., *The Social Gospel in America, 1870–1920* (New York: Oxford University Press, 1966), and Christopher H. Evans, *The Social Gospel in American Religion: A History* (New York: NYU Press, 2019).

80. Walter Rauschenbusch, *Christianity and the Social Crisis* (New York: Macmillan, 1907), 332, 343.

81. Elcott et al., *Faith, Nationalism, and the Future of Liberal Democracy*, 86.

82. William A. Walker, "What the New Testament Says about Homosexuality," Westar Institute, May 2008, https://www.westarinstitute.org/editorials/what-the-new-testament-says-about-homosexuality.

83. Tony Keddie, *Republican Jesus* (Oakland: University of California Press, 2021), 159, 161, 162.

84. Jack W. Cottrell, "Abortion and the Mosaic Law," *Christianity Today*, March 1973, https://www.christianitytoday.com/1973/03/abortion-and-mosaic-law/; Patricia Wilson-Kastner and B. Blair, "Biblical Views on Abortion: An Episcopal Perspective," *Conscience* 6 (1985): 4.

85. David Galston, "The Bible and Abortion," Westar Institute, 23 May 2019, https://www.westarinstitute.org/blog/the-bible-and-abortion.

86. Yehuda Shurpin, "Is Hillel's Teaching the Same as the Golden Rule?," Chabad.org, https://www.chabad.org/library/article_cdo/aid/5410546/jewish/Is-Hillels-Teaching-the-Same-as-the-Golden-Rule.htm.

87. Rabbi Danya Ruttenberg, "Why Are Jews So Pro-Choice," *The Forward*, 30 January 2018, https://forward.com/opinion/393168/why-are-jews-so-pro -choice/.

88. Keddie, *Republican Jesus*, 9–10.

89. Emilio Gentile, *Politics as Religion* (Princeton, NJ: Princeton University Press, 2006), 211.

90. See https://www.christianbiblereference.org/.

91. Tim Chester, "What Did Jesus Teach about the Poor?," Crossway, https:// www.crossway.org/articles/what-did-jesus-teach-about-the-poor/.

92. Elcott et al., *Faith, Nationalism, and the Future of Liberal Democracy*, 92–93.

93. John Blake, "There's Another Christian Movement That's Changing Our Politics," CNN, 13 November 2023, https://www.cnn.com/2023/11/13/us /social-gospel-movement-uaw-strike-blake-cec/index.html; Alec Ryrie, *Protestants: The Faith That Made the Modern World* (New York: Viking, 2017), 7.

94. "Here Are the Richest Pastors in America," Reddit, https://www.reddit .com/r/atheism/comments/g02epm/here_are_the_richest_pastors_in_america/.

95. Lynn Sherr, *Failure Is Impossible: Susan B. Anthony in Her Own Words* (New York: Crown, 1995), 255.

96. Henry Grabar, "The Pithiest Critique of Modern Conservativism Keeps Getting Credited to the Wrong Man," *Slate*, 3 June 2022, https://slate.com /business/2022/06/wilhoits-law-conservatives-frank-wilhoit.html.

CHAPTER 3.   Free Enterprise

1. A. B. Kendall, "Our Duty as Christian Citizens," *Herald of Gospel Lib- erty*, 10 February 1927, 133; Rolf Lundén, *Business and Religion in the American 1920s* (New York: Greenwood Press, 1988), 15–16.

2. "Christians Rule Trade Says Bible Teacher," *Los Angeles Times*, 14 January 1930, 2.

3. Mary Sennholz, *Faith and Freedom*, (Grove City, PA: Grove City Col- lege, 1975), 149.

4. Elizabeth Fones-Wolf, *Selling Free Enterprise: The Business Assault on Labor and Liberalism, 1945–1960* (Champaign: University of Illinois Press, 1994); Kim Phillips-Fein, *Invisible Hands: The Businessmen's Crusade against the New Deal* (New York: W. W. Norton, 2010); Lawrence Glickman, *Free Enterprise* (New Haven, CT: Yale University Press, 2019); Naomi Oreskes and Erik M. Conway: *The Big Myth: How American Business Taught Us to Loathe Government and Love the Free Market* (New York: Bloomsbury Publishing, 2023).

5. "Editorial," *Barron's*, 1 February 1954, 1.

6. Calvin Coolidge, "Government and Business," address to the New York State Chamber of Commerce, 19 September 1925, Calvin Coolidge Presidential Foundation, https://coolidgefoundation.org/resources/government-and-business/.

7. National Association of Manufacturers (NAM), NIIC, "Analysis of Basic Public Relations Problems Facing NAM," 13 January 1945, NAM Papers, Series III, Box 842, Hagley; NAM, Minutes of the Committee on Public Relations, 18 March 1935, NAM Papers, Series V, Box 1; Richard S. Tedlow, *Keeping the Corporate Image: Public Relations and Business, 1900–1950* (Greenwich, CT: JAI Press, 1979), 59–79; Elizabeth Fones-Wolf, "Creating a Favorable Business Climate: Corporations and Radio Broadcasting, 1934 to 1954," *Business History Review* 73 (Summer 1999): 221–55; Orestes and Conway, *The Big Myth*, 129–40.

8. Bess Furman, "Free Enterprise Won by GOP," *New York Times*, 12 November 1946, 32.

9. Milton Friedman, "The Goldwater View of Economics," *New York Times*, 11 October 1964, SM 35.

10. Phyllis Schlafly, *A Choice Not an Echo* (Phyllis Schlafly, 1964), 28–29.

11. Ronald Reagan, "President Ronald Reagan's Speech on Project Economic Justice," Center for Economic and Social Justice, 3 August 1987, https://www .cesj.org/about-cesj-in-brief/history-accomplishments/pres-reagans-speech-on -project-economic-justice/.

12. Ted Cruz, "Delivers Remarks to the Federalist Society's 'Role of Economic Liberty in the United States' Luncheon," 28 March 2017, https://www.cruz.senate .gov/newsroom/press-releases/sen-cruz-and-lsquowhen-we-think-boldly-and -creatively-we-can-unleash-the-free-enterprise-system-and-rsquo.

13. 1932 Democratic Party Platform, The American Presidency Project, https://www.presidency.ucsb.edu/documents/1932-democratic-party-platform.

14. "Address of Snell in Reply to Roosevelt," *New York Times*, 26 August 1935, 10.

15. "New Deal Policy Attacked by Knox," *Atlanta Constitution*, 31 July 1936, 1.

16. "Talmadge Renews New Deal Attack," *New York Times*, 5 July 1935, 2.

17. "Gov. Talmadge Left Off Atlanta Program," *Baltimore Sun*, 9 October 1935, 2.

18. Fess to Lowell Fess, 29 May 1933, Simeon Fess Papers, Box 842, Library of Congress, Washington, DC.

19. George Wolfskill and John A. Hudson, *All but the People* (Toronto: Macmillan, 1969), 93.

20. George Wolfskill, *The Revolt of the Conservatives* (Boston: Houghton Mifflin, 1962), 85–98; Robert F. Burk, *The Corporate State, and the Broker State* (Cambridge, MA: Harvard University Press, 1960), 159–63.

21. "Frank Urges Faith in Free Enterprise," *New York Times*, 13 January 1938, 1.

22. Orestes and Conway, *The Big Myth*, 116–17.

23. Clarence E. Wunderlin Jr., ed., *The Papers of Robert A. Taft*, Vol. 3, *1945–1948* (Kent, OH: Kent State University Press, 2003), 177–78.

24. Thomas W. Evans, *The Education of Ronald Reagan: The General Electric Years and the Untold Story of His Conversion to Conservatism* (New York: Columbia University Press: 2006), 230.

25. Earl Mazo, "Alcorn Has Talk with Eisenhower: Charges Democrats' Ultimate Aim Is Free-Enterprise Destruction," *New York Herald Tribune*, 22 May 1957, 15.

26. William Chapman, "Senator Charges Free Enterprise Being Smothered," *Washington Post*, 22 October 1964, B1.

27. Glickman, *Free Enterprise*, 9.

28. "Armey to Republicans," 1 November 1993, Richard Armey Papers, Box 842, Carl Albert Center Archives, Norman, Oklahoma.

29. Cal Thomas, "Clintons Promise Medical Socialism," *St. Louis Post-Dispatch*, 6 October 1993, 7B.

30. "Steele Calls Obama Health Plan 'Socialism,'" CBS News, 20 July 2009, https://www.cbsnews.com/news/steele-calls-obama-health-plan-socialism/.

31. Hearing before the Committee on Banking, Housing, and Urban Affairs, United States Senate, Examining the Opportunities That Clean Energy Investment Can Help Our Communities and Economy, 22 April 2021, 22–23, https://www.govinfo.gov/app/details/CHRG-117shrg47912.

32. U.S. Senate Committee on Environment and Public Works, "Barrasso on Green New Deal: We Need Solutions, Not Socialism," 12 February 2019, https://www.epw.senate.gov/public/index.cfm/2019/2/barrasso-on-green-new-deal-we-need-solutions-not-socialism.

33. Jason Le Miere, "Alexandria Ocasio-Cortez Wants to 'Take Away Your Hamburgers,' Ex-Trump Aide Gorka Claims in Bizarre Attack," *Newsweek*, 28 February 2019, https://www.newsweek.com/trump-alexandria-ocasio-cortez-sebastian-gorka-1348364.

34. Trump White House, "Remarks by President Trump in State of the Union Address," 6 February 2019, https://trumpwhitehouse.archives.gov/briefings-statements/remarks-president-trump-state-union-address-2/.

35. Alan S. Blinder, "Free Trade," in *Concise Encyclopedia of Economics*, https://www.econlib.org/library/Enc1/FreeTrade.html.

36. Republican Party Platform of 1916, The American Presidency Project, https://www.presidency.ucsb.edu/documents/republican-party-platform-1916.

37. Sheldon L. Richman, "The Reagan Record on Trade: Rhetoric v. Reality," CATO Institute, 20 May 1988, https://www.cato.org/sites/cato.org/files

/pubs/pdf/pa107.pdf; Milton Friedman, "Outdoing Smoot–Hawley," *Wall Street Journal*, 20 April 1987, https://miltonfriedman.hoover.org/internal/media/dispatcher/214378/full.

38.　Katie Lobosco, "Trump Wants More Tariffs, His Trade Wars Already Cost Americans $230 Billion to Date," CNN, 18 March 2024, https://www.cnn.com/2024/03/18/politics/donald-trump-tariffs-trade-war/index.html; Joseph Fong, "Trump Threatens to Slap '100% Tariff' on Cars Made in Mexico by China Firms," *YouTube*, 18 March 2024, https://www.youtube.com/watch?v=JAgG964trTE.

39.　Ellis W. Hawley, *The Great War and the Search for a Modern Order: A History of the American People and Their Institutions, 1917–1933* (New York: St. Martin's, 1979), 80–117; Ruth O'Brien, *Workers' Paradox: The Republican Origins of New Deal Labor Policy, 1886–1935* (Chapel Hill: University of North Carolina Press, 1998), 120–47; Andrew Gibson and Arthur Donovan, *The Abandoned Ocean: A History of United States Maritime Policy* (Columbia: University of South Carolina Press, 2000); Thomas W. Hazlett, "The Rationality of U.S. Regulation of the Broadcast Spectrum," *Journal of Law and Economics* 33 (1990): 133–75.

40.　Rinehart John Swenson, *The National Government and Business* (New York: Century Company, 1924), 3–4. For all quotations in this book, any emphasis is original.

41.　Cathy Bussewitz, "Unprecedented Profits for Exxon, as Travel, and War, Heated Up," Associated Press, 31 January 2023, https://apnews.com/article/russia-ukraine-exxon-mobil-corp-business-0de95b8421a658f020717a148a63c9c5; "GDP by Country, 2022," *Worldometer*, https://www.worldometers.info/gdp/gdp-by-country/.

42.　Allison Winter, "Billions in Federal Farm Payments Flow to a Select Group of Producers, Report Shows," *Iowa Capital Dispatch*, 1 February 2023, https://iowacapitaldispatch.com/2023/02/01/billions-in-federal-farm-payments-flow-to-a-select-group-of-producers-report-shows/.

43.　Mike McIntire, "Bailout Is a Windfall to Banks, If Not to Depositors," *New York Times*, 7 January 2009, https://www.nytimes.com/2009/01/18/business/18bank.html.

44.　Subsidy Tracker, https://subsidytracker.goodjobsfirst.org/, and "Top 100 Parent Companies," https://subsidytracker.goodjobsfirst.org/parent-totals.

45.　Chris Edwards, "Special Interests and Corporate Welfare," CATO Institute, 2022, https://www.cato.org/cato-handbook-policymakers/cato-handbook-policymakers-9th-edition-2022/special-interests-corporate-welfare.

46.　Thomas Brunell, "The Relationship between Political Parties and Interest Groups: Explaining Patterns of PAC Contributions to Candidates for Congress," *Political Research Quarterly* 58 (2005), 685.

47. Esther Whieldon, "Political Donations by U.S. Public Company CEOs Favor Republicans," S&P Global, 2 April 2019, https://www.spglobal.com/market intelligence/en/news-insights/trending/0Nm-AZgRKeGzfWZhvSWTFw2.

48. For an analysis of conservative forms of populism, see Michael Kazin, *The Populist Persuasion* (Ithaca, NY: Cornell University Press, 1995).

49. Open Secrets, "Who are the Biggest Donors?" (2022 cycle), https://www.opensecrets.org/elections-overview/biggest-donors.

50. Open Secrets, "Who are the Biggest Donors?" (2024 cycle), https://www.opensecrets.org/elections-overview/biggest-donors.

51. Liz Mineo, "Top Business Execs More Polarized Than Nation as Whole," *The Harvard Gazette*, 15 August 2022, https://news.harvard.edu/gazette/story/2022/08/top-business-execs-more-polarized-than-nation-as-whole/.

52. A. Barton Hinkle, "The High Price of Republican Hypocrisy," *Reason*, 11 November 2011, https://reason.com/2011/11/11/the-high-price-of-republican-hypocrisy/.

CHAPTER 4.   Limited Government

1. James Bryce, *The American Commonwealth* (London: Macmillan, 1888), 2:404.

2. Art Lindsley, "Does the Bible Support Limited Government?," Institute for Faith, Work & Economics, 19 February 2018, https://tifwe.org/bible-support-limited-government/.

3. Anne Bradley, "Why Limited Government Is Integral to Biblical Flourishing," Institute for Faith, Work & Economics, 19 November 2018, https://tifwe.org/why-limited-government-is-integral-to-biblical-flourishing/.

4. Roper Poll, search engine at https://ropercenter.cornell.edu/ipoll/.

5. Lydia Saad, "Public Firm in View Government Is Doing Too Much, Too Powerful," Gallup, 24 October 2023, https://news.gallup.com/poll/512900/public-firm-view-government-doing-powerful.aspx.

6. "Steiwer's Keynote Address," *New York Herald Tribune*, 10 June 1936, 1.

7. Gary M. Pecquet and Clifford F. Thies, "Reputation Overrides Record: How Warren G. Harding Mistakenly Became the 'Worst' President of the United States," *The Independent Review* 21 (2016): 37.

8. Don Irwin, "Group Seeking Bipartisan Role in '52 Election," *New York Herald Tribune*, 18 September 1951, 11.

9. Barry Goldwater 1964 Campaign, "Pledged to Enforce the Constitution and Restore the Republic," *The Imaginative Conservative*, https://theimaginative conservative.org/2012/10/pledged-to-enforce-constitution-and.html.

10. M. Stanton Evans, "The Case for Republican Negativism," *Human Events*, 25 March 1967, 8.

11. Ronald Reagan, "Farewell Address to the Nation," 11 January 1989, https://www.reaganfoundation.org/ronald-reagan/reagan-quotes-speeches/farewell-address-to-the-nation-1/.

12. Republican Party Platform of 2000, The American Presidency Project, https://www.presidency.ucsb.edu/documents/2000-republican-party-platform.

13. Cal Thomas, "True Conservatives Could Rebel," *PressReader*, 31 January 2004, https://www.pressreader.com/usa/texarkana-gazette/20040131/281638195502820.

14. Marco Rubio, CPAC, 18 February 2010, https://www.c-span.org/video/?292148-3/marco-rubio-remarks.

15. "The Mount Vernon Statement Recommits Conservatives to the American Founding," *First Principles*, 17 February 2010, https://static.heritage.org/CPP/FP_PS40w.pdf.

16. U.S. Congressman Mike Johnson, "7 Core Principles of Conservatism," https://mikejohnson.house.gov/7-core-principles-of-conservatism/.

17. Larry Kudlow, "The GOP Should Stick with Limited Government and Economic Growth," Fox Business, 14 April 2023, https://www.foxbusiness.com/media/larry-kudlow-gop-stick-limited-government-economic-growth.

18. "Meeting of the Republican National Committee, 5 June 1934," Meetings of the Republican National Committee, 1911–1980, Reel 4, Library of Congress; David Sherman Beach to William A. Borah, December 4, 1934, William A. Borah Papers, Box 751, Library of Congress.

19. Lewis Gould, *The Republicans: A History of the Grand Old Party* (New York: Oxford University Press, 2014), 194.

20. Bertrand Snell, Radio Address, 5 November 1934, Papers of Bertrand H. Snell, Box C1.1, State University of New York, Potsdam, NY.

21. Herbert H. Hoover, "Crisis to Free Men," Republican National Convention, 10 June 1936, https://publicpolicy.pepperdine.edu/academics/research/faculty-research/new-deal/hoover-speeches/hh061036.htm.

22. Robert A. Taft, "A Declaration of Republican Principles," *Vital Speeches of the Day*, January 1940, https://www.peterpappas.com/journals/debates/unit_9.pdf.

23. John O'Laughlin to Charles Hilles, 23 November 1938, Charles D. Hilles Papers, Box 129, Microfilm; "Vandenberg Asks Neutrality Stand," *New York Times*, 7 May 1939, 39.

24. "Text of Senator Taft's Rebuttal to Truman's Recent Addresses," *New York Times*, 17 May 1950, 16.

25. Harold Smith, "G.O.P. Nominee Hits Spendthrift Ways of Truman," *Chicago Tribune*, 16 July 1950, SW3.

26. "Banker's Resolutions Deplore Bureaucracy; Call Taxes 'Excessive,'" *Wall Street Journal*, 2 October 1952, 13.

27. Victor Lasky, "How the Cities Can Defeat Lyndon Johnson," *Human Events*, 29 February 1964, 11.

28. "Humphrey Invades GOP Area; Miller Raps Foreign Policy," *Philadelphia Inquirer*, 30 October 1964, 4.

29. Roman Hruska, "The Choice Is Yours," *Human Events*, 26 June 1965, 8.

30. Dan Gonyea, "From the Start Obama Struggled with Fallout from a Kind of Fake News," NPR, 10 January 2017, https://www.npr.org/2017/01/10/509164679/from-the-start-obama-struggled-with-fallout-from-a-kind-of-fake-news.

31. "The Return of Obamacare's Death Panels," Transcript of Hannity, Fox News, 30 July 2013, https://www.foxnews.com/transcript/the-return-of-obamacares-death-panels.

32. Louis Jacobson, "Michele Bachmann Decries 'Huge National Database' Run by IRS with 'Personal, Intimate' Health Care Details," PolitiFact, 20 May 2013, https://www.politifact.com/factchecks/2013/may/20/michele-bachmann/michele-bachmann-decries-huge-national-database-ru/.

33. Newt Gingrich, "Biden and the Big-Government Socialists' Cost-of-Living Disaster," *Newsweek*, 19 September 2022, https://www.newsweek.com/biden-big-government-socialists-cost-living-crisis-opinion-1743844.

34. Senator Tommy Tuberville, "Tuberville Responds to Biden's State of the Union Address," News Release, 7 February 2023, https://www.tuberville.senate.gov/newsroom/press-releases/tuberville-responds-to-bidens-state-of-the-union-address/.

35. David Kyvig, *Repealing National Prohibition* (Chicago: University of Chicago Press, 1979).

36. *Gitlow v. New York*, 268 U.S. 652 (1925).

37. Kenneth Ackerman, *Young J. Edgar: Hoover, the Red Scare, and the Assault on Civil Liberties* (New York: Carroll & Graff, 2007).

38. William Pencak, *For God and Country: The American Legion, 1919–1941* (Boston: Northeastern University Press, 1989); American Legion, Summary of Proceedings, 1921 and 1925 National Conventions, American Legion Archives, Indianapolis, Indiana.

39. George Seldes, *Facts and Fascists* (In Fact, 1943), 109–110.

40. "Fascisti of Rome Warmly Welcome American Legion," *Washington Post*, 28 September 1927, 1.

41. John P. Diggins, *Mussolini and Fascism: The View From America* (Princeton, NJ: Princeton University Press, 1972), 77–110; Wilson D. Miscamble, "The Limits of American Catholic Antifascism: The Case of John A. Ryan, *Church History* 59 (December 1990): 523–38; Harold Lord Varney to Henry P. Fletcher, 30 October 1933, Henry P. Fletcher Papers, Box 15, Library of Congress.

42. Bruce W. Dearstyne, "Lessons from the Textbook Wars of the 1920s," *History News Network*, 20 February 2022, https://historynewsnetwork.org /article/182475; Greg Huffman, "Twisted Sources: How Confederate Propaganda Ended Up in the South's Schoolbooks," *Facing South*, 10 April 2019, https://www .facingsouth.org/2019/04/twisted-sources-how-confederate-propaganda-ended -souths-schoolbooks; Adam Laats, "Conservatives Try to Control What Kids Learn, but It May Backfire," *Washington Post*, 7 February 2023, https://www .washingtonpost.com/made-by-history/2023/02/07/desantis-history-education/.

43. Laats, "Conservatives Try to Control."

44. Donald Yacovone, *Teaching White Supremacy: America's Democratic Ordeal and the Forging of Our National Identity* (New York: Pantheon Books, 2022); Huffman, "Twisted Sources."

45. Alvin W. Johnson and Frank H. Yost, *Separation of Church and State in the United States* (Minneapolis: University of Minnesota Press, 1948), 33; Jerome K. Jackson and Constantine F. Malmberg, *Religious Education and the State* (Garden City, NY: Doubleday, 1928), 1–80; Edward J. Larson, *Summer for the Gods: The Scopes Trial and America's Continuing Debate over Science and Religion* (New York: Basic Books, 1997), 230–31.

46. David H. Price, *The American Surveillance State* (London: Pluto Press, 2022), 25; Anthon G. Theoharis, *The Boss: J. Edgar Hoover and the Great American Inquisition* (Philadelphia: Temple University Press, 1988), 312–14; U.S. Senate, Hearings before the Select Committee to Study Governmental Operations with Respect to Intelligence Activities, 94th Cong., 1st Sess., Vol. 6, 1975, 393. See, generally, Final Report of the Select Committee to Study Governmental Operations, "Intelligence Activities and the Rights of Americans," 94th Cong., 2nd Sess., Book II, 1976.

47. "Eisenhower Hits Corrupt Officials," *Los Angeles Times*, 21 September 1952, 1.

48. "Homosexuality and Citizenship in Florida, a Report of the Florida Legislation Investigation Committee," January 1964, 14, 18–19, http://palmm .digital.flvc.org/islandora/object/uf%3A35645#page/cover1/mode/2up.

49. "University of Florida Apologizes for Honoring Antigay Alumnus," *Advocate*, 1 July 2005, https://www.advocate.com/news/2005/07/01/florida-alumni -group-apologizes-honoring-antigay-graduate.

50. "Florida Board of Education Extends 'Don't Say Gay' Ban to All Grades," *Politico*, 19 April 2023, https://www.politico.com/news/2023/04/19 /florida-expands-dont-say-gay-00092821.

51. Annika Kim Constantino, "Businesses Oppose Florida's 'Don't Say Gay' Ban on Discussion of LGBTQ Issues in Public Schools," CNBC, 29 March 2021, https://www.cnbc.com/2022/03/29/businesses-oppose-floridas-dont-say -gay-bill-banning-talk-of-lgbtq-issues-in-public-schools.html.

52. Christine Pushaw, Twitter, 3 March 2022, https://twitter.com/equalityfl /status/1500522197760327683.

53. Shrai Popat and Holly Honderich, "Florida Lawmakers Pass 'Don't Say Gay' Bill," BBC, 8 March 2022, https://www.bbc.com/news/world-us-canada -60576847.

54. "Settlement Agreement," Equality Florida and State of Florida, 5 March 2024, https://www.the74million.org/wp-content/uploads/2024/03/Settlement -Agreement.03.11.24.pdf.

55. "Governor Ron DeSantis Signs Sweeping Legislation to Protect the Innocence of Florida's Children," Ron DeSantis, 17 May 2023, https://www .flgov.com/2023/governor-ron-desantis-signs-sweeping-legislation-to -protect-the-innocence-of-floridas-children/.

56. Mark Sherman "Supreme Court Will Hear Case on Law Banning Gender-Affirming Care for Minors," PBS, 24 June 2024, https://www.pbs.org /newshour/politics/supreme-court-will-hear-case-on-law-banning-gender -affirming-care-for-minors.

57. "Critical Race Theory Ban Status," *World Population Review*, April 2023, https://worldpopulationreview.com/state-rankings/critical-race-theory -ban-states. James Forman Jr., *Locking Up Our Own: Crime and Punishment in Black America* (New York: Farrar, Straus & Giroux, 2016) (Pulitzer Prize); Douglas A. Blackmon, *Slavery by Another Name: The Re-Enslavement of Black Americans from the Civil War to World War II* (New York: Doubleday, 2006) (Pulitzer Prize); Carol Anderson, *White Rage: The Unspoken Truth of Our Racial Divide* (New York: Bloomsbury, 2017) (National Book Critics Circle Award); Ibram X. Kendi, *Stamped from the Beginning: The Definitive History of Racist Ideas in America* (New York: Nation Books, 2016) (National Book Award); Isabel Wilkerson, *Caste: The Origins of Our Discontent* (New York: Random House, 2020) (Time #1 Nonfiction Book of the Year); Michelle Alexander, *The New Jim Crow: Mass Incarceration in the Age of Colorblindness* (New York: New Press, 2012) (*Chronicle of Higher Education*'s one of the eleven best scholarly books of the 2010s); Eduardo Bonilla-Silva, *Racism without Racists: Colorblind Racism and the Persistence of Racial Inequality in the United States*, 5th ed. (Lanham, MD: Rowman & Littlefield, 2017) (American Library Association Book Award);

Richard Rothstein, *The Color of Law: A Forgotten History of How Our Government Segregated America* (New York: Liveright, 2018) (Hillman Prize for Nonfiction).

58. Benjamin Wallace-Wells, "How a Conservative Activist Invented the Conflict over Critical Race Theory," *The New Yorker*, 18 June 2021, https://www.newyorker.com/news/annals-of-inquiry/how-a-conservative-activist-invented-the-conflict-over-critical-race-theory; Laura Meckler and Josh Dawsey, "Republicans, Spurred on by an Obscure Figure, See Political Promise in Targeting Critical Race Theory," *Washington Post*, 21 June 2021, https://www.washingtonpost.com/education/2021/06/19/critical-race-theory-rufo-republicans/.

59. Tennessee State Legislature, Amendment No. 2 to HB0580, 2021, https://www.capitol.tn.gov/Bills/112/Amend/HA0441.pdf.

60. Terry Gross, "Uncovering Who Is Driving the Fight against Critical Race Theory in Schools: Interview with Tyler Kingkade," NPR, 24 June 2021, https://www.npr.org/2021/06/24/1009839021/uncovering-who-is-driving-the-fight-against-critical-race-theory-in-schools; American Legislative Exchange Council, "Workshop: Against Critical Election Theory's Onslaught: Reclaiming Education and the American Dream," 8 December 2021, https://www.alec.org/article/reclaiming-education-and-the-american-dream-against-critical-theorys-onslaught/.

61. Heritage Foundation, "Critical Race Theory," https://www.heritage.org/crt; Heritage Foundation, "Learn How to Spot Critical Race Theory—And What You Can Do to Fight It," https://secured.heritage.org/critical-race-theory-ebook-offer.

62. Jacob Grumbach, "Laboratories of Democratic Backsliding," *American Political Science Review*, 1 December 2022, https://www.cambridge.org/core/journals/american-political-science-review/article/laboratories-of-democratic-backsliding/0742F08306EFDD8612539F089853E4FE.

63. Sergei Guriev and Daniel Treisman, *Spin Dictators: The Changing Face of Tyranny in the 21st Century* (Princeton, NJ: Princeton University Press, 2022), 16.

64. Richard Corcoran, "Education Is Freedom," Hillsdale College, YouTube, https://www.youtube.com/watch?v=HVujpIator0&t=2299s.

65. Kasey Meehan, "Banned Book Update, 2022–2023 School Year," PEN America, https://pen.org/report/banned-in-the-usa-state-laws-supercharge-book-suppression-in-schools/.

66. Matthew C. MacWilliams, *On Fascism: 12 Lessons from American History* (New York: St. Martin's, 2020) 123–31.

67. Shane Harris, "Giving in to the Surveillance State," *New York Times*, 22 August 2012, https://www.nytimes.com/2012/08/23/opinion/whos-watching-the-nsa-watchers.html.

68. Jacob Weisberg, "Drug Addled," *Slate*, 18 January 2006, https://slate.com/news-and-politics/2006/01/why-bush-s-prescription-drug-plan-is-a-fiasco.html.

69. Frederick M. Hess and Michael J. Petrilli, *No Child Left Behind Primer* (New York: Peter Lang, 2006).

70. Gareth Davies, "Towards Big-government Conservatism: Conservatives and Federal Aid to Education in the 1970s," *Journal of Contemporary History* 43 (2008): 621–35.

71. Jonathan Cohen, "When Government Failed New Orleans, Again," *The New Republic*, 17 August 2010.

72. James Bovard, "Sins of Commission," *American Conservative*, 18 December 2006, 38.

73. Rob Garver, "Trump's Vow of 'Revenge' against His Opponents Gains Volume," Voice of America, 10 June 2024, https://www.voanews.com/a/trump-s-vows-of-revenge-against-his-opponents-gain-volume-/7650528.html.

74. Michelle L. Price, "Trump Shares Social Media Posts with QAnon Phrases and Calls for Jailing Lawmakers, Special Counsel," ABC News, 28 August 2024, https://apnews.com/article/trump-social-media-conspiracy-e3bbd855a2710d6b4bb4f480dd77e190.

75. Charlie Savage, Maggie Haberman, and Jonathan Swan, "Sweeping Raids, Giant Camps, and Mass Deportations: Inside Trump's 2025 Immigration Plans," *New York Times*, 11 November 2023, https://www.nytimes.com/2023/11/11/us/politics/trump-2025-immigration-agenda.html.

76. Jesse Helms, "Conservative Principles and Leadership," *Washington Post*, 22 August 1976, 35.

77. Ronald Reagan, "Peace: Restoring the Margin of Safety," 18 August 1980, https://www.reaganlibrary.gov/archives/speech/peace-restoring-margin-safety.

78. The White House, "Composition of Outlays, 1940–2028," table 10.1, https://www.whitehouse.gov/omb/budget/historical-tables/.

79. Robert S. Dudney, "Questions for the Candidates," *Air & Space Forces Magazine*, 1 May 2008, https://www.airandspaceforces.com/article/0508edit/.

80. Joshua Fechter, "Texas AG Ken Paxton Sues Harris County to Block Program That Would Give Cash to Poorest Households," *Texas Tribune*, 9 April 2024, https://www.texastribune.org/2024/04/09/texas-harris-county-guaranteed-income/.

81. Jamelle Bouie, "It Turns Out Republicans Don't Hate Big Government," *New York Times*, 21 April 2023, https://www.nytimes.com/2023/04/21/opinion/republicans-abortion-guns-big-government.html.

82. Andrew Egger, "Republicans Take Aim at ESG Investing," *The Dispatch*, 2 May 2022, https://thedispatch.com/article/republicans-take-aim-at-esg-investing.

83. Akielly Hu, "What Is ESG Investment, the Strategy under Attack by Republicans?," Grist, 24 March 2023, https://grist.org/economics/what-is-esg-the -investment-strategy-under-attack-by-republicans/; Jacob Soll, "Don't Take Financial Advice from Ron DeSantis," *Politico*, 4 June 2023, https://www.politico .com/news/magazine/2023/06/04/what-ben-franklin-could-teach-ron-desantis -00099483.

84. Soll, "Don't Take Financial Advice."

85. Mike Pence, "Republicans Can Stop ESG Political Bias," *Wall Street Journal*, 26 May 2022, https://www.wsj.com/articles/only-republicans-can-stop -the-esg-madness-woke-musk-consumer-demand-free-speech-corporate-america -11653574189.

86. "House GOP Fails to Override Biden's Veto of ESG Investing Ban," AP News, 23 March 2023, https://apnews.com/article/house-republicans-veto -override-esg-woke-investment-1fb8a23144d68b59c820c48c34152664.

87. Veronique De Rugy, "Stop Calling the GOP the Party of Small Government," *Reason*, June 2018, https://reason.com/2018/05/19/stop-calling-the-gop -the-party/.

CHAPTER 5.   Fiscal Responsibility

1. Gallup Poll, April 1937, https://ropercenter.cornell.edu/ipoll/study /31087062/questions#5f7a2032-640f-48bf-95f8-99f060c38710.

2. "Federal Budget Deficit," Gallup, March 2023, https://news.gallup .com/poll/147626/federal-budget-deficit.aspx.

3. Ralph Drollinger, "Solomon's Advice on How to Eliminate a $20.5 Trillion National Debt," Capitol Ministries, 16 January 2018, https://capmin .org/solomons-advice-eliminate-19-trillion-debt/. All italics original.

4. "A Stupendous Feat," Coolidge and the Budget, https://www.coolidge andthebudget.com/.

5. Republican Party Platform of 1936, The American Presidency Project, https://www.presidency.ucsb.edu/documents/republican-party-platform-1936.

6. See the Gallup Polls from 1939–40, https://ropercenter.cornell.edu/ipoll /search?collection=LSM&end=1940-12-31&experimental=ANY&q=war&start =1939-01-01.

7. Republican Party Platform of 1940, The American Presidency Project, https://www.presidency.ucsb.edu/documents/republican-party-platform-1940.

8. "Debt, Tax Cuts, and Balanced Budget Urged," *Chicago Tribune*, 28 October 1964, A3.

9. Republican Staff Report U.S. House Committee Budget Committee, House Report, *Toward a Balanced Budget*, 13 April 1979, 95 (found through Proquest Congressional).

10. President Ronald Reagan, "Remarks at a Rally Supporting the Proposed Constitutional Amendment for a Balanced Federal Budget," 20 July 1982, https://www.reaganlibrary.gov/archives/speech/remarks-rally-supporting-proposed-constitutional-amendment-balanced-federal-budget.

11. Republican Contract with America, Teaching American History, 27 September 1994, https://teachingamericanhistory.org/document/republican-contract-with-america/.

12. Republican Party Platform of 2016, The American Presidency Project, https://www.presidency.ucsb.edu/documents/2016-republican-party-platform.

13. Eliza Collins, "House Fails to Advance a Balanced Budget Amendment to Counter High Spending Levels," *USA Today*, 12 April 2018, https://www.usatoday.com/story/news/politics/2018/04/12/house-fails-advance-balanced-budget-amendment-counter-high-spending-levels/508665002/.

14. Mike Johnson, "7 Core Principles of Conservatism," 2018, https://mikejohnson.house.gov/7-core-principles-of-conservatism/.

15. Rachel del Guidice, "'True North' Outlines 14 Conservative Principles," *The Daily Signal*, 21 October 2019, https://www.dailysignal.com/2019/10/21/true-north-outlines-14-conservative-principles/.

16. 1932 Democratic Party Platform, The American Presidency Project, https://www.presidency.ucsb.edu/documents/1932-democratic-party-platform.

17. Parke Brown, "GOP Speaker Hits 'Humbug' at Washington," *Chicago Tribune*, 14 March 1935, 13.

18. "'Restore Republic,' Vandenberg's Plea to all Opponents," *Baltimore Sun*, 13 February 1936, 1.

19. "Hoover Gives Eleven Steps to Recovery," *Baltimore Sun*, 6 May 1938, 1.

20. 84 Cong. Rec. S3536 (30 Mar. 1939).

21. Joseph A. Loftus, "Proposal Assailed: 10% Reduction Pledged by Republicans," *New York Times*, 10 January 1953, 1.

22. Phyllis Schlafly, *A Choice Not an Echo* (Phyllis Schlafly, 1964), 115.

23. "LBJ's Revenue Outlook Draws Fire from GOP," *Washington Post*, 25 January 1966, A10.

24. William F. Buckley Jr., "The High Cost of Governing," *Los Angeles Times*, 2 February 1968, A5.

25. "Cornyn Urges Congress to Adopt Strong Balanced Budget Amendment," *Federal Information & News Dispatch*, 11 November 2011.

26. David Espo, "Balanced Budget Provision Rankles Dems," Associated Press, 30 July 2011.

27. Ed O'Keefe, "Mitch McConnell, John Boehner Double Down on Deficit Concerns," *Washington Post*, 20 May 2012, https://www.washingtonpost .com/blogs/2chambers/post/republican-leaders-double-down-on-deficit -concerns/2012/05/20/gIQABJ5DdU_blog.html.

28. Matthew Dickerson, "Statutory PAYGO Presents an Opportunity to Cut Spending," Heritage Foundation, 31 August 2022, https://www.heritage.org /budget-and-spending/report/statutory-paygo-presents-opportunity-cut-spending.

29. "Buchanan Calls for Spending Cuts, Balanced Budget Amendment," Congressman Vern Buchanan, Press Release, 23 January 2023, https://buchanan .house.gov/2023/1/buchanan-calls-spending-cuts-balanced-budget-amendment -part-debt-limit.

30. Franco Ordoñez, "Biden Signs Bipartisan Deal to Avert Debt Default," NPR, 3 June 2023, https://www.npr.org/2023/06/02/1179658326/biden-debt -ceiling.

31. Andrew Glass, "House Approves Balanced Budget Amendment, Jan. 26, 1995," *Politico*, 26 January 2017, https://www.politico.com/story/2017/01 /house-approves-balanced-budget-amendment-jan-26-1995-234003.

32. Kjetil Storesletten, Fabrizio Zilibotti, and Andreas Müller, "The Political Colour of Fiscal Responsibility: Trump's Fiscal Policy Is in the Wake of Republican Tradition," Centre for Economic Policy Research (CEPR), 12 November 2019, https://cepr.org/voxeu/columns/political-colour-fiscal-responsibility -trumps-fiscal-policy-wake-republican-tradition.

33. Aaron Blake, "How GOP Debt Ceiling Votes Decline under Democratic Presidents," *Washington Post*, 20 January 2023, https://www.washingtonpost .com/politics/2023/01/20/debt-ceiling-votes-white-house/.

34. Michael A. Cohen, "GOP Debate Rhetoric Rings Hollow," *Politico*, 17 July 2011, https://www.politico.com/story/2011/07/gop-debt-rhetoric-rings -hollow-059214.

CHAPTER 6.   States' Rights

1. Constitution of the Confederate States of America, Article 4, Section 2, Clause 1, and Article 4, Section 3, Clause 3, Avalon Project, https://avalon.law .yale.edu/19th_century/csa_csa.asp.

2. Michael DeMarco, "States' Rights," *Encyclopedia Virginia*, 2020, 7 December 2020, https://encyclopediavirginia.org/entries/states-rights/.

3. Gallup Poll, January 1936, https://ropercenter.cornell.edu/ipoll/study /31103047/questions#20e012da-afa1-4106-8bc2-2ee910170cc5.

4. Pew Research Center Poll, April 2010, https://ropercenter.cornell.edu /ipoll/study/31095989/questions#4bf57a25-f727-4aa3-af9d-fb68a9d05a57.

5. Calvin Coolidge, "Address at the College of William and Mary, Williamsburg, Va.," The American Presidency Project, 15 May 1926, https://www.presidency .ucsb.edu/documents/address-the-college-william-and-mary-williamsburg-va.

6. "Party Back to States' Rights, Landon Asserts," *Washington Post*, 5 June 1936, X3.

7. "Texts of the Republican Conference Resolutions on Foreign and Domestic Problems," *New York Times*, 8 September 1943, 11.

8. Barry Goldwater, "Return of Power to the States Would Help Cause of Freedom," *Los Angeles Times*, 26 April 1960, B5.

9. "Text of Declaration of Principle and Policy Issued by G.O.P. in Congress," *New York Times*, 8 June 1962, 18.

10. Richard Nixon, "Annual Message to the Congress on the State of the Union," The American Presidency Project, 22 January 1971, https://www .presidency.ucsb.edu/documents/annual-message-the-congress-the-state-the -union-1.

11. "Executive Order 12612—Federalism," Ronald Reagan Presidential Library and Museum, 18 October 1987, https://www.reaganlibrary.gov/archives/speech /executive-order-12612-federalism.

12. Editors, "Federalism the Decisive Issue in Campaign," *Daily Pennsylvanian via U-WIRE*, 24 October 2000.

13. Stephanie Hall Bradley, "Retained by the People: Federalism, the Ultimate Sovereign, and Natural Limits on Government Power," *William & Mary Bill of Rights Journal* 23 (2014–2015): 261; Michael Falcone, "Say to Feds: Stay off Our Turf," *Politico*, 9 June 2009, https://www.politico.com/story/2009/06 /states-say-to-feds-get-off-our-turf-023502.

14. Adam Wren, "Four Years Ago, Mike Pence Hated Presidential Overreach," *Politico*, 15 April 2020, https://www.politico.com/news/magazine/2020/04/15 /pence-presidential-overreach-186818.

15. Michael Laris, "Virginia's Giant-Killer Showed the Powers-That-Be," *Philadelphia Inquirer*, 12 June 2014, https://www.inquirer.com/philly/news /nation_world/20140612_Virginia_s_giant-killer_showed_the_powers-that -be.html.

16. "Pro-Family Legislators Conference—With Mike Johnson," Wallbuilders, 9 December 2021, https://www.podcast24.fr/episodes/wallbuilders-live-with -david-barton-rick-green/profamily-legislators-conference-with-congressman -mike-johnson-cMQIPshoUb.

17. "Views Voiced by Roosevelt on U.S. Issues: Defended States' Rights," *New York Herald Tribune*, 2 July 1932, 4.

18. 79 Cong. Rec. H14796, 14797 (26 Aug. 1935).

19. 79 Cong. Rec. H14796, 14797 (26 Aug. 1935).

20. "Mrs. Barney Heads Landon Coalition Here," *New York Herald Tribune*, 11 August 1936, 7.

21. 83 Cong. Rec. S432 (13 Jan. 1938).

22. 83 Cong. Rec. S382 (12 Jan. 1938).

23. "A Challenge to the South," *Atlanta Constitution*, 29 August 1937, 6K.

24. "Southern Editors Call for Return to Democratic Principles," *Atlanta Constitution*, 12 September 1937, 7B.

25. James T. Patterson, *Congressional Conservatism and the New Deal: The Growth of the Conservative Coalition in Congress, 1933–1939* (Westport, CT: Praeger, 1981).

26. "Governor Talmadge Issues Call to the South," *New York Times*, 5 January 1936, 34.

27. "Liberty Leaguers Backed Talmadge," *New York Times*, 16 April 1936, 2.

28. Russell to Thurmond, 2 February 1948, J. Strom Thurmond Papers, Boxes 146, 145, Robert Muldrow Cooper Library, Clemson, SC.

29. Statement of the Southern Governors Committee, 23 February 1948, Thurmond Papers, MSS 100.

30. Howard Smith, "Southern Manifesto," 12 March 1956, Teaching American History, https://teachingamericanhistory.org/document/southern -manifesto/.

31. 111 Cong. Rec. S10742 (17 May 1965).

32. 111 Cong. Rec. S10032 (10 May 1965).

33. Ryan Grim, "Mitch McConnell Lays Down Radical Marker on Voting Rights: 'This Is Not a Federal Issue,'" *The Intercept*, 23 June 2021, https://theinter cept.com/2021/06/23/mitch-mcconnell-voting-rights-protection-federal/.

34. 167 Cong. Rec. H975–76 (2 Mar. 2021).

35. 167 Cong. Rec. H994–95 (2 Mar. 2021).

36. "Ryan Williams, "Bidenomics: Big Government, Industrial Policy, and Centralized Control," *Epoch Times*, 4 July 2023, https://www.theepoch times.com/bidenomics-big-government-industrial-policy-and-centralized -control_5373031.html.

37. "Thomas Sees Peril to Life of Republic," *New York Times*, 17 January 1920, 3.

38. "Says That Drug Addicts Become AntiSocial," *Los Angeles Times*, 2 October 1928, I18; "Snatched by Dealers in Human Souls!," *Washington Post*, 22 June 1924, SM1; David F. Musto, *The American Disease: Origins of Narcotic Control* (New Haven, CT: Yale University Press, 1973), 91–229; Joseph F. Spillane, "Building a Drug Control Regime, 1919–1930," in *Federal Drug Control: The*

Evolution of Policy and Practice, ed. Jonathon Erlen and Joseph F. Spillane (New York: Pharmaceutical Products, 2004), 25–59; David Farber, ed., *The War on Drugs: A History* (New York: NYU Press, 2021).

39. Alexandra Chasin, *Assassin of Youth: A Kaleidoscopic History of Harry J. Anslinger's War on Drugs* (Chicago: University of Chicago Press, 2016).

40. John He, "Fights over Federalism," *Harvard Political Review*, 24 November 2009, https://harvardpolitics.com/fights-over-federalism/.

41. R. Shep Melnick, *Between the Lines: Interpreting Welfare Rights* (Washington, DC: Brookings Institution, 1994), 116.

42. U.S. House of Representatives, *Report 104-664, Defense of Marriage Act*, 9 July 1996, 2, 6. It should be noted that as part of his "new Democrat" positions, President Clinton backed the act. It eventually passed both chambers by wide margins, with all opposition from Democrats. See "All Actions: H.R.3396—104th Congress (1995–1996)," https://www.congress.gov/bill/104th-congress /house-bill/3396/all-actions.

43. John McElhenny, "States Urge Supreme Court Not to Intervene in Recount," Associated Press, 30 November 2000.

44. *Oregon v. Gonzalez*, 546 U.S. 243 (2006).

45. Craig Shirley, *Reagan's Revolution: The Untold Story of the Campaign That Started It All* (Nashville, TN: Thomas Nelson, 2010), 83.

46. Allan J. Lichtman, *White Protestant Nation: The Rise of the American Conservative Movement* (New York: Grove/Atlantic, 2008), 450, 454.

47. Anthony Bertuca, "House Sends Bill to President That Would Protect Gun Industry from Lawsuits," BU Study Abroad: Washington, 20 October 2005, https://www.bu.edu/washington/2005/10/20/house-sends-bill-to-president-that -would-protect-gun-industry-from-lawsuits/.

48. Alexander Bolton, "Lindsey Graham Breaks With Trump on Abortion Ban," *The Hill*, 8 April 2024, https://thehill.com/homenews/senate/4580756 -graham-trump-abortion-ban/.

49. Philip Wegmann, "Mike Pence: 'Abortion Bans More Important Than Short-Term Politics,'" Real Clear Politics, 14 September 2022, https://www .realclearpolitics.com/articles/2022/09/14/mike_pence_abortion_bans_more _important_than_short-term_politics_148191.html.

50. Maggie Astor, "Trump Indicates He Would Back a 15-Week Federal Abortion Ban," *New York Times*, 20 March 2024, https://www.nytimes .com/2024/03/20/us/politics/trump-15-week-federal-abortion-ban.html; Kate Sullivan, Kristen Holmes, Steve Contorno, and Daniel Dale, "Trump Says Abortion Legislation Should Be Left to States," CNN, 8 April 2024, https://www .cnn.com/2024/04/08/politics/donald-trump-abortion-2024/index.html.

51. Curt Devine, Casey Tolan, Audrey Ash, and Kyung Lah, "Hidden-Camera Video Shows Project 2025 Co-Author Discussing His Secret Work

Preparing for a Second Trump Term," CNN, 15 August 2024, https://www.cnn
.com/2024/08/15/politics/russ-vought-project-2025-trump-secret-recording-invs
/index.html.

52. *Mandate for Leadership: The Conservative Promise* (2023), Project 2025,
Heritage Foundation, 455, 472, 553, https://static.project2025.org/2025_Man
dateForLeadership_FULL.pdf.

53. Zolan Kanno-Youngs and Erica L. Green, "Trump Disavowed Project
2025 during the Campaign. Not Anymore," *New York Times*, 29 November 2024,
https://www.nytimes.com/2024/11/29/us/politics/trump-project-2025.html.

54. Joe Yurcaba and Jay Valle, "A National 'Don't Say Gay Bill'? Republicans
Introduce Bill to Restrict LGBTQ-Related Programs," NBC News, 19 October
2022, https://www.nbcnews.com/nbc-out/out-politics-and-policy/national-dont
-say-gay-law-republicans-introduce-bill-restrict-lgbtq-re-rcna53064.

55. "Florida Board of Education Extends 'Don't Say Gay' Classroom Ban
to All Grades," PBS.org, 19 April 2023, https://www.pbs.org/newshour/politics
/florida-board-of-education-expands-dont-say-gay-classroom-ban-to-all-grades.

56. Ronald Brownstein, "Mike Johnson Symbolizes a New Turn for the
Religious Right," CNN, 31 October 2023, https://www.cnn.com/2023/10/31
/politics/mike-johnson-donald-trump-religious-right/index.html.

57. Charlie Sykes, "Trump's 'Total Authority' Boast Should Have Enraged
Republicans. Instead, They Shrugged," NBC News, 16 April 2020, https://www
.nbcnews.com/think/opinion/trump-s-total-authority-boast-should-ve-enraged
-republicans-instead-ncna1184806.

58. GovTrack.us, "Child Welfare Provider Inclusion Act Would Allow Federal
Funds to Adoption or Foster Care Providers That Exclude Same-Sex Couples Who
Want to Adopt," Medium, 5 May 2021, https://govtrackinsider.com/child-welfare
-provider-inclusion-act-would-allow-federal-funds-to-adoption-or-foster-care
-providers-12882b60e6fd.

59. Marcy Gordon and Ken Thomas, "Paul Ryan Blasts High Tax States
Even Though They Send Billions to Federal Government," *Chicago Tribune*, 12
October 2017, https://www.chicagotribune.com/nation-world/ct-ryan-high-tax
-states-20171012-story.html.

60. Mary C. Curtis, "What's the State of Our Rights? Stay Tuned," *Roll Call*,
12 May 2022, https://rollcall.com/2022/05/12/state-of-our-rights-stay-tuned/.

CHAPTER 7.   Personal Morality and Responsibility

1. William F. Buckley Jr., "The Conservative Reply," *New York Times*, 16
February 1971, 33.

2. "Coolidge Points Out Business Moral Path," *Baltimore Sun*, 5 December 1920, 14.

3. Charles Mohr, "Goldwater Says Morality Is Demanded by the Nation," *New York Times*, 15 October 1964, 1; Andrew E. Busch, "The Goldwater Myth," *Claremont Review of Books*, Winter 2005/2006, https://claremontreviewofbooks .com/the-goldwater-myth/.

4. Muriel Dobbin, "Evangelical Lobby Gears Up to Shepard Its Extensive Flock to the Polls," *Baltimore Sun*, 21 October 1979, A3.

5. Russell Kirk, "Ten Conservative Principles," *Policy Commons*, 7 January 1987, https://policycommons.net/artifacts/1171064/ten-conservative-principles /1724193/.

6. Doug Willis, "Republican to Challenge Issa, Fong," *Daily News*, 17 February 1998, N3.

7. George W. Bush, *A Charge to Keep* (New York: William Morrow, 1999), 25–26.

8. Pat Buchanan, "Which Values Are American Values?," *Stillwater News Press*, 12 June 2019, https://www.stwnewspress.com/opinion/pat-buchanan -which-values-are-american-values/article_5f5e2fbc-8c8e-11e9-affe-7ff80ce71a81 .html.

9. Nolan A. Goodyear, "Pros and Cons of Political Situation Discussed by Prominent Georgians," *Atlanta Constitution*, 12 August 1928, 5K.

10. 72 Cong. Rec. S5414 (17 Mar. 1930).

11. 72 Cong. Rec. S5494 (18 Mar. 1930).

12 Joe Conason, *The Hunting of the President: The Ten-Year Campaign to Destroy Bill and Hillary Clinton* (New York: St. Martin's Griffin, 2000); Lou Kilzer, "Coors Funds Take on Clinton," *Rocky Mountain News*, 23 August 1998, 5A.

13. Franklin Graham, "Clinton's Sins Aren't Private," *Wall Street Journal*, 27 August 1998, https://www.wsj.com/articles/SB904162265981632000.

14. Edward Walsh, "Bauer Airs Ads Calling for Clinton to Resign," *Washington Post*, 9 September 1998, https://www.washingtonpost.com/wp-srv/politics /special/clinton/stories/bauer090998.htm.

15. James Dobson, "Dear Friends," Focus on the Family, September 1998, https://ontology.buffalo.edu/smith/clinton/character.html.

16. Thomas B. Edsall, "Resignation 'Too Easy' Robertson Tells Christian Coalition," *Washington Post*, 9 September 1998, https://www.washingtonpost .com/wp-srv/politics/special/clinton/stories/coalition091998.htm.

17. William Bennett, *The Death of Outrage: Bill Clinton and the Assault on American Values* (New York: Simon & Schuster, 1998), 45.

18. Bennett, *The Death of Outrage*, 118, 138, 140.

19. Mike Pence: Congress, "Why Clinton Must Resign or Be Impeached," http://web.archive.org/web/20010306205858fw_/http:/www.cybertext.net/pence/pres.html.

20. Southern Baptist Convention, "Resolution on Moral Character of Public Officials," 1 June 1998, https://www.sbc.net/resource-library/resolutions/resolution-on-moral-character-of-public-officials/.

21. Joseph Farah, "Democrats Are Immoral," *WND*, 20 November 2003, https://www.wnd.com/2003/11/21897/.

22. Summer Concepcion, "Marjorie Taylor Greene Defends Calling Democrats 'Pedophiles,'" NBC News, 3 April 2023, https://www.nbcnews.com/politics/congress/marjorie-taylor-greene-defends-calling-democrats-pedophiles-rcna77869.

23. Colin Martin, "Partisan Hostility Is Rising: 72% of GOP Calls Dems 'Immoral' in New Poll," WWJ News Radio, 10 August 2022, https://www.audacy.com/wwjnewsradio/news/national/72-of-gop-calls-dems-immoral-in-new-poll.

24. Paul Blest, "Nearly Half of Republicans Now Think Democrats Are Running Pedophile Cabals," *Vice*, 6 April 2022, https://www.vice.com/en/article/jgm9vd/republicans-democrats-pedophiles-poll.

25. Jordan Michael Smith, "America's Horniest President," *Politico*, 16 August 2015, https://www.politico.com/magazine/story/2015/08/warren-harding-child-sex-sandal-121404/.

26. Peter Baker, "DNA Is Said to Solve a Mystery of Warren Harding's Love Life," *New York Times*, 13 August 2015, https://www.nytimes.com/2015/08/13/us/dna-is-said-to-solve-a-mystery-of-warren-hardings-love-life.html.

27. Miriam Kleiman, "Was Harding's Mistress a Spy? The National Archives Knows and Tells," The National Archives, 17 November 2014, https://prologue.blogs.archives.gov/2014/11/17/was-hardings-mistress-a-spy-the-national-archives-knows-and-tells/.

28. "Book on Harding Scorned in House," *Atlanta Constitution*, 27 January 1928, 16.

29. "Rumors Cause Postponing of Tomb Dedication," *New Journal and Guide*, 18 October 1930, 2.

30. "Shouts Harding Defense in Suit of Nan Britton," *Chicago Tribune*, 5 November 1931, 18.

31. "Address at the Dedication of the Harding Memorial at Marion, Ohio," in *Public Papers of Herbert Hoover* (Washington DC: Government Printing Office, 1976), 16 June 1931, 228, 229.

32. William Neikirk and Mike Dorning, "Speaker-Elect Admits to Illicit Affairs," *Chicago Tribune*, 18 December 1998, https://www.chicagotribune.com/news/ct-xpm-1998-12-18-9812180366-story.html.

33. Tweet, @NewtGingrich, 28 June 2023, https://twitter.com/newtging rich/status/1674171804733022208.

34. David Gibson, "Wheaton Group Blasts College's Silence over Hastert Confession," *National Catholic Reporter*, 2 May 2016, https://www.ncronline .org/wheaton-group-blasts-colleges-silence-over-hastert-confession.

35. Hannah Trudo and Josh Gerstein, "Tom DeLay, Others Defend Hastert in Letters to Court," *Politico*, 26 April 2016, https://www.politico.com/story/2016 /04/dennis-hastert-tom-delay-letters-court-sentencing-222344.

36. Charles Sykes, "How Conservatives Betrayed Virtue for Donald Trump," *USA Today*, 13 June 2017, https://www.usatoday.com/story/opinion/2017/06/13 /how-conservatism-lost-its-role-models-charles-sykes-column/102402728/.

37. Kyle Morris, "Trump Has a 'Great Legacy,' Should 'Step Aside' in 2024, says Former Education Secretary Bill Bennett," Fox News, 16 November 2022, https://www.foxnews.com/politics/trump-great-legacy-step-aside-2024-former -education-sec-bill-bennett.

38. Gary Bauer, "America's Justice System Weaponized against President Trump," Dr. James Dobson Family Institute, 4 April 2023, https://www.drjames dobson.org/articles/americas-justice-system-weaponized-against-president-trump.

39. Gary Bauer, "Biden's Corruption," *The Patriot Post*, 11 May 2023, https://patriotpost.us/opinion/97229-bidens-corruption-2023-05-11.

40. Jon Brown, "Franklin Graham Denounces 'Politically Motivated' Charges, Urges Prayer for US amid Anti-Trump 'Onslaught,'" Fox News, 23 March 2023, https://www.foxnews.com/politics/franklin-graham-denounces -politically-motivated-charges-urges-prayer-us-amid-anti-trump-onslaught.

41. @FranklinGraham, 10 May 2023, https://twitter.com/Franklin_Graham /status/1656430619935617024.

42. Mark Wingfield, "Denial of Trump's Abusive Behavior Has 'Devastating Implications,' Russel Moore Said," *Baptist News Global*, 14 May 2023, https:// baptistnews.com/article/denial-of-trumps-abusive-behavior-has-devastating -implications-russell-moore-says/; Loren del Valle, "What E. Jean Carroll Had to Prove to Win the Case," CNN, 9 May 2023, https://www.cnn.com/2023/05/09/politics /carroll-trump-jury-deliberations/index.html.

43. Brian Blackwell, "Who's Who of Southern Baptists on Trump's Advisory Board," *The Baptist Message*, 30 June 2016, https://www.baptistmessage.com /whos-who-of-southern-baptists-on-trump-advisory-board/.

44. Bob Allen, "Former SBC President Jack Graham Calls Evangelical Support for Trump a 'No- Brainer.'" *Baptist News Global*, 19 January 2020, https:// baptistnews.com/article/former-sbc-president-jack-graham-calls-evangelical -support-for-trump-a-no-brainer/.

45. Scott Barkley, "Southern Baptist Leaders Congratulate Trump-Vance on Overwhelming Victory," *Kentucky Today*, 6 November 2024, https://www.kentuckytoday.com/news/southern-baptist-leaders-congratulate-trump-vance-on-overwhelming-victory/article_3ccc42a6-9cb2-11ef-b72a-075847af2fc6.html; Mike Hixenbaugh, "Evangelical Leaders Celebrate Trump's Victory as a Prophecy Fulfilled," NBC News, 6 November 2024, https://www.nbcnews.com/politics/2024-election/trump-wins-election-evangelical-christians-celebrate-rcna178946.

46. Carol Kuruvilla, "Trump Has Changed White Evangelicals Views on Morality in One Major Way," *Huffpost*, 26 April 2019, https://www.huffpost.com/entry/white-evangelicals-trump-morality_n_5cc20d6de4b031dc07efb940.

47. Olivia Olander and Kelly Hooper, "'Do You Care about Family Values?': Walker's Son Denounces Father's Campaign," *Politico*, 4 October 2022, https://www.politico.com/news/2022/10/03/herschel-walker-daily-beast-abortion-00060160.

48. Daniel Straus and Amanda Chen, "Clip and Save: Herschel Walker's Nine Most Stupendous, Ridiculous, and Offensive Lies," *The New Republic*, 14 October 2022, https://newrepublic.com/article/168148/herschel-walker-nine-stupendous-ridiculous-offensive-lies.

49. Eva McKend and Michael Warren, "Republican Sen. Rick Scott to Campaign for Herschel Walker in Georgia This Week," CNN, 9 October 2022, https://www.cnn.com/2022/10/08/politics/warnock-walker-georgia-senate-rick-scott/index.html.

50. Joe O'Dea, "Why Can't Republicans Jettison Herschel Walker," Colorado Pols, 12 October 2022, https://www.coloradopols.com/diary/181366/why-cant-republicans-jettison-herschel-walker-joe-odea.

51. "Top Republicans Rally with Herschel Walker amid Abortion Allegations," *Daily Caller*, 11 October 2022, https://dailycaller.com/2022/10/11/tom-cotton-rick-scott-rally-herschel-walker-georgia/.

52. Katherine Fung, "Republicans Brush Off New Herschel Walker Abortion Claims: 'Desperate,'" *Newsweek*, 22 October 2022, https://www.newsweek.com/republicans-brush-off-new-herschel-walker-abortion-claims-georgia-midterm-senate-race-1754956.

53. "Republicans Unite to Back Herschel Walker after Personal Accusations," *Noticias English*, 5 October 2022.

54. Mark Winfield, "It's Not Your Imagination: Polling Data Confirm Conservatives' Flip on Morality in Candidates, and Herschel Walker Is Exhibit B," *Baptist News Global*, 10 October 2022, https://baptistnews.com/article/its-not-your-imagination-polling-data-confirm-conservatives-flip-on-morality-in-candidates-and-hershel-walker-is-exhibit-b/.

55. "United States Political Sex Scandals Per Year, by Party," Imgur, 2013, https://imgur.com/a/ycyGg.

56. Stephanie Stark and Sofia Collignon, "Sexual Predators in Context for Public Office," *Political Studies Review* 20 (2022): 329, 335.

57. Stephen C. Craig and Pauline S. Cossette, "Eye of the Beholder: Partisanship, Identity, and Politics of Sexual Harassment," *Political Behavior* 44 (2022): 750.

58. Southern Baptist Convention, "Baptist Faith & Message 2000," https://bfm.sbc.net/bfm2000/.

59. Guidepost, "Report of the Independent Investigation," 15 May 2022, https://www.baptiststandard.com/wp-content/uploads/SBC-Guidepost -report.pdf.

60. Christa Brown, "Clergy Sex Abuse: The Damage Done When Faith Is Weaponized," *Baptist News Global*, 29 July 2019, https://baptistnews.com /article/clergy-sex-abuse-the-damage-done-when-faith-is-weaponized/.

61. Conservative Baptist Network, "The Evidences of Concern within the Southern Baptist Convention," January 2023, https://capstonereport.com/wp -content/uploads/2023/01/The-Evidences-of-Concern-Within-the-Southern -Baptist-Convention.pdf.

62. Commonwealth of Kentucky, Supreme Court, No. 22-SC-0303, Amicus Brief of Southern Baptist Convention, Southern Baptist Convention, Executive Committee, Baptist Theological Seminary, and Lifeway Christian Resources, 1, https://appellatepublic.kycourts.net/api/api/v1/publicaccessdocuments/2d37 43b787049b565212d3c2d5d8274cfe679406f2fea9d1701cb62bbf328c0c /download.

63. Christa Brown, David Clohessy, and Dave Pittman, "The Duplicity of an SBC Amicus Brief," BishopAccountability.org, 26 October 2023, https:// www.bishop-accountability.org/2023/10/the-duplicity-of-an-sbc-amicus-brief/.

64. Yonat Shimron, "Disgraced Pastor Ted Haggard Faces New Allegations," *Religion News Service*, 26 July 2022, https://religionnews.com/2022/07/26 /disgraced-pastor-ted-haggard-faces-new-allegations/.

65. "Baptist Leader Coy Privette Dies," *Baptist Recorder*, 25 March 2015, https://www.brnow.org/news/Baptist-leader-Coy-Privette-dies/.

66. "A Final Lesson," NBC News, 20 October 2023, https://www.nbcnews .com/podcast/grapevine/grapevine-episode-6-transcript-final-lesson-rcna120662.

67. Jamiel Lynch, "Megachurch Pastor Admits Past 'Inappropriate' Behavior with 'Young Lady' after Accusation of Molesting 12-Year-Old," CNN, 17 June 2024, https://www.cnn.com/2024/06/17/us/robert-morris-gateway-church -sexual-abuse-allegations/index.html; Kaleem Kahn, "Robert Morris, Net Worth and Biography 2024," Impact Wealth, 1 February 2024, https://impactwealth.org

/robert-morris-net-worth-and-biography-2024/; Robert Hixenbaugh, "Gateway Church Elder Says Accepting Resignation of Pastor in Sex Abuse Scandal Was 'Difficult' Decision," NBC News, 20 June 2024, https://www.nbcnews.com/news /us-news/gateway-church-leader-announces-robert-morris-resignation-audio -rcna158026.

68. "Full List of Texas Pastors Charged with Abusing Children This Year," *Newsweek*, 6 December 2022, https://www.newsweek.com/full-list-texas-pastors -charged-abusing-children-1765910.

69. Sari Horwitz, Dana Hedgpeth, Emmanuel Martinez, Scott Higham, and Salwan Georges, "'In the Name of God,'" *Washington Post*, 26 May 2024, https://www.washingtonpost.com/investigations/interactive/2024/sexual -abuse-native-american-boarding-schools/.

70. Larry Eubanks, "As Long as Patriarchy Reigns, Church Sexual Abuse Will Persist," God, Faith, Media, 17 June 2019, https://goodfaithmedia.org/as-long -as-patriarchy-reigns-church-sexual-abuse-will-persist/.

71. Christa Brown, "Why I'm Not Engaging with the SBC's Abuse Reform Implementation Task Force," BishopAccountability.org, 17 February 2023, https://www.bishop-accountability.org/2023/02/why-im-not-engaging-with-the -sbcs-abuse-reform-implementation-task-force/.

72. Sheila Wray Gregoire, "Is the Evangelical View of Sex at the Root of Our Sex Scandals?," *Religion News*, 18 February 2021, https://religionnews.com /2021/02/18/ravi-zacharias-carl-lentz-is-the-evangelical-view-of-sex-at-the-root -of-our-sex-scandals/.

73. M. D. White and K. J. Terry, "Child Sexual Abuse in the Catholic Church: Revisiting the Rotten Apples Explanation," *Criminal Justice and Behavior* 35 (2008): 674.

74. Geoff Bennett, "Investigation Reveals Widespread Sexual Abuse and Cover-ups by Archdiocese of Baltimore," PBS, 6 April 2023, https://www.pbs .org/newshour/show/investigation-reveals-widespread-sexual-abuse-and-cover -ups-by-archdiocese-of-baltimore.

75. Joshua Kaplan, Justin Elliott, and Alex Mierjeski, "Justice Clarence Thomas Acknowledges That He Should Have Disclosed Free Trips from Billionaire," *ProPublica*, 7 June 2024, https://www.propublica.org/article/clarence -thomas-gift-disclosures-harlan-crow.

76. Brian Niemietz, "Huge Clarence Thomas R.V. Loan Forgiven by Wealthy Businessman, Senate Investigation Finds," *New York Daily News*, 20 October 2023, https://www.nydailynews.com/2023/10/25/clarence-thomas -rv-loan-forgiven-businessman-ethics/. See also the report of the Democratic majority on the Senate Judiciary Committee, *An Investigation of the Ethics Chal-*

lenges at the Supreme Court, 21 December 2024, https://drive.google.com/file/d/1ze1Xu95W-NCafPNP-mWhyeX3rENdkyM9/view.

77. Emma Brown, Shawn Boburg, and Jonathan O'Connell, "Judicial Activist Directed Fees to Clarence Thomas's Wife, 'Urges No Mention of 'Ginni,'" *Washington Post*, 4 May 2023, https://www.washingtonpost.com/investigations/2023/05/04/leonard-leo-clarence-ginni-thomas-conway/.

78. Shawn Boburg, Emma Brown, and Ann E. Marinow, "Influential Activist Leonard Leo Helped Fund Media Campaign Lionizing Clarence Thomas," *Washington Post*, 20 July 2023, https://www.washingtonpost.com/investigations/2023/07/20/leonard-leo-clarence-thomas-paoletta/.

79. Robert O'Harrow Jr. and Shawn Boburg, "A Conservative Activist's Behind-the-Scenes Campaign to Remake the Nation's Courts," *Washington Post*, 21 May 2019, https://www.washingtonpost.com/graphics/2019/investigations/leonard-leo-federalists-society-courts.

80. Senator Dick Durbin, "Durbin Reveals Omissions of Gifted Private Travel to Justice Clarence Thomas from Harlan Crow," Press Release, 7 June 2024, https://www.durbin.senate.gov/newsroom/press-releases/durbin-reveals-omissions-of-gifted-private-travel-to-justice-clarence-thomas-from-harlan-crow.

81. Jeff Zymeri, "'Thuggish Takedown,' Republican Senators Accuse Democrats, Media Allies, of Smear Campaign against Conservative Justices," *National Review*, 23 May 2023, https://www.nationalreview.com/news/thuggish-takedown-senate-republicans-accuse-democrats-media-allies-of-smear-campaign-against-conservative-justices/; Senate Judiciary Committee, Hearing on Supreme Court Ethics Reform, 2 May 2023, https://www.judiciary.senate.gov/supreme-court-ethics-reform.

CHAPTER 8.   Law and Order

1. Richard Nixon, "Address Accepting the Presidential Nomination at the Republican National Convention in Miami Beach, Florida," The American Presidency Project, 8 August 1968, https://www.presidency.ucsb.edu/documents/address-accepting-the-presidential-nomination-the-republican-national-convention-miami.

2. "Poll Finds Crime Top Fear at Home," *New York Times*, 27 February 1968, 29.

3. "Crime," Gallup, 2024, https://news.gallup.com/poll/1603/crime.aspx.

4. "Coolidge Apostle of Law and Order," *New York Times*, 13 June 1920, 5.

5. "Police Strike Issue in Bay State Election," *New York Herald Tribune*, 30 October 1919, 1.

6. William Howard Taft, "Reviewing Candidates," *Los Angeles Times*, 6 January 1920, 15.

7. "Wood Urges Law and Order," *Baltimore Sun*, 9 February 1920, 2.

8. Warren G. Harding, "Address Accepting Republican Nomination," 22 July 1920, The American Presidency Project, https://www.presidency.ucsb.edu/documents/address-accepting-the-republican-presidential-nomination-marion-ohio.

9. "Union League Plans Ratification Rally," *Philadelphia Inquirer*, 14 June 1920, 5.

10. "Willis Outlines 10-Point Platform," *New York Times*, 12 February 1928, 7.

11. "Snell Rallies Party to Fight 'Dictatorship,'" *Baltimore Sun*, 11 June 1936, 5.

12. Edward H. Miller, *A Conspiratorial Life: Robert Welch, the John Birch Society and the Revolution of American Conservatism* (Chicago: University of Chicago Press, 2021), 370-71. Matthew Dallek, *Birchers: How the John Birch Society Radicalized the American Right* (New York: Basic Books, 2023), reaches a similar conclusion.

13. The John Birch Society, "Support Your Local Police," https://jbs.org/sylp/.

14. G. Edward Griffin, *The Life and Words of Robert Welch, Founder of the John Birch Society* (Thousand Oaks, CA: American Media, 1975), 207.

15. "John Birch Pamphlets Distributed," *Baltimore Sun*, 31 August 1964, 32.

16. Roy Reed, "Birch Society Is Growing in the South," *New York Times*, 8 November 1965, 1.

17. Charles Mohr, "Goldwater Hits U.S. Moral Rot," *New York Times*, 11 October 1964, 76; "Text of Goldwater Kickoff Talk," *Los Angeles Times*, 4 September 1964, 16.

18. Republican Party Platform of 1980, The American Presidency Project, https://www.presidency.ucsb.edu/documents/republican-party-platform-1980.

19. Ronald Reagan, "Remarks at the Annual Meeting of the International Association of Chiefs of Police in New Orleans, Louisiana," Ronald Reagan Presidential Library and Museum, 28 September 1981, https://www.reaganlibrary.gov/archives/speech/remarks-annual-meeting-international-association-chiefs-police-new-orleans.

20. Cathleen Decker, "Offers Conservative Law-and-Order Agenda," *Los Angeles Times*, 23 June 1988, 18.

21. Charles May, "Riot-Area Visit Brief on Bush L.A. Trip: Critics Were Kept Away as The President Spoke of Law and Order," *Philadelphia Inquirer*, 30 May 1992, A4.

22. Fox Butterfield, "Bush's Law and Order Adds Up to Tough and Popular," *New York Times*, 8 August 1999, A1.

23. 2000 Republican Party Platform, The American Presidency Project, https://www.presidency.ucsb.edu/documents/2000-republican-party-platform.

24. David Lightman, "Trump in St. Louis, Fends Off Hecklers, Says Clinton and Obama 'Destroying' Country," *Miami Herald*, 13 March 2016, https://www.miamiherald.com/article65517272.html.

25. "Donald Trump's Acceptance Speech at the Republican Convention," *Time*, 21 July 2016, https://time.com/4418493/republican-convention-donald-trump-transcript/.

26. U.S. Department of Justice, "Attorney General Sessions Delivers Remarks at the Reagan Alumni Association's Celebration of President Reagan's Birthday," 6 February 2018, https://www.justice.gov/opa/speech/attorney-general-sessions-delivers-remarks-reagan-alumni-associations-celebration.

27. Michael Wines, "'Looting' Comment from Trump Dates Back to Racial Unrest of the 1960s," *New York Times*, 29 May 2020, https://www.nytimes.com/2020/05/29/us/looting-starts-shooting-starts.html.

28. Herbert Hoover, "Address to the Associated Press: Law Enforcement and Respect for the Law," 22 April 1929, The American Presidency Project, https://www.presidency.ucsb.edu/documents/address-the-associated-press-law-enforcement-and-respect-for-the-law.

29. "McGonigle Promises 'Integrity' on Pardons," *Philadelphia Inquirer*, 12 September 1958, 8.

30. Michael William Flamm, "'Law and Order': Street Crime, Civil Disorder, and the Crisis of Liberalism" (PhD diss., Columbia University, 1998), 101–2.

31. "Text of Goldwater's Speech Formally Opening Presidential Campaign," *New York Times*, 4 September 1964, https://www.nytimes.com/1964/09/04/archives/text-of-goldwaters-speech-formally-opening-presidential-campaign.html.

32. "The Nixon Menace," *Bay State Banner*, 15 August 1968, 4.

33. John Elmer, "Agnew Rips Democrats on Law and Order," *Chicago Tribune*, 16 September 1968, 1.

34. Richard Bergholz, "Nixon Backs Agnew on Law, Order," *Los Angeles Times*, 18 September 1968, 1.

35. "Where the Candidates Stand," *Statecraft*, October 1968.

36. "Reagan Accuses Democrats of Blocking Law and Order," *Globe and Mail*, 7 July 1984, 2.

37. Andrew Rosenthal, "Bush and Dukakis Trade Accusations over Crime," *New York Times*, 21 October 1988, 1.

38. Peter Baker, "Bush Made Willie Horton an Issue in 1988, and the Racial Scars Are Still Fresh," *New York Times*, 3 December 2020, https://www .nytimes.com/2018/12/03/us/politics/bush-willie-horton.html; "Independent Ads: The National Security Political Action Committee 'Willie Horton,'" *Inside Politics*, http://www.insidepolitics.org/ps111/independentads.html.

39. "Excerpts From Dec. 18 Impeachment Debate," *Washington Post*, 18 December 1998, https://www.washingtonpost.com/wp-srv/politics/special/clinton /stories/excerpts121898.htm.

40. 144 Cong. Rec. H11774–H11870 (18 Dec. 1998).

41. Rhea Mahbubani, "The Indictment against Donald Trump Quotes His Own 2016 Campaign Promises Slamming Hillary Clinton's Emails," *Business Insider*, 8 June 2023, https://www.businessinsider.com/trump-indictment -2016-campaign-promises-slamming-hillary-clinton-emails-2023-6.

42. Erik Uebelacker, "Trump Signed Law Making Mishandling Classified Docs a Felony," *Newsweek*, 13 June 2023, https://www.thedailybeast.com/trump -signed-a-law-making-mishandling-classified-docs-a-felony.

43. MSNBC, "Trump Campaign Ad Slammed as Overtly Racist," 14 September 2020, https://www.youtube.com/watch?v=sh38D1a7L9o.

44. @realdonaldtrump, 22 August 2020, https://twitter.com/realDonald Trump/status/1297138033918173184.

45. "You Won't Be Safe in Joe Biden's America," YouTube, https://www .youtube.com/watch?v=JK6K-sWTAtM.

46. Daniel Bice and Bill Glauber, "Supporters of Mandela Barnes Accuse Republicans of Running Racist Ads in Support of Ron Johnson," *Milwaukee Journal Sentinel*, 22 September 2022, https://www.jsonline.com/story/news /politics/elections/2022/09/22/mandela-barnes-supporters-accuse-republicans -airing-racist-ads-race-us-senate-race-ron-johnson/8074904001/.

47. Greg Bluestein, "Georgia Senate: In TV Attack, Loeffler Targets Collins' Legal Record," *AJC Politics*, 17 July 2020, https://www.ajc.com/politics /politics-blog/georgia-senate-in-tv-attack-loeffler-targets-collins-legal-record /SX4JCA7UIJF3XPBUTY5R5KSXLM/.

48. "Candace Valenzuela, Extreme Agenda," YouTube, 6 October 2020, https://www.youtube.com/watch?v=K0TjGT5bar4.

49. Tom Reed for Congress, "Can't Trust Tracy," https://www.youtube.com /@TomReedforCongress.

50. "Handel Ad Casts McBath as Anti-Police with Footage from March with Roswell Chief," *Atlanta Journal-Constitution*. 26 August 2020, https://www.ajc .com/politics/politics-blog/handel-ad-casts-mcbath-as-anti-police-with-footage -from-march-with-roswell-chief/ORUXBCQEJZG6BOU4DFVWEQICQE/.

51. Madeline Holcombe, "Her Son Was Killed in a 'Stand Your Ground' Shooting. Read Her Message to Him on What Would Have Been His 25th Birthday," CNN, 18 February 2020, https://www.cnn.com/2020/02/18/us/lucy-mcbath -jordan-stand-your-ground-birthday-message-trnd/index.html.

52. "Liberal Bob Trammel Loves Protesting," YouTube, 15 July 2020, https:// www.youtube.com/watch?v=na5BZ3TfpXQ&t=11s.

53. *Albuquerque Journal* Editorial Board, "NM GOP Needs to Explain Doctored Mailer," *Albuquerque Journal*, 29 September 2022, https://www.abq journal.com/2536044/nm-gop-needs-to-explain-doctored-mailer.html.

54. "Senator: Dems. Back Reparations for Those Who 'Do the Crime,'" Associated Press, 9 October 2022, https://apnews.com/article/tuberville-comments -reparations-19d58a87c23b57c1e9a6c8ca7f8fcb70.

55. National Republican Senatorial Campaign Committee, "We Can't Trust Cheri Beasley to Protect Our Families," YouTube, 13 May 2022, https://www .youtube.com/watch?v=TidAbar7E2U.

56. "Vote Against Liberal Laura Gillen: Endorsed by Anti-Police Groups," YouTube, 2 November 2022, https://www.youtube.com/watch?v=P6KETyq _MDg.

57. Meg Kinnard, "Trump Addresses Fraternal Order of Police in Battleground North Carolina," PBS, 6 September 2024, https://www.pbs.org/newshour /politics/watch-live-trump-addresses-fraternal-order-of-police-in-battleground -north-carolina.

58. Lauren Sforza, "Newt Gingrich Claims Democrats Have a 'Passion' for Stealing Elections," *The Hill*, 4 June 2023, https://thehill.com/blogs/blog-briefing -room/4033936-newt-gingrich-claims-democrats-have-a-passion-for-stealing -elections/.

59. Molly Bohannon, "Trump Promises 'Long-term Prison Sentences' for Election Cheating Despite No Evidence of Major Fraud," *Forbes*, 2 September 2024, https://www.forbes.com/sites/mollybohannon/2024/09/08/trump-vows -long-term-prison-sentences-for-election-cheating-despite-no-evidence-of -major-fraud/.

60. 65 Cong. Rec. S5559 (4 Apr. 1924).

61. Republican Party Platform of 1924, The American Presidency Project, https://www.presidency.ucsb.edu/documents/republican-party-platform-1924.

62. Richard Nixon, "The President's News Conference," 29 August 1972, The American Presidency Project, https://www.presidency.ucsb.edu/documents /the-presidents-news-conference-90.

63. "Mr. Nixon's Supporters Don't Take it Lightly," *New York Times*, 21 July 1974, https://www.nytimes.com/1974/07/21/archives/mr-nixons-supporters -dont-take-it-quietly-aides-and-outsiders-damn.html.

64. Amelia Thompson-DeVeaux, "It Took a Long Time for Conservatives to Abandon Nixon," 538.com, 9 October 2019, https://fivethirtyeight.com/features/it-took-a-long-time-for-republicans-to-abandon-nixon/.

65. "President Nixon's Speech on Cambodia," 30 April 1970, Vassar, https://www.vassar.edu/vietnam/documents/doc15.html.

66. Malcolm Byrne and Peter Kornbluh, *The Iran–Contra Affair: The Making of a Scandal, 1983–1988* (Alexandria, VA: Chadwyck-Healey, 1990); Lawrence E. Walsh, "Final Report of the Independent Counsel for Iran/Contra Matters," 4 August 1993, https://irp.fas.org/offdocs/walsh/.

67. Walsh, "Final Report of the Independent Counsel," 186–92.

68. Walsh, "Final Report of the Independent Counsel," 445.

69. "*United States v. John M. Poindexter*," Federation of American Scientists, https://irp.fas.org/offdocs/walsh/chap_03.htm.

70. Evans Witt, "Conservative Torn by Iran Contra Affair," *Gettysburg Times*, 14 January 1987, 5.

71. Sidney Blumenthal, "North the Charge of the Right Brigade," *Washington Post*, 5 August 1987, https://www.washingtonpost.com/archive/lifestyle/1987/08/05/north-the-charge-of-the-right-brigade/5beda80c-1667-4095-9337-d379c098299d/.

72. U.S. Attorney's Office, Southern District of New York, "Former Congressman Christopher Collins Sentencing for Insider Trading and Lying to Federal Law Enforcement Officers," 17 January 2020, https://www.justice.gov/usao-sdny/pr/former-congressman-christopher-collins-sentenced-insider-trading-scheme-and-lying.

73. U.S. Attorney's Office, Southern District of California, "Former Congressman Duncan Hunter Sentenced to Eleven Months in Prison for Stealing Campaign Funds," 17 March 2020, https://www.justice.gov/usao-sdca/pr/former-congressman-duncan-d-hunter-sentenced-11-months-prison-stealing-campaign-funds.

74. Kevin Freking, "Expel George Santos? Republican Leaders Aren't Ready to Take That Step," Associated Press, 11 May 2023, https://apnews.com/article/george-santos-congress-republican-leaders-15d7172c7388198f77fbcc392c5a19d3.

75. Kevin Freking, "The House Expels Rep. George Santos," Associated Press, 1 December 2023, https://apnews.com/article/george-santos-expulsion-vote-ethics-investigation-fd0f1524065883c6b2fe3e6f9afd84db.

76. "Special Election: New York District 3," CNN, 11 March 2024, https://www.cnn.com/election/2024/results/new-york/special-election/us-house-district-3.

77. U.S. Attorney's Office, Eastern District of New York, "Former Congressman George Santos Pleads Guilty to Wire Fraud and Aggravated Identity

Theft," 19 August 2024, https://www.justice.gov/usao-edny/pr/former-congress man-george-santos-pleads-guilty-wire-fraud-and-aggravated-identity.

78. Mueller Letter to Barr, 27 March 2019, https://apps.npr.org/documents /document.html?id=5984399-Mueller-Letter-to-Barr.

79. Michael C. Bender and Maggie Haberman, "Republicans Erupt in Outrage and Rush to Defend the Defendant," *New York Times*, 30 March 2023, https://www.nytimes.com/2023/03/30/us/politics/trump-indicted-republican -response.html.

80. Mary Clare Jalonick, "Republican Lawmakers React with Fury to Trump Verdict and Rally to His Defense," Associated Press, 30 May 2024, https://apnews .com/article/trump-verdict-republicans-guilty-reaction-congress-election -c8193404866565c55b093086890cbef8.

81. Matthew Choi and Olivia Alafriz, "Texas Republicans in Congress Stand by Donald Trump after Federal Indictment," *Texas Tribune*, 9 June 2023, https:// www.texastribune.org/2023/06/09/donald-trump-indicted-texas-republicans/; Sarah Fortinsky, "Republicans Rally round Trump Amid Reported DOJ Indict- ment," *The Hill*, 8 June 2023, https://thehill.com/homenews/4041744-republicans -rally-around-trump-amid-indictment-news/.

82. Jared Gans, "House GOP Leaders Defend Trump on Day of Arraign- ment: 'A Dark Day for Our Country,'" *The Hill*, 13 June 2023, https://thehill .com/homenews/house/4048322-house-gop-leaders-defend-trump-after -arraignment/.

83. Robert Farley, "The Facts on Manhattan Crime," FactCheck.org, 14 April 2023, https://www.factcheck.org/2023/04/the-facts-on-manhattan-crime/.

84. Steven Vago and Kevin Crane, "Kevin McCarthy and Gov. Hochul Trade Blows as GOP House Leader Slams NYC Crime," *New York Post*, 4 Au- gust 2022, https://nypost.com/2022/08/04/mccarthy-and-hochul-trade-blows -as-gop-house-leader-slams-nyc-crime/.

85. Albert R. Hunt, "Verbal Violence Begets Physical Violence," *Wall Street Journal*, 9 November 1995, A21.

86. Kitchener, "Talk Show Hosts Turn Up Rhetoric after Bomb Blast," *The Listener*, 25 April 1995, A7.

87. Patrick Goldstein, "Yakity Yak Please Talk Back," *Los Angeles Times*, 16 July 1995, 16.

88. Jamison Foser, "Limbaugh Flashback: In 1995 Limbaugh Predicted 'Sec- ond Violent American Revolution,'" Media Matters for America, 19 April 2010, https://www.mediamatters.org/rush-limbaugh/limbaugh-flashback-1995-rush -predicted-second-violent-american-revolution.

89. Elvia Diaz, "Donald Trump Jr. Calls for 'Total War' over 2020 Election. That's beyond Irresponsible," *Arizona Republic*, November 2020, https://www

.azcentral.com/story/opinion/op-ed/elviadiaz/2020/11/05/donald-trump-jr-call -total-war-beyond-irresponsible/6181504002/.

90. Jaclyn Peiser, "Twitter Bans Steve Bannon for Suggesting Violence against Fauci, FBI Director Wray," *Washington Post*, 20 November 2020, https:// www.washingtonpost.com/nation/2020/11/06/twitter-bannon-beheaded-fauci -wray/.

91. "Citing the America Revolution, Rush Limbaugh Implicitly Endorses Political Violence," Media Matters for America, 7 January 2021, https://www.media matters.org/january-6-insurrection/citing-american-revolution-rush-limbaugh -implicitly-endorses-political.

92. "Rudy Giuliana's Speech Transcripts at Trump's Washington DC Rally, Wants 'Trial by Combat,'" Rev, 6 January 2021, https://www.rev.com/blog /transcripts/rudy-giuliani-speech-transcript-at-trumps-washington-d-c-rally-wants -trial-by-combat.

93. Kim Bellware, "There Will be 'Riots in the Streets,' If Trump Is Prosecuted, Graham Says," *Washington Post*, 29 August 2022, https://www.washington post.com/politics/2022/08/29/lindsey-graham-riots/.

94. Fatma Khaled, "Republican Confronted over Shooting Video Tweet with Hashtag 'Fire Pelosi,'" *Newsweek*, 27 October 2022, https://www.newsweek.com /republican-confronted-over-shooting-video-tweet-fire-pelosi-hashtag-1755661.

95. John Avlon, "Trump Backers Are Going Bonkers with Dangerous Threats," CNN, 13 June 2013, https://www.cnn.com/2023/06/12/opinions/trump -indictment-violent-rhetoric-avlon/index.html.

96. Allan J. Lichtman, *13 Cracks: Repairing American Democracy after Trump* (Lanham, MD: Rowman & Littlefield, 2022), 170–73; Andrew Restuccia and Sioban Holmes, "Trump's Tweet about Pence Seen as Critical Moment in Riot," *Wall Street Journal*, 21 July 2022, https://www.wsj.com/livecoverage /jan-6-hearing-today-trump/card/trump-s-tweet-about-pence-seen-as-critical -moment-during-riot-fmPxoFkeoTKxi0NqPLCL.

97. Timothy H. J. Nerozzi, "Trump Comment about Punishing Gen. Milley with 'Death' Causes Major Outcry from GOP Rivals," Fox News, 29 September 2023, https://www.foxnews.com/politics/trump-comment-punishing-gen-milley -death-causes-major-outcry-gop.

98. Martin Pengelly, "Trump Warns of 'Bedlam' If Criminal Cases Bar Him from the White House," *The Guardian*, 10 January 2024, https://www .theguardian.com/us-news/2024/jan/10/donald-trump-bedlam-criminal-cases.

99. Myah Ward, "Trump Says Country Faces a 'Bloodbath' If Biden Wins," Yahoo News, 16 March 2024, https://news.yahoo.com/trump-says-country-faces -bloodbath-223215044.html.

100. "Trump Hog-tied Biden, Drawing a Rebuke from the Democratic Campaign," Associated Press, 29 March 2024, https://apnews.com/article/trump -biden-hogtied-post-4fb29b80ed926c20c2fbbed05fd03755.

101. Andrew Howard, "Suggesting 'Nine Barrels Shooting' at Cheney, Trump Reverts to Violent Rhetoric," *Politico*, 1 November 2024, https://www.politico .com/news/2024/11/01/cheney-trump-firing-squad-threats-are-how-dictators -destroy-free-nations-00186707.

102. Jacob Rosen and Olivia Rinaldi, "Trump Says 'I Don't Mind' If Some-one Had to Shoot Through Media," CBS News, 3 November 2024, https:// www.cbsnews.com/news/donald-trump-lititz-pennsylvania-rally-shoot-through -media-bulletproof-glass/.

CHAPTER 9.   Strict Construction

1. "A New Chief Justice," *Chicago Tribune*, 11 June 1969, 28.

2. "Judges 1: 'A Downward Death Spiral,'" NPR, 25 July 2019, https:// www.npr.org/2019/07/25/745488893/judges-1-a-downward-death-spiral.

3. Robert H. Bork, "The Constitution, Original Intent, and Economic Rights," *San Diego Law Review* 23 (1988): 823, 826, 832.

4. "Taking a Stand on Confirmation: Senatorial Voice for and against Bork," *New York Times*, 6 October 1987, B6.

5. Ronald Reagan, "Remarks to the Federalist Society for Law and Public Policy," Ronald Reagan Library and Museum, 9 September 1988, https://www .reaganlibrary.gov/archives/speech/remarks-federalist-society-law-and-public -policy-studies.

6. Second Bush–Kerry Debate, in St. Louis, MO, 8 October, 2004; The White House, "President Bush Discusses Judicial Philosophy and Appointments," 6 October 2008, https://georgewbush-whitehouse.archives.gov/news/releases /2008/10/20081006-5.html.

7. America's Election Headquarters for October 23, 2008, Fox News, 23 October 2008.

8. Craig R. Bowden, *Common Sense: How to Restore America* (Scotts Valley, CA: Create Space, 2012), 65.

9. Reuters Staff, "Trump to Nominate 'Strict Constructionist' to the Supreme Court," Reuters, 26 January 2017, https://www.reuters.com/article /us-usa-court-pence/trump-to-nominate-strict-constructionist-to-supreme-court -pence-idUSKBN15A2RR.

10. "Trump Announces Brett Kavanaugh as Supreme Court Nominee," *New York Times*, 9 July 2018, https://www.nytimes.com/2018/07/09/us/politics /trump-supreme-court-announcement-transcript.html.

11. "Ron DeSantis' Inaugural Speech: Read the Full Transcript," WFTS Digital Staff, 8 January 2019, https://www.abcactionnews.com/news/state/ron -desantis-inaugural-speech-read-the-full-transcript.

12. 100 Cong. Rec. S6748 (18 May 1954).

13. John N. Popham, "Reaction of South," *New York Times*, 18 May 1954, 1.

14. "Southern Manifesto on Integration," Thirteen PBS, 12 March 1956, https://www.thirteen.org/wnet/supremecourt/rights/sources_document2.html.

15. 100 Cong. Rec. H6874 (19 May 1954).

16. 100 Cong. Rec. A4632 (24 June 1954).

17. William F. Buckley Jr., "Why the South Must Prevail," *National Review*, 24 August 1957, https://adamgomez.wordpress.com/wp-content/uploads /2012/03/whythesouthmustprevail-1957.pdf.

18. "State Chief Justices Chide Supreme Court," *Baltimore Sun*, 24 August 1958, 1.

19. "Butler Raps Foes of Bill," *Baltimore Sun*, 4 May 1958, 24.

20. Anthony Lewis, "Johnson Shows Mastery Again," *New York Times*, 25 August 1958, 8.

21. 104 Cong. Rec. S18964 (20 Aug. 1958).

22. "Partial Text of Goldwater Speech," *Washington Post*, 12 September 1964, A6.

23. Anthony Lewis, "News Analysis; Campaign Issues—VIII; Goldwater Criticisms of Supreme Court Seen as Part of Attack on Centralization," *New York Times*, 1 November 1964, 79.

24. Senator Everett Dirksen, "Press Release, 26 June 1964, Papers of Everett M. Dirksen, Campaigns and Politics, Folder 50, Dirksen Congressional Center, Pekin, IL.

25. American Independent Party Platform of 1968, The American Presidency Project, https://www.presidency.ucsb.edu/documents/american-independent -party-platform-1968.

26. Fred D. Graham, "Bar Speakers Critical of the Warren Court," *New York Times*, 17 July 1971, 1.

27. Robert Bork, "Neutral Principles and Some First Amendment Problems," *Indiana Law Journal* 47 (1971): 18.

28. James J. Kilpatrick, "High Marks for the High Court Except on the Abortion Ruling," *Baltimore Sun*, 12 August 1973, K5.

29. *Roe v. Wade*, U.S. 35 L. Ed. 2d (1972), Dissent (Rehnquist), 197–98.

30. Warren Richey, "Reagan Switches Strategy on Abortion Challenge in Court," *Christian Science Monitor*, 17 July 1985, https://www.csmonitor.com /1985/0717/aroe-f.html.

31. *Obergefell v. Hodges*, 576 U.S. 644 (2015), Dissent (Roberts), Justia: U.S. Supreme Court, https://supreme.justia.com/cases/federal/us/576/14-556/#tab -opinion-3427258.

32. Travis Weber, "Critical Analysis of *Obergefell v. Hodges*," Family Research Council, https://downloads.frc.org/EF/EF15G67.pdf.

33. "'This Decision Will Not Stand,' Republicans Seek Common Ground against Same-Sex Marriage," *The Guardian*, 4 July 2015, https://www.theguard ian.com/us-news/2015/jul/04/republicans-against-same-sex-marriage.

34. Adam Cohen, "The Lord Justice Hath Ruled: Pringles Are Potato Chips," *New York Times*, 31 May 2009, https://www.nytimes.com/2009/06/01 /opinion/01mon4.html?_r=2&em.

35. Edward Hallett Carr, *What Is History?* (London: Cambridge University Press, 1961), 10.

36. Franklin D. Roosevelt, "March 9, 1937: Fireside Chat 9: On 'Court-Packing,'" Miller Center, https://millercenter.org/the-presidency/presidential -speeches/march-9-1937-fireside-chat-9-court-packing. See, generally, Marian C. McKenna, *Franklin Roosevelt and the Great Constitutional War: The Court-Packing Crisis of 1937* (New York. Fordham University Press, 2002).

37. Gallup poll, November 1936, https://ropercenter.cornell.edu/ipoll/study /31087041/questions#1aa52a3f-1c92-406b-bc0a-3923d8a9654d.

38. Edmund P. Grice to James Byrnes, 23 February 1937, in William E. Leuchtenburg, *The Supreme Court Reborn: The Constitutional Revolution in the Age of Roosevelt* (Oxford: Oxford University Press, 1995), 136–37. On the battle over the Court, see also Barry Cushman, *Rethinking the New Deal Court: The Structure of a Constitutional Revolution* (New York: Oxford University Press, 1998); McKenna, *Franklin Roosevelt and the Great Constitutional War*.

39. "Amendment for School Prayer Suggested by Nixon at Stop Here," *New York Times*, 1 July 1962, 48.

40. Studies confirm that the rulings advantaged Republicans. See Tilman Klumpp, Hugo M. Mialon, and Michael A. Williams, "The Business of American Democracy: *Citizens United*, Independent Spending, and Elections," *Journal of Law and Economics* 59 (2016): 1–43; Nour Abdul-Razzak, Carlo Prato, and Stephane Wolton, "How Citizens United Gave Republicans a Bonanza of Seats in U.S. State Legislatures," *Washington Post*, 24 February 2017, https://www .washingtonpost.com/news/monkey-cage/wp/2017/02/24/how-citizens-united -gave-republicans-a-bonanza-of-seats-in-u-s-state-legislatures/.

41. E. J. Dionne Jr., "Supreme Court Ruling Calls for a Populist Revolt," *Washington Post*, 25 January 2010, https://www.washingtonpost.com/wp-dyn/content/article/2010/01/24/AR2010012402298.html.

42. Manu Raju, "Democrats Cry Injustice," *Politico*, 29 January 2010, https://www.politico.com/news/stories/0110/32200_Page2.html.

43. Alex Gangitano, "*Citizens United* Decision Weathers 10 Years of Controversy," *The Hill*, 21 January 2020, https://thehill.com/business-a-lobbying/business-a-lobbying/478852-citizens-united-decision-weathers-10-years-of/.

44. Senator Sheldon Whitehouse, "Senate Session," 29 January 2910, C-SPAN, https://www.c-span.org/program/us-senate/senate-session/218850.

45. Subcommittee on the Constitution and Civil Justice of the Committee on the Judiciary, Hearing, "The Voting Rights Act after the Supreme Court's Decision in Shelby County," 18 July 2013, 3, 5.

46. Ian Millhiser, "Chief Justice Roberts's Lifelong Crusade against Voting Rights Explained," *Vox*, 18 September 2020, https://www.vox.com/21211880/supreme-court-chief-justice-john-roberts-voting-rights-act-election-2020.

47. Emmet J. Bondurant, "*Rucho v. Common Cause*: A Critique," *Emory Law Journal* 70 (2021): 1.

48. *Brnovich v. Democratic National Committee*, 594 U.S. 647 2021.

49. Richard L. Hasen, "The Supreme Court's Latest Voting Rights Opinion Is Even Worse Than It Seems," *Slate*, 8 July 2021, https://slate.com/news-and-politics/2021/07/supreme-court-sam-alito-brnovich-angry.html.

50. David G. Savage, "How the Supreme Court Has Tilted Election Law to Favor the Republican Party," *Los Angeles Times*, 4 June 2021, https://www.latimes.com/politics/story/2021-06-04/how-supreme-court-tilted-election-law-favor-gop.

51. Enrique Schaerer, "What the Heller: An Originalist Critique of Justice Scalia's Second Amendment Jurisprudence," *University of Cincinnati Law Review* 82 (2018): 795.

52. Chris Coons, "Senator Coons Statement on Dobbs v. Jackson Women's Health Organization Decision," 24 June 2022, https://www.coons.senate.gov/news/press-releases/sen-coons-statement-on-dobbs-v-jackson-womens-health-organization-decision.

53. Alan B. Morrison, "Selective Judicial Activism in the Roberts Court," *GW Law: Scholarly Commons*, 2022, https://scholarship.law.gwu.edu/faculty_publications/1612/.

54. *Trump v. Anderson*, 601 U.S. 100 (2024), Justice Barrett, concurring in part and concurring in the judgment.

55. Garrett Epps, "The Origin of Specious," *Washington Monthly*, 25 August 2024, https://washingtonmonthly.com/2024/08/25/the-origin-of-specious-2/.

56. Mitch McConnell, "Democrats Are Disgracefully Eager to Burn Down the Institutions of Our Constitutional Government," Republican Leader, 3 May 2022, https://www.republicanleader.senate.gov/newsroom/research/democrats -are-disgracefully-eager-to-burn-down-the-institutions-of-our-constitutional -government.

57. Kristen Holmes, "Trump Calls for Termination of the Constitution in Truth Social Post," CNN, 4 December 2022, https://www.cnn.com/2022/12/03 /politics/trump-constitution-truth-social/index.html.

58. Lauren White and Lama Elsharif, "Nine out of Ten Republicans Silent on Trump's Call to Terminate the Constitution," CREW, 25 April 2023, https://www.citizensforethics.org/reports-investigations/crew-reports/9-out-of-10 -republicans-silent-on-trumps-calls-to-terminate-the-constitution/.

59. Ted Hesson, "Trump Vows to End Birthright Citizenship for Children of Immigrants in US Illegally," Reuters, 30 May 2023, https://www.reuters.com /world/us/trump-vows-end-birthright-citizenship-children-immigrants-us -illegally-2023-05-30/.

60. Jill Colvin and Bill Barrow, "Trumps Vows to Be a Dictator on 'Day One,' Follows Growing Worry over His Authoritarian Rhetoric," Associated Press, 7 December 2023, https://apnews.com/article/trump-hannity-dictator-authoritarian -presidential-election-f27e7e9d7c13fabbe3ae7dd7f1235c72.

61. Cohen, "The Lord Justice."

CHAPTER 10.   U.S. Sovereignty

1. Herbert Hoover, "Address on the 150th Anniversary of the Battle of King's Mountain," 7 October 1930, The American Presidency Project, https:// www.presidency.ucsb.edu/documents/address-the-150th-anniversary-the-battle -kings-mountain.

2. Richard A. Koenigsberg, "National Boundaries as Fear of Penetration," Library of Social Science, Newsletter, April 2024. Available from author.

3. U.S. Congressman Chris Smith, Press Release: "Panel of Experts Raises the Alarm on Growing Concerns surrounding Looming WHO 'Pandemic Treaty,'" 6 February 2024, https://chrissmith.house.gov/news/documentsingle.aspx ?DocumentID=411866; Ariel Cohen, "GOP Lawmakers Argue That Pandemic Treaty Threatens U.S. Sovereignty," *Roll Call*, 5 February 2024, https://rollcall .com/2024/02/05/gop-lawmakers-argue-pandemic-treaty-threatens-us -sovereignty/.

4. Warren G. Harding, "June 12, 1920: Speech Accepting the Republican Nomination," Miller Center, https://millercenter.org/the-presidency/presidential -speeches/june-12-1920-speech-accepting-republican-nomination.

5.   Inaugural Address of Warren G. Harding, 4 March 1921, The Avalon Project, https://avalon.law.yale.edu/20th_century/harding.asp.

6.   Markku Routsila, "The Origins of Christian Anti-Internationalism," EBIN, 2007, https://ebin.pub/the-origins-of-christian-anti-internationalism -conservative-evangelicals-and-the-league-of-nations-1nbsped-9781589014527 -9781589011915.html.

7.   "Quiz Speaker on League of Nations," *Baltimore Sun*, 6 October 1920, 4.

8.   Calvin Coolidge, "First Annual Message to the Congress of the United States," 6 December 1923, Calvin Coolidge Presidential Foundation, https:// coolidgefoundation.org/resources/first-annual-message-to-the-congress/.

9.   87 Cong. Rec. S4364, 4365 (25 Sept. 1941).

10.   Robert A. Taft, "Speech on the North Atlantic Treaty," 26 July 1949, Teaching American History, https://teachingamericanhistory.org/document /speech-on-the-north-atlantic-treaty/.

11.   J. Reuben Clark, "Our Dwindling Sovereignty," 98 Cong. Rec. S170612 (3 Mar. 1952).

12.   "Bricker Rips U.N. Plan to Curb Rights," *Chicago Tribune*, 13 November 1951, 1.

13.   "Interview with General Eisenhower," July 1951, Henry Cabot Lodge Papers, II, Reel 28, Massachusetts Historical Society, Boston; "Demolish The Enemy," unsigned, undated campaign memorandum 1952, Thomas E. Stephens Papers, Box 7, Dwight David Eisenhower Presidential Library; Abilene, Kansas.

14.   William S. White, "Knowland Demands Set Trend." *Los Angeles Times*, 25 November 1954, 1.

15.   Bess Furman, "DAR Urges Curb on United Nations," *New York Times*, 23 April 1953, 11.

16.   "'One Worlders' Route Drawn by Sen. Bricker," *Chicago Tribune*, 5 June 1954, 7.

17.   Natalie Hevener Kaufman, *Human Rights Treaties and the Senate: A History of Opposition* (Chapel Hill: University of North Carolina Press, 1990), 84.

18.   Phyllis Schlafly, *A Choice Not an Echo* (Phyllis Schlafly, 1964), 63.

19.   John Stormer, *None Dare Call It Treason* (Florissant, MO: Liberty Bell Press, 1964).

20.   Daniel Pipes, "*None Dare Call It Treason*—25 Years Later," *Orbis*, Spring 1991, https://www.danielpipes.org/526/none-dare-call-it-treason-25-years-later.

21.   "NRA Delivers Remarks at United Nations," 14 July 2011, Library of Congress, Web Archives Collection, http://webarchive.loc.gov/all/20120518020635 /http://www.nraila.org/Legislation/Read.aspx?ID=6993.

22.   Jeff Abramson and Greg Webb, "U.S. to Quit Arms Trade Treaty," Arms Control Association, May 2019, https://www.armscontrol.org/act/2019-05/news /us-quit-arms-trade-treaty.

23. "Buchanan on the Issues," *Human Events*, 8 February 1992, 10–17.

24. Jesse Helms, "American Sovereignty and the UN," *National Interest* 62 (Winter 2000/2001), 31–34.

25. Eric Patterson and Kendra Puryear, "Outlaws Barbarians: The Bush Administration's Revolution in Sovereignty," *The Whitehead Journal of Diplomacy and International Relations* 7 (2006): 204–5.

26. Michael Barkun, *A Culture of Conspiracy: Apocalyptic Visions in Contemporary America* (Oakland: University of California Press, 2013).

27. Lisa Friedman "Trump Serves Notice to Quit Paris Climate Agreement," *New York Times*, 4 November 2019, https://www.nytimes.com/2019/11/04/climate/trump-paris-agreement-climate.html.

28. "The Full Transcript of Trump's Speech on the Iran Nuclear Deal," *New York Times*, 8 May 2018, https://www.nytimes.com/2018/05/08/us/politics/trump-speech-iran-deal.html.

29. "Laura Ingraham Interviews Donald Trump on Fox's Ingraham Angle—Part 1," 31 August 2020, https://rollcall.com/factbase/trump/transcript/donald-trump-interview-laura-ingraham-fox-news-august-31-2020/.

30. Michael Gold and Maggie Haberman, "Trump's Newest Venture? A $60 Bible," *New York Times*, 26 March 2024, https://www.nytimes.com/2024/03/26/us/politics/trump-bible.html.

31. Nadia Schadlow, "Conservative U.S. Statecraft for the 21st Century," *Foreign Policy*, 7 November 2022, https://foreignpolicy.com/2022/11/07/us-republicans-conservative-foreign-policy-principles/.

32. Charles Lindbergh, "Des Moines Speech," 11 September 1941, http://www.charleslindbergh.com/americanfirst/speech.asp.

33. "Jessup Appointment Scorned," *Human Events*, 24 November 1960, 579.

34. "A Strange Choice," *Chicago Tribune*, 9 November 1960, 20.

35. "Wants Jessup Barred from World Court," *New York Herald Tribune*, 16 November 1960, 5.

36. Seymour Korman, "Reagan Lashes Left Wing Democrats," *Chicago Tribune*, 2 May 1965, B2.

37. "Reagan Scores Sovereignty Loss in Canal Treaty," *Chicago Tribune*, 26 August 1977, 12.

38. Robert M. Bleiberg, "The U.S. Ought to Harden Its Stance on the Canal Zone," *Barron's* 27 June 1977, 7.

39. Strom Thurmond, "No: No to the Treaties," *Chicago Tribune*, 11 September 1977, A1.

40. 121 Cong. Rec. S5071 (4 Mar. 1975).

41. John Bolton, *How Obama Is Endangering Our National Sovereignty* (New York: Encounter, 2011), 40–47.

42. Andrew R. Arthur, "Open Borders Is in Biden's 'DNA,'" Center for Immigration Studies, 18 January 2023, https://cis.org/Arthur/Open-Borders -Bidens-DNA.

43. Warren L. Cohen, *Empire without Tears: American Foreign Relations, 1921–1933* (Philadelphia: Temple University Press, 1987), 18–44; Jeffrey W. Legro, "Whence American Internationalism," *International Organization* 54 (April 2000): 253–89.

44. Edwin Black, *IBM and the Holocaust: The Strategic Alliance between Nazi Germany and America's Most Powerful Corporation* (New York: Crown Publishers, 2001); Reinhold Billstein, Karola Fings, Anita Kugler, and Nicholas Levis, *Working for the Enemy: Ford, General Motors, and Forced Labor in Germany during the Second World War* (New York: Berghahn Books, 2000); Gabriel Kolko, "American Business and Germany, 1930–1941," *Western Political Quarterly* 15 (December 1962): 725.

45. "Text of Lindbergh's Speech Appealing to Peace in Europe," *New York Times*, 5 August 1940, 4.

46. Vernon Van Dyke and Edward Lane Davis, "Senator Taft and American Security," *Journal of Politics* 14 (1952): 179, 181, 182.

47. 85 Cong. Rec. Appendix (2 Oct. 1939).

48. Clarence Manion to Hamilton Fish, 22 September 1941, Clarence E. Manion Papers, Box 1, Chicago Historical Society, Chicago.

49. Justus D. Doenecke, *In Danger Undaunted: The Anti-Interventionist Movement of 1940–1941 as Revealed in the Papers of the America First Committee* (Stanford, CA: Hoover Institution, 1990), 469; Lindbergh to "Members of the America First Committee," 14 December 1941, Robert E. Wood Papers, Box 9, Herbert Hoover Presidential Library, West Branch, Iowa; Herbert Hoover to Robert Taft, 8 December 1941, Robert A. Taft Papers, Box 286, Library of Congress; R. Douglas Stuart, Jr., "TO ALL CHAPTER CHAIRMEN," 8 December 1941, Sterling Morton to Stuart, 12 December 1941, Sterling Morton Papers, Box 6, Chicago Historical Society.

50. Lawrence E. Walsh, *Final Report of the Independent Counsel for Iran/ Contra Affairs*, Vol. 1, *Investigations and Prosecutions*, 4 August 1993, 561–66, https://irp.fas.org/offdocs/walsh/.

51. Jen Kirby, "Is It Actually Illegal to Accept 'Campaign Dirt' from Foreigners," VOX, 14 June 2019, https://www.vox.com/2019/6/14/18677631/trump -campaign-finance-law-fec-illegal-fbi.

52. Jason Daley, "How Adlai Stevenson Stopped Russian Interference in the 1960 Election," *Smithsonian Magazine*, 4 January 2017, https://www.smith sonianmag.com/smart-news/how-adlai-stevenson-stopped-russian-interference -1960-election-180961681/.

53. Casey Michel, "Russia's Long and Mostly Unsuccessful Efforts to Influence U.S. Presidential Elections," *Politico Magazine*, 26 October 2019, https://www.politico.com/magazine/story/2019/10/26/russias-long-and-mostly-unsuccessful-history-of-election-interference-229884/.

54. Luke Broadwater and Glenn Thrush, "Ignoring Warnings, GOP Trumpeted Now-Discredited Allegation against Biden," *New York Times*, 23 February 2024, https://www.nytimes.com/2024/02/23/us/politics/gop-smirnov-allegation-biden.html; Matt Gertz, "Hannity Once Touted Smirnov Bribe Claims as 'The Biggest Story of the Year.' Now He's Running for Cover," Media Matters, 26 February 2024, https://www.mediamatters.org/fox-news/hannity-once-touted-smirnovs-bribe-claims-biggest-story-year-now-hes-running-cover.

55. Zoe Richards, "Ex-FBI Informant Pleads Guilty to Making False Bribery Allegations about the Bidens," NBC News, 16 December 2024, https://www.nbcnews.com/politics/politics-news/ex-fbi-informant-pleads-guilty-false-allegations-bidens-rcna184448.

56. Gregory J. Wallance, "The Far Right Has Replaced the Old Left as Russia's Propaganda Tool," *The Hill*, 27 February 2024, https://thehill.com/opinion/international/4489496-the-far-right-has-replaced-the-old-left-as-russias-propaganda-tool/.

57. Stewart Patrick, *The Sovereignty Wars: Reconciling America with the World*, Brookings, https://www.brookings.edu/books/the-sovereignty-wars/.

CHAPTER 11.   Religion, Race, Immigrants, and Sex

1. U.S. Senate, Hearing before the Subcommittee on the Judiciary, German and Bolshevik Propaganda, 66th Cong., 1st Sess., February 1919, 11–15, 112, 113, 116.

2. Hearing before the Subcommittee on the Judiciary, German and Bolshevik Propaganda, 115, 136.

3. U.S. House of Representatives, *Report of the Special Committee to Investigate Communist Activities in the United States,* 71st Cong., 1st Sess., 17 January 1931, 14.

4. David Nasaw, *The Chief: The Life of William Randolph Hearst* (Boston: Houghton Mifflin, 2000), 778.

5. Chamber of Commerce of the United States, "Twenty-Second Annual Meeting 1934," Chamber of Commerce Papers, Box 7, Hagley; Frank Buxton to Bainbridge Colby, 17 June 1934, Bainbridge Colby Papers, Box 30, Library of Congress.

6. "Three Stations Reject Coughlin," *Broadcasting*, 1 December 1938, 79.

7. Edwin E. Slosson, "The Anti-Semite Scare," *The Independent*, 25 December 1920, 427.

8. Hiram Wesley Evans, "The Klan's Fight for Americanism," *North American Review*, 1 March 1926, 2, 10–11, 28.

9. "Evans Tells Why Klan Objects to 3 Classes," *Washington Post*, 25 October 1923, 5.

10. Charles Lindbergh, "Des Moines Speech," 11 September 1941, http://www.charleslindbergh.com/americanfirst/speech.asp.

11. Joshua Muravchik, "Patrick J. Buchanan and the Jews," American Enterprise Institute, 1 January 1991, https://www.aei.org/articles/patrick-j-buchanan-and-the-jews/.

12. Patrick J. Buchanan, "The Dispossession of Christian America," Patrick J. Buchanan, 27 November 1998, https://buchanan.org/blog/pjb-the-dispossession-of-christian-americans-241.

13. Jeremy Diamond, "Trump's 'Star of David' Tweet Controversy Explained," CNN, 5 July 2016, https://www.cnn.com/2016/07/04/politics/donald-trump-star-of-david-tweet-explained/index.html.

14. Niraj Chockshi, "Trump Accuses Hillary Clinton of Guiding Global Elites against U.S. Working Class," *New York Times*, 13 October 2016, https://www.nytimes.com/2016/10/14/us/politics/trump-comments-linked-to-antisemitism.html.

15. Jonathan Weisman, "Jewish Allies Call Trump's Dinner with Antisemites a Breaking Point," *New York Times*, 28 November 2022, https://www.nytimes.com/2022/11/28/us/politics/trump-kanye-west-nick-fuentes-antisemitism.html; "Nicholas J. Fuentes: Five Things to Know," Anti-Defamation League, 8 July 2021, https://www.adl.org/resources/blog/nicholas-j-fuentes-five-things-know.

16. Felicia Sonmez, "Trump Says Jewish People Who Vote for Democrats Are 'Very Disloyal to Israel,' Denies Remarks Are Anti-Semitic," *Washington Post*, 21 April 2019, https://www.washingtonpost.com/politics/trump-says-that-jewish-people-who-vote-for-democrats-are-very-disloyal-to-israel-denies-his-remarks-are-anti-semitic/2019/08/21/055e53bc-c42d-11e9-b5e4-54aa56d5b7ce_story.html.

17. Dana Milbank, "The Bloodbath Trump Promised Has Already Begun," *Washington Post*, 22 March 2024, https://www.washingtonpost.com/opinions/2024/03/22/trump-jews-schumer-vote-democrats-israel-bloodbath/.

18. Jonathan Weisman, "Trump's Suggestion That Jews Could Cost Him Race Creates Fear of Antisemitic Reprisal," *New York Times*, 20 September 2024, https://www.nytimes.com/2024/09/20/us/politics/trump-jews-antisemitism.html.

19. Ben Sales, "Marjorie Taylor Greene Shares Anti-Semitic and Islamophobic Video," *Jerusalem Post*, 27 August 2020, https://www.jpost.com/diaspora/antisemitism/marjorie-taylor-greene-shared-antisemitic-and-islamophobic-video-640093.

20. Jack Rosen, "George Santos and American Antisemitism," 6 January 2023, *New York Daily News*, https://www.nydailynews.com/opinion/ny-oped-george-santos-antisemitism-20230106-57mc6f53qnbajjuif4qzb4wwf4-story.html; Andrew Lapin, "George Santos, US Congressman Who Lied about Jewish Heritage, Once Praised Hitler," *The Times of Israel*, 28 January 2023, https://www.timesofisrael.com/george-santos-congressman-who-lied-about-jewish-heritage-once-praised-hitler/.

21. "Sterilization of All Negroes Is Ku Klux Aim," *Afro American*, 7 July 1922, 7.

22. "Evans Tells Why Klan Objects to 3 Classes," 5.

23. "Inside the Ku Klux Klan as Revealed by a Former Member in an Exclusive Interview," *Pittsburgh Courier*, 16 February 1957, B5.

24. Cecilia O'Leary, *To Die For: The Paradox of American Patriotism* (Princeton, NJ: Princeton University Press, 1999); David W. Blight, *Race and Reunion: The Civil War and American Memory* (Cambridge, MA: Harvard University Press, 2001).

25. "Reds Try to Stir Negroes to Revolt," *New York Times*, 28 July 1919, 4.

26. Theodore Kornweibel Jr., *Seeing Red: Federal Campaigns against Black Militancy, 1919–1925* (Bloomington: Indiana University Press, 1998), xiv.

27. Mark Robert Schneider, *We Return Fighting: The Civil Rights Movement in the Jazz Age* (Boston: Northeastern University Press, 2002); Kornweibel, *Seeing Red*; E. David Cronon, *Black Moses: The Story of Marcus Garvey and the Universal Negro Improvement Association* (Madison: University of Wisconsin Press, 1969).

28. Frank L. Kluckhohn, "Lindbergh Urges We Shun War," *New York Times*, 16 September 1939, 9, 14; "Lindbergh's Talk on Arms Embargo," *New York Times*, October 14, 1939, 10; Johnpeter Horst Grill and Robert L. Jenkins, "The Nazis and the American South in the 1930s: A Mirror Image?," *Journal of Southern History* 58 (November 1992): 675; Daniel W. Aldridge III, "A War for the Colored Races: Anti-Interventionism and the African American Intelligentsia, 1939–1941," *Diplomatic History* 28 (June 2004): 321–52; Justus D. Doenecke, *In Danger Undaunted: The Anti-Interventionist Movement of 1940–1941 as Revealed in the Papers of the America First Committee* (Stanford, CA: Hoover Institution, 1990), 30.

29. Republican State Party, "South Carolina Election Analysis," 1965, Thurmond Papers, Box 17.

30. Jeremy D. Mayer, "The Racial Politics of the 1964 Presidential Campaign," *Prologue* 33 (2001): 6–29.

31. "Accuses Goldwater of Trying to Win Votes by Exploiting Bigotry," *The Call*, 1 December 1961, 4.

32. Joshua D. Farrington, "Evicted from the Party: Black Republicans and the Election of 1964," *Journal of Arizona History* 61 (2020): 127–48.

33. Robert J. Donovan, "GOP Candidate Talks States' Rights and Delights Dixie People," *Los Angeles Times*, 20 September 1964, B1.

34. Charles Mohr, "Goldwater Says He'd Curb Court," *New York Times*, 16 September 1964, 1.

35. Claude Sitton, "Goldwater Gets Backing in South," *New York Times*, 16 August 1964, 1.

36. "Carolina Crowds Hail Goldwater," *New York Sunday Times*, 1 November 1964, 76.

37. "Negro Spokesmen Bitter on Goldwater Nomination, Saying It Will Aid Racists," *New York Times*, 17 July 1964, 2.

38. Angie Maxwell and Todd Shields, *The Long Southern Strategy* (New York: Oxford University Press, 2019), 37–38.

39. Angie Maxwell, "What We Get Wrong about the Southern Strategy," *Washington Post*, 26 July 2019, https://www.washingtonpost.com/outlook/2019/07/26/what-we-get-wrong-about-southern-strategy/.

40. Homer Bigart, "Agnew Asserts Busing of Children Uproots Them from Neighborhoods," *New York Times*, 15 September 1968, 76.

41. Theo Lippman Jr., "Agnew Gives Slum Views," *Baltimore Sun*, 19 October 1968, A6.

42. "George Wallace's Candidacy," *Los Angeles Times*, 26 July 1968, A4.

43. "Where the Candidates Stand," *Statecraft*, October 1968, Walter Judd Papers, Box 213, Hoover Institution; Dan T. Carter, *The Politics of Rage: George Wallace, the Origins of the New Conservatism, and the Transformation of American Politics* (New York: Simon & Schuster, 1995), 324–70; Michael Kazin, *The Populist Persuasion: An American History* (New York: Basic Books, 1995), 221–42; Thomas Bryne Edsall and Mary D. Edsall, *Chain Reaction: The Impact of Race, Rights, and Taxes on American Politics* (New York: Norton, 1992), 76–82.

44. Dan T. Carter. *From George Wallace to Newt Gingrich: Race in the Conservative Counterrevolution, 1963–1994* (Baton Rouge: Louisiana State University Press, 1996), 20

45. Carter, *From George Wallace to Newt Gingrich*, 30; John D. Ehrlichman, notes, 9 August 1970, 29 December 1969, 16 March 1970, 27 January 1972, 7 December 1972, Ehrlichman Papers, Hoover Institution, Boxes 1, 3; Oval Office Conversation, 13 May 1971, Presidential Recordings Program, Miller Center of

Public Affairs, University of Virginia, https://www.nixonlibrary.gov/white-house
-tapes/498.

46. Christi Parsons, "Limbaugh Draws Fire on Obama Parody," *Seattle Times*, 6 May 2007, https://www.seattletimes.com/nation-world/limbaugh-draws
-fire-on-obama-parody/.

47. Diane J. Cho, "Rush Limbaugh's Most Controversial Quotes," *People*, 17 February 2021, https://people.com/politics/rush-limbaugh-most-controversial
-moments/.

48. Mara Liasson, "Trump Questions Harris's Eligibility to Be the Vice Presidential Candidate," NPR, 20 August 2020, https://www.npr.org/2020/08
/13/902351379/trump-questions-harris-eligibility-to-be-the-vice-presidential
-candidate.

49. Eric Bradner and Aaron Pellish, "Trump Falsely Suggests Kamala Harris 'Happened to Turn Black,'" CNN 31 July 2024, https://www.cnn.com/2024
/07/31/politics/donald-trump-kamala-harris-black-nabj/index.html.

50. Merlyn Thomas and Mike Wendling, "Trump Repeats Baseless Claim about Immigrants Eating Pets," BBC, 15 September 2024, https://www.bbc
.com/news/articles/c77l28myezko.

51. "Communism Hits South with Non-Segregation," *Common Sense*, 1 July 1954, 1–2.

52. "Charlottesville Lawmaker on Negroes and Jews," *New Journal and Guide*, 22 September 1956, A28.

53. Reese Cleghorn, "The Segs," *Esquire*, January 1964, 133; Claude Sitton, "Citizens' Council Fuels Louisiana Resistance, *New York Times*, 27 November 1960, E6.

54. "The Truth about Liberty Lobby," *Liberty Letter*, March 1965; "Happy Birthday to Liberty Lobby," *Liberty Letter*, July 1965, Iowa Collection, Reel 69; Frank P. Mintz, *The Liberty Lobby and the American Right: Race, Conspiracy, and Culture* (Westport, CT: Greenwood Press, 1985); John P. Jackson Jr., "The Pre-History of American Holocaust Denial," *American Jewish History* 105 (2021): 25–48; Ben A. Franklin, "Passman Seeking Outside Help in His Fight on Foreign Aid," *New York Times*, 15 January 1965, 12.

55. Jackson, "Pre-History of American Holocaust Denial," 25.

56. Frank Meyer, Memos, 5 September 1961, 17 January 1962, 4 February 1962, William Rusher Papers, Reel 9, Library of Congress; Rusher to L. Brent Bozell, 28 September 1961, William F. Buckley Jr. Papers, Box 14, Sterling Memorial Library, Yale University, New Haven, CT.

57. "GOP Ad Channels Anti-Semitism to Portray George Soros as Puppetmaster," *Daily Beast*, 18 October 2018, https://www.thedailybeast.com/gop-ad
-taps-anti-semitism-to-portray-george-soros-as-puppet-master.

58. Reuters Staff, "Fact Check: A Flyer Showing a Job Listing to Become a 'Professional Anarchist," Reuters, 5 June 2020, https://www.reuters.com/article /uk-factcheck-fake-flyer-anarchist-soros/fact-check-fake-flyer-showing-a-job -listing-to-become-a-professional-anarchist-idUSKBN23926L.

59. Alex Samuels, "In False Facebook Posts, Texas Agriculture Commissioner Sid Miller Accused George Soros of Paying Protesters to 'Destroy' the Country," *The Texas Tribune*, 5 June 2020, https://www.texastribune.org/2020/06/05/sid -miller-george-floyd-protests/.

60. Candace Owens, @RealCandaceO, 20 May 2020, @reatlestmercury, 28 May 2020, https://twitter.com/RealCandaceO/status/1266061954285740033.

61. Peter Holley, "KKK's Official Newspaper Supports Donald Trump for President," *Washington Post*, 2 November 2016, https://www.washingtonpost.com /news/post-politics/wp/2016/11/01/the-kkks-official-newspaper-has-endorsed -donald-trump-for-president/.

62. John H. Pelletier, "Would Bar Out Undesirables," *Los Angeles Times*, 4 September 1921, 111.

63. Clinton Stoddard Burr, *America's Race Heritage* (Washington, DC: National Historical Society, 1922), 6.

64. 65 Cong. Rec. H5443 (2 Apr. 1924).

65. 65 Cong. Rec. H5641 (5 Apr. 1924).

66. "Race Suicide Menace," *Chicago Tribune*, 24 October 1924, 23.

67. "Eugenists Dread Tainted Aliens," *New York Times*, 25 September 1921, 25.

68. U.S. House of Representatives, Committee on Immigration and Naturalization, 86th Cong., 1st Sess., "Europe as an Emigrant-Exporting Country and the United States as an Immigrant-Receiving Country," 8 March 1924, 1297.

69. "Europe as an Emigrant-Exporting Country," 1278, tables.

70. Rosalind Crone, "Europe in the Inter-War Period," Open Learn, https:// www.open.edu/openlearn/history-the-arts/roaring-twenties-europe-the-interwar -period/content-section-2/.

71. Dennis Wepman, *Immigration: From the Founding of Virginia to the Closing of Ellis Island* (Facts on File, 2002), 242.

72. David A. Reed, "America of the Melting Pot Comes to an End," *New York Sunday Times*, 27 April 1924, 3.

73. *U.S. v. Thind*, 261 U.S. 204 (1923); *Gong Lum v. Rice*, 275 U.S. 78 (1927).

74. "Alien Law Defended in Biological Study," *Washington Post*, 2 January 1925, 3; John Trevor, "The Immigration Act," *New York Times*, 1 February 1927, 26; Louis Marshall et al. to Coolidge, 22 May 1924, Calvin Coolidge Papers, Reel 78, Library of Congress.

75. Jackie Hogan and Kristin Haltinner, "Floods, Invaders, and Parasites: Immigration Threat Narratives and Right-Wing Populism in the USA, UK and Australia," *Journal of Cultural Studies* 36 (2015): 530.

76. Jason DeParle, "The Anti-Immigrant Crusader," *New York Times*, 17 April 2011, https://www.nytimes.com/2011/04/17/us/17immig.html.

77. Carly Goodman, "John Tanton Has Died: He Made America Less Open to Immigrants—and More Open to Trump," *Washington Post*, 19 July 2019, https://www.washingtonpost.com/outlook/2019/07/18/john-tanton-has -died-how-he-made-america-less-open-immigrants-more-open-trump/.

78. DeParle, "The Anti-Immigration Crusader."

79. Donald A. Collins, FAIR Board Chair, VDARE.com, "Time's Up: Democrats and Republicans! Immigration Has to Be Fixed Now," 24 June 2014, https://vdare.pub/articles/time-s-up-democrats-and-republicans-immigration -has-to-be-fixed-now.

80. FAIR, "We Need Your Help!," https://www.fairus.org/.

81. Cassie Miller and Caleb Kieffer, "The Year in Hate and Extremism 2022," Southern Poverty Law Center, 6 June 2023, https://www.splcenter.org /year-hate-extremism-2022/introduction.

82. Video at Texas GOP Vote: https://www.texasgopvote.com/immigration /anti-immigration-groups-founded-and-backed-radical-environmentalists -and-005712.

83. Brendan Farrington, "Bill to Ban Sanctuary Policies Draws Raucous Debate," Associated Press, 18 April 2019, https://news.wgcu.org/2019-04-18 /florida-bill-to-ban-sanctuary-policies-draws-raucous-debate.

84. Liz Goodwin, "Racist GOP Appeals Heat Up in Final Weeks before Midterms," *Washington Post*, 15 October 2022, https://www.washingtonpost .com/politics/2022/10/15/racist-appeals-heat-up-final-weeks-before-mid terms/.

85. Donald J. Trump, @realDonaldTrump, https://twitter.com/realDonald Trump/status/1056919064906469376.

86. Meryl Kornfield and Marianne LeVine, "Trump Lambastes Immigrants Using False Homicide Claims," *Washington Post*, 29 September 2024, https:// www.washingtonpost.com/politics/2024/09/29/trump-false-claims-immigrants -homicide/.

87. Jenna Johnson and Abigail Hauslohner, "'I Think Islam Hates Us'; A Timeline of Trump's Comments on Islam and Muslims," *Washington Post*, 20 May 2017, https://www.washingtonpost.com/news/post-politics/wp/2017/05 /20/i-think-islam-hates-us-a-timeline-of-trumps-comments-about-islam -and-muslims/.

88. FAIR, "Fair's Statement on Donald Trump's Muslim Immigration Comments," 15 December 2015, https://www.fairus.org/press-releases/fairs-statement-donald-trumps-muslim-immigration-comments.

89. Jonathan Tilove, "David Vitter Ad Slammed as Racist by Advocates for Immigrants," *The Times-Picayune*, 9 October 2010, https://www.nola.com/news/politics/david-vitter-ad-slammed-as-racist-by-advocates-for-immigrants/article_7cb50f69-5e87-5ae9-98a3-2f14d67a6a9f.html. Video at https://www.youtube.com/watch?v=9uvp0Jljh6U.

90. Campaign Legal Center, "Race in Our Politics," https://campaignlegal.org/race-our-politics-catalog-campaign-materials.

91. Monivette Cordeiro, "Corcoran Runs 'Sanctuary Cities' Ad in Sad Attempt to Be Most Racist Candidate," *Orlando Weekly*, 31 January 2018 (includes YouTube video of ad), https://www.orlandoweekly.com/news/corcoran-runs-sanctuary-cities-ad-in-sad-attempt-to-be-floridas-most-racist-candidate-10386010.

92. "Ron DeSantis for Governor," YouTube, 2 August 2018, https://www.youtube.com/watch?v=z1YP_zZJFXs.

93. Donald Trump for President, Campaign Ad, YouTube, 11 September 2024, https://www.youtube.com/watch?v=wic8ykS18Xg.

94. Casey Cagle, "Sanctuary Cities," YouTube, 3 May 2018, https://www.youtube.com/watch?v=zbwE4JrrRpQ/.

95. Michael Hiltzik, "That Unbelievably Racist Ad during the Dodgers Playoff? Ex-Trump Aides Were Behind It," *Los Angeles Times*, 17 October 2022, https://www.latimes.com/business/story/2022-10-17/stephen-miller-behind-racist-ad-dodgers-game.

96. "Republicans Zero in on Crime, Immigration in Midterm Ads," YouTube, 12 October 2022, https://www.youtube.com/watch?v=gHscw4fa2IA.

97. Talal Ansari, "An Election Flier in Kansas Depicts ISIS as the New Neighbors," *Buzzfeed News*, 31 October 2016, https://www.buzzfeednews.com/article/talalansari/an-election-flyer-in-kansas-depicts-isis-as-the-neighbors.

98. "Secure America Now Ad 'Islamic States of America,'" YouTube, 6 February 2020, https://www.youtube.com/watch?v=DVSw8w77Oi4.

99. Sara Rathod, "7 Ads That Prove This Has Been the Worst Election Ever," *Mother Jones*, 2 November 2016, https://www.motherjones.com/politics/2016/11/islamophobic-republican-campaign-ads/.

100. Elizabeth Landers and James Masters, "Trump Retweets Anti-Muslim Videos," CNN, 30 November 2017, https://www.cnn.com/2017/11/29/politics/donald-trump-retweet-jayda-fransen/index.html.

101. Wardlow Mailers, https://www.scribd.com/document/391114701/Wardlow-Mailers.

102. Dean Obeidallah, "Laura Loomer, Trumpy Bigot Embraced by the Florida GOP Could Actually Get to Congress," *Daily Beast*, 9 February 2020, https://www.thedailybeast.com/laura-loomer-trumpy-bigot-embraced-by-the-florida-gop-could-actually-get-to-congress.

103. Maggie Haberman and Jonathan Swan, "Trump Wanted to Hire Laura Loomer, anti-Muslim Activist," *New York Times*, 23 April 2023, https://www.nytimes.com/2023/04/07/us/politics/trump-laura-loomer.html.

104. Aymann Ismail, "What Happened in the *Tennessean*'s Newsroom after That Anti-Muslim Ad," *Slate*, 23 June 2020, https://slate.com/news-and-politics/2020/06/tennessean-islam-ad-editor-interview.html.

105. Megan Lebowitz, "Trump Sparks Republican Backlash after Saying Immigrants Are 'Poisoning the Blood' of the U.S." NBC News, 19 December 2023, https://www.nbcnews.com/politics/donald-trump/trump-sparks-republican-backlash-saying-immigrants-are-poisoning-blood-rcna130493.

106. Maggie Haberman and Michael Gold, "Trump, at Fund-raiser, Says He Wants Immigrants From 'Nice' Countries," *New York Times*, 7 April 2024, https://www.nytimes.com/2024/04/07/us/politics/trump-immigrants-nice-countries.html.

107. Ko Bragg, "First Came Suffrage. Then Came Women of the Ku Klux Klan," The 19th, 28 December 2020, https://19thnews.org/2020/12/first-came-suffrage-then-came-the-women-of-the-ku-klux-klan/.

108. Nancy K. MacLean, *Behind the Mask of Chivalry: The Making of the Second Ku Klux Klan* (New York: Oxford University Press, 1994), 114–18.

109. By the 1920s, the media used "conservative" and "liberal" in ways recognizable today, with the term "progressive" applied mainly to Republicans in the tradition of Theodore Roosevelt. See Anna Shaw Faulkner, "Does Jazz Put the Sin in Syncopation," *Ladies Home Journal*, August 1921, 16.

110. Frank R. Kent, "Filth on Main Street," *The Independent*, 20 June 1925, 687–88; Nellie B. Miller, "Fighting Filth on Main Street," *The Independent*, 10 October 1925, 411–13.

111. Jay A. Gertzman, *Bookleggers and Smuthounds*: *The Trade in Erotica, 1920–1940* (Philadelphia: University of Pennsylvania Press, 1999); Will Durant, "The New Morality," *Forum* 81 (May 1929), 309–12.

112. John S. Sumner, "Are American Morals Disintegrating?," *Current Opinion* 70 (May 1921), 608–12.

113. Gaines M. Foster, "Conservative Social Christianity, the Law, and Personal Morality: Wilbur F. Crafts in Washington," *Church History* 71 (December 2002): 799–819.

114. Thomas Doherty, *Pre-Code Hollywood: Sex, Immorality, and Insurrection in American Cinema, 1930–1934* (New York: Columbia University Press,

1999), the Code on 347–67. Daniel A. Lord, *Played by Ear: The Autobiography of Daniel A. Lord* (Chicago: Loyola University Press, 1956), 298.

115. "The Pill and the Sexual Revolution," PBS: *American Experience*, https://www.pbs.org/wgbh/americanexperience/features/pill-and-sexual-revolution/.

116. Pat Buchanan, Graduation Address, Rosemont College, 22 May 1971, William A. Rusher Papers, Box 13, Library of Congress.

117. Donald T. Critchlow, *Phyllis Schlafly and Grassroots Conservatism: A Woman's Crusade* (Princeton, NJ: Princeton University Press, 2005), 212–53; Ethel B. Jones, "ERA Voting: Labor Force Attachment, Marriage, and Religion," *Journal of Legal Studies*, 12 (January 1983): 157–68; Bill Curry, "15,000 Hold Opposition Rally," *Washington Post*, 20 November 1977, 1, 23; Sally Quinn, "The Pedestal Has Crashed," *Washington Post*, 23 November 1977, B1.

118. "Patrick Joseph Buchanan, 'Culture War Speech: Address to the Republican National Convention' (17 August 1992)," Voices of Democracy, https://voicesofdemocracy.umd.edu/buchanan-culture-war-speech-speech-text/.

119. Maureen Dowd, "Hillary Clinton Provocateur?," *New Orleans Times-Picayune*, 1 December 1996, B7.

120. Laura Ingraham, "Hillary Clinton as Feminist Heroine," *The American Enterprise* 11 (2000), 35–36.

121. Kristin Ellison, "Confronted on GMA with 'Stereotypical Bitch' Statement about Clinton, Beck Said, 'Probably a Better Word Was "Nag,"'" Media Matters for America, 30 May 2007, https://www.mediamatters.org/abc/confronted-gma-stereotypical-bitch-statement-about-clinton-beck-said-probably-better-word-was.

122. Rush Limbaugh, "Does Our Looks-Obsessed Culture Want to Stare at an Aging Woman," 17 December 2007, https://www.rushlimbaugh.com/daily/2007/12/17/does_our_looks_obsessed_culture_want_to_stare_at_an_aging_woman6/.

123. Aaron Blake, "McConnell: Dems' 2016 Field Looks Like 'a Rerun of the 'Golden Girls,'" *Washington Post*, 15 March 2013, https://www.washingtonpost.com/news/post-politics/wp/2013/03/15/mcconnell-dems-2016-field-looks-like-a-re-run-of-the-golden-girls/.

124. The Rush Limbaugh Show, Transcript, 29 February 2012, https://web.archive.org/web/20120306050417/http://www.rushlimbaugh.com/daily/2012/02/29/butt_sisters_are_safe_from_newt_and_rick.

125. "Limbaugh: Contraception Advocate Should Post Online Sex Videos," NBC News, 1 March 2012, https://www.nbcnews.com/news/world/limbaugh-contraception-advocate-should-post-online-sex-videos-flna282595.

126. Tamara Keith, "Sexism Is out in the Open in the 2016 Campaign. That May Have Been Inevitable," NPR, 23 October 2016, https://www.npr.org/2016

/10/23/498878356/sexism-is-out-in-the-open-in-the-2016-campaign-that-may
-have-been-inevitable.

127. "Trump Ad Targets Hillary Clinton's Health," CNN, YouTube, https://
www.youtube.com/watch?v=h6FUt8DVCug.

128. Sammy Nickalls, "Newt Gingrich Had a Coughing Fit While Criticizing Hillary Clinton for Coughing," *Esquire*, 6 September 2016, https://www
.esquire.com/news-politics/news/a48381/newt-gingrich-coughing/.

129. Katherine Q. Seelye, "Gingrich's 'Piglets' Poked," *New York Times*, 19
January 1995, 20.

130. Matt K. Lewis, "Trump Is Making Paternalistic, Delusional Promises
to Women," *The Hill*, 25 September 2024, https://thehill.com/opinion/campaign
/4896829-trump-is-making-paternalistic-and-delusional-promises-to-women/.

131. Rachel Treisman, "J. D. Vance Went Viral for 'Cat Lady' Comments.
The Century-Old Trope Has a Long Tail," PBS, WHYY, 29 July 2024, https://
whyy.org/articles/jd-vance-viral-cat-lady-comments-history/.

132. Pat Campbell, "Husbands, Wives, Headship, and Submission," SBC
Life, 1 April 1999, https://www.baptistpress.com/resource-library/sbc-life-articles
/husbands-wives-headship-and-submission/.

133. David Siders, "The 'Shrinking Baptist Convention' Is Doubling-Down on
Its Culture Wars," *Politico*, 3 July 2023, https://www.politico.com/news/magazine
/2023/07/03/the-shrinking-baptist-convention-is-doubling-down-on-the-culture
-wars-00104174.

134. Siders, "The Shrinking Baptist Convention."

135. Geoff Bennett and Shoshana Dubnow, "Southern Baptist Convention
Bans Female Pastors, Ejecting Several Churches in the Process," PBS, 15 June
2023, https://www.pbs.org/newshour/show/southern-baptist-convention-bans
-female-pastors-ejecting-several-churches-in-the-process; Elizabeth Dias and Ruth
Graham, "Southern Baptists' Fight over Female Leaders Shows Power of Insurgent
Right," *New York Times*, 16 June 2023, https://www.nytimes.com/2023/06/16
/us/southern-baptist-women-pastors-church.html.

136. Elizabeth Dias and Ruth Graham, "Southern Baptists Move to Purge
Churches with Female Pastors," *New York Times*, 13 June 2023, https://www
.nytimes.com/2023/06/13/us/southern-baptist-movement-women-pastors.html;
Bennett and Dubnow, "Southern Baptist Convention Bans Female Pastors."

137. "US Denominations and Their Stances on Women in Leadership," CBE
International, April 2007, https://www2.cbeinternational.org/new/E-Journal
/2007/07spring/denominations%20first%20installment--FINAL.pdf.

138. "How Women in the Southern Baptist Convention Have Fought for
Decades to be Ordained," *The Conversation*, 1 June 2021, https://theconversation

.com/how-women-in-the-southern-baptist-convention-have-fought-for-decades
-to-be-ordained-161061.

139.　Kate Shellnutt, "Southern Baptists Committed to Abuse Reform. What Happened?," *Christianity Today*, 14 June 2023, https://www.christianitytoday .com/news/2023/june/southern-baptist-abuse-reform-response-task-force-data base.html.

140.　Christa Brown, "Why I'm Not Engaging With the SBC's Abuse Reform Implementation Task Force," BishopAccountability.org, 17 February 2023, https://www.bishop-accountability.org/2023/02/why-im-not-engaging-with-the -sbcs-abuse-reform-implementation-task-force/.

141.　Pope John Paul II, *Ordinatio sacerdotalis*, "Apostolic Letter on Reserving Priestly Ordination to Men Alone," 1994, https://www.vatican.va/content /john-paul-ii/en/apost_letters/1994/documents/hf_jp-ii_apl_19940522_ordinatio -sacerdotalis.html.

142.　Saul Gonzalez, "Roman Catholic Women Priests," *Religion and Ethics News Weekly*," 11 January 2023, https://www.pbs.org/wnet/religionandethics /2013/01/11/january-11-2013-roman-catholic-women-priests/14476.

143.　The Editors, "Pope Francis Discusses Ukraine, U.S. Bishops and More," *America: The Jesuit Review*, 28 November 2022, https://www.americamagazine .org/faith/2022/11/28/pope-francis-interview-america-244225.

144.　Lawrence Hurley, "Chief Justice Roberts Says Building a Fence around the Supreme Court Was the 'Hardest Decision' of His Tenure," NBC News, 24 May 2023, https://www.nbcnews.com/politics/supreme-court/roberts-calls -building-fence-supreme-court-hardest-decision-tenure-rcna85956.

145.　Allan M. Brandt, *No Magic Bullet: A Social History of Venereal Disease in the United States since 1880* (New York: Oxford University Press, 1987), 122–125.

146.　Randolph W. Baxter, "'Homo-Hunting' in the Early Cold War: Senator Kenneth Wherry and the Homophobic Side of McCarthyism," *Nebraska History* 84 (2003): 125.

147.　Baxter, "'Homo-Hunting' in the Early Cold War," 129.

148.　"Singer Pledges Anti-Gay Drive Nationwide," *Washington Post*, 28 March 1977, D 12; Save Our Children, Inc., "The Civil Rights of Parents," Advertisement, *Miami Herald*, 21 March 1977, 3A.

149.　Jim Peron, "The New Theocracy," *Libertarian Review* (September 1981), 30; David Brudnoy to William Rusher, 15 June 1977 and 20 August 1977, Rusher Papers, Box 12.

150.　Mark Ballard, "Speaker Mike Johnson's Views on Same-Sex Marriage Were Forged in Louisiana Evangelical Movement," *The Advocate*, 4 November 2023, https://www.theadvocate.com/baton_rouge/news/politics/mike-johnson

-anti-gay-views-same-as-evangelical-conservative/article_fc10696e-5928-5ae2
-a09a-d1950268d8a4.html.

151. Annika Kim Constantino, "Businesses Oppose Florida's 'Don't Say Gay' Ban on Discussion of LGBTQ Issues in Public Schools," CNBC, 29 March 2021, https://www.cnbc.com/2022/03/29/businesses-oppose-floridas-dont-say -gay-bill-banning-talk-of-lgbtq-issues-in-public-schools.html.

152. Shrai Popat and Holly Honderich, "Florida Lawmakers Pass 'Don't Say Gay' Bill," BBC, 8 March 2022, https://www.bbc.com/news/world-us -canada-60576847.

153. Taylor Orth, "Which Group of Americans Are Most Likely to Believe Conspiracy Theories?," YouGov, 30 March 2022, https://today.yougov.com/topics /politics/articles-reports/2022/03/30/which-groups-americans-believe -conspiracies.

154. "Second Baptist School Alumnus Responds to Church's Anti-Gay Stance on Proposed Houston Equal Rights Ordinance," *Out Smart*, 21 May 2014, https://www.outsmartmagazine.com/2014/05/second-baptist-school-alumnus -responds-churchs-anti-gay-stance-proposed-houston-equal-rights-ordinance/.

155. Julia Serano, "Transgender Peoples, Bathrooms, and Sexual Predators: What the Data Say," *Medium*, 17 June 2021, https://juliaserano.medium.com /transgender-people-bathrooms-and-sexual-predators-what-the-data-say-2f31 ae2a7c06.

156. Adam Nagourney and Jeremy W. Peters, "How a Campaign against Transgender Rights Mobilized Conservatives," *New York Times*, 16 April 2023, https://www.nytimes.com/2023/04/16/us/politics/transgender-conservative -campaign.html.

157. Rick Vachon and Mark Cohen, "The Dark Money Funding Conservative Anti-Trans Groups," *AJNEWS*, 31 May 2023, https://americanjournalnews .com/dark-money-conservative-anti-trans-movement/.

158. Dylan Abad, "Why Ron DeSantis Is Emailing Supporters about Pregnant Men," News Channel 8, 30 June 2023, https://www.wfla.com/news/politics /why-ron-desantis-is-emailing-supporters-about-pregnant-men/.

159. "President Trump's Plan to Protect Children from Left-Wing Gender Insanity," Trump Vance, 1 February 2023, https://www.donaldjtrump.com /agenda47/president-trumps-plan-to-protect-children-from-left-wing-gender -insanity.

160. Christopher Lamb, "Gender-Affirming Surgery Threatens 'Unique Dignity' of a Person, Vatican Says," CNN, 8 April 2024, https://www.cnn.com /2024/04/08/world/gender-affirming-surgery-threatens-unique-dignity-of-a -person-vatican-says-intl/index.html.

161. Rosalind S. Helderman and Jon Cohen, "As Republican Convention Emphasizes Diversity, Racial Incidents Intrude," *Washington Post*, 29 August 2012, https://www.washingtonpost.com/politics/2012/08/29/b9023a52-f1ec-11e1 -892d-bc92fee603a7_story.html.

162. "Full NBC News April 2023 Poll," https://www.documentcloud.org /documents/23789655-full-nbc-news-april-2023-poll/.

163. Jim Geraghty, "Everything Is the Culture War Now," *National Review*, 27 April 2023, https://www.nationalreview.com/the-morning-jolt/everything -is-the-culture-war-now/.

CHAPTER 12.   Donald Trump and Conservatism

1. S. E. Cupp, "Don't Dare Call It Conservative—Republicans Who Follow Trump Have Betrayed Their Philosophy," *Deseret News*, 13 January 2021, https:// www.deseret.com/opinion/2021/1/13/22229519/capitol-riots-republicans-donald -trump-conservative-gop-election-fraud.

2. Brian Stewart, "Revolution Betrayed," Quillette, 4 May 2022, https:// quillette.com/2022/05/04/revolution-betrayed/.

3. Charles J. Sykes, "As a Conservative, I Despair at Republicans' Support for Trump. His Vision Is Not Conservatism," *The Guardian*, 22 July 2018, https://www.theguardian.com/commentisfree/2018/jul/22/conservative-despair -republicans-trump.

4. Zack Stanton, "Does 'Conservatism' Actually Mean Anything Anymore?," *Politico*, 17 September 2021, https://www.politico.com/news/magazine/2021 /09/17/future-politics-conservatism-george-will-512308.

5. Greg Sargent, "A Longtime Conservative Insider Warns: The GOP Can't be Saved," *Washington Post*, 6 September 2022, https://www.washingtonpost .com/opinions/2022/09/06/trump-gop-bill-kristol-jan-6-mar-a-lago/.

6. Linda Feldman and Sophie Hills, "What Trump's Four Indictments Tell Us about America," *Christian Science Monitor*, 25 August 2023, https://www.csmonitor .com/USA/Politics/2023/0821/What-Trump-s-four-indictments-tell-us-about -America.

7. McKay Coppins, "How Trump Is Changing What 'Conservative' Means," *The Atlantic*, 12 April 2017, https://www.theatlantic.com/politics/archive /2017/04/what-does-moderate-mean-in-the-trump-era/522642/.

8. Patrick Ruffini, "The Six Republican Parties," *The Intersection*, 23 May 2023, https://www.patrickruffini.com/p/the-six-republican-parties.

9. Aaron Parsley, "What Happened to the Ten House Republicans Who Voted for Trump's Second Impeachment," *People*, 13 November 2022, https://

people.com/politics/elections-house-republicans-who-voted-trump-second
-impeachment/.

10. Manu Raju, "Lisa Murkowski, Done with Trump, Won't Rule Out
Leaving GOP," CNN, 24 March 2024, https://www.cnn.com/2024/03/24
/politics/lisa-murkowski-done-with-trump/index.html.

11. Barbara Sprunt, "7 GOP Senators Voted to Convict Trump; Only 1
Faces Voters Next Year," NPR, 15 February 2021, https://www.npr.org/sections
/trump-impeachment-trial-live-updates/2021/02/15/967878039/7-gop-senators
-voted-to-convict-trump-only-1-faces-voters-next-year.

12. Meredith McGraw and Alex Isenstadt, "'I Killed Him': How Trump
Torpedoed Tom Emmer's Speaker Bid," *Politico*, 24 October 2023, https://www
.politico.com/news/2023/10/24/i-killed-him-how-trump-torpedoed-tom-emmers
-speaker-bid-00123329.

13. Richard A. Viguerie, *Conservatives Betrayed: How George W. Bush and
Other Big Government Republicans Hijacked the Conservative Cause* (Los Angeles:
Bonus, 2006); Bruce Bartlett, *Impostor: How George W. Bush Bankrupted America
and Betrayed the Reagan Legacy* (New York: Doubleday, 2006); Amy Clark,
"Buckley: Bush Not a True Conservative," CBS News, 22 July 2006, https://
www.cbsnews.com/news/buckley-bush-not-a-true-conservative/.

14. Patrick J. Buchanan, "1992 Republican National Convention Speech,"
17 August 1992, https://buchanan.org/blog/1992-republican-national-convention
-speech-148.

15. Colin Campbell, "Trump: If I'm President 'Christianity Will Have
Power in the US,'" Insider, 23 January 2016, https://www.businessinsider.com
/donald-trump-christianity-merry-christmas-2016-1.

16. Elizabeth Dias, "'Christianity Will Have Power,'" *New York Times*, 9 August
2020, https://www.nytimes.com/2020/08/09/us/evangelicals-trump-christianity
.html.

17. David Crary, "Some Critics See Trump's Behavior as un-Christian.
His Conservative Backers See a Hero," Associated Press, 21 July 2023, https://
apnews.com/article/trump-evangelicals-christians-politics-jesus-2024-election
-2850284ccf3e7155273131b7344a0dd0.

18. Crary, "Some Critics See Trump's Behavior as un-Christian."

19. David Norman Smith and Eric Hanley, "The Anger Games: Who Voted
for Donald Trump in the 2016 Election and Why?," *Critical Sociology* 44 (2008):
195–212.

20. Joanne Freeman, "This Isn't Democracy. It's the Heartbeat of Authoritarianism," *Politico*, 6 October 2023, https://www.politico.com/news/magazine
/2023/10/06/republican-leaders-mccarthy-expert-roundup-00120170.

21. Jonathan Chait, "Donald Trump Is the Most Pure Conservative President Ever," *Intelligencer*, 23 February 2018, https://nymag.com/intelligencer/2018/02/donald-trump-is-the-most-pure-conservative-president-ever.html.

22. Anthea Butler, "Forum: Studying Religion in the Age of Trump," *Religion and American Culture* 27 (2017): 13.

23. Douglas Craig, *After Wilson: The Struggle for the Democratic Party, 1920–1934* (Chapel Hill: University of North Carolina Press, 1992); William Starr Myers, *The State Papers and Other Writings of Herbert Hoover*, Vol. 2 (New York: Doubleday, 1934), addresses of 31 October 1932, 418, and 5 November 1932, 452.

24. "Gingrich: The Left Redefining America," NBC, Today, 17 May 2010, https://www.today.com/popculture/gingrich-left-redefining-american-wbna37194394.

25. Bob Moser, "Rush Limbaugh Did His Best to Ruin America," *Rolling Stone*, 17 February 2021, https://www.rollingstone.com/politics/politics-features/rush-limbaugh-dead-trump-ruined-america-1129222/.

26. Glenn Ellmers, "'Conservatism' Is No Longer Enough," *The American Mind*, 24 March 2021, https://americanmind.org/salvo/why-the-claremont-institute-is-not-conservative-and-you-shouldnt-be-either/.

27. Patrick J. Deneen, *Regime Change: Toward a Postliberal Future* (New York: Penguin Random House, 2023), https://www.penguinrandomhouse.com/books/618154/regime-change-by-patrick-j-deneen/.

28. J. D. Wolf and Brad Meiselas, "Trump Echoes Hitler: Threatens to Rid America of 'Vermin' from Within," MTN, 11 November 2023, https://www.meidastouch.com/news/trump-echoes-hitler-threatens-to-rid-america-of-vermin-from-within.

29. Julianne McShane, "Trump Campaign Defends Nazi-Era "Vermin" Threat with . . . Another Incendiary Threat," *Mother Jones*, 13 November 2023, https://www.motherjones.com/politics/2023/11/trump-vermin-hitler-threat/.

30. David M. Elcott et al., *Faith, Nationalism, and the Future of Liberal Democracy* (Notre Dame, IN: University of Notre Dame Press, 2021), 12.

31. "Epistemological Modesty: An Interview With Peter Berger," Religion Online, October 1997, https://www.religion-online.org/article/epistemological-modesty-an-interview-with-peter-berger./

EPILOGUE

1. I write this in December 2024.

2. Brianna Navarre, "The Christian Voted for Trump: Will He Deliver a 'Kingdom of Christ?,'" *U.S. News*, 13 November 2024, https://www.usnews.com

/opinion/articles/2024-11-13/the-christian-right-voted-for-trump-will-he-deliver-a-kingdom-of-christ.

3. "Elon Musk Gave $20 Million to a Super PAC Comparing Trump to Ginsburg on Abortion," PBS, 6 December 2024, https://www.pbs.org/newshour/politics/elon-musk-gave-20-million-to-a-super-pac-comparing-trump-to-ginsburg-on-abortion.

4. The math for the two calculations: $(152.3*.49*.93) - (152.3*.46*.96)$ and $(152.3*.54*.93) - (152.3*.42*.96)$.

5. Claire Cain Miller, Ruth Igielnik, and Margot Sanger-Katz, "17% of Voters Blame Biden for the End of *Roe*," *New York Times*, 15 May 2024, https://www.nytimes.com/2024/05/15/upshot/abortion-biden-trump-blame.html.

6. Chiarra Vercellone et al., "2024 U.S. Election Misinformation Monitor," NewsGuard, November 2024, https://www.newsguardtech.com/special-reports/2024-elections-misinformation-tracker/.

7. Darrell M. West, "How Disinformation Defined the 2024 Election Narrative," Brookings Institute, 7 November 2024, https://www.brookings.edu/articles/how-disinformation-defined-the-2024-election-narrative/.

8. Sarah Steffen, "Fact Check: Disinformation's Impact on the U.S. Election," *In Focus*, 7 November 2024, https://www.dw.com/en/fact-check-what-role-did-disinformation-play-in-the-us-election/a-70729575.

9. Michael Ende, *The Neverending Story* (New York: Penguin Young Readers, 1993), 152.

10. Hannah Arendt, *The Origins of Totalitarianism* (New York: Mariner Books Classics, 2024), 361.

INDEX

ALLAN J. LICHTMAN is distinguished professor of history at American University. He is the author or co-author of thirteen books, including *Thirteen Cracks: Repairing American Democracy after Trump.*